HIGH PRIEST

HIGH PRIEST

by
Timothy Leary

Original art by Allen Atwell
and Michael Green

AN NAL BOOK

The World Publishing Company
New York   Cleveland

Excerpts from *The Divine Comedy* by Dante Alighieri, translated by
Lawrence Grant White, reprinted by permission of Random House, Inc.
Excerpts from *The Magus* by John Fowles reprinted by permission of
Little, Brown and Company. Excerpts from *Steppenwolf* by Hermann
Hesse, translated by Basil Creighton, Copyright 1927, © 1957 by Holt,
Rinehart and Winston, Inc.; reprinted by permission of Holt, Rinehart
and Winston, Inc. "Within and Without" by Hermann Hesse, Copyright
1954 by Suhrkamp Verlag, Berlin; reprinted by permission of
Suhrkamp Verlag. Excerpts from *Doors of Perception* by Aldous Huxley,
Copyright © 1954, reprinted by permission of Harper & Row.
Excerpts from *Island* by Aldous Huxley, Copyright © 1962, reprinted
by permission of Harper & Row. Excerpts from *The Lotus and the Robot*
by Arthur Koestler, Copyright © 1961 by Arthur Koestler, reprinted
by permission of The Macmillan Company. Excerpts from *The Epic
of Gilgamesh* translated by N. K. Sandars reprinted by permission of
Penguin Books Ltd. Excerpts from *The Religions of Man* by Huston
Smith, Copyright © 1958, reprinted by permission of Harper & Row.
Excerpts from *The Lord of the Rings* by J. R. R. Tolkien reprinted by
permission of Houghton Mifflin Company. Excerpts from *The I Ching
or Book of Changes*, translated by R. Wilhelm and C. F. Baynes,
Bollingen Series XIX (Princeton University Press, 1967), Copyright
© 1950, 1967 by The Bollingen Foundation, New York; reprinted by
permission of Princeton University Press. Excerpts from "Minutes to Go"
by William Burroughs reprinted by permission of Beach Books, Texts
& Documents. Excerpts from the Boston *Herald Traveler* reprinted by
permission of the Boston Herald Traveler Corporation. Excerpts from
"LSD—Hollywood's Status Drug" (*Cosmopolitan*, September, 1963),
Copyright © 1963 by Hearst Magazines, Inc.; reprinted by permission
of *Cosmopolitan*. Excerpts from letters and writings of Allen Ginsberg
reprinted by permission of the author. Excerpts from letters of
Michael Hollingshead reprinted by permission of the author.
Excerpts from *Inner Space* reprinted by permission of The Rt. Rev.
Michael Augustine Francis Itkin. Excerpts from an interview with
Timothy Leary originally appeared in *Playboy* magazine; Copyright
© 1966 by HMH Publishing Co. Inc.; reprinted by permission of *Playboy*.
Excerpts from "The Hallucinogenic Drug Cult" by Noah Gordon
(*The Reporter*, August 15, 1963), Copyright © 1963 by The Reporter
Magazine Company; reprinted by permission of *The Reporter* and
the author. Excerpts from "Return Trip to Nirvana" by Arthur Koestler
reprinted by permission of the *Sunday Telegraph*, London. Excerpts from
"Instant Mysticism" (*Time*, October 25, 1963) and "An Epidemic of Acid
Heads" (*Time*, March 11, 1966); Copyright © 1963 by Time, Inc.;
Copyright © 1966 by Time, Inc.; reprinted by permission of Time, Inc.
Illustration facing pages 46 and 184: Courtesy of Richard Davis Studio.
Illustration facing page 128: Courtesy of Fred W. McDarrah.
Portions of Trip 6 appeared in *Esquire* Magazine.

First Printing

Published by The New American Library, Inc.
in association with The World Publishing Company
2231 West 110th Street, Cleveland, Ohio 44102
Library of Congress Catalog Card Number: 68–9031
Printed in the United States of America.

This Manuscript Is Entrusted to
My Daughter, SUSAN LEARY,
and My Son, JOHN LEARY

But I—why should I go? By whose decree?
I am not Paul, nor am I yet Aeneas,
      but deemed
unworthy by myself and others. Wherefore, if I
allow myself to go, I fear it would be folly.

Dante to Vergil

ACKNOWLEDGMENTS

The events related in this history reflect the collective consciousness and collaborative behavior of several thousand people—spiritual researchers who have shared dark confusions and bright hopes, given their emotion, muscle, brain, and risked scorn and social isolation to pursue the psychedelic yoga.

Homage and gratitude to these fellow explorers.

Richard Alpert and Ralph Metzner have participated in every phase of the long ascent and continue to climb higher. His-story is their story.

Three tender elvish flowers, Rosemary Woodruff, Susan Leary, and Jack Leary, have endured the harshest ordeals of the journey—at home and in prison—and have survived, blossoming.

Loving thanks to the psychologists and religious philosophers who counseled at our centers in Cambridge, Boston, Zihuatanejo, Antigua, Millbrook, and Manhattan.

The original art for this manuscript is the illuminated work of Allen Atwell and Michael Green.

The editorial acts of love were performed by Susan Firestone, Lorraine Schwartz, and Jean McCreedy.

The psychedelic revolution is a religious renaissance of the young, for the young, by the young. This volume presents Old Testament background for the new witness of those born after 1946, children of the Atomic Age.

The authentic priests, the real prophets of this great movement are the rock-and-roll musicians. Acid-rock is the hymns, odes, chants of the turned-on love generation. For the first time in history, teen-agers (our new advanced mutant species) have written their own songs, beat their own rhythm, created their own religion.

The work of the psychedelic scholar-politicians (described in this history) is over, with love and confidence we turn our work and our planet over to the young and their prophets:

The Beatles	Country Joe and the Fish
The Byrds	Charlie Lloyd
The Rolling Stones	The Monkees

The Beach Boys   Donovan
The Jefferson Airplane   The Association
The Mamas and the Papas   Buffalo Springfield
The Grateful Dead   The Animals
Moby Grape   Big Brother
The Daily Flash   and the Holding Company
The Doors   The Quicksilver Messenger Service
and many other ecstatic combinations.

CHRONOLOGY OF TRIPS

NOTE

The League for Spiritual Discovery is a legally incorporated religion dedicated to the ancient sacred sequence of turning-on, tuning-in, and dropping-out. Its aim is to help recreate every man as God and every woman as Goddess.

This book is the first of a four-volume biblical account of the birth, structural growth, exile, return, persecution, redemption, and flowering of the LSD religious cult.

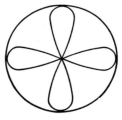

The seal of the League is a mandala—the end-less circle circumscribing a four-leaf lotus made by the double infinity sign. This interweaving of the infinite universe of male (8) with the infinite universe of female (∞) forms the flower, symbol of seed-life—centered in the void-eye of God.

HIGH PRIEST

Death of the Mind:

January 1959

Guide: GODSDOG

Oracle: III

Difficulty at the Beginning

The Abysmal, Water

The Arousing, Thunder

Clouds and thunder:
The image of DIFFICULTY AT THE BEGINNING.
Thus the superior man
Brings order out of confusion.

(I Ching)

In the beginning God created the heavens and the earth.

The earth was without form and void, and darkness was on the face of the deep.

Nicholas in *The Magus* by John Fowles:

For a while I let my mind wander into a bottomless madness.

Supposing all my life that last year had been the very opposite of what Conchis so often said—so often, to trick me once again—about life in general.

That is, the very opposite of hazard.

And God said let there be light; and there was light. And God saw that the light was good; and God separated the light from the darkness.

In the beginning was the TURN ON. The flash, the illumination. The electric trip. The sudden bolt of energy that starts the new system.

The TURN ON was God.

All things were made from the TURN ON and without Him was not any thing made.

In this TURN ON was life; and the life was the light of men.

It has always been the same.

It was the flash that exploded the galaxies, from which all energy flows. It was the spark that ignites in the mysterious welding of amino-acid strands that creates the humming vine of organic life. It is the brilliant neurological glare that illuminates the shadows of man's mind. The God-intoxicated revelation. The Divine union. The vision of harmony, samadhi, satori, ecstasy which we now call psychedelic.

What happens when you turn on? Where do you go when you take the trip? You go within. Consciousness changes. Your nerve endings, neural cameras, cellular memory banks, protein structures become broadcasting instruments for the timeless humming message of God located inside your body.

The external world doesn't change, but your experience of it becomes drastically altered.

You close your eyes and the thirteen billion cell brain computer flashes multiple kaleidoscopic messages. Symbolic thought merges with sensory explosions; symbolic thoughts fuse with somatic-tissue events; ideas combine with memories—personal, cellular, evolutionary, embryonic—thoughts collapse into molecular patterns.

You open your eyes and you see your tidy television-studio world of labeled stage-props fusing with sensory, somatic, cellular, molecular flashes.

2

Your nervous system is prepared to register and coordinate up to one thousand million units of flashing information each second.

A psychedelic trip lasts from five to twelve hours. Each trip takes off from a stage-set structured by the physical surroundings and the cast of characters present. Each person in the session is a universe of two billion years of protein, protean memories, and sensations. A heady mix.

How to describe this multiple, jumbled, rapidly changing process? What do you do after you TURN ON?

The Light shineth in the darkness and the darkness comprehendeth it not.

You TUNE IN.

TUNE IN means to bear witness to the Light, that all men might believe.

The TURN ON bolt shatters structure. Reveals the frozen nature of the artificial stage-set men call reality. Certitude collapses. There is nothing but the energy which lighteneth every man that cometh into the world. $E = MC^2$.

We discover we are not television actors born onto the American stage-set of a commercially sponsored program twenty centuries old. We are two-billion-year-old carriers of the Light, born not just of blood nor of the will of the flesh, nor of the will of man, but of the Light that flashed in the Precambrian mud, the Light made flesh.

TUNE IN means that you sit in the debris of your shattered illusions, and discover that there is nothing, you are nothing except the bearer of the wire-coil of life, that your body is the temple of the Light and you begin once again to build a structure to preserve and glorify the Light. You bear witness crying, the Sun that comes after me is preferred before me, and your days are spent preparing the earth for the Son to come. That is TUNING IN.

And to TUNE IN you must DROP OUT.

DROP OUT means detach yourself tenderly, aesthetically, harmoniously from the fake-prop studio of the empire game and do nothing but guard and glorify the Light.

My first trip came in the middle of the journey of this life (when I was thirty-five years old) and

Nicholas in *The Magus:*

I stared at myself. They were trying to drive me mad, to brainwash me in some astounding way. But I clung to reality.

∞

And God saw that it was good.

∞

From *The Magus:*

I cannot believe Maurice is evil. You will understand.

∞

And God made the beasts of the earth according to their kinds and the cattle

according to their kinds, and everything that creeps upon the ground according to its kind. And God saw that it was good.

∞

awoke to the consciousness that I was trapped in a dark room, in a hastily constructed, thin-walled stage-prop home in Berkeley, California, and the ribbon of light had been lost.

I was a rootless city-dweller. An anonymous institutional employee who drove to work each morning in a long line of commuter cars, and drove home each night and drank martinis and looked like and thought like and acted like several million middle-class liberal intellectual robots.

Woke up, fell out of dead
Made the bus in fleconds flat

There was no connection with soil or with my racial past. My clan gods slumbered. My tribal banners were hidden, forgotten in cellular repositories.

How I entered this flimsy stage-set I cannot well recall, so full was I of sleep at the time.

I dropped out, taking leave from my job (as Director of Psychological Research for the Kaiser Foundation Hospital) and sailing for Spain on the S.S. *Independence,* American Export Lines, with my two children, Susan, age nine, and Jack, age seven.

We settled in a villa in Torremolinos on the Costa del Sol. There the kids trooped off across the field to school each morning while I stayed home to die messily.

The coast of Spain Málaga to Gibraltar is the southernmost part of Europe, and down to this bottom sift and fall the psychological dregs of the Continent—drunken Swedes, cashiered Danes, twisted Germans, sodden British.

The main occupation of the Torremolinos colony was drug taking—and the drug was alcohol.

Found my way upstairs and had a poke

I had brought with me a trunk full of psychological data—thousands of test scores and numerical indices which demonstrated with precision why psychotherapy did not work. In America, I had a staff of statisticians and clerks and rooms of calculators and computers to handle the data. But I had said good-bye to all that and sat sweating in a small room in a Spanish house adding and subtracting long columns of figures. Hour after hour.

Then the man said, "This at last is bone of my bones and flesh of my flesh; she shall be called woman, because she was taken out of man."

∞

But I just had a book
Having read the look
It was a brutal yoga. Each laborious calculation was proving that psychology was just a mind-game, an eccentric head trip on the part of psychologists, and that psychotherapy was an arduous, expensive, ineffective, unimaginative attempt to impose the mind of the doctor on the mind of the patient.

Each arithmetical index was pushing me farther and farther from my chosen profession.
And though the moles were rather small
I had to count them all
The dying process was slow.

I would throw down the ballpoint pen and walk fast to the main street of the village and sit in a bar and drink and talk detached-zombie-fashion with the expatriates and leave abruptly and run back to the house and continue the paralyzing calculations, sweating in panic.
Now he knows how many moles it takes to fill
*   the Alpert Hall*
Boredom, black depression, flashes of frantic, restless anxiety. No place to go.
I led the news today oh joy
And though the views was rather mad
In December the rains came and the Mediterranean was gray and cold. On Christmas Eve I met a young, runaway prostitute from Valencia and took her home. By New Years I had the clap.

Times of growth are beset with difficulties. They resemble a first birth. But these difficulties arise from the very profusion of all that is struggling to attain form. Everything is in motion: therefore if one perseveres there is a prospect of great success, in spite of the existing danger. When it is a man's fate to undertake such new beginnings, everything is still unformed, dark. (I Ching III)

From *The Magus:*

"You may search the house." She watched me, chin on hand, in the yellow chair; unnettled; in possession. Of what, I didn't know; but in possession. I felt like a green young dog in pursuit of a cunning old hare; every time I leapt, I bit brown air.

∞

In the middle of January I moved with the kids to a steam-heated hotel, but Jack's un-house-trained puppy and my distant gloom freaked the owner, so I moved to an apartment tunneled into the rock at the foot of Calle San Miguel. It was a cave with oozing stone walls. The beds were always damp.

Well I just had to graph

There the break-through-break-down started.

It began in the head. One morning my scalp began to itch. By noon it was unbearable. Each hair root was a burning rod of sensation. My hair was a cap of fire. I ran down the beach and cut my feet on rocks to keep from ripping my fingers through my scalp.

By evening my face began to swell and huge water blisters erupted from my cheeks. A young Danish doctor came, injected me with a huge needle, and gave me sleeping pills.

Somebody broke and I went into a steam

In the morning I was blind—eyes shut tight by swollen tissue and caked with dried pus. I felt my way to the bathroom, lit a candle, and pried open one eye before the mirror.

Broke up, sell out of bed

In the oblong glass I saw the twisted, tormented face of an insane stranger.

I saw the rotograph

A Spanish doctor came and gave me more shots and more sleeping pills. He had never seen such a case before. Jack and Susan crept into the room to look at me with big sorrowful eyes. The bed was cold and soggy but I slept.

The third day the disease had spread to my body. Huge watery welts blossomed on my back, stomach, and flanks. Both the Danish and the Spanish doctors shook their heads, and both injected me from large metal hypodermics.

In the afternoon I hired a taxi and was driven to Málaga to consult the specialist. His eyes bulged and he shook his head and gave me two injections.

I'd ove turned you on

Before returning to Torremolinos I sat at a sidewalk cafe and drank a Coca-Cola. A pretty, young Swedish girl joined me. She was traveling with her parents and was bored and rebellious, hungry for adventure. She steamed with erotic vapor. I looked at her and smiled weakly. See you later.

Back at Torremolinos the doctors agreed I should move to a steam-heated hotel. We had to smuggle the dog in. Jack and Susan left to stay with a

But the serpent said to the woman, "You will not die. For God knows that when you eat of it your eyes will be opened, and you will be like God, knowing good and evil."

∞

From *The Magus:*

"Responsibility!" I wheeled round on her again. "Do you really think we do this just for you? Do you really believe we are not . . . charting the voyage?"

∞

But the Lord God called to the man, and said to him, "Where are you?" And he said, "I heard the sound of thee in the garden, and I was afraid, because I was naked; and I hid myself."

∞

From *The Magus:*

"With all the necessity of a very complex experiment." "I like my experiments simple." "The days of simple experiments are over."

∞

The Lord God said to the serpent, ". . . I will put enmity between you and the woman, and between your seed and her seed. . . ."

∞

Therefore the Lord God sent him forth from the garden of Eden, to till the ground from which he was taken. He drove out the man; and at the east of the garden of Eden he placed the cherubim, and a flaming sword which turned every way, to guard the way to the tree of life.

∞

sabbatical family from the University of Pennsylvania.

By night the disease had spread to my extremities. My wrists and hands were swollen to arthritic paralysis. My ankles and feet ballooned. I couldn't walk or move my fingers. I sat in the darkness for several hours and then came the scent of decay. Overpowering odor of disintegration.

I got up from the chair, but my feet buckled and I fell to my knees. I crawled across the room to the electric switch and pulled myself up to flick on the light.

He didn't notice that the frights had changed

Jack's puppy had been very sick and a rivulet of yellow shit ran along the floor. We would be expelled from the hotel if the chambermaid found the evidence. I crawled to the bathroom and pulled down a roll of toilet paper. For the next hour I crept along the tile floor cleaning up the mess. It was slimy mucus. The color of peanut butter.

I crawled to the bathroom. The toilet didn't work. I crawled to the window which overlooked the back yard of the hotel and heaved out the wad of toilet paper.

There were electric wires about four feet below the window and the discolored strings of paper caught on the wires and hung down like banners swaying in the breeze. Flag of my action.

Using an umbrella as a cane, I hobbled along the hallway, down the back stairs, and across the rutted muddy back yard. Each step was torture. I fell several times. I stood on a packing crate and flailed at the paper banner like a madman fighting vultures.

Clouds and thunder are represented by definite decorative lines; this means that in the chaos of difficulty at the beginning, order is already implicit. So too the superior man has to arrange and organize the inchoate profusion of such times of beginning, just as one sorts out silk threads from a knotted tangle and binds them into skeins. In order to find one's place in the infinity of being, one must be able both to separate and to unite. (I Ching III)

By the time I wrenched back to the room, two hours had elapsed. I was weak and trembling. I slumped in the chair for the rest of the dark night, wrapped in a Burberry mackintosh.

I died. I let go. Surrendered.

I slowly let every tie to my old life slip away. My career, my ambitions, my home. My identity. The guilts. The wants.

With a sudden snap, all the ropes of my social self were gone. I was a thirty-eight-year-old male animal with two cubs. High, completely free.

I could feel some seed of life stirring inside and energy uncoil. When the dawn came I moved my hands. The swelling was gone. I found a pen and paper. I wrote three letters. One to my employers, telling them I was not returning to my job. A second to my insurance agent to cash in my policies. And a third long manuscript to a colleague, spelling out certain revelations about the new psychology, the limiting artifactual nature of the mind, the unfolding possibilities of mind-free consciousness, the liberating effect of the ancient rebirth process that comes only through death of the mind.

The ordeal in Spain was the first of some four hundred death-rebirth trips I have experienced since 1958. The first step was non-chemical. Or was it?

Conchis in *The Magus:*

He leant forward, after a long silence, and turned up the lamp; then stared at me.

"The disadvantage of our new drama is that in your role you do not know what you can believe and what you cannot."

∞

DIFFICULTY AT THE BEGINNING:
Works supreme success,
Furthering through perseverance.
Nothing should be undertaken.
It furthers one to appoint helpers.
(I Ching)

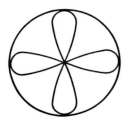

God Reveals Himself
in Mysterious Forms:

THE SACRED MUSHROOMS OF MEXICO

August 1960

Guide: ROBERT GORDON WASSON

Oracle: XVI

Enthusiasm

The Arousing, Thunder

The Receptive, Earth

Thunder comes resounding out of the earth:
The image of ENTHUSIASM.
Thus the ancient kings made music
In order to honor merit,
And offered it with splendor

(I Ching)

From *Hallucinogenic Fungi of Mexico* by Robert Gordon Wasson:

I do not recall which of us, my wife or I, first dared to put into words back in the forties the surmise that our own remote ancestors, perhaps 4,000 years ago, worshipped a divine mushroom.

In the fall of 1952 we learned that the 16th century writers, describing the Indian cultures of Mexico, had recorded that certain mushrooms played a divine role in the religion of the natives.

The so-called mushroom stones really represented mushrooms, and that they were the symbol of a religion, like the cross in the Christian religion or the star of Judea or the crescent of the Moslems.

I was first drugged out of my mind in Cuernavaca, August 1960. I ate seven of the Sacred Mushrooms of Mexico and discovered that beauty, revelation, sensuality, the cellular history of the past, God, the Devil—all lie inside my body, outside my mind.

In the days of Montezuma this town called horn-of-the-cow was the center of soothsayers, wise-men, and magicians. Cuernavaca is the southern anchor point of a line running from the fabled volcanic peaks Popo and Iztaccihuatl over to the volcano of Toluca. On the high slopes of the volcanoes, east and west of the capital, grow the Sacred Mushrooms of Mexico, divinatory fungi, Teonanacatl, flesh of the Gods.

In the summer of 1960 Cuernavaca was the site of considerable activity by American psychologists—soothsayers, medicine men, would-be magicians—from the North—vacationing on research grants and working in the lush valley of Morelos in sight of the snowy peaks of the legendary volcanoes.

Erich Fromm was running an experimental project down the highway, studying the social and emotional currents of Indian village life.

Over in Tepoztlan, ten miles to the east, Professor David McClelland, on vacation from Harvard, was working on plans to help underdeveloped countries raise their economic standards through psychological techniques and the Protestant ethic. His statistics showed that Catholic, Moslem, Buddhist countries were poor.

Elliot Danzig, Mexico's leading industrial psychologist, was a few cornfields away in his villa which sits next to the cliff under the altar of the God Tepozteco. It was at this altar, often shrouded in rain clouds, that the Aztecs had worshipped the God, Tepozteco, to drumrolls of the arousing thunder and bolts of lightning, the clinging flame. It was he who showered down blessings including the gift of *pulque* . . . a milky beer fermented from cactus, which contains its own abundance of thunder over the earth.

In Cuernavaca another villa served as summer headquarters for four American psychologists—Timothy Leary and Richard Alpert of Harvard, Frank Barron of California, and Richard Dettering of San Francisco.

Thus we find a mushroom in the center of the cult with perhaps the longest continuous history in the world.

The happenings of that summer in quiet Cuernavaca were to set up reverberations which have echoed now for years. Many of the scientists who were working and vacationing there that season have had their lives dramatically changed, and none of them will ever completely escape from the mysterious power, the challenge, the paradox of what started to unfold.

We have found this cult of the divine mushroom a revelation, in the true meaning of that abused word, though for the Indians it is an everyday feature, albeit a holy mystery, of their lives.

I was working on a book about the philosophy of the behavioral sciences. I was dissatisfied with the theory and methods of psychology and trying to develop an existential-transactional approach to the study of human events.

Existential means you study natural events as they unfold without prejudging them with your own concepts. You surrender your mind to the events.

Transactional means you see the research situation as a social network, of which the experimenter is one part. The psychologist doesn't stand outside the event, but recognizes his part in it, and works collaboratively with the subject towards mutually selected goals.

There are no apt words . . . to characterize your state when you are, shall we say, "Bemushroomed."

This philosophic position, when applied, generates a lot of emotion. For one thing, it bypasses the traditional experimenter-subject and doctor-patient relationships. It tells the doctor and the scientist to relax his control. It urges that everyman be his own scientist. Do his own research. It bypasses the controlled experiment in favor of the natural sequence of behavior. You don't have to design an experiment, Dr. Jones, you are already part of one.

The 1967 phenomenon of several million Americans taking LSD on their own, exploring their own consciousness, doing it themselves, developing their

What we need is a vocabulary to describe all the modalities of a divine inebriant.

These difficulties in communicating have played their part in certain amusing situations. Two psychiatrists who have taken the mushroom and known the experience in its full dimensions have been criticized in professional circles as being no longer "objective."

Thus we are all divided into two classes: those who have taken the mushroom and are disqualified by our subjective experience and those who have not taken the mushroom and are disqualified by their total ignorance of the subject.

I am profoundly grateful to my Indian friends for having initiated me into the tremendous mystery of the mushroom.

Of alcohol they speak with the same jocular vulgarity that we do. But about mushrooms they prefer not to speak at all, at least when they are in company and especially when strangers, white strangers, are present.

own methods of turning-on, is nothing less than an existential-transactional revolution in psychology. The professionals—the doctors and the experimentalists and the government officials—don't like it. The idea of people going out and solving their own problems, changing their own consciousness, irritates the doctors. They say it's indiscriminate, unsupervised, uncontrolled, and basically for kicks. They are right. It is and it should be. That's what life itself is. An indiscriminate, unsupervised, uncontrolled two-billion-year-old energy dance with ecstatic communion as the goal.

These laws are not forces external to things but represent the harmony of movement immanent in them. That is why the celestial bodies do not deviate from their orbits and why all events in nature occur with fixed regularity. (I Ching XVI)

The villa in Cuernavaca, which became the backdrop for my mushroom revelations, needs to be described. The setting, the surrounding, is a key factor in the outcome of any visionary voyage whether you use mushrooms or marijuana or LSD or rosary beads, and in this regard the Cuernavaca mushroom eaters were fortunate.

The Spanish-style villa was out on the Acapulco road near the golf course. It was a rambling white stucco house with scarlet trim, surrounded by gray stone walls. The walls were pierced by two red-iron scroll gates and there was a long veranda and a wide staircase leading down to a carriage drive. Down below was a sloping lawn ringed by flowers. Two rows of red urns flanked the stairs.

The villa had been built by Mexican Moslems and remodeled by Mexican Viennese. It was colorful, open, and lush.

Next to the upper terrace was the swimming pool, lake blue, and the lawn fell away downslope to a lower green terraced lawn. The close-cropped turf was thick rough Cuernavaca grass, good to look at but matting into heavy piled green carpet, scraping your bare feet and leaving tattooed welts on your back after you lay on it.

The lower lawn was shaded by lacy Ahuehuate trees, and on the walls of the villa, vines, green, splashed with red, yellow, orange, and the clear blue of the mile-high Morelos sky and the lush green of the golf course fairway down below the wall.

Summer days . . . swimming trunks before breakfast . . . ontological discussions . . . the cold grapefruit eaten by hot poolside . . . the egocentric fallacy of the doctor-patient relationship . . . touch football on the lawn . . . the imposition of psychological categories on the flow of life . . . clear hot sun burning tanned skin . . . the need to collaborate with subjects . . . the startle value of iced drinks . . . the anti-existential impact of the Mexico City *News* with its Aristotelian structure of essences and abstractions . . . the shouts of Jack Leary and the Mexican boy, Pepe, chasing ducks on the lower lawn . . . visitors from Mexico City defined wider bounds for inquiry . . . the sudden cooling splash of the evening rain . . . Dewey and Bentley . . . Kennedy and Nixon . . . thunder and earth . . . the sky over the volcanoes . . . candles at dinner.

Be like the sun at midday.

A frequent visitor was Gerhart Braun, anthropologist-historian-linguist from the University of Mexico. With him would come Joan, his girl friend, and Betty, an English major from the University of California, who wrote poetry and cracked jokes and played touch football with the kids.

Gerhart had been studying the Aztec culture and translating old texts written in Nahuatl, the language used by the Aztecs before the conquest. He had discovered repeated references to the use of Sacred Mushrooms by Aztec soothsayers on ceremonial occasions to predict the future, to feel better, to solve mental problems.

On the eve of the Emperor's coronation Mexico City got high on mushrooms. But the Spanish historians, most of them priests, rarely mentioned the magic mushrooms. And when they did it was in prudish, frightened terms. Evil! Danger! Fear!

Then, when evening and darkness come and you are alone with a wise old man or woman whose confidence you have won, by the light of a candle held in the hand and talking in a whisper, you may bring up the subject.

They are never exposed in the marketplace but pass from hand to hand by prearrangement.

The Aztecs before the Spanish arrived called them Teonanacatl, **God's** flesh. I need hardly remind you of a disquieting para' lel, the designation of **the** elements in our Eucharist:

"Take, eat, this is my body . . .", and again, "Grant us therefore, gracious Lord, so to eat the flesh of Thy dear son. . . ."

The orthodox Christian must accept by faith the miracle of the conversion of the bread into God's flesh: That is what is meant by the Doctrine of Transubstantiation.

By contrast, the mushroom of the Aztecs carries its own conviction; every communicant will testify to the miracle that he has experienced.

In the language of the Mazatecs the sacred mushrooms are called 'nti si tho. The first word, 'nti, is a particle expressing reverence and endearment. The second element means "that which springs forth."

Gerhart's curiosity was aroused and he had asked around about the mushrooms and discovered that they grew on the volcanic slopes near Mexico City.

So one day we drove up to the village of San Pedro near the volcano of Toluca and walked around the marketplace asking about the Sacred Mushrooms. Bruce Conner came with us shooting movies, dancing around filming the sides of meat hanging in the butcher shops and the swarms of black flies and the piles of fruit, the sidewalk displays of cloth woven in red and yellow seed and cell designs.

There was much thoughtful shaking of heads by the shopkeepers when the mushrooms were mentioned—and conversation in low Spanish in the back rooms. Old Juana was the one to see. Where did one find Juana? She would come to the market. Wait right here under the arch. She'll come soon.

We stood there for an hour while the sandaled market-day crowds padded by. An old woman, backbent, gray stringy hair, black shawl, eyes down, creaking stiffly, Señora Juana. She brushed by us, not responding to our hail, not stopping or looking up at us.

She passed through the market street and turned at the corner and walked away from the village. We followed along the rutted dirt road, and on the outskirts of town Gerhart walked faster and caught up with Juana. She stopped and they began to talk.

We stood back and waited and watched. Juana seemed to be listening, then she looked up at Gerhart, nodded her head, pointed up to the mountain, turned, pointed back to the town, and then started off down the road.

Gerhart returned to us smiling. Okay. It's all set. She'll get the mushrooms next Wednesday and I'll meet her in the marketplace next Thursday.

The following Thursday Gerhart phoned from Mexico City. Excited. He had met Juana in the market. They had gone away from the tumult of the market to the shade of a church wall. He asked her if she was sure they were safe. She popped two of them in her mouth before his eyes. He washed them in cold water, and they are resting now on the center shelf of his refrigerator. See you Saturday.

Saturday, the day of visions, dawned sunny and clear. Around noon Gerhart and his group arrived from Mexico City. Joan and Betty the poet.

I met them on the lawn and the group stood in a welcoming circle. My son Jack's iguana, a four-foot dinosaur, crawled up and lay on his belly, blinking his black ancient ebony eyes, and everyone stooped to inspect the long blunt snout, the patterned design of his canvas skin, our old friend who crawled up from the crevice of our planet's history and breathed slowly and flicked his lids and watched us live and die. They said he was a hundred years old.

The maid was surprised when we walked into the kitchen to wash the *hongos* and she was even more surprised to learn that we weren't planning to cook them. *Crudos?* Her dark eyes narrowed. Then the resigned shrug. Americans are eccentric.

Gerhart had talked with the University botanists and had researched the field thoroughly. So while he supervised the cleaning he started to lecture on the mushrooms. Known and used by the Aztecs. Banned by the Catholic church. Said by leading botanists not even to exist! The trance-giving mushrooms. Pushed out of history's notice until the last decade when they had been discovered by Weitlinger and Schultes and the American mycologists, Valentina and Gordon Wasson. Pause to clear throat. By now they had been eaten by a few scientists, a few poets, a few intellectuals looking for mystical experiences. They produced wondrous trances. Oh yeah? What does he mean by that?

There were two kinds, females and males. The lady mushrooms were the familiar umbrella shape, but black, ominous, bitter-looking. The male's anatomy was so phallic there was no need to ask why they were called males. Wondrous trances. The words meant nothing. We moved out to the pool.

The mushrooms were in two large bowls, male and female separate, on the table under the huge beach umbrella. Gerhart was still lecturing, now about the dosage. Six females and six males. The effect should begin after an hour. Then he stuffed a big, black, moldy-damp mushroom in his mouth and made a face and chewed and I watched his

"The little mushroom comes of itself, no one knows whence, like the wind that comes we know not whence nor why."

For more than four centuries the Indians have kept the divine mushroom close to their hearts, sheltered from desecration by white men, a precious secret.

We know that today there are many *curanderos* who carry on the cult, each according to his lights, some of them consummate artists, performing the ancient liturgy in remote huts before minuscule congregations.

They are hard to reach, these *curanderos*.

Do not think that it is a question of money.

Perhaps you will learn the names of a number of renowned *curanderos,* and your emissaries will even promise to deliver them to you, but then you wait and wait and they never come.

You will brush past them in the marketplace, they will know you, but you will not know them.

The judge in the town hall may be the very man you are seeking: And you may pass the time of day with him, yet never learn that he is your *curandero.*

After all, would you have it any different? What priest of the Catholic Church will perform mass to satisfy an unbeliever's curiosity?

Adam's apple bounce as it went down. Gerhart was voyager number one.

I picked one up. It stank of forest damp and crumbling logs and New England basement. Are you sure they are not poisonous?

Gerhart shrugged. That's what I asked the old witch and she swore that they were okay and she popped a few in her mouth to demonstrate.

I looked around. Joan, following Gerhart's example, was munching somewhat unhappily. She was explorer number two.

Mandy, my girl friend, was miserably chewing. She was number three.

Dick Dettering was looking down so that the loose pouches under his eyes sagged. Well, Dicko? He gave a fierce scared look and began to nibble at his palm with squirrelly movement. He was number four.

I went next. They tasted worse than they looked. Bitter, stringy. Filthy. I took a slug of Carta Blanca and jammed the rest in my mouth and washed them down. Number five.

Poet Betty standing by the edge of the terrace was suddenly vomiting black strings in the bushes. Then she ate more. She was number six.

Gerhart was telling us that the males had no effect and served only a ceremonial function. Everyone was listening to his own stomach expecting to be poisoned. Quite a picture, six of us sitting around on the sunlit terrace in our bathing suits waiting, waiting: asking each other, how many did you take? Males or females? Do you feel anything?

Two people fasted. Ruth Dettering was eager to eat but she was pregnant and Dick scolded her with froggy harumphs until she agreed to wait. She had been a nurse and I was glad that she was going to be out of trance. I talked to her about how to call for an ambulance and stomach pumps.

And Whiskers fasted.

Whiskers was a friend of a friend and had arrived the night before. He was slight in build, sweet in demeanor—a sensitive logician just flunked out of Michigan, clipping his words, hesitant, pedantic, anxious about sending a cable to his mother. To his mother?

He claimed he suffered from nervous fits and so he passed up the visions. He was sitting next to Gerhart and was dressed in bathing trunks over flowered undershorts, and green garters and black socks and leather shoes and a silken robe. He had been appointed scientist and was taking elaborate notes of Gerhart's reactions.

Religion in primitive society was an awesome reality, "terrible" in the original meaning of the word, pervading all life and culminating in ceremonies that were forbidden to the profane.

Suddenly
      I begin
           to feel
Strange.
Going under dental gas. Good-bye.
Mildly nauseous. Detached. Moving away
               away
                  away

Let me point out certain parallels between our Mexican rite and the mystery performed at Eleusis.

From the group in bathing suits.
On a terrace
      under the bright
           Mexican sky.
When I tell this the others scoff
Hah, hah. Him. Power of suggestion.
Skepticism? Of my mind? Of me? Of mind? Of my?
Oh, now no. No matter.
Dettering says he feels it too.

O muses, O great genius, aid me now! O memory that wrote down what I saw, here shall your noble character be shown. (Inferno II)

At the heart of the mystery of Eleusis lay a secret. In the surviving texts there are numerous references to the secret, but in none is it revealed.

Oh my friend. Do you feel tingling in face?
Yes.
Dental gas?
Yes.
Slight dizziness?
Yes. Exactly.
Whiskers making notes. Rapid whiz pencil.
Lips obscene gash brown stained beard.
Flowered underpants peeping out
from bathing trunks, green socks, black shoes,
thin shoulders
Bending over note pad.
Viennese analyst.
Comic. Laugh. Laugh. Laugh. Laugh. Can't stop.

From the writings of the Greeks, from a fresco in Pompeii, we know that the initiate drank a potion.

Then, in the depths of the night, he beheld a great vision, and the next day he was still so awestruck that he felt he would never be the same man as before.

Laugh. Laugh.
All look at me.
Astonishment
More laugh laugh laugh laugh
Whiskers looks up, red tongue flicks from shrubbery.
Lick lips.
Stomach laugh. So funny that I. . . .
Laughing pointing. . . .
The rabbi! Psychoanalytic rabbinical rabbit!
Convulsed in laughahafter.

When, at the beginning of summer, thunder—electrical energy—comes rushing forth from the earth again, and the first thunderstorm refreshes nature, a prolonged state of tension is resolved. Joy and relief make themselves felt. (I Ching XVI)

What the initiate experienced was "new, astonishing, inaccessible to rational cognition."

pomposity of scholars
impudence of the mind
smug naïveté of words
If Whiskers could only see!
Stagger in hahahouse. Roaring. Into bedroom.
Fahahalling on bed
Doubled in laughahafter.
Detterings follow, watch curiously, maybe scared.
Funnier.
Then
Dettering begins to lafhahahaf.
Yes, he laughs too.
You see, Dickohoho? The impudent mind?
Comedy? Yes.
Only Ruth standing there grinning quizzically.

The king is told not to be anxious, but to study how he may always be like the sun in his meridian height, cheering and enlightening all.

It also seems significant that the Greeks were wont to refer to mushrooms as "the food of the gods," *broma theon,* and that Porphyrius is quoted as having called them "nurslings of the gods," *Theotrophos.*

Starting back to terrace
My walk has changed
Rubber legs
Room is full of water
Under water
Floating
Floating in air-sea

Room
Terrace
People
All
Under
Water
BUT NO WORDS CAN DESCRIBE

Out on terrace
Trance has hit the others.
Gerhart
Sprawling on chair, staring up at umbrella
Eyes popping, big as melons
Gone
Gone
Gone
Babbling.

No, see Whisker pencil flying
Hear Gerhart voice
        an orange spot, I should say twenty
        centimeters in diameter, now changing
        to purple, now being approached at an
        angle of forty-five degrees by an
        alternating band of yellow and red. . . .
Scientists at work
Funny, funny too.
Long, lanky Gerhart in straw sombrero
Gleaming, staring eyes fixed in space
Tufted goatee bobbing up and down as he tapes
out visions.

Dettering swims up.
Point to Gerhart
We lafhafhafhaf
Swim to poet-Betty
On the beach by flowers.
Face turns up
Gone, gone, gone.
I took nine.
Nine, she sighs.
Betty makes hissing noise.
Eyes tender. All woman inviting.

Ruth Dettering standing by the door.

They were not for mortal man to eat, at least not every day. We might be dealing with what was in origin a religious tabu. . . .

I do not suggest that St. John of Patmos ate mushrooms in order to write the book of Revelation.

Yet the succession of images in his vision, so clearly seen but such a phantasmagoria, means for me that he was in the same state as one bemushroomed.

The advantage of the mushroom is that it puts many (if not everyone) within reach of this state without having to suffer the mortifications of Blake and St. John.

It permits you to see, more clearly than our perishing mortal eye can see, vistas beyond the horizons of this life, to travel backwards and forwards in time. To enter other planes of existence, even (as the Indians say) to know God.

All that you see during this night has a pristine quality: the landscape, the edifices, the carvings, the animals— they look as though they had come straight from the Maker's workshop.

This newness of everything —it is as if the world had just dawned—overwhelms you and melts you with its beauty.

Swim to her through water, suddenly
Ominous.
Have you ever swum
On moonless night
In southern sea
Where sharks may be?
And felt that dread
Of unknown
Black peril?
Swimming in ocean of energy
With no mind to guide.

Look, Ruth. I can tell you that this
thing is going to hit me real hard.
Harder than anything that has ever
happened to me. And to the others too.
Ruth listens hard, nodding her good
nurse head. You may have six psychotic nuts
on your hands. I think you should send
the kids downtown to the movies, and
the maid too, get her out of here, and lock
the gates and for god's sake stay close
and keep your eyes on things.

How do you feel having all this
Going on around you?
Ruth grins.
So envious I could
Scream.
Sitting on chair
Feeling cold doom
Sky dark, air still
Soundless like
Ocean
Bottom
World stops spinning
Somewhere
The big celestial motor
Which keeps universe moving
Is turned off and the whole business
Terrace, house, lawn, city, world
coasting
    coasting
      dropping
        through space
          without
            sound

Mandy floats from beach chair
Swims by, I watch her go
Inside door loosens hair
Falls down over shoulders
Looks out in bikini wet tresses trailing
Mermaid eyes see far away.

Old Dettering floats over
sea-toad face
bloated
purple green warts
froggy
We stand looking down over
allgreen grass blade leaf petal in
focus sharp clear shining
changing waves color
like
floodlight slides
at summer dance hall
kaleidoscope

Behold! You are come to Cerin Amroth, said Haldir.
For this is the heart of the ancient realm as it was
long ago, and here is the mound of Amroth, where
in happier days his high house was built. Here ever
bloom the winter flowers in the unfading grass.
(The Lord of the Rings)

mandy and i lie side by side on beach chair
her knee hits mine they merge
no difference between skins
last abstraction of self and self's body gone
hairs on leg (my leg?) tripled move in sharp
perspective
like little fleas in Tivoli sideshow in Copenhagen
no word spoken
five us sit on terrace
still staring space
catatonic silent withdrawn
sitting in heavenly asylum
Ruth I talk
She psychiatric nurse
I good patient.
She talks earnestly about . . . reality.
You must try LSD
and mescaline and

All these things you see
with an immediacy of vision
that leads you to say to
yourself, "Now I am seeing
for the first time, seeing direct, without the intervention of mortal eyes."

It is clear to me where
Plato found his ideas. It was
clear to his contemporaries
too. Plato had drunk of the
potion in the Temple of
Eleusis and had spent the
night seeing the great vision.

And all the time you are
seeing these things, the
priestess sings, not loud
but with authority.

Your body lies in the darkness, heavy as lead, but your spirit seems to soar and leave the hut,

see if they are
different from
mushrooms

Listen tolerantly.
Pity her.
Poor creature.
Think such affairs important.
Mind games. Head trips.

Whiskers walks in kitchen completely dressed, he is going to town to send another wire to mother. He is so serious about the comic game in which he is trapped. Whiskers seems so can't bear funny.

and with the speed of thought to travel where it wishes in time and space, accompanied by the shaman's singing and by the ejaculations of her percussive chant.

On patio
Scientist Gerhart giggly, sitting peacefully,
Lost contemplation.
Joan by side
But
She is fighting spell
Fluttering,
Talking
Refusing to relax.

Of great importance, furthermore, is the law of movement along the line of least resistance, which in this hexagram is enunciated as the law for natural events and for human life.

What you are seeing and what you are hearing appears as one:

Holds bowl of mushrooms in hand
Hostess pushing cookies at church tea.
Have another, one more makes all the difference.
I eat a second.
Have another, one more makes all the difference.
I eat third.

Swim along veranda to bedroom
Shades drawn. Dark.
Betty feels isolated. All woman un-tilled earth. I am sorry tender.
Her black hair
drawn back big pony tail.
Cherokee princess great beauty.
Humming bird words swoop from mouth.
How do you feel?

The music assumes harmonious shapes, giving visual form to its harmonies, and what you are seeing takes on the modalities of music—the music of the spheres.

I sit trying answer. Can't talk.
Can only look jeweled patterns,
swirling tapestry work in closed eyes.
What is she asking me? Oh yes, how do I feel.
Far far gone.
She sits silently behind bead-work face. Do you
have anything on your mind? Do you want to talk?
She wants close. Intimacy. But,
I drift off to cavern of sea light.

All your senses are similarly affected:

The cigarette with which you occasionally break the tension of the night smells as no cigarette before had ever smelled: The glass of water is infinitely better than champagne.

Gerhart and Joan come in.
Fall on another bed.

In Mandy's arms
Her body warm foam rubber
Marshmallow flesh
My body gone
Fallen into her
Two leafy water plants
Twined together, undulating warm bermuda sea
deep
Entangled so that no one
Not even plants themselves can tell
Which leaf
Which stem
Belongs to which.

The bemushroomed person is poised in space, a disembodied eye, invisible, incorporeal, seeing but not seen.

Gone again, gone into
Palace by Nile
Temple near Hong Kong
Babylonian boudoir, Bedouin pleasure tent
Gem-flash jewel
Woven color silk gown movement
Mosaics flaming color Muzo emerald Burma rubies
Ceylon sapphire
Mosaics lighted from within glowing, moving,
changing.
Hundred reptiles, Jewel encrusted. Hammered
Moorish patterned
Snakeskin.
Snake mosaic, reptiles piled in
Giant, mile-square chest
Slide, slither, tumble down central
                           drain
                          One

In truth, he is the five senses disembodied, all of them keyed to the height of sensitivity and awareness, all of them blending into one another most strangely, until the person, utterly passive, becomes a pure receptor, infinitely delicate, of sensations.

As your body lies there in its sleeping bag, your soul is free, loses all sense of time, alert as it never was before, living an eternity in a night, seeing infinity in a grain of sand.

By
One
One
By
One

Such happy beauty
I lift up head to laugh
From around come answering chuckles.
Who? There are others here?
Eye open
Gerhart and Joan on next bed laughing
Next to me mermaid, laughing.
Put hand on hip where
Skin pokes through bikini lacings
Hand up soft back until fingers
Sink in quicksand of flesh through skin through ribs
Closed eyes
Moving belts like
Inlaid Moorish patterns

What you have seen and heard is cut as with a burin into your memory, never to be effaced.

Plummeting back through time,
                    snake time,
                        fish time
Down through giant jungle palm time,
            greeny lacy ferny leaf time.
Watching first life oozing,
                writhing,
                    twisting up.
Watching first sea thing crawl to shore
        Lie with her. Sand-rasp under cheek
            Then float sea-thing, down
                Deep green sea dark
                    I am first living
                        Thing I
                        Am

Laughter in dark room IT IS INTERESTING TO CON-
TEMPLATE A TANGLED BANK CLOTHED WITH MANY
PLANTS OF MANY KINDS Gerhart sitting up in dark
shouting WITH BIRDS SINGING ON THE BUSHES WITH
VARIOUS INSECTS FLITTING ABOUT Oh God don't let

At last you know what the ineffable is and what ec-stasy means.

The mind harks back to the origin of that word. For the Greeks *ekstasis* meant the flight of the soul from the body. I can find no better word to describe the bemushroomed state.

In common parlance, among the many who have not experienced ecstasy, ecstasy is fun, and I am frequently asked why I do not reach for mushrooms every night.

But ecstasy is not fun. Your very soul is seized and shaken until it tingles.

this end AND WITH WORMS CRAWLING THROUGH THE DAMP EARTH Gerhart goatee bobbing AND TO REFLECT THAT THESE ELABORATELY CONSTRUCTED FORMS SO DIFFERENT FROM EACH OTHER Gerhart gone in ecstasy AND DEPENDENT ON EACH OTHER IN SO COMPLEX A MANNER I know his ecstasy HAVE ALL BEEN PRODUCED BY LAWS ACTING AROUND US We are high. High Priests

THESE LAWS TAKEN IN ancient evolution trail THUS FROM THE WAR OF NATURE, FROM FAMINE AND DEATH down to fishy bottom Float with plankton THE MOST EXALTED OBJECT WHICH WE ARE CAPABLE OF CONCEIVING NAMELY down the littoral Tumbling past coral reef THE PRODUCTION OF THE HIGHER ANIMALS DIRECTLY FOLLOWS AND barnacled sea cliff Fathoms down through tangled jungle THERE IS GRANDEUR IN THIS VIEW OF LIFE Once we were all double-celled creatures Remember THAT WHILE THIS PLANET HAS GONE ON CYCLING ON ACCORDING TO THE FIXED LAWS OF GRAVITY Once we all drifted down soft red-walled caverns FROM SO SIMPLE A BEGINNING ENDLESS FORMS MOST BEAUTIFUL AND MOST WONDERFUL Our neurons remember HAVE BEEN AND ARE BEING EVOLVED Do you remember

Then begins Blake's long red voyage EVERY TIME LESS THAN A PULSATION OF THE ARTERY down the blood stream IS EQUAL IN ITS PERIOD AND VALUE TO SIX THOUSAND YEARS floating, bouncing along labyrinthian tunnels FOR IN THIS MOMENT THE POET'S WORK IS DONE artery, arteriole AND ALL THE GREAT EVENTS OF TIME START FORTH through every capillary AND ARE CONCEIVED IN SUCH A PERIOD through pink honey-comb tissue world WITHIN A MOMENT: A PULSATION OF ARTERY along soft watermelon channels EVERY SPACE LARGER THAN A RED GLOBULE OF MAN'S BLOOD part clotted scarlet swamps coagulate IS VISIONARY, AND IS CREATED BY THE HAMMER OF LOS tumbling thru caverned heart hall, ventricular AND EVERY SPACE SMALLER THAN A GLOBULE sliding down the smooth aortic shute OF MAN'S BLOOD OPENS slow bumping into narrow tunneled plexus INTO ETERNITY, OF WHICH THE VEGETABLE EARTH feel heart's muscle motor prodding us

Chuckles from across room
All fall in soft laugh
Some scene
Four sprawl in darkened room
Opium den of purest dreams
     Oh you worldling looking in think
     you evil no you wrong evil in your
     mental coin your evil makes me
     compassion laugh
     here is no evil
     but
Diamond virtue
Pure blue pureness
Beyond desire
Only
Needle moment
Buddha unity

This uniting of the human past with the Divinity in solemn moments of religious inspiration established the bond between God and man. The ruler who revered the Divinity in revering his ancestors became thereby the Son of Heaven, in whom the heavenly and the earthly world met in mystical contact. (I Ching XVI)

     That's
     why we laugh do you understand
     thinking about that paradox
     of mental evil and
     the mind-less clean diamond that's
     why we laugh
Words and thinking
Are not as important as we
Said and thought
And so we four drugged ontologists
Lift up heads and laugh
Mandy stone carved semitic mask above water
don't sleep don't sleep
Miss the beauty if you sleep
No one sleeps

Head fall back on bed. Floating, tumble weed, wind driven. CERTAIN SEEDS, FALLING ON WATER BECOME

After all, who will choose to feel undiluted awe, or to float through that door yonder into the divine presence?

The unknowing abuse the word, but we must recapture its full and terrifying sense.

As man emerged from his brutish past, thousands of years ago, there was a stage in the evolution of his awareness when the discovery of a mushroom (or perhaps a higher plant) with miraculous properties was a revelation to him,

a veritable detonator to his soul, arousing in him sentiments of awe and reverence, and gentleness and love, to the highest pitch of which mankind is capable, all those sentiments and virtues that mankind has ever since regarded as the highest attributes of his kind.

It made him see what the perishing mortal eye cannot see. The Greeks were right to hedge about this mystery, this imbibing of the potion, with secrecy and surveillance.

What today is resolved into the effects of a mere drug, a tryptamine or lysergic acid derivative, was for them a prodigious miracle, inspiring in them poetry and philosophy and religion.

Perhaps with all our modern knowledge we do not need the divine mushrooms any more. Perhaps we need them more than ever.

Some are shocked that the key to religion might be reduced to a drug.

DUCKWEED. Dropping again down shaft of time. WHEN THEY REACH THE JUNCTION OF THE LAND AND THE WATER THEY BECOME LICHEN. See tiger jungle cats, sinewy. Good-bye. REACHING RICH SOIL, THEY BECOME WU-TSU, THE ROOT OF WHICH BECOMES GRUBS, WHILE THE LEAVES COME FROM BUTTERFLIES, OR HSU. See reptiles jewelry. Good-bye. SO GOD CREATED THE GREAT SEA MONSTERS AND EVERY LIVING CREATURE THAT MOVES, WITH WHICH THE WATERS SWARM. Now I see the straggly shore creatures. Good-bye, dear friends. THE YANG CHI GRAFTED TO AN OLD BAMBOO WHICH HAS FOR A LONG TIME PUT FORTH NO SHOOTS, PRODUCES THE CH'ING-NING. I am drifting down past flowering sea life. Good-bye. AND GOD MADE THE BEASTS OF THE EARTH ACCORDING TO THEIR KINDS AND THE CATTLE ACCORDING TO ITS KIND. Drifting down through the history of my body which is all body down to the red, wet, warm beginnings. AND GOD SAW EVERYTHING HE MADE, AND BEHOLD IT WAS VERY GOOD. I am down to the center. To the single point of origin. Hello.
lay pulsing softly center
of all life and time
I the giant eye . . .
Giant eye I
Giant eye
Eye
I

Lying ecstatic eyes closed on a Triassic-Jurassic sedentary rock formation, one hand on Mandy's vertebrae hearing interstellar voices from the Mexican patio, light years away. Voice calls. Where are you? Here! I am lying unicelled looking up up up through the spiral unfolding of two billion years, seeing it all ahead of me, ovum, segmentation, differentiation of organs, plant, fish, mammal, monkey, baby, grammar school, college, Harvard, Mexico, Cuernavaca. They want me way up there. Is it worth the whole journey? To start the two-billion-year cycle once again? No. Why bother? Let's move over to the Precambrian sludge, no too wet, abysses, overlying waters, narrow littoral rocks, let's try that Cenozoic snaky jungle. Ah, yes.

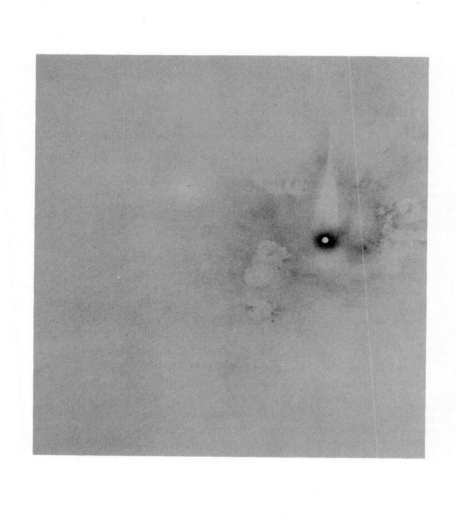

On the other hand, the drug is as mysterious as it ever was: Like the wind it cometh we know not whence nor why.

IT IS NOW EIGHT O'CLOCK STOP MUSHROOM EATING BEGUN AT FIVE O'CLOCK STOP EFFECT STARTING TO WEAR OFF STOP WANT TO STAY HERE BUT CANT STOP RETURNING SOON STOP HAVING MOMENTS OF NONTRANCE CONSCIOUSNESS STOP STOP STOP BUT THEN ENRAPTURING VISIONS RETURN AND CLUTCH OF MIND LOOSENS STOP IMPACT OF NOW-WORLD HITS RETINA AND DON'T STOP

Mandy and I peer out of cage at earthlings
Acapulco friends who have just arrived
Humor of situation pushes over brink to laughter

If our classical scholars were given the opportunity to attend the rite at Eleusis, to talk with the priestess, they would exchange anything for that chance.

Friends listen Dicko orate
Shoots nervous glances in our direction
Wildly funny
  then i realize responsibility
  and role as host
  and walk out to porch and have
  friendly conversation with new arrivals
  explaining what is
  happening and telling them to go to
  kitchen for drink and we will be
  eating supper in hour or so they are
  relieved and we conclude our
  perfectly normal conversation

They would approach the precincts, enter the hallowed chamber with the reverence born of the texts venerated by scholars for millennia.

Quiet waters roll and Dettering
Old rumpled crocodile paddles up
  Dettering reports that the rest of the
  crowd had landed back on shore and
  were gathered around the kitchen
  table
  Whiskers had returned and Gerhart
  was dictating notes to him.

I INTEND REMAINING OUT HERE LONG AS POSSIBLE STOP HAVING WONDERFUL TIME STOP WISH EVERYONE WERE HERE

on livingroom couch
head in flesh pool of Mandy lap
Plastic forms spinning in eyelid

And that would be their frame of mind if they were invited to partake of the potion?

Ruth standing above us
¿Qué tal?

Join us in the kitchen, everyone talking
No, Ruth.
Good-bye Ruth.
¿Adónde vas?
To slinky sea bottom.
Ruth leans down and shakes my shoulder.
Take me with you. Tell me what you see
No. No. Dear nurse Ruth.
I can't.
Ask marlin to take you with him on slippery,
divy,
     skimming jumping run for joy across and
        under the sun-specked ocean
Ask your blood to sing the song of voyage
       down to wine-red cavern of your
       heart.
Can they speak your language? No?
Neither me. My voice trails off as I head
                down
                   again

Head falls through
Butter belly and
Melon womb to
Sofa cushions
    Mandy is getting up to check
    on guests
At the far end of the pool Mandy and I sit
on beach chairs. She climbs on lap. We throw
heads back and watch gray clouds skudding along
black sky.
Magic mushrooms
Sculpting clouds
Into Roman emperors
    Greek gods
    Football scrimmages
    Cavalry charges
We sit for full half-hour
No words
Soft laughter at secret we share
Then
The gray masses change back to clouds for
longer and longer and longer periods and all
at once my legs feel cramped and the chill of
night air and
the trance is over.

Well, those rites take place now, unbeknownst to the classical scholars, in scattered dwellings, humble, thatched, without windows, far from the beaten track.

If it is the rainy season, perhaps the mystery is accomplished by torrential rains and punctuated by terrifying thunderbolts.

Then, indeed, as you lie there bemushroomed, listening to the music and seeing visions, you know a soul-shattering experience,

recalling as you do the belief of some primitive peoples that mushrooms, the sacred mushrooms, are divinely engendered by Jupiter Fulminans,

The time was 9:07 and the journey into the other half of the cerebral cortex had lasted four hours and seven minutes from the time of eating.

And that was the trip.

It was the classic visionary voyage and I came back a changed man. You are never the same after you've had that one flash glimpse down the cellular time tunnel. You are never the same after you've had the veil drawn.

In the seven years since eating seven mushrooms in a garden in Mexico I have devoted all of my time and energy to the exploration and description of these strange deep realms.

the god of the lightning-bolt, in the soft mother earth.

∞

ENTHUSIASM.

It furthers one to install helpers
And to set armies marching.
(I Ching)

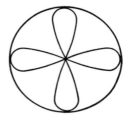

The Revelation Is Awe-Full:

September 1960

Guide: JACK LEARY

Oracle: IX

The taming power of the small

The Gentle, Wind

The Creative, Heaven

The wind drives across heaven:
The image of THE TAMING POWER OF THE
   SMALL.
Thus the superior man
Refines the outward aspect of his nature.
                                              (I Ching)

On a sunny Saturday afternoon in 1960, beside the swimming pool of his rented summer villa in Cuernavaca, a 39-year-old American ate a handful of odd-looking mushrooms he'd bought from the witch doctor of a nearby village.

Within minutes, he recalled later, he felt himself "being swept over the edge of a sensory Niagara into a maelstrom of transcendental visions and hallucinations."

The fungi were legendary "sacred mushrooms" that have since become known and feared by many, as one of the psychedelic (literally, mind-manifesting) chemicals that have created a national fad among the nation's young and a scandal in the press.

The American was a Harvard psychotherapist named Timothy Leary, who has since found himself transmogrified from scientist and researcher into progenitor and high priest of a revolutionary movement.

At dinner the night after the visions, the maid asked if she could take the mushrooms over to the servants' cottage to show her husband. Ah, Lola, you want him to find you some? Lola's eyes narrowed and she made a gesture of disgust. *No, Señor. Malos. Muy malos.* Ruth leaned forward, rapid Spanish. Why do you want your husband to see them, Lola? The maid took a step backward, crouching. So he will see them, *Señora,* and know them, and never eat them. The plate with black twisted mushrooms was on the mantel. When I picked it up several flies spiraled away. Lola held the plate at arm's length and scuttled from the room.

Lola's face had a look of bitter dread. I didn't know then that we were to meet this same fear of the visionary unknown at every step along the road to come.

Ruth was looking out the window and she turned with a puzzled smile on her face. Strange sight, she said. Lola's half-running across the lawn with the plate of mushrooms in one hand and crossing herself with the other.

There was fear in the air the next day in Mexico City. I sensed it on the Paseo de la Reforma, the broad, grand pride of Mexico. Twelve cars wide, split by grass strips and tree lanes, lined with statues, sweeping into round wide *glorietas,* humming like a power-line with speeding cars. As I drove along near Sanborns, the traffic slowed. The American embassy building was ringed with hundreds of police troopers, black boots, black leather belts. They looked half-fierce and half-embarrassed. I remembered reading about the left-wing student riots. *Cuba sí. Yanqui, no.* The government was moving with a nervous show of force.

I was having lunch with a sociologist named Lewis. Trouble as usual parking, and I found him waiting at a table in Prendes. He declined a cigarette and hesitated when I ordered a vermouth and then decided to join me. He talked about his studies of village life in southern Mexico and Guatemala. He had lifted the lid and poked around inside and what he described wasn't pretty. The sick. The miserable. The bullies. The victims. The hopeless. The grinding pressure of no money, lousy food, distrust, waking before dawn in a cold hut, your body stiff and crusted with yesterday's sweat and dirt, your mouth sour, your bowels running, haunted by your debts, your fearful ignorance of why it all works out this way and what to do. Lewis really told you how it was in concrete terms. Human helplessness. No happy theories to explain it away either. I liked him for that.

We ordered seafood and I had a half-bottle of smoky Mexican white wine. Lewis was a sensitive man. He was disturbed by what he had seen and had to write about. He loved the Mexicans and hated sociological theory. He was bitter because he had been attacked by the political book reviewers, and the psychoanalytic book reviewers and the theorists and his American colleagues who saw a rich, pássionate, Freudian warmth in his villagers. He had heard vaguely of the sacred mushrooms but had never paid much attention to the reports about them.

Mandy and I took the elevator way up to the skytop restaurant of the Latino-American building. We sat drinking tequila and looking through the glass wall out over the valley of Mexico. The air was hazy blue except where some white clouds hung over the western volcanic peaks. The whole historic bit was right there in front of us. There was the dusty flatland around the airport which used to be a lake and the old colonial section with crumbling *tezontle* churches and palaces, and the skyscrapers running out to the modern sections and there out beyond, the acres of tenements. We watched airliners sliding down sloping trajectories and I thought of Dick Alpert flying to Mexico to pick me up in his Cessna, at this moment, somewhere a mile high over Jalisco, poring over his airmaps and checking the green patterns below,

A movement spawned not by an idea but by a substance that's been called "the spiritual equivalent of the hydrogen bomb."

Few men, in their youth, would have seemed less likely to emerge as a religious leader, let alone as a rebel with a cause.

At the age of 19, Leary distressed his Roman Catholic mother by abandoning Holy Cross two years before graduation ("The scholastic approach to religion didn't turn me on").

Then he affronted his father, a retired army career officer, by walking out of West Point after 18 months ("My interests were philosophic rather than militaristic").

Not until he transferred to the University of Alabama did he begin to settle down academically—to work for his B.A. in psychology.

On graduation in 1942, he enlisted as an army psychologist, served in a Pennsylvania hospital until the end of the war.

He then resumed his schooling and earned his Ph.D. at the University of California at Berkeley.

Acquiring both eminence and enemies with his first major jobs—as director of Oakland's progressive Kaiser Foundation hospital and as an assistant professor at UC's school of medicine in San Francisco.

Leary began to display the courage and sometimes rash iconoclasm that have since marked every phase of his checkered career.

Contending that traditional psychiatric methods were hurting as many patients as they helped, he resigned in 1958 and signed up as a lecturer on clinical psychology at Harvard.

Here he began to evolve and enunciate the theory of social interplay and personal behavior as so many stylized games, since popularized by Dr. Eric Berne in his best-selling book, Games People Play.

looking for the landmarks to guide him in to the Guadalajara airport.

I had started taking narcotics too early in the day, wine at lunch, tequila in the cocktail lounge and by the time the good restaurants were serving dinner, I was heavy and tired. Liquor contracts consciousness. Soggy symbols. Mandy was being very college-girl. I was missing the semitic mermaid with the sculptured lines and got bored and irritable.

A classic liquor high. Around midnight we ran into Poet Betty in the *mariachi* section. By this time, the taste of tequila was perfumey obnoxious and the lime taste was acrid and the musicians were puffy, pouter pigeons buttoned into their fake *ranchero* costumes just as sick of singing the same old ballads as I was of hearing them. When Guadalajara de Noche closed at one o'clock, we had coffee in the *mariachi* market and I drove Poet Betty home and then stood in the hallway of Mandy's house and for a moment I felt the message of the mushrooms which is the wordless, mindless rapture of the moment. I started a miserable debate with myself about the next move. I wanted to drive to Cuernavaca but I knew that I'd have to come back to meet Dick Alpert at the airport next afternoon.

Around three in the morning I was standing in front of the hotel, Virreyes, leaning against a lamppost, sodden, tired, hung on the hooks of indecision, deciding whether to drive back or sleep the rest of the night in the city. The coin came down stay. As I turned to walk to the hotel entrance, my shoe caught in a metal hook sticking from the bottom of the post. I moved forward. My shoe caught. I fell. Crouched on the sidewalk, on my hands and knees, I looked up. A group of taxi-drivers and Mexican hotel hangers-on were standing at the lobby entrance. Their talk stopped and they turned to stare down at me. My eyes moved from one face to the next, to the next. Then I lifted myself up slowly, slapped the dirt from my hands and walked into the hotel.

When I got to Mandy's house for lunch there was a message. Dick Alpert had phoned from Guadalajara and would be landing at Mexico City airport in an hour. I found him closing his flight plan in the operations office. Dick is tall, blond, and boyish, full of silly enthusiasms—and during his three-day flight down the west coast and over the mountains he had fallen in love with Mexico. We piled his luggage in the car and stopped at a *tienda* for beer and potato chips and headed out past the university on to the toll road and started climbing through the cloudy passes out of the valley. Dick stretched out his legs in the front seat and began telling me how happy the Mexican people were and how much more sensible their life was than the American. On his flight down, there was always a cab driver who would see him circling over the town and by the time Dick had set the plane down on the cow-pasture runway, the taxi would be waiting for him and sometimes there would be not one but two or three girls in the cab for him to take his pick.

They're relaxed. They smile. They love music. They know what the important values are.

That's right, Dick, I said. And when they get bored with their small town and their cab and the whorehouse where they work, why they just jump in their plane and fly away to the next country that hits their fancy.

Dick flashed his modest boy smile. I suppose I'm talking like the typical naïve American tourist. The happy native bit.

They're stuck. They have no choice. Is that right?

I told him that I didn't know. Because I didn't know. But I was sure that the Mexicans had no secrets that Americans lack, because there weren't any Mexicans at all but fifty million men and women with eyes and ears and brains and hearts more or less hung up on their own mental chess-boards, different from our chess pieces maybe, but hung up all the same.

So, I didn't know. Ever since last weekend and the mushrooms I didn't know as much any more. I had started the slow process of throwing things out of mind, junking mental furniture that had been clogging up my brain. I used to know a lot about Mexico, generalizations, theories.

Now I was beginning to see that all I knew were

He began to both preach and practice the effective but unconventional new psychiatric research technique of sending his students to study emotional problems such as alcoholism where they germinate —rather than in the textbook or the laboratory.

At the time, predictably enough, few of these novel notions went over very well with Leary's hidebound colleagues.

But their rumblings of skepticism rose to a chorus of outrage when Leary returned to Harvard in 1960 from his pioneering voyage into inner space.

He began experimenting on himself, his associates, and hundreds of volunteer subjects with measured doses of psilocybin, the chemical derivative of the sacred mushrooms,

vowing "to dedicate the rest of my life as a psychologist to the systematic exploration of this new instrument."

He and his rapidly multiplying followers began to turn on with the other psychedelic drugs:

morning glory seeds, nutmeg, marijuana, peyote, mescaline and a colorless, odorless, tasteless but incredibly potent laboratory compound called LSD 25.

LSD was first synthesized in 1938 by a Swiss biochemist seeking a pain-killer for migraine headaches.

faded memories of a few hundred conversations with Mexicans about Mexico and faded memories of a few books written by American minds in American words. An American head-trip imposed on a different way of life. I knew nothing, really
> my words, lies
>> just memories of myself
>> strung along the
>> wires of my mind

Dick spinning theories about Mexicans
Started the chuckling
Mild replica of the
Mushroom
Laughter

We had just passed the summit at Tres Marías and were heading down the long descent to Morelos. I began to tell Dick about the mushrooms. He listened to my story and then he surprised me with his response.

A hundred times stronger than psilocybin, LSD sent its hallucinated users on multihued, multileveled roller coaster rides so spectacular that it soon became Leary's primary tool for research.

Sounds very much like marijuana. You've never tried it? Same reaction. Feelings of detachment. Intensification of color and sound. Euphoria. Sense of having discovered some great wisdom. Everyone's been smoking pot for years around San Francisco and Greenwich Village. There are regular cults of tea-heads. A friend of mine gave me two pounds of pot when he left for Europe. I smoked it for awhile but got bored with it and finally it dried up and I threw most of it away.

And as word began to circulate about the fantastic, phantasmagorical "trips" taken by his students, it soon became a clandestine campus kick.

This was some development! Was that all I had experienced? Were the mystic visions and the oriental dreams just a stronger version of a Greenwich Village pot high? I had been sure we were on the verge of something new and great. A pushing back of the frontiers of consciousness. But now it looked as though I was just a naïve, sheltered intellectual discovering what hip teen-agers on the North Beach had been experiencing for years.

The late afternoon thunderstorm was going full blast as we rolled down the last long straight grade into Cuernavaca. Dick decided to spend the first night in Tepoztlan with the McClellands, who were renting a house for the summer. The Tepoztlan road at sundown. Herdsmen nudging along their cattle. Indians trudging home from the *milpas* with

By 1962 it had become an underground cult among the young avant-garde from Los Angeles.

machetes and rakes over their shoulders. The rain makes for a greater scene. The headlights on the white ponchos slumped over plodding burros. The valley of Tepoztlan is haunted. It's the nave of a prehistoric cathedral with the roof blown off and the huge pillared cliff walls still standing, and the land is always damp, and dark-green, and teeming with sad memories. Dick's story about the marijuana and the rain, and the tequila fatigue from last night, they all began to hit and I felt disillusioned.

The hexagram presents a configuration of circumstances in which a strong element is temporarily held in leash by a weak element. It is only through gentleness that this can have a successful outcome. (I Ching IX)

Thursday was clear and sunny. I spent that afternoon lying by the pool. I was way behind on my writing, but all I did was soak up sun and sweat and think. I tried to ask Dick Dettering about the mushrooms but he didn't want to talk. He was worrying about giving a lecture in Spanish. He had given the speech a hundred times in English, but he had no ear for Spanish and when he read the translation he sounded like a Midwesterner reading names from the Cuernavaca telephone book. He seemed to have forgotten the mushrooms.

When the sun would get too hot, I'd take my son Jack's rubber water goggles and his snorkle breathing tube and swim in the pool. The mask made everything under water seem sharp,

clean,
clear,
clear. . . .

grained surface of pool . . . abstract canvas . . . blue tile border glowing . . . sapphire ribbon . . . living green threads . . . hung in azure . . . sun-specked water . . . before . . . pool was . . . pool blue water . . . felt good when hot . . . now . . . giant . . . fluid . . . gem box. . . .

The pool had not changed. My retina and the brain stuff behind it had changed, turned-on. The water hadn't been drained in two weeks and all that green algae stuff, however beautiful to the

Playboy: How many times have you used LSD, Dr. Leary?

Leary: Up to this moment, I've had 311 psychedelic sessions.

Playboy: What do you think it's done for you—and to you?

Leary: That's difficult to answer easily. Let me say this: when I was 39 I had my first psychedelic experience. At that time I was a middle-aged man involved in the middle-aged process of dying.

My joy in life, my sensual openness, my creativity were all sliding downhill.

Since that time, six years ago, my life has been renewed in almost every dimension.

Most of my colleagues at the University of California and at Harvard, of course, feel that I've become eccentric and a kook.

I would estimate that fewer than 15 percent of my professional colleagues understand and support what I'm doing.

The ones who do, as you might expect, tend to be among the younger psychologists. Psychedelic drugs are the medium of the young. As you move up the age scale—into the 30's, 40's, and 50's—fewer and fewer people are open to the possibilities that these chemicals offer.

Playboy: Why is that?

Leary: To the person over 35 or 40, the word "drug" means one of two things: doctor-disease or dope fiend-crime.

Nothing you can say to a person who has this neurological fix on the word "drug" is going to change his mind.

mushroomed eye, had to go. The next morning we were expecting special guests. The Soviet cultural attaché coming down for the day. I had met him twice at cocktail parties where he had been surrounded by my countrymen, politically wise beyond their years from reading *Time* magazine and liquored up enough to think they could win the great debate. Both times I had felt shame at the spectacle and had moved in to talk friendly with him about Russian education and his impressions of Mexico and Cuba. He was young, new at his job, eager to be liked, well-informed, terribly confident, proud of his country, and, when tight, pathetically puzzled at why Americans misunderstood him and his peaceful intentions.

I wanted things to go smoothly when Leonov and his friends arrived for lunch. The pool should be emptied and cleaned. This meant a clash with Lola the maid. To her it meant extra work and a larger water bill to explain to her absentee landlords. Nothing for her to gain. Something to lose. Passive resistance. Also, she had changed since I took the mushrooms. She was suspicious. I had angered her somehow. Made her afraid of me. I knew she'd stall until 3:30 so our water would drain on the eighth green of the golf club after sunset.

At 3:30 I mobilized my son and Pepe his friend. If we cleaned it now and started filling at sundown it would be full enough for the Russians to swim the next day. Pepe, go tell your mother we are going to clean the pool.

Lola came darting out of her cottage. She shook her head as we talked. The gardener was at school. *Mañana. Mañana es mejor.* Hear me, Lola, Tomorrow is Friday. Come friends tomorrow from Mexico. Necessitates much time to fill the pool. Correct? We must clean the pool today or wait until Monday. True? Okay, Lola, you are the director. We shall wait. But she didn't.

In the morning the pool was clean but empty. A thin trickle of fresh water puddled on the bottom. No one would swim today, Russians or Americans. Ruth was drinking coffee. She was calm and amused at my anger. She defended the maid. Lola was in the kitchen. When I finished giving her my opinion I banged my hand on the metal sink. Ruth's cool disapproving eyes followed me into the bedroom. I was in a rage, undercut by both women. Gone mushroom tranquility.

I was still smarting when the Russian came. The day went badly. It was hot and they had brought their bathing suits. Aztec duplicity exposed American inhospitality to Communist diplomat. We sat by the end of the pool listening to the thin splash of water and drank too much too early in the day. I talked to him about the mushrooms, but he wasn't interested and became irritable. The weary pushing of alcohol-soggy symbols back and forth across the board. He wanted to know why Americans used germ warfare in Korea. The only mistake the Russians made in Hungary was to delay sending in troops. Russian women were by far the most beautiful in the world. The American secret police would arrest me if he came to see me in America. I was going to give him my address so that he would be sure to visit me in Cambridge anyway, but after they left, I remembered that I had forgotten.

Lola had stayed out of sight most of the day, and when she appeared down on the lawn feeding the animals, our eyes never met.

The next day was my last day at the villa. Dick Alpert and my son and I were to fly back to California after the weekend. And the weekend continued bad. Gerhart and Joan and Mandy arrived at noon. They brought no mushrooms. Gerhart had climbed for three hours to reach the village, but Juana the witch was nowhere to be found. No one knew where she was nor when she'd come back. The villagers were mysterious and evasive.

This didn't bother any of last week's veterans. No one really wanted to repeat. I was expecting one prospective mushroomer later in the day, but I wasn't disturbed by the thought of his missing out. He was an anthropologist who had spent three years in a Mexican village, which he now called "my village," and he and his wife sang Mexican ballads together and produced endless facts about Mexican life. He was a pleasant intellectual chap

He's frozen like a Pavlovian dog to this conditioned reflex. To people under 25, on the other hand, the word "drug" refers to a wide range of mind benders running from alcohol, energizers, and stupefiers to marijuana and the other psychedelic drugs.

To middle-aged America, it may be synonymous with instant insanity, but to most Americans under 25, the psychedelic drug means ecstasy, sensual unfolding, religious experience, revelation, illumination, contact with nature.

There's not a teen-ager or young person in the United States today who doesn't know at least one person who has had a good experience with marijuana or LSD.

The horizons of the current younger generation, in terms of expanded consciousness, are light-years beyond those of their parents.

The breakthrough has occurred; there's no going back. The psychedelic battle is won.

Playboy: Why, then, have you called for a one-year "cease-fire" on the use of LSD and marijuana?

Leary: Because there have never been two generations of human beings so far apart—living essentially in two different worlds, speaking two different languages —as the people over 25 and the younger generation.

Evolutionary misunderstanding causes bloodshed and imprisonment.

To relieve this situation I have asked the younger generation to cool it for a year and to use this moratorium period to explain to their parents—and to their jailers—what LSD and marijuana are, and why we want and intend to use them.

I have made clear that this is a voluntary waiving of the constitutional right to change your own consciousness.

But I suggested this as a conciliatory gesture to mollify and educate the older generation and to allow time for the younger people to learn more about how to turn on.

but scared stiff of the mushrooms. He wanted to take them because it was like a duty. If he was to know Mexico he should know the native ritual.

Gerhart had an idea. We can give him the mushrooms left over from last week. They're dried by now, but that's all right. They retain their potency indefinitely. Just to make sure, we can start him out on a stronger dose.

The anthropologist and his wife arrived at two and when I went to the gate to let them in, there were three American college kids about to ring the bell. They were friends of Poet Betty. The boy was a Princeton sophomore and the girls were just starting at Mount Holyoke College. The college crowd went inside to change into swimming suits and I mixed drinks and sat in the dining room talking with the anthropologist about the mushroom situation. He said he was willing to try them dried. His wife would watch. He was extremely nervous.

Do you wish to look, Frodo? said the Lady Galadriel. You did not wish to see Elf-magic and were content.

Do you advise me to look? asked Frodo.

No, she said. I do not counsel you one way or another. I am not a counsellor. You may learn something, and whether what you see be fair or evil, that may be profitable, and yet it may not. Seeing is both good and perilous. Yet I think, Frodo, that you have courage and wisdom enough for the venture, or I would not have brought you here. Do as you will!

I will look, said Frodo, and he climbed on the pedestal and bent over the dark water. (The Lord of the Rings)

I was worried a bit about the anthropological panic and decided to round up someone to take the visions with him. If necessary, I was resolved to join him myself, although I had no desire to do so. The college kids were the only ones around the villa who hadn't mushroomed and when I asked them, they said sure, why not. The young kids were the first people I had talked to who were not automatically, reflexedly frightened at the idea of expanding consciousness. The psychedelic generation.

So we all sat around the dining room table while I counted the black twisted knobs into five bowls. Eight for anthro. Eight for Princeton. Eight to tall Mount Holyoke, eight to short.

And eight in the fifth bowl which I kept in front of me. Three college kids examined the dried sticks curiously and popped them in their mouths. They went through their bowls quickly. Good little children. Then they sat back happily waiting for the trance.

Not anthro. He picked up a knob, studied it from every angle, sniffed it, asked several questions about their origin and their effect. I could see drops of sweat on his brow just below the hair line. He didn't look happy. Finally, seeing that we were all watching him, waiting, he bit the end of the plant and made tasting sounds. Then his face scrunched up. Whew, they taste rotten. Are you sure they aren't poisonous? He took another bite and asked about dysentery. He continued to eat very slowly, forcing them down.

The green bowl in front of me became a magnet. Why not take them and return to the garden of ecstasy? More wisdom waits there. My mind argued for taking the mushrooms. So simple. There they are in the bowl ten inches from your mouth. But there wasn't one shred of desire pushing me towards them. My brain said yes. The second experience will be more enlightening. It will give you a basis for comparison. But I was scared too. I must have spent five minutes sitting there holding a black knob between my thumb and forefinger. Finally, I threw it back and pushed the bowl away. I'll take them if Dick Alpert wants to join me when he arrives.

The college crowd had long since drifted out to the patio, lying on beach chairs, waiting. Anthro still sat stiffly in front of his half-emptied bowl. He never did finish them. His wife sat next to him in solemn silence.

After thirty minutes, after forty minutes, after fifty minutes, nothing had happened. After an hour the colleges ate the rest of the mushrooms and after

I'm demanding that this period also be a moratorium on hysterical legislation and on punitive arrests of young people for the possession of LSD and marijuana.

If at the end of one year, the older generation has not taken advantage of this cease-fire, I predict and indeed urge a firm statement on the part of everyone involved that they intend to resume the use of psychedelics.

That they will exercise their constitutional rights to expand their own consciousness—whatever the cost.

Playboy: What do you say to the standard charge that LSD is too powerful and dangerous to entrust to the young?

Leary: Well, none of us yet knows exactly how LSD can be used for the growth and benefit of the human being.

It is a powerful releaser of energy as yet not fully understood. But if I'm confronted with the possibility that a 15-year-old or a 50-year-old is going to use a new form of energy that he doesn't understand, I'll back the 15-year-old every time.

Why? Because a 15-year-old is going to use a new form of energy to have fun, to intensify sensation, to make love, for curiosity, for personal growth.

Many 50-year-olds have lost their curiosity, have lost their ability to make love, have dulled their openness to new sensations, and would use any form of new energy for power, control, and warfare.

So it doesn't concern me at all that young people are taking time out from the educational and occupational assembly lines to experiment with consciousness, to dabble with new forms of experience and artistic expression.

The present generation under the age of 25 is the wisest and holiest generation that the human race has ever seen.

And, by God, instead of lamenting, derogating and imprisoning them, we should support them, listen to them, and turn on with them.

∞

two hours there was nothing to do but to apologize like a poor host. The college faces were fallen in disappointment, but anthro and wife didn't seem to mind.

Dick Alpert and the McClellands from Tepoztlan arrived and some more people from the capital dropped in and a professor from Amherst got lecturing drunk and a State Department officer, who was bitter about his job and our Latin policy and his boss, got very funny, sarcastic drunk and the others sat around the table and made intellectual talk. And that was about the way the summer in Cuernavaca ended.

Oh no, there was one final incident on Sunday morning. I went through that saddest routine of packing and checking the house over and over again, finding things that I had forgotten. Not enough room in the trunks and all this with a hangover and not enough sleep and the lousy feeling that had persisted all week since Dick Alpert told me about marijuana.

Lola was still keeping out of sight and when I did intersect her in the dining room, she looked at me with distrust and narrowed her eyes as though I were dangerous somehow.

When the last suitcase was locked, my son made the inevitable discovery that a toy had been left out. It was a plastic machine gun that shot corks. He and Pepe had been ambushing enemy all summer with their guns. It was large and bulky and impossible to pack. Then an image of Lola in the final scene occurred to me. Look, Jack, I want you to leave the gun here, okay? All right, but why? Pepe already has one. Never mind. Watch and you'll see.

When I took the last suitcase out to the car, I was carrying the gun. I laid it carefully on the driver's seat. Then I gave Lola two hundred and fifty pesos and we said good-bye and promised to write and we moved out to the sidewalk. Dick Alpert and Jack were in the car. I called Jack out and handed him the machine gun. Jack, give this to Lola and say this is for her. You see, it was my wish to drive off waving to Lola and to have her standing by the gate with the gun in her hand. Victorious defender. *Soldatera.*

From *The Reporter:*

When the International Federation for Internal Freedom was formed in Cambridge, Massachusetts, during the autumn of 1962, it was unique even in New England, a region not unfamiliar with eccentric social movements.

IFIF (pronounced "if-if," as if the speaker is stuttering over some terrifying cosmic question).

IFIF preaches the gospel that man's salvation lies in the expansion of his own consciousness, a state which, it is asserted, can be achieved through the ingestion of such substances as LSD-25, psilocybin, mescaline or even the right type of morning-glory seeds.

Although a handful of well-known people—most of the philosophers, mystics, and theologians—have lent IFIF support of their names, scientific circles have in general been quite critical of many of its expressed beliefs and goals.

The support of the theologians and mystics, in combination with the fact that IFIF's cause was unwittingly nurtured within Harvard University, has composed the movement's principal credentials.

I stood behind the car and watched Jack come up to Lola and make his speech and watched her take the gun and look surprised and then laugh. She seemed to understand and she seemed pleased. She called something to me. I be back soon, I said. She was nodding and smiling when the gun went off. Her face froze as she saw the cork bounce off my chest. Her eyes dropped down to the trigger still held taut by her finger. Then when she saw me laughing, she lifted the gun in front of her face as though it were an apron to hide behind and she began to giggle.

We were all grinning like pleased idiots as I got back in the car and made the U-turn. And as we rolled off and waved *adiós*, I was laughing and she was standing with the gun in her right hand.

Hence the image of many clouds, promising moisture and blessing to the land, although as yet no rain falls. The situation is not unfavorable; there is a prospect of ultimate success, but there are still obstacles in the way, and we can merely take preparatory measures. Only through the small means of friendly persuasion can we exert any influence. The time has not yet come for sweeping measures. However, we may be able, to a limited extent, to act as a restraining and subduing influence. To carry out our purpose we need firm determination within and gentleness and adaptability in external relations. (Wind over Heaven)

Next morning, I had trouble giving my car to the government, and it was mid-afternoon by the time I got to the airport. Dick went up to meteorology to see if we could beat the evening thunderstorm out of the valley, and my son collected a crowd around him and his iguana in the airport lobby. Dick came down, saying we had fifteen minutes of clear weather and Acapulco was blue and clean, so we rushed down to the Cessna and we stuck the iguana on the shelf behind the rear seat and we kissed Betty good-bye, and Dick ran up the engine and we turned the corner onto the main runway and rolled down the wide concrete highway and faster and faster and lifted up over the brown swamp flats and when the tower said okay, we left the frequency and flight pattern of the field and turned right and began climbing to make the height of the Tres Marías and when we didn't make it at the first run, we circled to gain altitude, looking down at the dozens of round, green-hollow-coned volcanoes scattered over the valley of Mexico and finally squeezed over the pass at 14,000 feet and in a half-hour dropped down over Tepoztlan and ran the length of the valley twice, buzzing the McClellands' ranch and dipping the wings when they came running out to wave and turned towards Cuernavaca and circled the villa and saw Lola and Pepe standing by the swimming pool (now quite full, thank you) and were surprised to see how many jet blue *albercas* were set alongside of how many lush villas in this rich little town that Hernando thought he conquered.

We are high
In the sky
Good-bye
Down there
There's a fog on U.S.A.
And my friends have frost their way
We'll be up there soon they said
But they've ground themselves instead
Please don't be down

After we passed Lake Tequesquetengo, Dick began to teach me how to fly and I began learning about the two new dimensions and, not knowing how to trim the plane, fighting the sliding of the horizon, while Dick bent over the map and drew red lines and made calculations.

It was all pretty mushroomy, sitting up there a mile high, beating our own path where no one else had ever been, beyond games, in touch with only the living moment. Should we climb those clouds or sidestep them through that gap to the north? In touch with only this immediate reality—is Acapulco there or there? Realizing (as we fail to realize down below, although it is as true down below) that we are a moment away from death and not caring for even that abstraction, death, because it's not a word

For many initiates, the credentials have been sufficient.

IFIF offers by its very existence, a certain amount of justification and rationale to those who submit to the dangerous attraction drug-taking holds for college students and young people in general.

"Drugs have always attracted college students," I was told recently by Dr. Dana L. Farnsworth, Director of the Harvard University Health Services.

"But this is the first time in history that an organization has existed to promote their use."

Caught unprepared by the utilization of a variety of hallucinogenic drugs in many areas of the U.S., law-enforcement officials and health authorities do not appear at present to possess the means of coping with the problem.

They are hampered by a net of vague, ineffectual and contradictory legal structure.

Meanwhile, in IFIF's four-room ground-floor head-quarters at 14 Storey Street, Cambridge, a varying number of blue-jeaned young people perform the clerical chores of a growing organization.

They work to spread its chapters and outposts through the country and the world, and push an aggressive, promotional drive that has all the earmarks of a proselytizing campaign.

∞

From *LSD* by Alpert, Cohen, and Schiller:

It is hard to imagine the fantastic growth of LSD use in the United States since 1962.

I believe approximately four million Americans took LSD last year, judging from conversation with suppliers.

Perhaps as many as 70 percent of all users now are high school and college students. . . .

∞

or a concept but a right-now decision about this peak, that cloud, this push on the rudder which turns us towards Acapulco airport or the mountain cliff.

We were flying at 110 miles per hour, with the jagged cotton fields ten feet below stretched out as far as we could see. The world was completely shut off. Somewhere down below were the mountains of Guerrero and Acapulco Bay and the Pacific. But we were above and out of it, skudding along the mile-high, white-capped ocean.

Dick was leaning forward studying the horizon and sweeping his eyes down and over the instruments and then back to the front. He turned to brief me. Here's the situation. We're okay up here. We're high enough to miss this stuff (he was pointing to the orange peaks on the map) but sooner or later we'll have to land and that means diving down blind through this white crud.

We can't turn back? No, that's no good. Mexico City is already socked in tight. And, if we tried to chance it north or south, there's no guarantee that the clouds will break. AT 5:45 THE ACAPULCO TOWER RECEIVED A CALL FROM AN AIRCRAFT ON THE UNICON. What we'll have to do is keep flying high and wide until we get well beyond the coast, out over the ocean, and then we plough down through the clouds until we hit the clear above the ocean and then we'll have to turn back and run the coast until we find Acapulco. All we have to do is be sure we fly far enough to miss the coastal range and hope there's enough ceiling over the Pacific. BUT THE AIRCRAFT IDENTIFICATION WAS UNINTELLIGIBLE DUE TO POOR TRANSMISSION. I'll see if I can get Acapulco tower for a reading on their ceiling.

Dick fiddled with the radio dial with his left hand and then he took the black plastic mouthpiece in his right hand. Acapulco, this is Cessna four-six Bravo. Do you hear me? REPEATED ATTEMPTS TO ESTABLISH RADIO CONTACT WERE UNSUCCESSFUL. We waited, listening to the engine hum and the rush of air past the cabin windows. Acapulco tower. This is Cessna four-six Bravo. Come in Acapulco. No answer. Maybe they don't catch the English. You call them in Spanish. Just push the knob here and talk.

NOTHING WAS SEEN OF THE PLANE, OR ITS OCCUPANTS, UNTIL FOURTEEN DAYS LATER.

The mouthpiece was cool and the black wire curled away and down below the instrument panel. I looked back at Jack strapped in the rear seat. His eyes were big and calm-serious. A FARMER CHECKING TIMBER IN THE MOUNTAINS CAME UPON THE BURNED WRECKAGE OF THE MISSING CESSNA. I cleared my voice. Acapulco. *Somos Cessna cuatro-seis Bravo. Acapulco, Cessna cuatro-seis Bravo hablando.* No answer.

Dick made a disgusted noise. Maybe they're on a different frequency. Or maybe they're out to supper. Or maybe they don't have an operator.

So what do we do now?

Dick motioned with his hand for me to take the wheel. Here, you take over. I'll try to figure out where we are and when we should hit the coast. Keep the compass on 270 and for God's sake keep the altitude where it is and just fly her straight. EXAMINATION OF THE WRECKAGE SHOWED THAT THE AIRCRAFT STRUCK TREES WHILE FLYING IN A STRAIGHT AND LEVEL ALTITUDE.

And I was all of a sudden sitting there a mile high in the sky with three people and an iguana and several suitcases and a ton-heavy plane holding the whole business up with just my two hands glued to the co-pilot stick. It was obvious that my hands clutched to the wheel wouldn't hold up the plane and its load. IT CUT THROUGH THE TREES FOR A DISTANCE OF 416 FEET BEFORE IT FINALLY CAME TO REST. I held on tight squeezing the metal circle in my hands afraid to move my feet on the rudder or relax my grip because then we'd drop like a stone in a mile-deep well. I could feel drops of sweat rolling down from my armpits. The gray snowdrifts ahead seemed to be rushing at us. I squeezed the wheel harder. IT COULD NOT BE DETERMINED WHETHER OR NOT THE PILOT HAD RECEIVED A WEATHER BRIEFING PRIOR TO TAKE OFF. Panic. Control. Frozen panic. My mind hung up rigid. Panic.

Hey. You're losing altitude. Pull her back. I sat not moving except to pivot my head to look at Dick. FOR THE AREA IN WHICH THE CRASH OCCURRED THE FIRECARTS CALLED FOR WIDESPREAD STRATUS AND FOG.

From *Psychedelic Prayers:*

What one values in the game—
    is the play
    fluid

What one values in the form—
    is the moment of
    forming
    fluid

What one values in the house—
    is the moment of
    dwelling
    fluid

What one values in the heart—
    is the beat
    pulsing

What one values in the action—
    is the timing
    fluid

Indeed
because you flow like water
you can neither win
nor lose

∞

From *Time:*

An epidemic of "acid heads"—the disease is striking in beachside beatnik pads and in the dormitories of expensive prep schools;

It has grown into an alarming problem at U.C.L.A. and on the U.C. campus at Berkeley.

And everywhere the diagnosis is the same: psychotic illness resulting from unauthorized, nonmedical use of the drug LSD-25.

Patients with post-LSD symptoms are providing the U.C.L.A. neuropsychiatric institute with 10% to 15% of its cases: more are flocking to the university's general medical center and the county general hospital.

By best estimates, 10,000 students in the University of California system have tried LSD (though not all have suffered detectable ill effects).

No one can even guess how many more selfstyled "acid heads" there are among oddball cult groups.

He had a puzzled look and moved his fingers lightly to his stick and nudged it gently back. The nose of the plane rose and I saw the indicator level off. Dick was grinning at me. Keep us up there, old man. CEILINGS WERE EXPECTED TO BE 800 TO 1200 FEET OVERCAST WITH VISIBILITIES OF FROM TWO TO FOUR MILES IN FOG, VARIABLE TO 200 FEET.

The confident smile of the experienced guide broke the spell. I let off squeezing the stick and pulled it up towards me and felt the rushing air pushing under the plane, solidly holding it up there a mile high, and pushed the rudder left foot and saw the needle swing slowly back to 270, and I and the plane were flying along just so smooth up there above the white caps and I began to grin and to feel with it. High. IT WAS DECIDED THAT THERE THE AIRPLANE STRUCK THE MOUNTAINSIDE AT 2,700 FEET MSL. I turned my head around and squeezed Jack's leg and grinned at him and thought about how great and brave he was and how I loved him and I looked over at Dick bending over the charts and thought about how lucky it was that I trusted him and how he trusted me and that was it, the goodness of the moment, the three of us together, and this was the way it always should be on the trip. IT WAS THEN IN SOLID INSTRUMENT WEATHER CONDITIONS — No worry. No worry about getting down or coming back to the ground. Dick was wise and skilled and trustworthy. You couldn't ask for better there. —WHICH PRECLUDED THE POSSIBILITY OF THE PILOT EVER HAVING SEEN THE TERRAIN—UNTIL IT WAS TOO LATE. And son Jack back there with his blue shorts and his sunburned legs and his tousled hair and his always dirty face smiling back at me and not worried, trusting me, and I was thinking that life is really no different anywhere in air or down there. Aren't we always just a breath away from death, and all that counts up here or down there is to be with people you love and trust and not caring about the future, or the past, gone and done and less meaning than that air pocket we bounced over a mile there a minute back.

We should be over Acapulco right about now, said Dick. His head was still turned down to the charts. Then he looked up and said, Hey. Hey, look

"Florid & terrifying."

Southern California devotees proclaim the alleged benefits of LSD with evangelistic fervor. They say it brings supernatural powers.

It does not, say U.C.L.A. psychiatrists.

Some say it is an aphrodisiac. It is not.

They say it helps the user to solve his emotional problems.

It may—but only if the solution is already in the mind, hidden behind an emotional block.

What LSD actually has done for far too many users, says U.C.L.A.'s psychiatric resident Duke D. Fisher, is to produce "florid psychoses with terrifying visual and auditory hallucinations, marked depression, often with serious suicide attempts and anxiety bordering on panic."

One patient tried to kill himself when he thought his body was melting, and he remained suicidal for more than two weeks, after only one dose of LSD.

at this. He was pointing over there to the left to a hole, a tiny hole in the gray clouds, a peep hole, a rent in the cotton fabric and through it glistening the blue water, the ocean.

Let me take her down, that hole is closing fast. He swung the stick over and rolled the plane dizzyingly on its side and we began to fall sideways, stomach gasping, ears hurting, and by now the hole in the clouds was smaller than our wingspread but we needled through it, falling sideways, left cheek pointing to the lovely gray-green endless rippling world of water below.

The next problem is to find land and then run up the coast to Acapulco. Dick was banking sharply to the right and as we turned the long corner and leveled off, there were the high cliffs on one side with the hotels stuck on top and there way over to the right was the high promontory rolling to the sea, with the villas and hotels nailed to the slopes, and we were slicing a line right smack down the middle of Acapulco Bay. We had hit it blindly right on the center.

The wind can indeed drive the clouds together in the sky; yet, being nothing but air, without solid body, it does not produce great or lasting effects. So also an individual, in times when he can produce no great effect in the outer world, can do nothing except refine the expression of his nature in small ways. (I Ching IX)

We had breakfast next morning on the open terrace of Caleta looking down at the morning beach and the red surfboards bobbing on the blue bay and over to Roqueta, the island, palmy and green. Then Jack sprang again the question he had been springing all summer and never answered— how about skin diving? It was now or never because we were flying north at summer's end. Dick pulled out a map and checked the mileage and we counted up the flying hours on our fingers and Dick looked at Jack's hopeful eyes and said, sure, we can afford an hour or two for something important like skin diving and Jack began to grin.

I rented a set for Jack and me and we walked with José the instructor down to the beach, all of us in swimming trunks and Jack carrying the heavy air tank. I was to dive first for a half-hour while Jack watched and then he was to take over. I stood knee-deep in the warm surf and José lifted the tank on my back and began strapping me in while I braced my legs against the weight. The belt of round lead slugs got tied around my waist and the rubber mask over my eyes and José showed me how to clear the mask of water by tilting the corner and blowing and he stuck the rubber tube end in my mouth and I felt the cold surgical taste of oxygen and heard the hiss hiss of the air rush and a cast-iron mechanical duck waddled with finned feet out beyond the breakers and José's brown arms motioned down and I took a deep gulp of the cool rubbery air in the mouthpiece and pushed down under the surface.

Down to no place. I didn't sink and I didn't rise, just stayed there suspended a foot or so under water getting used to breathing through a tube and fighting the panic, the panic bred of the lifelong habit of rising to the surface to breathe. José was right there by me and I watched the bubbles up around his face and looked inside his mask at the black eyes glaring out and saw his hands motioning down and his sleek brown legs pumping and him slicing down fishy deeper, hands and feet finning him along. He stopped and turned and made wavy gill motions and I got the point and pushed clumsy with my hands up and kicked and started dropping down and there was the bottom, sandy and clear, every brown grain in sharp focus and the bottom creatures, tawny purple shells and spiny quilled animals breathing softly, and clean rocks.

We were swimming along together slowly, two giant humpbacked fish nosing across this new bottom world. José turned and put his thumb and forefinger together to ask okay and I made the same sign, sure okay and I saw his eyes inside the mask smiling at me and right there at that moment everything became okay, exultant new world vision, a new thrilly freedom

> down
>> down
>>> down
>>>> in the blue glass
>>>> light world.

Other patients have required more than two months of psychiatric hospitalization.

Still others have been sent to state hospitals for long-term treatment.

Adds U.C.L.A. psychiatrist J. Thomas Ungerleider: "The symptoms may recur in their original intensity long after the last dose of the drug.

Many users have had this experience."

The varied types of LSD users include vast numbers of thrill seekers.

Most have tried marijuana, then the amphetamines, before "graduating" themselves to what they regard as the ultimate in kicks.

In the rebellious student groups like those at Berkeley many are trying LSD because they feel lost on an impersonal, bustling campus:

Others have been squeezed by the need to make better grades to avoid the draft.

One of the most disturbing aspects of the LSD binge is that it has hit high schools and prep schools.

∞

From the Associated Press:

LSD-25 and similar drugs that drastically alter sensory perception have the power to permanently cripple the mind, an editorial in the Sept. 14 *Journal* of the American Medical Association warned today.

∞

From *Cosmopolitan:*

So serious do physicians and psychiatrists view the fad for this drug that Dr. Roy Grinker, chief editor of the AMA's *Archives of General Psychiatry,* recently wrote an editorial in his publication warning that the drug could be fatal if used indiscriminately

and that many psychiatrists had become so enamored with its "mystical, hallucinatory state" that they were "disqualified as competent investigators."

He further complained the drug was being imprudently publicized and endorsed by "movie actors and television artists."

This last crack was a direct slap at Hollywood, where LSD received its first major burst of publicity, and where some of its most devoted rooters live.

Actually, Hollywood was buzzing over LSD as far back as 1959.

Free
Weightless, fin-driven
Free from earth
Free from air
For the first time free from
Gravity grasp
Dirt free, talk free
Path, road, and sidewalk free
Free
To slide through trackless sea space

Thinking of the world above
Did it ever?
Do they really walk around up there?
    Bodies draped in cloth
    Feet in leather boxes
    Fixed, dimension flat paths
    Through dust and spit and dung
    And cigarette butts
    Through cooking smells
    Exhaust fumes

Through noise
Horn, screech, fart, squeal, cough, clash
And talk clatter?
Here clear water still
Sliding silence of the deep deaf
Only hiss hiss of tube
Spilling upward, bouncing, bubbly
Laughter.

Down there it's not a wet world
Wet is land talk.

Down there it's not a worry world
Worry is land think.
    no job
    no worry
    no money
    no hurry
    no past
    no future
    no think talk walk
    no hating
    no waiting

no striving
no reading writing
Just
Everything
So new

My teeth were clenched hard on the rubber mouthpiece . . . jaw muscles taut and hurting . . . snap . . . molars clank together . . . mouthpiece bit through . . . can't hold tight in mouth . . . water seeping in mask . . . did he say swallow or blow out . . . vision blurry from water in mask . . . hiss hiss of air . . . keep cool . . . what's situation . . . ten feet under . . . 100-pound tank on back . . . 100-pound leads on belt . . . water in mask . . . trouble holding shredded mouthpiece with teeth . . . fear fear panic fear . . . can I go back? . . . weighted down with metal . . . trapped . . . can I get back . . . want to get back . . . want my dirty world back . . . maybe trapped . . . want go back . . . now!

I squatted down with my feet on the sandy bottom and pushed up, uncoiling torpedoing up, whoosh, breaking up through surface with splash, ripping off mouthpiece, mask, gulping free air blinking at sunlight. Splash beside me, José, face amused, worried, back on the worry dimension. *Con calma. Con calma, hombre.* I was breaststroking, lunging towards shore, wounded walrus, white air tube dangling on side. José holding me with one arm, holding my mask with his other hand.

Standing in waist-high surf, gasping for breath, shoulders heaving, heart pounding, shaking off water and fear. Not listening to José's voice soothing, advising. I was thinking about the rapture of the sea deep and the far-out visions and the clean unity, and of the sudden panic coming, the fear that you can't go back, back to the world you love to leave, and thinking of the fear of mushroom rapture. Will I ever get back? Panic. Loss of control. Panic.

I had had my daily ration of expanded consciousness and was glad to feel dry sand underfoot. Jack was eager to take over the diving. He stood casual, almost bored, while José and I strapped him in the metal uniform. He didn't seem to be listening

It began when two Los Angeles doctors published the results of an experimental therapy program they had conducted with 110 patients—

including Cary Grant, his wife Betsy Drake and several more Hollywood actors, publicists, and writers. The reaction to the paper was explosive.

Joe Hyams, Hollywood correspondent for the New York *Herald Tribune,* who did one of the first interviews with Cary Grant about LSD therapy, told me recently, "After my series came out, the phone began to ring wildly. Psychiatrists called, complaining their patients were now begging them for LSD. Every actor in town under analysis wanted it. In all, I got close to eight hundred letters."

Cary Grant today is still eager to offer this testimony to the efficacy of the drug: "If I drop dead within the next ten years, I will have enjoyed more living in the latter part of my life than most people ever know."

When I asked Grant if he thought his association with the drug had helped or hindered its development, he said brusquely, "A Hollywood name might have created some resistance, but many people will seek any reason to oppose a new idea, you know."

More and more of the California intelligentsia began to push the drug.

From his houseboat in Sausalito, philosopher Alan Watts spoke of a society where LSD pills would be taken two or three times a year, like aspirin, to relieve temporary emotional headaches.

Aldous Huxley wrote glowingly of his mystical LSD flights.

Poet Allen Ginsberg urged that the drug be given to Khrushchev and Kennedy in the interests of world peace.

∞

to my words of advice and when José nodded to him he pulled on the mask and stuck in the mouthpiece and waded out knee-, waist-, shoulder-high and sank out of sight. I stood on the shore watching the two lines of bubbles moving out into the bay. Jack was gone, dropped down and out of the world and I was standing there, scared, worried, stuck on the sandy shelf of mind but Jack was gone beyond it all.

Four Mexican kids had followed the divers' trail across the bay. They had goggles but no tank and kept bobbing under for a breath-length to watch the underwater action. I called one of them back to shore and asked him how it was going with *el niño.* White teeth grin. He had seen my panic. *Perfecto, Señor.*

I walked over to the beach-bar and ordered a planters punch and sat the half-hour out watching the bubbles and the boys moving around the bay out beyond the fishing boats and then circling back, and finally Jack's black head bobbed up and he scoffed through the shallow water bent over a little from the heavy tank still looking bored but also cocky proud. The natural, non-conceptual confidence of the young. The psychedelic generation.

We walked back to the diving shop and José started making out the bill. The owner asked him in Spanish how it had gone and José grinned and said *muy bien. El hijo es mucho mas mejor que el padre.* Jack looked at me and I winked and he creased his face in a big grin and that was the diving trip.

THE TAMING POWER OF THE SMALL

Has success.
Dense clouds, no rain from our
   western region.

(I Ching)

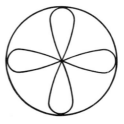

The Sacrament Solves No Problems:

October 1960

Guide: ALDOUS HUXLEY

Oracle: XXXVI

Darkening of the light

The Receptive, Earth

The Clinging, Fire

The light has sunk into the earth:
The image of DARKENING OF THE LIGHT.
Thus does the superior man live with the great
    mass:
He veils his light, yet still shines.

(I Ching)

Lease:

Witnesseth that for and in consideration of the payment of the rents and the performance of the covenants

said parties of the first part do hereby lease, demise and let unto the said parties of the second part

that certain three-story dwelling house and appurtenances. . . .

From *The Saturday Evening Post*:

Leary returned to Harvard longing to journey still further beyond his mind and his ardor infected Alpert, another clinical psychologist and McClelland protege.

∞

We got back to the East Coast early September and located in Newton Center. The house was big. A three-story baronial mansion on a hill with trees and lawns and a three-car garage and a garden house and 185 stone steps leading up to the front door. Inside it were books and woodwork and thick rugs and metal-work lamps and a wide staircase winding up from the entrance hall.

Took a couple of days to get settled. And on the third day I drove down to Newton Corner and crossed to Charlesbank Road and along the curving river towards Cambridge. At this point the Charles is a wide, slow stream. On the other side a Norman tower sticks up from the trees, and down aways the bridge on the Watertown Road loops across in three arches, simple and clean like Ponte Santa Trinita, reflected in the water below.

After a while the river swings to the left towards Cambridge and then back again in a grand slow sweep, and there on the right is Soldier's Field and beyond it the roofs of the Harvard Business School, very European (Copenhagen, mostly), with dozens of little chimneys sticking up, and over to the left the three shiny colored domes—red, green, blue— and the Harvard brick. All clear like color slides. I was glad to be back and glad that it all looked so fresh and sharp. Even the traffic lights seemed to glisten, gem flashes, red and green. The fact that they told you Stop and Go was incidental to what they told you about color and light. I was still turned on.

My office was in the Center for Personality Research, Harvard University. The house was named after Morton Prince, one of the first American psychologists to recognize alterations in consciousness as a critical area for study. In the days when psychologists were gentlemen scholars, he published classic works on unconscious states, coconscious states, the varieties of awareness consequences, and was the founder of the Center for Personality Research at Harvard. Today he would be considered a far-out scholar with his curious and bold interests in multiple personality, hypnosis, trances, and visions. It was somehow most natural and proper that we would be initiating studies into altered states of consciousness in Morton Prince House.

The precedent for our psychedelic research did not begin with Morton Prince, however, but traced back to the turn of the century, to that most venerable and greatest of American psychologists, William James, who had mystic experiences using nitrous oxide and saw God and scandalized people by running drug parties in Boston's stuffy Back Bay.

After Morton Prince and William James, the genealogical line of consciousness expansion research at Harvard was continued by another giant in the history of psychology: Harry A. Murray and his visionary scene of green shirts, white whales, Freud-Jung-Melville.

When Harry Murray retired and moved his office to a house next door and nailed his whale emblem over the threshold, a new director came into the Center. David C. McClelland is a non-visionary Quaker, a Protestant-ethic man, intelligent, tall, puritan, dedicated to external achievement.

Professor McClelland had visited the villa in Cuernavaca the week after I took the magic mushrooms, and was shocked and grumpy when I told him about my trip. He was the first person I had wanted to try the mushrooms, and his instinctive withdrawal jolted me.

The Quakers were founded by a flipped-out hallucinating visionary named George Fox, who turned-on and dropped-out and spent six years in prison for passing on the same message I got from the Aztec plant. I couldn't understand then why any psychologist, especially a member of a mystic sect like the Quakers, wouldn't rush to have the experience.

When I opened the front door of Harvard's Center for Personality Research, there in the library

From *The Varieties of Religious Experience* by William James:

Our normal waking consciousness parted from the filmiest of screens, there lie potential forms of consciousness entirely different.

No account of the universe in its totality can be final which leaves these other forms of consciousness quite disregarded.

How to regard them is the question—for they are so discontinuous with ordinary consciousness.

were two bright graduate students, George and Mike. They came to my office and began telling me right away about their summer research and then I began telling them about the mushrooms. This was nothing new to them. George had spent several months running mescaline experiments the year before and used to drop into my office to tell me about the visions and insights and perceptual fireworks. I used to listen politely but not caring. I had no concepts, no mental hooks on which to hang his words, and no intuitive electricity to get turned-on. Like every educated savage, I automatically discredited anything that I didn't understand.

Now it was different. The visionary flash had come and George had seen and felt it too and we leaned forward talking fast and drugging each other with vision talk. Mike was swept into the spell too. He had been wanting George to give him mescaline for several months but they never got around to it. He was eager to start. What a great research tool!

Looking back on my own (drug) experiences, they all converge towards a kind of insight to which I cannot help ascribing some metaphysical significance.

The word research stopped me. Psychiatric science. Good God, here we go again. Using drugs to do something to somebody else. Drug them. Then test the changes. Measuring the impact of chemicals on the mind. It was this sort of manipulatory business that had repelled me from experimental drug research in the past.

A Ring of Power looks after itself, Frodo. It may slip off treacherously, but its keeper never abandons it. At most he plays with the idea of handing it on to someone else's care—and that only at an early stage, when it first begins to grip. But as far as I know, Bilbo alone in history has ever gone beyond playing, and really done it. He needed all my help, too. And even so he would never have just forsaken it, or cast it aside. It was not Gollum, Frodo, but the Ring itself that decided things. The Ring left him. (The Lord of the Rings)

Those who have ears to hear, let them hear: To me the living sense of its reality only comes in the artificial mystic state of mind.

∞

For thousands of years men have used any chemicals they could get their hands on to change consciousness and for fifty years psychologists have been developing methods including probing people's minds, getting behind the screens and protections which we all maintain. What does the patient really think? What does he really feel? Psychoanalysis, the study of dreams. Slips of the tongue. Tests of fantasy expression in which the subject unwittingly gives away his secret inclinations. It was natural that men would use mescaline and LSD to get high and it was also natural that psychologists would see mescaline and LSD as new manipulatory instruments for cutting through defenses and exposing inner feelings. New ways of knocking out the social man and laying bare the sick, evil man within.

To interpret the visionary experience laymen use the language of ecstasy, and psychiatrists use the language which is familiar and natural to them— the dialect of diagnosis. Now the curious thing about psychiatric language is that it's almost completely negative, a pompous, gloomy lexicon of troubles, symptoms, abnormalities, eccentricities.

To read through the psychiatric literature is to descend into the modern Freudian *Inferno*—prim, prudish catalogue of anguish and conflict.

The psychiatric trip is worried and nervous. Revelation is a dirty word. When they observe mystical reactions to the southern vegetables, psychiatrists employ the labels of pathology. Peyote and mescaline and LSD produce thoughts and behavior which are not conventionally normal. These events are called ABNORMAL. Very unconventional. Therefore very abnormal! Psychotic!

The psychiatrists are hung up on psychosis, whatever that is. And so the new consciousness-expanding substances in 1960 were classed as psychotomimetic. Psychiatrists thought that LSD causes normal people to act like psychotics! And glorious mescaline too! And the mushroom!

So when I heard Mike asking me about research plans for the mushrooms, my first reaction was, oh, no, baby! No! No! No! No selecting of subjects. No testing them before and after. No explaining away the mushroom effect in terms of my favorite variables or your favorite variables. No chemical procedures ripping away people's protections and watching them deal with the sudden confrontation

Psychiatric Report:

The volunteers selected were told only that they might receive a substance which would produce temporary changes in perception and bodily feelings or an inert substance.

A baseline EEG, mental status and checklist of symptoms was completed before the drug was administered.

Results in visual hallucinations, illusions, a form of hyperacusis, body image distortions, . . .

. . . euphoria, anxiety, depression, flight of ideas, clang associations, inability to abstract.

A subject in response to the proverb, people in glass houses shouldn't throw stones, said before the drug.

of the real-reality. And then calling them diagnostic names. Like psychotic. No sir.

Well, Mike, it depends what you mean by research. I'd love to take the mushrooms again. And I'd like to give them to my friends and have them see what I saw. In fact I'd be glad to spend the rest of my life teaching people how to use them. And I'd like everyone who takes the mushrooms to write down afterwards what he saw and felt and visioned and how the whole scene affected his life.

George and Mike were listening and nodding and swinging along with this and began to throw in ideas. Why not start a research like this. There would be no scientists vs. people-studied in our research. Everyone would take turns taking the mushrooms and observing and keeping careful records of how we change and what we experience. And we'd all meet together to plan the sessions and there would be no withholding of information or results, it would all be out on the table for everyone to know. No calling people names. No diagnosing. And we would try to get a variety of people involved in the group. Not just psychologists and behavioral scientists but writers and poets and housewives and cab drivers.

I was particularly pleased with the collaborative, no-leader aspect of the plan. I wanted to avoid selecting the members of the mushroom research group. I told George and Mike that they knew more people around the university and the town of Cambridge than I did and that they should do the selecting of collaborators to take the mushrooms with us. George and Mike said sure and began talking together excitedly throwing names back and forth. Plenty of spirit around.

Then George began to talk about the literature on visionary states and asked me if I had read Aldous Huxley's books on mescaline, *Doors to Perception* and *Heaven and Hell,* and when I said I hadn't he rushed down the hall to his office and brought them back. Small, thin rectangles. I stuck them in my jacket pockets.

The final issue was the big one. Where would we get the mushrooms? Someone had told me that the Public Health Service had succeeded in synthesizing the mushrooms and I said I'd write to Washington and try to check on that lead. Gerhart back in Mexico had told me that he'd continue the search for Juana the witch and if he found her he'd get a large supply and send some up to me. And Frank Barron back in Berkeley had told me that the people at the University of Mexico had cultivated mushrooms and maybe we could get some from them.

That night I read Huxley. And then I read those two books again. And again. It was all there. All my vision. And more too. Huxley had taken mescaline in a garden and shucked off the mind and awakened to eternity.

About a week later someone at a party told me that Aldous Huxley was spending the fall in town and that sounded like a good omen, so I sat down and wrote him a letter.

Two days later, during one of our planning conferences, Mr. Huxley telephoned to say he was interested and lunch was arranged.

Aldous Huxley was staying in a new M.I.T. apartment overlooking the Charles River. He answered the bell—tall, pale, frail—joined me, and we drove to the Harvard Faculty Club. He read the menu slowly through his magnifying glass. I asked him if he wanted soup and he asked what kind and I looked at the menu and it was mushroom soup so we laughed and we had mushrooms for lunch.

Aldous Huxley: stooped, towering, gray Buddha. A wise and good man. Head like a multi-lingual encyclopedia. Voice elegant and chuckling except when the pitch rose in momentary amused indignation about over-population or the pomposity of psychiatrists.

We talked about how to study and use the consciousness-expanding drugs and we clicked along agreeably on the do's and the not-to-do's. We would avoid the behaviorist approach to others' awareness. Avoid labeling or depersonalizing the subject. We should not impose our own jargon or our own experimental games on others. We were not out to discover new laws, which is to say, to discover the redundant implications of our own

You shouldn't point out faults in others that might exist in yourself. After the drug he said, At who? That depends on a lot of things.

Autonomic responses, pupillary dilation, nausea, dizziness, flushing, abdominal complaints, blood pressure, and pulse. . . .

Psilocybin, LSD, and mescaline are extremely potent agents capable of producing acute psychotic behavior in many individuals.

premises. We were not to be limited by the pathological point of view. We were not to interpret ecstasy as mania, or calm serenity as catatonia; we were not to diagnose Buddha as a detached schizoid; nor Christ as an exhibitionistic masochist; nor the mystic experience as a symptom; nor the visionary state as a model psychosis. Aldous Huxley chuckling away with compassionate humor at human folly.

And with such erudition! Moving back and forth in history, quoting the mystics. Wordsworth. Plotinus. The Areopagite. William James. Ranging from the esoteric past, back to the biochemical present: Humphrey Osmond curing alcoholics in Saskatchewan with LSD; Keith Ditman's plans to clean out Skid Row in Los Angeles with LSD; Roger Heim taking his bag of Mexican mushrooms to the Parisian chemists who couldn't isolate the active ingredient, and then going to Albert Hoffman the great Swiss, who did it and called it psilocybin. They had sent the pills back to the *curandera* in Oaxaca state and she tried them and had divinatory visions and was happy that her practice could now be year-round and not restricted to the three rainy mushroom months.

Aldous Huxley was shrewdly aware of the political complications and the expected opposition from the Murugans, the name he gave to power people in his novel, *Island.*

"*Dope . . . Murugan was telling me about the fungi that are used here as a source of dope.*

"*What's in a name? . . . Answer, practically everything. Murugan calls it dope and feels about it all the disapproval that, by conditioned reflex, the dirty word evokes. We on the contrary, give the stuff good names—the* moksha *medicine, the reality revealer, the truth-and-beauty pill. And we know, by direct experience, that the good names are deserved. Whereas our young friend here has no firsthand knowledge of the stuff and can't be persuaded even to give it a try. For him it's dope and dope is something that, by definition, no decent person ever indulges in.*"

Aldous Huxley advised and counseled and joked and told stories and we listened and our research project was shaped accordingly. Huxley offered to sit in on our planning meetings and was ready to take mushrooms with us when the research was under way.

From these meetings grew the design for a naturalistic pilot study, in which the subjects would be treated like astronauts—carefully prepared, briefed with all available facts, and then expected to run their own spacecraft, make their own observations, and report back to ground control. Our subjects were not passive patients but hero-explorers.

During the weeks of October and November of 1960 there were many meetings to plan the research. Aldous Huxley would come and listen and then close his eyes and detach himself from the scene and go into his controlled meditation trance, which was unnerving to some of the Harvard people who equate consciousness with talk, and then he would open his eyes and make a diamond-pure comment.

We talked about having tape recordings and music and reproductions of paintings and mystical quotations, and people volunteered to round up the props and there was only one thing wrong with the meetings and that was that it was all talk and no action. That is, no mushrooms. It was like sitting around planning and talking about sex: we were all hungry and impatient for the mushrooms to arrive. We hoped that they would come that week and if so we'd have the first session on Sunday.

By Friday they hadn't come and we made careful plans to pick up the package at the post office if it came on Saturday. I didn't realize until later how eager and anxious people were. The tension was mounting and it kept mounting Saturday morning until George phoned everyone and said that they weren't at the post office, and the first session was postponed a week. Big letdown and then the tension started up again.

On Wednesday afternoon I came into the office and my secretary Clair said, Oh, by the way, the mushrooms just arrived. Where are they? George and Mike took them and are keeping the package in their office. I walked down the hall to their office

From the Boston *Record American* Mailbag:

Your editorial, Controlling LSD, was excellent, but it did not go far enough. Walter Winchell, in your paper recently, made a statement which might do more to discourage its use. He stated emphatically that LSD can make a person blind.

From the Washington *Evening Star:*

Sen. Robert F. Kennedy, D-N.Y., today rapped former Harvard University psychologist Timothy Leary for not sufficiently stressing the dangers of LSD in his speaking tours.

The impression that the vision-producing drug can be used indiscriminately "has damaged the minds of many of our young people," Kennedy said.

Dr. Robert in *Island* by Aldous Huxley.

"Which brings me back to those American doctors.

but they were gone and the mushrooms were nowhere to be found. This gave me a funny feeling of frustration. The mushrooms had arrived but I couldn't see them. Out of my hands, out of my control.

The next morning Mike came by my office to chat about the session coming up that weekend. He didn't mention that the mushrooms had arrived. I said, Oh, by the way, I understand that the package arrived from Sandoz. Mike took a step backward and blinked. Oh, yes, they came yesterday.

Where are they now?

His face darkened and took on a pinched expression.

Well . . . I . . . We, George and I . . . took them. We didn't want to leave them around.

He was embarrassed, half defiant. I felt irritated.

"Three of them were psychiatrists, and one of the psychiatrists smoked cigars without stopping and had a German accent. . . . I never heard anything like it.

Gandalf looked again very hard at Bilbo, and there was a gleam in his eye. I think, Bilbo, he said quietly, I should leave it behind. Don't you want to?

Well yes—and no. Now it comes to it, I don't like parting with it at all, I may say. And I don't really see why I should. Why do you want me to? he asked, and a curious change came over his voice. It was sharp with suspicion and annoyance. You are always badgering me about my ring. (The Lord of the Rings)

I'd like to look at them.

He hesitated and then said, Okay.

A few minutes later he returned with a brown cardboard box. There were four small gray pill-boxes inside labeled PS 39, and printed on the label, NOT TO BE SOLD, FOR RESEARCH INVESTIGATION. There was a plastic stopper and a wad of cotton in the neck of the little brown bottle and then I shook out in my hand the round pink pills, glistening like pearls on my hand. There they were. Keys to the doors to perception. I poured them back in the bottle and stuffed the bottle back in the box and said, let's keep them here in my filing cabinet. I was sensitive about control of the pills and felt better having them in my office. In my power. Not that I had any intention of using them unilaterally.

". . . the way they treat people with neurotic symptoms . . . they never attack on all the fronts; they only attack on about half of one front.

That evening I had a date with a girl named Joan and instead of going to the city to dinner I took her home because I had promised to buy favors and decorations for a big Halloween party which my daughter was giving the next night. After we shopped and came home I filled the ice-cooler and brought a bottle of whisky and soda into the study and we sat drinking until dinner, and every time the whisky would start to relax me the kids would get into a quarrel and I'd bound out to stop it, or the phone would ring and then I'd mix another drink to quiet down again. We had a bottle of Burgundy with the steak and by dinner's end I was feeling a fine alcohol stupor.

In the living room Joan was lying in front of the fire, and a friend Joe O'Donell had come in and was mixing drinks and we started joking and laughing at O'Donell's crazy stories.

Then Rhona and Charlie came down from the third floor to join in the noise. They were the young couple who took care of the house, pretty little blonde Rhona and big happy Charlie finishing his fourth year at Boston University.

After a while we fell to talking about the mushrooms. Right from the start O'Donell had been amused and worldly about the research. This shocked me. He was a scientist and serious about studying behavior and here he was taking a casual attitude towards the mushrooms. The hell with all this phony talk and measurement business, let's get the mushrooms and start swinging.

O'Donell was talking along this way, hard-boiled and cynical and then he popped the question that brought me up short, why don't we have some mushrooms right now? Big Charlie had been hearing all this mushroom talk for days and he jumped at this suggestion. Hey, that's a great idea. Let's try them out tonight and see what happens. I had been lecturing all year on research philosophy and ethics and how you should be collaborative and not use your position as a scientist to get an unfair advantage and about sharing information and sharing the power to make decisions with the subjects. And that was the way we had set up the mushroom research. Collaborative all the way. No pulling

"So far as they are concerned, the physical fronts don't exist . . .

"mind abstracted from the body—that's the only front they attack on.

"And not even on the whole of that front. The man with the cigar kept talking about the unconscious.

"But the only unconscious they ever pay attention to is the negative unconscious,

"the garbage that people have tried to get rid of by burying it in the basement.

"Not a single word about the positive unconscious. No attempt to help the patient to open himself up to the life force or the Buddha nature.

rank. Everyone taking turns at giving mushrooms and taking them. Now O'Donell's suggestion that we take the pills without the rest of the team present complicated everything I had been saying and the agreement we had made with the rest of the group.

Besides, it will be a useful pilot study. We can try out a small dosage and see what happens and pave the way for a better session Sunday. That's right, said big Charlie, we'll be guinea pigs for the rest of them. O'Donell was looking at me coolly. Goddammit, don't be so square. You'll ruin the whole mushroom business if you try to make it rigid and organized and scheduled. In life you're either spontaneous or you're nothing.

Spontaneous. That was some word. About two weeks before, I had been standing around at a cocktail party in Middletown and composer John Cage walked up and asked if I wanted to try his mushrooms and I laughed and thought it was a joke, kidding about my mushroom obsession, and I said sure and he led me out into the kitchen and there on a plate were some sliced and broiled mushrooms, delicious with butter and salt. John told me about the fun of mushrooms—ordinary non-trance mushrooms that you eat, and how spontaneity was the key. You could go to a forest glade for ten days in a row and not see a mushroom and then on that eleventh day (or it might be the first day for you) there they are, the mushrooms, pushing up through the soil so fast you can see them growing. The magnificent intersection in space-time, you and the mushrooms. And you have to be there at the exact hour because if you're a few hours late then you're too late and the rot has set in or the insects have started eating them. It's the spontaneity, the planless meeting, the thing you can't push or hurry.

What troubles you? Why hesitate? Why is your heart oppressed by cowardice? Why do you lack in courage and zeal when I myself do prophesy such good? (Inferno III)

So when O'Donell started this talk that I'm square and rigid and you gotta be spontaneous, well, it stopped me short. The last thing in the world I wanted to be was a worrying square and the last thing I wanted to put down was spontaneity, so I worked out the quick compromise in my mind that I'd give them the mushrooms and let them have the experience but I wouldn't take them and so maybe I'd protect my contract with the absent researchers.

For by your arguments you have disposed my heart to such an eagerness to go that to my first intent I have returned. Lead on poet. (Inferno III)

We got in my car and drove down to Cambridge. I parked in the front of the office and went in for the pills. I came back out to the car carrying a glass of water and it was agreed that everyone take two pills right away in the car so that the high could start building up on the way home. The literature on mushroom research suggested using doses of 8 milligrams, and each pill was 2 milligrams, so that when they took two pills they were taking half of a normal dose. O'Donell suggested starting slow with half a dose and then taking the rest later if it was going well.

There was no reaction in the car and after we were settled in front of the fire, O'Donell and big Charlie and Joan took two more, and after an hour when the effect was working hardly at all, Joan took two more and Charlie and O'Donell took three more and I took two myself. The dosage for the group was 4 milligrams for me, 12 for Joan and 14 for Charlie and O'Donell. After about an hour and fifteen minutes it started to hit. Charlie started seeing the room in wonderful technicolor and began to pace up and down through the house raving about the beauty, the texture, the delicate shades.

His wife Rhona was watching him amused and a bit scared. Charlie was an ex-football guard, not an intellectual person and never sensitive to beauty. Here he was moving around possessed, chanting poetry about the shadows on the rug and the subtle play of light on the wall.

I was lying on the couch feeling good from the mood and the two pills and urging Charlie on and laughing happily at him. Joan came over and

"And no attempt even to teach him to be a little more conscious in his everyday life. . . ."

"These people just leave the unfortunate neurotic to wallow in his old bad habits of never being all there in present time. The whole thing is just pure idiocy!

"No, the man with the cigar didn't even have *that* excuse; he was as clever as clever can be. So it's not idiocy. . . ."

"It must be something voluntary, something self-induced

"—like getting drunk or talking yourself into believing some piece of foolishness because it happens to be in the Scriptures.

curled up in my arms and said she felt wonderful and how glad she was that I was there to take care of her.

That left poor O'Donell alone. In the molecular structure of the psychedelic group the lone atom whirls out of orbit. He was the only one not going along with the happy spirit. Face black with frown and wild-eye look. He was engaged to a girl in Seattle and missing her a lot and sick with love and loneliness and worry about the romance and he seemed to be falling apart under the mushrooms. Everything gets intensified—lover or loneliness. O'Donell was sitting next to me on the couch muttering and letting out weird laughs. He turned to us and smiled an evil sort of smile and spit on the rug. Now under any circumstances this is a show-stopper, the sudden violent act smashing through the social fabric. But under mushrooms shock comes even stronger. Underwater calm and bliss shattered by rude spit.

He had our attention all right. Our eyes were riveted to him as he reached down and took a package of cigarettes. He began to shake the package so that the white cylinders fell into a crazy pile on the coffee table. Again, like the spit, it was nothing more than a slight eccentric gesture but sent a creepy chill running through me.

O'Donell turned to me with the weird grin. Order. Order. Down with order. Again I felt the chill. Everything was going so mellow and smooth and the mushroom peace was so fine that I was surprised to see O'Donell getting worked up. Nothing seemed important at the moment except the loving calm. The idea that people worked themselves up, worrying about things, little things especially, was amusing. O'Donell, I said, it's all great. I had a girl and he didn't. He looked at me strangely and took his fist and pounded it in his hand and kept twisting it and turning his fist in his hand. Then he got up and walked to the bathroom and I could hear him urinating.

Joan was thirsty, the mushroom thirst, the dry throat of visions, so I went to the kitchen. Big Charlie standing by the refrigerator. He turned with a look of ecstasy. Look at this room. See those

"And then look at their idea of what's normal. Believe it or not, a normal human being is one who can have an orgasm and is adjusted to society. . . ."

"And then what about the society you're supposed to be adjusted to? Is it a mad society or a sane one? And even if it's pretty sane, is it right that everybody should be *completely* adjusted to it?"

∞

Harvard Psychedelic Research Project:

RESEARCH DESIGN FOR A STUDY OF CLINICAL REACTIONS TO PSILOCYBIN ADMINISTERED IN SUPPORTIVE ENVIRONMENT

walls glowing. It's seething with color. And look at these peaches. Look at that red blush on the yellow. They're glowing. They're alive. Dad-burn-it, those peaches are alive. They can talk.

Rhona walked in the room with a question on her face. What's going on? Your husband is talking to the beautiful peaches. Laughter. Charlie looking down at Rhona. Honey, if you could only see yourself. Why? The way you look. So fresh and wet. You look just like a newborn chicken just coming out of the shell. I looked at her. I could see what he meant. Blonde-yellow and fresh and young. Laughter. Charlie was looking at me with wonder. You're beautiful, he said. Your face is the most beautiful thing I've ever seen. Those lines in your face and your hair, the blue and gray, looks like a halo. Rhona was laughing too. She started out the door. Go tell Joan that Charlie thinks I'm beautiful and that I have a halo.

Charlie back talking to the beautiful peach. It was a great peach with its red patch and the fuzzy yellow glow.

Then O'Donell at the door. Still had the funny secret smile. Looked down at a kitchen knife on the table. Ah, that's what we need—a knife. Picked it up and looked around. In front of his face was the kitchen lamp hung from a long cord. O'Donell snarled and slashed at the cord with the knife. Horror and violence in paradise. O'Donell, for God's sake, behave. He laughed. Behave. That's what you want me to do. Behave. Be good.

O'Donell walked around the table towards Charlie with the knife in his hand. Some scene. Charlie's face was a picture. Disbelief. Fright. O'Donell, for God's sake, put that knife down. You scare me waving that knife at me. O'Donell laughed. That's what we need. Knives. Fear. Better than order. Threw the knife on the table. Big clatter noise.

I walked back out to the fire. Joan put her head in my lap. I missed you. Great abiding peace sitting close together. The good old love pill. No talk. Firewatching. Noise behind us. Big Charlie and O'Donell. Hey. Charlie and I want more pills. The two of them looked so worried. They want. Funny notion. To want. Who wants anything except peace and love. They want more pills.

Also the demand annoyed me. And the old power thing. I had two pills in me and was happy. They had seven in them and wanted more.

Look. It's two-thirty. The party is going great. Why not ride with it? Enjoy it. Don't worry about pills. Does it really matter? Do the pills really matter?

One must not unresistingly let himself be swept along by unfavorable circumstances, not permit his steadfastness to be shaken. He can avoid this by maintaining his inner light, while remaining outwardly yielding and tractable. With this attitude he can overcome even the greatest adversities. (I Ching XXXVI)

Charlie sent me his eye and looked sheepish. Yeah, you're right. It's late and why worry. Charlie walked off. I'm going to look out the window and read those lights, he said.

But O'Donell didn't move. He stood lurching above me. His face was twisted with rage. You've got those pills and I want them. Are you going to give them to me or do I have to start trouble. Control.

His face scared me. Animal leer. His lips drawn back and his teeth were wolf fangs. Trying his best to look fierce. He was succeeding. Looked fierce. As a matter of fact, I had never seen anyone in my life so dangerous. Same time, made me laugh. How could anyone get so upset, get so worried. Get so worked up about anything as inconsequential as a few more pills. Did it matter? Did anything matter except peace and love. O'Donell, for God's sake, relax. Swing with it.

The leer. Bared fangs. Face wolfish and the devil. Voice low and ominous. I'm going to have those pills or there'll be trouble.

I laughed. Threats. Pills. Trouble. What words. Those aren't mushroom words. Felt strong because I felt so moral. He was foolish to want and need and suffer and threaten. Smart, wise, good me.

O'Donell gave me a one last snarling look and

I PURPOSES OF RESEARCH

This investigation sets out to determine the factors—personal, social—which produce optimally positive reactions to psilocybin. "Positive reaction" in this study is defined as:

Pleasant, ecstatic, non-anxious experience

Broadening of awareness

Increased insight

An additional aim of the study is to determine if the reactions to psilocybin (positive or negative) are enduring.

II *PROCEDURE OF AD-MINISTRATION*

This study is guided by a set of ethical and interpersonal principles which stress collaboration, openness, humanistic interchange between researcher and subjects. These principles lead to the following operations:

1. Participants whenever possible will alternate roles of observer and subject.

2. Participants will be given all available information about the drug and its effects before the experiment. We will attempt to avoid an atmosphere of mystery and secret experimentation.

turned on his heel and went upstairs to bed. Glad to see him go. Done O'Donell.

Charlie paced back and kept up his funny raving about the beauty. He had changed. More confident. Coming on like a great teacher of men. The beauty and the color and now I see what artists are trying to do. Trying to get it all down on canvas, the way it glows and throbs and lives.

Good old footballer Charlie suddenly become lecturer on art. Giving us the aesthetic chalk-talk. And happy too. Pacing, raving, looking with wonder, throwing out his arms, wanting to embrace the whole scene. Rhona, if you could only see it. And I'm so happy. This is utopia. It's heaven. Why do we have to come back? Why can't it always be this way?

Charlie goes off to the dining room to dig the folds of the curtains. Joan stays there under my arm peaceful and quiet. Then after a while the sky through the windows beings to lighten and Joan says it's time to go and we take the long slow winding drive down the Charles bank my right hand holding her hand and on her front steps we stand watching the first sunlight caught in the tree leaves and it was all about as fresh and clean and lovely as you could want.

I had two hours sleep and then rushed back to Cambridge to meet a class. As I went by the main office I left word that I wanted to see Mike and George as soon as possible. I wanted to see them right away to tell them about the pilot-study session. I was still worried about jumping the gun, about using the mushrooms without their knowledge.

After the class Mike was waiting in my office and we sat down and I told him the whole story. About my indecision, about my not wanting to be square, about O'Donell, about Charlie, about Joan and me feeling so close. He didn't like it at all. He didn't like our using the mushrooms so frivolously, late at night after drinking, in a party fashion. All very unscientific. And the issue of trust and responsibility. Couldn't I be depended upon? Was I so easily influenced? All very unscientific and non-collaborative.

I apologized and said I felt bad about not in-

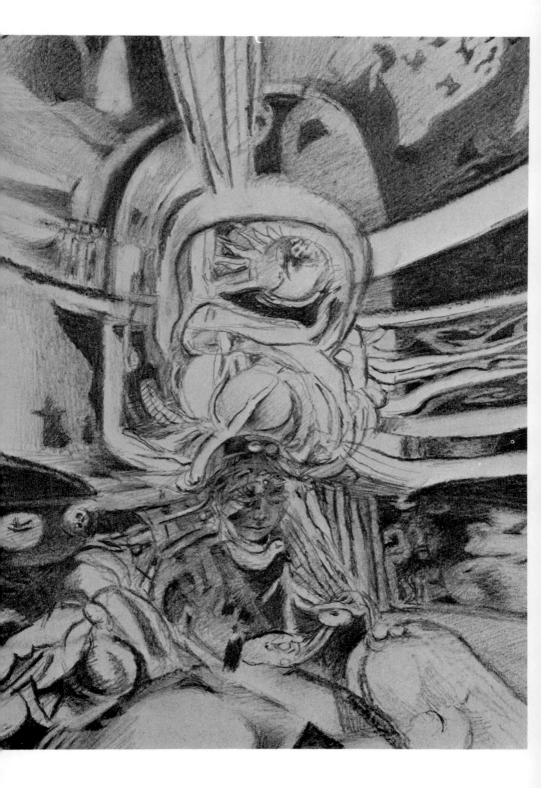

3. The participants will be given control of their own dosage. A maximum dosage will be determined by the principal investigators.

forming George and him. But also that I was glad it had happened because we had learned a lot. First of all about the dosage. It was clear that the articles in the scientific literature were way off. The psychiatric studies had been using four and five pills. Here we had Joan taking six and just feeling cozy. And here was Charlie taking seven and just getting sensitized to beauty and not coming anywhere near the deep visions and the falling down through the floor, through the earth surface down into the well of time the way we did in Mexico.

And the second thing we learned was timing of dosage. People could start with moderate amounts, like two or three pills, and then increase the dosage at their own speed so that they could control it themselves and not be suddenly clobbered by a big first dose. And then too it was obvious that observers could take small doses as well so that they could go along part of the way with the visionary voyagers.

This maximum number of tablets will be given the subject and he will be told to dose himself at the rate and amount he desires.

I explained to Mike that it was inevitable that Charlie and Rhona be made part of the group eventually. We couldn't keep them out of the mushroom scene taking place on the premises.

Mike remained disapproving, wrenching every drop of guilt from the dark raisin of my remorse, but after I apologized he was touched and at the end he wrung my hand in forgiveness.

After Mike left, O'Donell came by my office and I told him about Mike's punitive wrath. He nodded cool and wise. Sure. Sure. I understand the whole thing. It's those damn research meetings we've been having. Everyone gets all worked up. Anxious. They want to take the trip and they are scared to take the trip. The whole research business is fake anyway. There's too much fear around. This society is run on fear. Research is a phony ritual to counteract fear of the mystery. We should keep this thing secret. Have a good time with these mushroom pills. Learn with them. You can't research

4. The sessions will take place in pleasant, spacious, aesthetic surroundings. Music, art reproductions, sympathetic observers will be available.

ecstasy except on yourself and your friends. And all this collaborative research bullshit. How are you going to collaborate or have a good time with people who are afraid of fun and ecstasy and keep using science as a defense?

I knew he was right. It was some residual conformist, prudish cop-out feeling of mine to want to have ecstasy above ground. To make the joyous mystery public and socially acceptable. It was hard for me to accept the fact that you can't surrender to God's grace and win a Sunday school merit badge at the same time.

Another thing, said O'Donell, there's the power thing. Mike was sore because we went ahead last night without him. Well that's the way it's going to be. Everyone who isn't tripping himself because he's too scared or tired is going to resent our doing it. Sex, drugs, fun, travel, dancing, loafing. You name it. Anything that's pleasurable is going to bring down the wrath of the power-control people. Because the essence of ecstasy and the essence of religion and the essence of orgasm (and they're all pretty much the same) is that you give up power and swing with it. And the cats who can't do that end up with the power and they use it to punish the innocent and the happy. And they'll try to make us look bad and feel bad.

Yeah, and they can make it sound bad too. Can't you see the headlines they could have written about last night's trip? PROFS LURE GIRLS TO DRUG PARTIES. Or how about this one—PROFS, COEDS NABBED IN DRUG RAID—wasn't that what Mike was doing to your head?

I said, well, we are supposed to be scientists and we used the drugs last night in an informal social situation. We gave the drugs to our friends. Drugs! Listen to that word. Drugs! This country is hysterical about drugs. That word is a symbol more powerful than sex or communism. To the average American the word drug means doctor-disease or dope-degenerate. But underneath, everyone knows that the key to the mystery of life is chemical. The Elixir. The magic potion. The Holy Communion. The alchemist's powder. And everyone who wants to keep the status quo going is alarmed by the word drug. I was thinking of Lola, the Mexican maid, running across the lawn crossing herself in fear, fear of the mushrooms.

I was feeling fear in a double dose. From within and without. The fear of taking the trip and going

5. The subject will be allowed to bring a relative or friend to be his observer.

6. No subject should take the drug in a group where he is a stranger.

7. An attempt will be made to have one observer for each two subjects. The subjects will be given complete freedom of the house but cannot leave the premises. Observers will be available at all times for discussions.

III PROCEDURE FOR COLLECTING DATA

The basic data of the research are reports written by the subject after his experience.

Every participant who writes up a report receives copies of all other reports after completion of his own. This procedure increases the feeling of collaboration and, we believe, leads to frank description.

A second source of data are questionnaires filled out by each subject.

There is a third source of data: ratings executed by observers who watched the subjects and interviewed them during and after the experience.

out of my mind. And the fear of the wrath of the control people who were opposed to others' taking the trip. I was climbing on the tightrope I was to walk for the next seven years. I was scared by the freedom O'Donell was defending. And afraid of the prudish social forces which attack freedom.

In a time of darkness it is essential to be cautious and reserved. One should not needlessly awaken overwhelming enmity by inconsiderate behavior. In such times one ought not to fall in with the practices of others; neither should one drag them censoriously into the light. In social intercourse one should not try to be all-knowing. One should let many things pass, without being duped. (I Ching)

Any psychedelic session confronts you with paradoxes that man has struggled with for thousands of years. And this innocent little trip proposed by O'Donell had been a four-year college education. It destroyed my hopes that the mushroom pill was an automatic love-revelation pill.

This was a disturbing discovery. There seemed to be equal amounts of God and Devil (or whatever you want to call them) within the nervous system. Psychedelic drugs just open the door to the Magic Theatre, and the stages and dramas you encounter depend on what you are looking for, your state of mind when you begin, the pressure of your traveling companions.

The terrible truth began to dawn—and, no, I didn't want to face it—that our consciousness creates the universe we experience. We are the architects of the celestial and hellish stages we act upon.

I began to get a sinking feeling. Psychedelic drugs didn't solve any problems. They just magnified, mythified, clarified to jewel-like sharpness the basic problem of life and evolution.

I began to feel the frustration of the guy who invented the wheel at that horrid moment when he real-ized it could be harnessed to any damnable human game—to a war chariot, to a bulldozer, to a Las Vegas roulette table. The old games will always be with us: spontaneity vs. control, freedom vs. structure, love vs. isolation. The stage sets get bigger. The energies move faster, our insight into the divine plan becomes more awe-fully detailed. The razor-edge of paradox remains.

The thunderstorm has the effect of clearing the air; the superior man produces a similar effect when dealing with mistakes and sins of men that induce a condition of tension. . . . He forgives misdeeds . . . just as water washes everything clean. (I Ching XXXVI)

And the quizzical smile of O'Donell remained.

IV   *SUBJECTS*

All the subjects will be volunteers.

Three groups of subjects will be studied in this exploratory period: a group of professional and non-professional volunteers, a group of outstanding creative intellectuals, a group of persons psychologically addicted to and dependent on drug stimulation.

∞

DARKENING OF THE LIGHT.
*In adversity
It furthers one to be persevering.*
(I Ching)

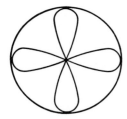

You Will Be Hurled Beyond
the Good and Evil Game:

THE RITE TO BE WRONG

November 1960

Guide: SUSAN LEARY

Oracle: X

Treading (Conduct)

The Creative, Heaven

The Joyous, Lake

Heaven above, the lake below:
The image of TREADING.
Thus the superior man discriminates between
   high and low,
And thereby fortifies the thinking of the
   people.

(I Ching)

Susan Leary:

My first memories about my father's research are of sessions in our house on Grant Avenue, in Newton, Massachusetts, in 1960.

I remember lots of people coming all the time and turning on, and uh, I remember doing things with the people.

I was thirteen years old at the time.

We had an enormous house, and uh, there was a huge living room with a shaggy green rug that looked like a field of grass.

And a sort of music room. We lived in this beautiful house sort of like a museum.

The house was in a big stir of excitement when I got home. The great Halloween party was in the works. Ten teen-age boys and nine girls. The girls were going to stay over for a slumber party. They were busy stringing up orange and black ribbons, creative over joyous, and trying out the record player and fixing each other's hair and giggling about costumes and boys. We were all whipped up into a pre-party frenzy and it didn't help when some parents, whom I had invited to come for a drink after the party, appeared beforehand expecting to be entertained.

Gradually the house began to fill up with sailors and tramps and clowns and pickaninnies and Japanese geishas and the adults assembled in the kitchen to keep out of the way. We had ordered two roast chickens but no one was hungry so we sat around the kitchen table putting away the Scotch and listening to the noise from the front rooms.

My tension kept building up. No sleep the night before, of course, and the moral donnybrook with Mike at the office and then I had to rush out to interfere when my daughter started fighting with her brother, who had burst a girl's balloon. And when we expected the party to settle down to dancing, it turned out that teen-age boys don't dance and the girls huddled disgustedly in the dining room near the record player while the boys started a football game in the living room, tackling any girl who got caught in midfield without interference. Just about at the point when the whistle should be blown I raced out of the kitchen and broke up three scrimmages and got everyone assembled in the dining room and sitting down for entertainment, except that we hadn't figured out any entertainment, and there were the twenty faces waiting intently to be entertained.

O'Donell and I got all the girls into the living room and told them to hide. And then we went into the dining room and gave the boys paper bags to put over their heads and told them to hunt around blind in the living room until they found a girl and then to sit on the couch with her. Well the game went like wildfire and why not since we had harnessed the strongest motive of all to make the wheels go round. For the next fifteen minutes we stood in the living room catching the lamps as they fell and umpiring the action and listening to the screams and giggles. When the last girl was caught a big cheer went up and then the girls said that they wanted to catch the boys and the whole act was repeated and when the last boy was caught they all screamed that they wanted to try it again and the boys went into the dining room and we started helping the girls to hide. The atmosphere was reeking of teen-age excitement, really indecent in its fervor, and when one flushed girl came up breathless and asked the name of this wonderful new game I told her, honey the game isn't really so new. It's as old as life and she said, well, we do need a name for it and I said we'll think of a good name sooner or later.

Now about four or five of the girls had just blossomed within the last few months and this didn't lower the temperature. They kept wanting to hide up on the ledges of the bookshelf and kept calling to O'Donell and Charlie and me to help boost them up and they kept falling back on top of us and we were struggling to lift them up and hold them from falling and then the boys came in and the screams commenced and O'Donell and I tottered back to the kitchen and poured a Scotch and looked at each other.

At eleven the boys departed and we got the nine girls herded upstairs to the master bedroom and set up the TV and the record player and good nights all around and back to the kitchen. The three of us, Charlie and O'Donell and I, were sitting around the kitchen table catching our breath and then the parade began. The girls kept coming down for hot chocolate and cookies and milk and ice cream. The girls were still flushed and wound up and couldn't

It was rented from a very rich professor who had traveled around the world collecting material objects and they were very beautiful.

There was a Moroccan lamp on the first floor at the bottom of the main stairway and it had lights inside.

It was very large and had all different-colored glass around it.

When you turned it on in the nighttime it glowed and radiated and people would get hung up looking at it.

I remember lots of graduate students coming for psychedelic sessions, and ministers and Harvard professors and religious people with robes, and poets.

I remember Charlie Olsen was one of the first.

I remember he was very big and tall, looked like a gigantic mountain of teddy bear. I came to about his waist.

Much of the time I was not involved in what was going on in the house.

I had my own social scene with kids in Newton. But I remember him being around the house, like a Santa Claus laughing.

He was very nice.

leave that kitchen alone. There was one long-legged girl in particular who was wearing pink underpants and a green sweater and she stood by the electric mixer waiting for a milk shake and kept pulling the sweater down over her underpants and when she let go the sweater snapped up and then she pulled it down and it snapped up and then she pulled it down and it snapped up. She made four trips to the kitchen and finally I asked her in a nice way to go back up and put on her overcoat or something. Charlie and O'Donell and I were trying to carry on a conversation and finally I called a curfew on the girls' kitchen visits and we went back to serious drinking.

We were all three tired and drawn out to a fine edge and the whisky was relaxing and we fell to discussing the mushrooms and the big moral struggle of the day. Good old solid Charlie was shocked and angry at the moral abuse we had taken from Mike. O'Donell had some creative theories explaining why *they* always persecute us. He was taking all the blame for the informal session.

The more we talked the more righteous I became and the madder I got at the moralists. Alcohol stirs up the emotions. Of course, the more I agreed with O'Donell, the more guilty I became about my resentment towards him and my blaming him for the session. So we were swinging along in the most cheerful style and then the question came up again. O'Donell said, well, why don't we have a mushroom or two just to see what a small dose would do. Now this sounded like a good experiment. And after all the turmoil, it seemed only just and true that we three comrades should cement our alliance with a touch of revelation. It so happened that I had the bottle in my pocket. I could feel it there everytime I reached for matches. I pulled it out and we each took two.

Charlie started again on his mushroom litany. They produced paradise, and oriental beauty, and he was twenty-two years old and had never dreamed that such heavenly bliss was available to mankind. I was out of cigarettes and when I asked Charlie for a Marlboro he grinned and said, sure, but it will cost you a mushroom. Good enough. I poured out a pink pearl and handed it to him. When I asked for a light he proposed the same bargain and then I realized more clearly the power-control position I had set up for myself. That moment in my office when I had taken the brown cardboard box from Mike and put it in my file, I had changed my relationships with everyone I dealt with. They all wanted the bread of dreams, the flesh of the gods. And I was changed with the one ring of power in my pocket. I was feeling that miserable pleasure of the millionaire. There was always the ploy behind the ploy. Can I tap him for nirvana? Can I work him for a vision? There was one easy way out.

Look, Charlie, let's stop all the playing around for the mushroom power. I have the ring of power. But I don't want it. I'm getting rid of it. I'm giving the precious mushroom bottle to you. Here, take it. Now you're stuck with it. Now you decide who gets them and how many and when. Let them come to you for the word. You decide. You dispense them. You take the responsibility.

I handed the bottle to Charlie and laughed at his big football face bewildered by my move. I felt great. The load was off my shoulders. Mushrooms had taught me this much, that the artificial differences between people, like age or role or prestige or control of the money or the land or the army or the mushrooms were irrelevant. I was damn glad to get rid of the role that I had put myself in—holder of the indole ring.

Less shame, my guide said, would wash away a greater fault than yours has been, my son. Therefore be unburdened of your sorrow. Remember, I am always at your side. (Inferno VII)

While I was laughing and enjoying my new release Charlie was whispering to O'Donell and then he began pouring them out in his hand, all of them, the whole bottle, pink-pearl cluster in his big hand and he counted out eight, a third of the total and handed them to O'Donell and then he pushed eight with his big finger into his right hand and

And another poet I remember is Allen Ginsberg.

I remember I was watching television in my room one night and my father was running a session downstairs.

I was watching a movie; the airplane movie where the airplane catches on fire.

What's the name of that movie? It was the one where the wing catches on fire and they throw all the luggage outside.

Allen Ginsberg was downstairs and my father would come up now and then to report.

And I remember one point, my father coming up into my room and saying that Allen thought that Kennedy and Khrushchev should have an LSD session together and end the Cold War.

So Allen got on the phone and I remember my father was worried about the phone bill, so Allen Ginsberg called Jack Kerouac instead.

I remember an Easter Sunday, 1961, Alan Watts the philosopher was running a session, very Christian.

They took LSD in goblets and read from the New Testament.

During the afternoon it began snowing very lightly outside.

gave them to me and pushed his finger around counting six, seven, eight, and let them drop into his right hand and popped them into his mouth and there was one left—the twenty-fifth—and he said, who gets this extra. O'Donell said, you carry the heaviest body weight so you deserve it, and down it went, the last pink-pearl pill. I was still holding eight in my hand. I was again surprised at the way Charlie and O'Donell were treating the mushrooms. They were applying the liquor ritual to this new commodity. We're hung up always on the rituals we've learned, and the old drinking pattern of bottoms up and share the supply was operating and at this moment you were either with it or you weren't. Besides, I had given the responsibility to Charlie. I was free so I threw the eight pink jewels into my mouth. To speed matters up O'Donell suggested that we chew them. Sweet chalky taste and we washed them down with Scotch and waited for the next scene.

From all the literature I had read on the subject, we had just surpassed the world's record for psilocybin consumption. The psychiatric people had been using 8 to 10 milligrams (that is, four to five pills), and I had just consumed 20 milligrams (ten pills) and so had O'Donell, and Charlie had wolfed down 22 milligrams.

It hit in about twenty minutes, the waves of sensation rippling down the body and the pressure on the ear drums. There were six doors to the kitchen and they were all closed. We were sealed in a bathysphere plunged down to sea bottom. The walls and ceilings glowed phosphorescent yellow, electric vibrating color. The floor was shimmering like lemon Jell-o. Some torn fragments of party decoration were scattered on the floor and they sparkled, dazzling, black shiny ebony jewels. Orange gems.

Some kid had left a cardboard top hat and Charlie tilted it on his head. His face was huge, yellow-stained with deep green shadows under his eyes. He had grown in stature, the leader, the keeper of the mushrooms. Top-hatted ringmaster of the cosmic circus. Chuckling, grinning impishly. Walking around the kitchen joking about the fortune in jewels on the floor, lifting his huge body in a comic tiptoe gait. The clown genius. He was the wisest and funniest person I had ever seen.

O'Donell the rebel was in a good mood too. We were three kitchen conspirators. Three gods romping around a spangly paradise. There were only the three of us in the yellow-walled universe. No one else existed but this rolling trinity. Then over the laughter I heard a noise, a door opening upstairs and a blast of rock-and-roll from the record player, and then the door closing and silence. Oh yes; from a thousand years back I remembered the party and the girls' slumber-group upstairs on that other distant planet. Vague *angst*. Are they all right? Are they doing well a million light-years away up there? Yes. Don't worry. Don't take the interstellar trip up there to see. . . .

> Then
> > suddenly
> > > it all
> > > > changes
> The play has started
> We
> Are puppets in that old
> Cosmological drama.

SCENE ONE

A large entrance hall leading to wide sweeping stairs. On the left of the stairs a huge oaken door closes off the dining room. On the right an archway leads into an enormous living room dimly lit. A small door leading into the kitchen is shut. The floor and stairs are covered with a deep-piled rug, no, it is really a desert expanse of sand. A wide stream of brown sand silently runs down the stairs and flows into a shifting pool on the hallway floor. The top half of the front door is set in polished diamond, three feet by five feet, flashing intense glass light. The woodwork and closet doors are carved ivory, solid, bone smooth and cool to the touch. A light green silk covers the walls and in the fabric are thousands of yellow diamonds in the form of fleur de lis gleaming. A golden picture frame outlines a large rectangular hole in the wall. Within the

And I remember at one point we all went outside and chased snowflakes, and were running around catching them like baseball players chasing fly balls.

I remember Aldous Huxley came over many times.

He was very tall and strange-looking and he had a funny accent and he was very nice.

He was tall and thin and sort of stoopy. He sort of reminded me of Gandalf the gray wizard in those books on the Fellowship of the Ring.

I was allowed to go anyplace in the house. The sessions were always open.

The doors were always open and the people always liked having my younger brother or myself come in.

They were always pleasant. They weren't very active, of course.

hole, about three feet back, sits a tall Spanish cardinal. He has a long, thin, dirty white beard which trembles as he breathes. An elongated Greco nose and deep-set eyes watching steadily, now frowning, now smiling, now turning down to the illuminated manuscript on which his hands rest and along which his slender fingers move. His thin pillar body is covered with the red folds of an episcopal robe, and his arms in yellow-white lace. He is watching, waiting, judging, preparing to render verdict.

They would smile and uh, they were always mellow and rather angelic.

On the opposite wall there hangs a four-foot Moroccan mosque lamp, burnished gold, pierced over its entire swollen surface with filigreed lace-work designs. Inside the lamp, behind orange, red, and green glass, burn three bulbs spilling colors over the wall, setting fire to the green silk and reflecting from the embedded, flowered diamonds.

The sand below the lamp is littered with piles of gems—ruby, emerald, orange-diamond—which have dropped down through the latticed holes.

If I walked in a room and, if I walked into the music room for example, and all the people were lying around listening to music, meditating, I would know then that they were in a session because that's not something that people do in their normal frame of consciousness.

Spotlights flood the stage with changing waves of color. Under the sand floor is an electric generator which emits a steady hum and charges the atmosphere with high-voltage currents.

For centuries there is no action, only the cardinal moving his thin fingers across his scrolled pages and breathing softly.

Then,

The kitchen door opens. Enter Charlie, pagan leader of rebel gang. He is nine feet tall, a mountain man with a huge meat-red face glowing with energy, grinning, chuckling over some rebel-triumph, eyes dancing. His black top hat is tilted. He doesn't walk. He soars in leaping, floating steps to center stage, looking around in pleased admiration. He turns and beckons to his two followers.

But with people who I really didn't know I couldn't tell because I had no way to compare their normal state of consciousness with the state of consciousness they were in when they had taken LSD.

Enter O'Donell and Leary. They are small, wiry, happy rebels. O'Donell's face is covered with freckled potato sacking through which his white animal teeth gleam with impish pleasure. Leary gazes around in wonder.

I don't remember how often my father was taking it, but I do remember that he would take it with all the guests.

I remember that there were many people who would come and many people who were involved in what he was doing.

Usually I could tell when my father was high, but sometimes I couldn't. It depended on how high he was.

I usually could tell, because his face would be glowing and he'd be radiating.

There's no way really to describe it.

It seemed natural and good.

Leader Charlie floats halfway up the stairs and sweeps his hand round in gesture.

CHARLIE: Look. Look at the emeralds. Look at the gold. Look at the diamonds.

(*Leary stands in dazed awe. O'Donell shuffles around the stage, his shoulders butting forward. He is grinning fiercely.*)

O'DONELL: They left them and now it's all ours.

(*All three roar with laughter.*)

Quick, get a paper bag and we'll scoop up all those jewels.

CHARLIE: And the sand. Look, rivers of it. The owners of this house are going to be surprised to find this desert in their hallway.

(*All laugh. And laugh.*)

What can we do with it?

LEARY: Tell the people who take care of the house to sweep it up. And clean up all these sloppy piles of jewels scattered around. Bad housekeeping.

(*All laugh. And laugh.*)

Tell them to put the sand into millions of hourglasses.

CHARLIE: Hourglasses. What are they for?

LEARY: I once heard about people who make machines to measure time.

CHARLIE: Measure time! They think they can measure time?

O'DONELL: Hah. Measure time? What crazy thing will they think of next?

LEARY: Why sure. People will sell the jewels to buy machines to measure time.

CHARLIE: Sell jewels? Next you know they'll be selling sunshine.

LEARY: And moonlight.

O'DONELL: I am time. Can they measure me? With an hourglass?

(*All laugh. And laugh.*)

(*Charlie soars down from the stairs and bounds around the stage. O'Donell and Leary follow him aimlessly.*)

CHARLIE: This stage is so empty.

LEARY: Yes, big and empty.

O'DONELL: They've all gone.

CHARLIE: Where did they go?

O'DONELL: They've been doing it forever.

LEARY: Yes, they do, don't they.

CHARLIE: What? Do what?

O'DONELL: Come and act on the stage set for a while and then go.

CHARLIE: Why do they do it?

O'DONELL: Nobody has ever figured it out.

(*Leary has been standing studying the jewels dropping from the burnished mosque lamp. He turns with a start.*)

LEARY: Figured what out?

O'DONELL: Where they come from. Why they come. Where they're going.

(*They stand, all three, in silence for . . . well, let's say eleven years. Then the cardinal sitting behind the gold frame in his rectangle cave turns and raises his left hand up to his chin so that it covers, merges with his elongated beard. His eyes smile compassionately. He speaks in a low voice in Spanish.*)

CARDINAL: Dear little ones. Do you really think that you can answer that riddle?

LEARY: Can you answer it?

(*The cardinal smiles, moves his arm down to the book, exposing his beard, then moves it back, tugging softly at his chin. He says nothing.*)

LEARY: Yes I can answer the riddle. There is no riddle. (*He is thinking of each grain in the river of sand swirling below his feet.*)

O'DONELL: That's right, there's no riddle. I've solved it all, many times.

CHARLIE: (*Reproachful leader-god, commanding.*) Why do you guys worry? With all this beauty? Why worry about riddles?

O'DONELL: What riddles?

CHARLIE: Exactly. What riddles?

O'DONELL: We were talking about all of them and where they went to.

CHARLIE: Who?

O'DONELL: Why, all the actors that were here before.

CHARLIE: It is funny when you think about it. Where did they go? Who?

LEARY: Well, there were the Landlords. They rented us the house and left. They think they own the set.

O'DONELL: Own the set? Own?

But I always believed in my father and what he was and I figured that what he was doing would . . . I . . . you know, he would not be doing anything for any useless, frivolous reason.

In spite of the fact that there were lots of people and lots of laughing there, it wasn't social.

Because all the communication—there was not all that much of verbal communication except when Alan Watts was there, who talked constantly.

But, usually there was not much verbal communication.

LEARY: And the land too. They think they own the land.

(*All laugh. And laugh.*)

CHARLIE: (*Still laughing.*) Stop it you guys. It's too much. You make it sound like a game of Monopoly. Own the land. (*He laughs.*)

LEARY: Damn right. They bought it with money, too.

O'DONELL: Money, hah.

It wasn't a social thing, really. It was much like people having telepathy.

CHARLIE: Money. You mean the green paper that you find in the cardboard box that the game comes in.

LEARY: Exactly.

CHARLIE: Good. Now I understand.

LEARY: Well, the Landlords bought it from the Cartwrights. And the Crabtrees, they sold it to the Cartwrights. That was much earlier in the game.

O'DONELL: All gone.

It wasn't social like a talky cocktail party.

LEARY: And here we are. With all the sand and the jewels and the ivory that goes with it.

O'DONELL: Well I think it's only right that we keep up the game. Why don't we buy it and sell it to each other?

CHARLIE: Yeah, good idea. It will pass the time. And then after we get tired buying and selling let's go in and listen to music in the study.

My father was teaching at Harvard at the time and when . . . I knew that it had something to do with his Harvard research.

(*Short pause. Charlie now leaps back up on the stairs.*)

It really is beautiful, isn't it. Shimmering and glowing.

O'DONELL: Strange, strange.

LEARY: Yes. What?

O'DONELL: That they did it all. The stage is set.

CHARLIE: (*Soaring down to the doors.*) You mean the way they made these ivory doors?

O'DONELL: Yes. Look at them. How they worked!

LEARY: And how they cared. They must have cared.

He never really explained it to me, but the people who were there were researchers and serious types, lots of Harvard graduate students and a lot of very intelligent people.

CHARLIE: And the old Arab lamp there. Some old Arab sitting in his tent hammering it and designing the holes and lacework.

LEARY: And all for us.

O'DONELL: They made the scene and left.

CHARLIE: Left it for us.

O'DONELL: (*Pointing.*) Hey, why is that big door to the dining room shut? I hate shut doors.

CHARLIE: It's stuck. I tried to open it.

O'DONELL: How did it get closed in the first place?

LEARY: I shut it during the game.

O'DONELL: What game?

LEARY: The game where the boys were searching blind after the girls. I had the boys shut up in there while the girls were hiding and it got stuck.

O'DONELL: (*He bends over shaking his head, wolf-like and muttering.*) Always a mistake.

LEARY: What?

O'DONELL: To shut people in. Always a mistake.

CHARLIE: (*The leader.*) Well, let's open the bars. Freedom. The three of us can push the gate back.

(*Charlie motions. O'Donell and Leary float over and they begin shoving and butting, trying to slide the door along its roller. It doesn't move. They try again. Then stop, all leaning in pushing positions against the door.*)

LEARY: Well, we've been able to open lots of things up tonight. But this one we can't do.

CHARLIE: Yeah. Can't win them all. We'll do it tomorrow when we're not under . . . when we feel stronger.

O'DONELL: (*He is frowning and gnashing his teeth slowly, hunched over.*) Well, I feel strong now. Stronger than anyone in the world. And I want doors open. I can't stand to be cooped in. (*He starts pushing violently, savagely, his eyes gleaming and his teeth white against his brown, cloth face. He can't move the door. Failure makes him angrier and he throws himself against the door again growling. The colored floodlights begin to dim and the room grows shadowy.*)

Jewels lose their sparkle. The gem shadows are puddles of drab color. Sand river turns into tan stained carpet. The white ivory woodwork gleams unpleasantly bright. Charlie becomes an ungainly young man, silly with child's hat on his head. Three drugged men in disheveled shirt sleeves wandering

And I figured it must have something to do with his work in psychology.

It was not a typical home life, but my father getting involved with LSD was not the beginning of my unusual life.

Even before he got involved with LSD I had no mother and we traveled a great deal in Europe and Mexico and I saw a lot of the world and interesting people.

When my father got involved with LSD it just took on new, sort of new dimension.

And it's true that all my friends just lived with their mother and father and so forth and they always had a tight, small family scene.

We used to have a lot of visitors come, and people staying for the weekend, and some staying for periods of time.

It was not the normal, it was not like my friends' home life.

Well, my friends weren't aware that my father was conducting LSD experiments.

They just figured that my father had a lot of friends coming and going all the time.

around at the foot of the wide, sweeping staircase. The bearded cardinal has frozen, two-dimensional against the wall. Three Beckett clowns on a vast, empty stage. Pointlessly milling around.

I heard O'Donell saying something about the teen-age girls upstairs. I frowned. Bad thought. Keep the other planets out of the action. Charlie tilted his top hat down over his eyes, giggling at O'Donell. No point in thinking about girls, O'Donell, you're impotent under the drug anyway. O'Donell scowled. Oh yeah. That's what you think. Talk about your own impotency but it doesn't hold for me. I may turn them on.

Charlie grinned. What would the girls' mothers think if they knew there were drugged men roving around the house. The girls have never been safer, I said. All the reports say that the drug turns sex off. Charlie laughed. That's right. Last night I could look at Rhona and Joan and they were beautiful but I had no lust and didn't even want to touch them.

O'Donell loosed a mocking laugh. The scene bothered me. I was feeling disjointed and rudderless. I felt a longing for someone loving. I missed Joan and wanted to hold her close. Charlie and O'Donell were arguing and the happy mood was lost. Life is pointless without love, I said. We're straggling, lost on an endless desert stage. It's all meaningless, but we have to do something.

O'Donell leered. Speak for yourself. I'm going upstairs.

It was crystal clear to me that life without love is an empty sham, senseless action, puppetry. But we have to do something. What had any point? I tried to use my mind, but there were no categories, no clichés, nothing inferential to hold on to. All loveless actions were ritual. Empty gestures. Where, where is the real right program? What, what to do and why? Where to begin? How to build up a life of loveless action? I was standing in the hallway with my eyes closed trying to find a philosophy, a way, a meaning. What is life about anyway, without love? I was pushing my mind back, back to some beginnings, to something basic. What action is any better than the other? What? What? What? Painful, clutching conflict. Then I reached something. Helping others. Yes, that's the beginning. Everywhere there is helpfulness and then we try to help. Yes. There's a difference that makes sense. It is better to help than hurt. The house is in a mess from the party. Rhona will have to clean it up tomorrow. I'll do it tonight. That makes sense. I'll start with the kitchen.

Charlie and O'Donell were still bantering sarcastically at the foot of the stairs. The only loveless action that makes sense is to clean up the mess, I said. Matter of fact, that's a form of love. Come on out and help me.

I left them and walked into the kitchen and started running water in the sink and rinsing dishes. The door opened and Charlie walked in. O'Donell's gone upstairs. Upstairs? I thought of upstairs and I thought of the girls and the slumber party. Waves of guilt washed over me for having dragged my kids around from country to country, school to school, house to house, and Susan missing friends and the warm cozy routine schedule and this was her first party, her first social event, and how excited she was and nothing must mar it, no clowning-around adults. Upstairs? Where did he go upstairs? To bed. I turned from the sink and looked at Charlie. My voice was harsh. Are you sure?

Charlie's face reacting to my rough tones. A look of terror. Yes, well, I'm sure . . . that's what he said. My voice ominous. Well, I gave you the pills and it's your party and you're responsible. More terror. Gee, I'll go upstairs to check. I stood by the sink thinking again about the dear, naïve, tender daughter, wanting so much a normal stable growing up. I dried my hands and started upstairs. In the upper hallway I could see the door to the girls' room open and Charlie's voice commanding. I was sick with the horror of it. O'Donell, drugged, lurching into the slumber party. Scandal. Susan's dream of social acceptance shattered. The girls were standing in the center of the room bug-eyed. O'Donell was lying on their bed. Charlie was bending over him pulling his arm. Come on

They were not aware until the Harvard business was publicized.

Well, um, I'm sure they noticed something unusual about it, but I never discussed it with them.

They were aware that something was going on, but it was like living in a church with jolly people.

Federal Court
Laredo, Texas

The Court: You may close for the government, Mr. Blask.

Mr. Blask: May it please the court. Ladies and gentlemen of the jury. I, too, would take a moment to express for Mr. Susman and myself appreciation for the patience with which you have listened to the testimony of the last two or three days.

To say that this was an unusual case would be gross understatement, and to say that it's an important case would be gross understatement, because, ladies and gentlemen, I have participated in what I feel is a considerable number of criminal cases and I cannot remember a case that I have felt more strongly about than I have this case, and I will tell you why:

Because we are dealing today in—and you will be dealing with it when you are deliberating—with a man who lives in your society. He may not live in your community but he lives here in the United States. He is no different than anybody else. Just because he may believe in a different religious aspect, that has nothing to do with it, or because he may be of a different race, that has nothing to do with it.

O'Donell, let's go downstairs. O'Donell's mocking sneer. Nah. I doan wanna go downstairs. I'm gonna stay here with the girls.

Charlie had pulled him up to a sitting position. Come on, O'Donell, you can't be in here. Nah. Who says I can't. I do what I like. I grabbed his other arm and we yanked him to his feet. O'Donell tried to throw us off but we held on. Come on, O'Donell. We don't belong here. This is the girls' party. Look at Susie. You love her, don't you? Do you want to spoil her party? I looked at Susan. She was watching us silently, curiously. We pulled O'Donell out the door. He was struggling but not too hard. We hustled him to the other end of the hallway and stopped.

Goddammit, O'Donell, knock it off. You have no right to butt in there.

Charlie and I were towering over him. He was shrinking back from us, his eyes glaring, his lips drawn back in animal rage. I had never seen such a visage of evil. He gnashed his teeth. He had shrunk in size and was crouching, possessed with malice. Shocking awful evil. Cornered rat, cornered rat was running through my mind.

Neah. Neah. Mocking whine. Who are you to say what is right? Maybe I know what's right for those girls. Pampered middle-class dears in there watching television and playing records, growing up to be miserable middle-class bitches. Maybe the greatest thing that can happen to them in their life is for me to stir them up a little.

O'Donell's words hit my empty mind like hammer strokes. Stunned me. My God, maybe he's right. What reason, real reason do I have to interfere? It's my own dirty mind. I was racking my brain looking for a moral rebuttal. I was on Mars, you understand, looking down at earth, seeing in a flash the absurdity of social fears, taboos, the insane rituals that enslave mankind, the horrid middle-class fear. The fear. The fear. Did I want to descend to Main Street and protect tribal codes? Identify with the New England middle class? Share their insane terror of non-conformity? Their fear? I felt somehow that what O'Donell was doing was wrong but I couldn't tell him why. My mind had been purged of cliché and irrational belief. The beautiful, pure empty mind faced with the existential moment. The moral crisis. Why shouldn't O'Donell do what he wanted? Who could tell in the long run whether his plan would or would not be good? He might be the sharp Zen master to shake the girls out of middle-class shackles.

I turned, puzzled, to Charlie. He was standing, holding O'Donell's arm. His face was dazed. Tell him, Charlie, why he shouldn't go into the girls' room. Charlie stared at me. I . . . I don't know why it's wrong for him to go there.

I could tell that Charlie was going through the same moral search. Listen, Charlie. Don't you think it's wrong for him to go back in the girls' room? Charlie nodded decisively. Yes. I know it's wrong. Well, Charlie, tell him why it's wrong. Again the puzzled, helpless look. I . . . I . . . I can't tell him. I don't know why. I can't think of any reason.

Plunged back into the cosmic vacuum. My mind ran through a hundred conventional, cliché reasons and rejected them. O'Donell was smiling with mean triumph. You see, you can't tell me I'm wrong. Do you want to set yourselves up as the great moralists? Telling me about your miserable shoulds and shouldn'ts. O'Donell made a move down the hall. Charlie and I grabbed him.

Wait a minute. I know you shouldn't go there. I can't tell you why, but I know you're wrong.

It was all perfectly clear to me. We were recapitulating the moral struggles of the human race. We were the first and only men on earth and we were faced with the first ethical decision. Of course we could use force. Charlie and I—the first cosmic police force—could bend his arms and drag him—the first and eternal criminal—away and overpower him. By force. But why? What justification besides force? It was the first moral choice of my life. The first time I was faced with a fresh, ethical crossroads. There was no learned, easy motto to parrot. Ethics had to be built right up from scratch and it had to be right not in terms of revealed dogma, or fear of punishment, but in terms of the basic issue. Now what was the basic issue? What is the unassailable first assumption? Suddenly it came to me. Moses on the mountain. A beautiful bolt of rightness.

When we live here in this United States, every law that is written on the books applies equally to us and we must live by them.

And the reason that this case is important and must be taken so importantly is because you are dealing with a man who has taken this stand during the time that he testified and told you, "My name is Dr. Timothy Leary and that I am a psychologist, that I know it is wrong to possess marijuana, but I know that there are certain ways that I can possess it legally and I know that if I had applied for such relief that I probably would not have been granted it because they would have conducted investigations up in Millbrook."

And he tells you that despite all of these things, "I am more than the law: I am Dr. Timothy Leary and the law does not apply to me."

And that is why this case is so important, because he is not above the law. None of us are.

Congress enacted these laws in this book and they enacted the laws concerning marijuana because they felt that it was an immense danger and that is why it was there.

Congress also recognized that there are uses that are good for marijuana but that in order to experiment with it, as he says, or to research with it, as he says, he is a researcher, you must be licensed.

And the government will not allow somebody irresponsible to be licensed. And I think that he is irresponsible and I believe that is why he could not be licensed and had never made an application for it.

What about the facts in this case?

He has admitted to you that he smokes marijuana. He told you that in 1964 or 1965, the first time he ever touched marijuana was in India.

I'll tell you why you can't go into Susan's room. Because it is her trip, her territory, her party, and *because she doesn't want you there.* You have the right to do anything you want to so long as you don't lay your trip on anyone else. No one has the right to force himself on someone else against his will. I was speaking slowly with the greatest seriousness. When I finished, Charlie shouted, Yes, of course, that's exactly right. You can't go there because the girls don't want you. Do your own thing. Let them do their thing.

Tremendous flood of relief. The first ethical law had been forged. Moses smiles. There was a right— not based on force, not based on fear, not based on irrational taboo or custom or dogma. But based on cellular equality. Mutual respect. Charlie and I were nodding at each other happily. O'Donell was making a mocking growling noise and suddenly he burst out of our grasp and started down the hall. We grabbed him and pulled him back and around the corner to the north wing of the house far away from the girls.

O'Donell was seething with futile rage. Again the rat-face and fangs, and his face even seemed gray and furry. We stood there blocking his way, arguing. You're cops. All cops are the same. Telling me what I can't do. Charlie and I were reasoning with him. Why don't we go back downstairs and have fun the way we were? Charlie was pleading. He had been swayed by O'Donell's violent rebuttal. We got no place. We were spoilsport, busybody policemen and O'Donell was going to have his own way. What can we do? Charlie was looking at me pleading.

Suddenly I felt a moral impatience with Charlie. He was no longer the wise, Olympian clown god. He was a whining, begging boy who had talked me into giving him the pills and caused all this mess. Goddammit, Charlie. See what you did giving out the pills that way? I never wanted you to start this mess. You were the big shot and it's your responsibility.

Now Charlie was mad. Oh? It's my responsibility, is it? Well, I quit! I resign! You're twice my age and you're twice as smart as I am and you handle it. I quit! Charlie dropped O'Donell's arm and started down the back stairs to the kitchen. Good, said O'Donell, all the cops quit and now I'm going back to see the girls. O'Donell started down the north-wing hallway and Charlie was moving down the stairs. I was panicked. I could follow O'Donell and leap on him and wrestle him back, but I feared the noise. I was obsessed by the dread of disturbing the girls. Fear of a scandal. I called down the stairs. Now I was pleading. Okay, Charlie. It's not your responsibility. But as one friend to another, as one human being to another, will you help me keep him away from the girls?

Charlie looked up in my eyes. We both understood. Responsibility and roles were nonsensical and Charlie had been right to see through this and reject it. Under the mushrooms there aren't roles and rituals. But the appeal to him as man to man couldn't be dismissed. Charlie bounded back up and ran to the corner of the hall. He grabbed O'Donell's arm. O'Donell snarled and tried to push past. Charlie laughed, ominous, confident. Oh, little man, you want to get rough with me. Football Charlie was a giant pushing back the tiny foe. Don't try to pull any force, O'Donell, because that just won't work.

The three of us standing in the north-wing hallway. O'Donell sunk in bitter passivity. He was still muttering about cops. Need for someone present who was not under the drugs. We were still the only three men in the universe and we needed help. Then I thought of Rhona. Charlie, go up and wake Rhona. Tell her we need her down here badly. Charlie nodded and started down the hall. He walked sheepishly and I shouted to him (again sore about his giving out the mushrooms irresponsibly), Ah, hah, you're guilty, aren't you? I was happy to see him guilty at waking his wife and exposing her to this drug mess. I was happy because it made me right and him wrong.

Rhona's face was pinched and sour. She was blinking at the light. I was glad to see her. Rhona, a terrible thing has happened. She was cool and businesslike. What's so terrible? I explained the situation. First of all, you must realize that the

This is research? This is a man who tells you that "I am above the law."

What kind of a man are you dealing with? What kind of a man do you have before you here today?

You have a man that says, "I believe in bringing up my children the old-fashioned way," and the "old-fashioned way," ladies and gentlemen,

is to expose them to marijuana, expose them to these other drugs that he has no right to dispense. And that is what we have here.

Is that irresponsibility?

I can think of no—no other situation that can be more irresponsible.

Mr. Fitzgibbon: If Your Honor please. I thought on the question of religion we weren't going to talk on it.

The Court: Religion?

Mr. Fitzgibbon: The right to bring up our children.

Mr. Blask: Now, getting back to the fact as it relates to Dr. Leary and this marijuana, as we are dealing with here today—

and you recognize it's not a question of the quantity, because if we wanted to railroad him into being punished, we could have manufactured something

—and I think you realize that we are bringing you the honest facts. That's all there was, was something about a half an ounce.

The question of the amount has nothing to do with it— nothing whatsoever.

What did this man admit to doing?

Whether we take it at face value or not, he admits that he obtained the marijuana in New York; he transported it from New York to Laredo, Texas. He has admitted that. There is no question about it.

He did not have the proper order forms. There is no question about that.

But he won't get a license because he knows they won't give it to him and he secretes the marijuana.

That is the responsible person for you.

three of us have taken a bigger dose of these pills than anyone in the world. Rhona was still cool. So what's so bad about that?

Then I told her about the scene in the girls' room and how O'Donell insisted on going back. Rhona listened thoughtfully and we were all watching her. She became the great judge and law-giver.

Who says I shouldn't do what I want to do. But, teen-age girls! Susan's party! We were pleading our cases. Rhona listened. The hallway was shadowy, a dim cave deep in the underworld. We finished.

Finally the silence breaks. Truth speaks.

Of course you can't go in there, O'Donell!

And his voice coming back, mocking Rhona's prim, proper British, Nyayah. Why can't I go in there? What law says I can't and who's law? My tight muscles loosened when Rhona had pronounced the verdict, but now they tightened again. Could she give a reason, a rule that went beyond the transient rules of the games that we all knew we didn't have to play?

And the reply, cool and so convincing. Impossible to think of going in there, O'Donell. *Grown-ups don't join pajama parties!* It just isn't done.

Wham! What a judgment. What legal logic. Moses, take your stone tablets. Justice Brandeis, forget your Blackstone. Rhona's words. Pinnacle of legal reasoning. Rhona, just two years out of teen-age herself, knew *the rule*—as relentless as Three strikes you're out. Adults don't infringe on the trip of the adolescent. I was swinging clear and happy. And loving Rhona. Admiration. O'Donell was stunned. You could see his tense squirming body begin to relax. Looking down at the floor. Nodding his head. We stood for a long time and then Rhona, briskly, case-dismissed, no-nonsense voice, said All right. All of you come down to the kitchen and I'll brew up some tea and cookies. The calm, sure voice of the British empire. Righto! Good show! Well done! Now let's have tea.

Rhona started down the back stairs. Charlie and I stood back waiting for O'Donell to go next. We were all thinking the same thing. O'Donell made an impatient gesture and Charlie glanced at me and went down. I followed. We were all listening and

But what does he do when he is finally exposed and they find out about it?

He makes a joke about it. Now, I don't mean to shout, for shouting's sake, but I feel so strongly about this case and his acts that I can't help myself, and I hope that you will forgive me.

But when anybody makes fun and thinks it such a joke to possess marijuana illegally—I think it is important and I think that you ought to consider it important—

and I ask that when you deliberate, you look at those counts two and three, and I think that you will find that he transported that marijuana against the laws of the United States; he did not pay the tax on it; that on count two, when he found out that that marijuana was in his possession, he knew it.

The Court: Dr. Leary, you and your counsel will step up here, please, sir.

Your case—the situation in which you find yourself here gives a great deal of concern. You are, of course, as I am sure you recognize, an unusual type of personality, unconventional in many respects.

turning our heads to see if O'Donell would come. He paused at the top of the stairs. We walked slowly down. Then he took two steps and stood, playing with us. I looked back and saw the sly, one-up grin, lips drawn back from the teeth. When I turned the corner of the stairs there was silence and then slowly O'Donell came down.

In terms of a human situation, one is handling wild, intractable people. In such a case one's purpose will be achieved if one behaves with decorum. Pleasant manners succeed even with irritable people. (I Ching X)

Rhona was putting the kettle on the stove. Hey, Rhona, go up and check on the girls, will you? All right. But why don't you men start cleaning up this mess.

I was ripped apart with guilt over lousy-father irresponsible stuff and scared of O'Donell. He had a wild gleam and was muttering to himself and moving with a clumsy madman plod. I feared him and sensed the insanity and understood the insanity and his confusion and sympathized with the confusion. Why? Who makes these rules? And why? And why do they hurt and humiliate? He just didn't understand the social game and was going through motions that were meaningless. Rinsing dishes. He wasn't happy about it. We could hear him muttering and the dishes breaking. I felt a closeness with him. We were all prisoners in a concentration camp of our own making. Pushed and punished by senseless rules. I went over to get the garbage can and quickly leaned over to him. Two Jews in the Nazi prison. Look, I whispered, the whole world is crazy. The whole system is insane. But don't try to fight it now. Play along. We got ourselves into it. It's the only way.

O'Donell shot me an understanding glance and nodded. Yeah, you're right, he whispered. We'll play it out.

I went outside to empty the cans, saying to myself, yeah, the world is crazy. They want order and I can't think of anything better than order so let's clean up. And anyway someone will have to clean up if we don't and that's doing good and makes some sense.

When I came back Charlie was standing by the stove, hands on hips, smiling and shrugging his shoulders. Look! O'Donell, what are you doing? O'Donell was cleaning up the table. He had a big brown bag and was dumping everything in the garbage—food, glasses, silver, cigarette lighter. The voice stopped him and he stood holding the bag, grinning. I took the bag from him and laughed. O'Donell just won't play the game. With that stupid look and moronic grin, he is making a joke of the whole business. It was kind of funny. Next the roast chickens, sitting on serving plates, untouched. O'Donell took an ashtray and dumped it on the first chicken.

Don't throw ashes on
My fresh roast chicken.
There's no celestial housemaid.

He was wrong. But why? In the great cosmic scheme of things why not throw silver in the garbage and ashes on the fresh roast chicken? Why? I stood there holding the garbage sack in my hands, brow furrowed. Why? Why not? Why? Then I understood. It's okay not to play the game if you are willing to deal yourself out of the game. Don't play house if you don't want to play house. But don't live in the house and expect the rewards of the house game. Yeah, O'Donell. Sure. Empty ashes on the chicken if you don't mind eating chicken with ashes. But don't infringe on others' games. Don't throw out Charlie's lighter and the family silver. And don't break up the teen-age girls' game.

Break up. Destroy. I remember him slashing the lamp cord with the knife and spitting on the carpet. Suppose your game is destroy. I thought of all the poor kids who had been left out of the rich games they saw all around them. Why? Explain it. Why? Because some games, most games, keep others out. Not because the kid can't play well enough. Not because he isn't willing to learn. But because no reason. So they create the game of destroy. If you play the game of keep-out, then you provoke the game of destroy. Smash the middle class. Down with the rich. Slash the Cadillac tires. Loot and

It is my duty, in due course, to impose sentence for these offenses.

Is there anything you want to tell me at this time in your own behalf or in mitigation or extenuation?

Defendant Leary: No, sir.

The Court: In that case under count two I impose a period of confinement of twenty years and a fine of $20,000.

On count three I impose a period of confinement of ten years and a fine of $20,000.

You may remain at large on bond until such time as you receive instructions through the District Attorney as to where to report for this examination that I have in mind.

Susan, come forward.

On your plea of not guilty, I have found you guilty of —on the third count of this indictment.

I hope you will understand that throughout this trial and now, and insofar as this court has jurisdiction of this matter in the future, my desire will be to take the action which is for your own best interests.

It occurs to me that you have been raised in very unusual surroundings and I cannot, in my own thinking, measure your conduct by the same standard that I might measure another eighteen-year-old.

In order to give me the best understanding on the imposition of sentence in your case, I order you committed to the custody of the Attorney General for observation and study at an appropriate classification center or agency, with report to be made to the court of its findings within a period of sixty days.

This is what I believe ultimately will be to your advantage.

Anything further?

Mr. Blask: We have nothing further.

trample the Roman villa. Rape the Alabama white woman. Jettison the Landlord's silver. Mangle the pajama party of the sleek, smug suburban teen-age girls. We all want to violate that fence that keeps us out.

Heaven and the lake show a difference of elevation that inheres in the natures of the two, hence no envy arises. Among mankind also there are necessarily differences of elevation; it is impossible to bring about universal equality. But it is important that differences in social rank should not be arbitrary and unjust, for if this occurs, envy and class struggle are the inevitable consequences. If, on the other hand, external differences in rank correspond with differences in inner worth, and if inner worth forms the criterion of external rank, people acquiesce and order reigns in society. (I Ching X)

Rhona was back. I had visions of outraged virtue. Drugged men wrestling and lurching through the pajama party. What would they tell their fierce social mothers? Were they terrified? Was Susan crushed? Rhona was calm and casual. Oh, they're doing fine. Pillow fights and rock-and-roll and only worried about when we'll make them turn off the record player.

Rhona was at one end of the table. O'Donell at the other. Charlie and I facing each other. I wanted Rhona's approval for something, for everything. Oh, Goddess, hear my story. Rhona was sleepy but resigned to the role and interested in my approval and my wisdom. I was ready to discuss how we had to leave Newton; drugs at a teen-age party. Guilt. Guilt. Guilt. Rhona was worried about the tea.

Charlie! You know you must scald the pot before you put the tea in. Wise words. Five hundred years of solid empire. That great little island and the game they invented and believed in and how they made it stand up. Society is a crazy made-up game. Riddled with confusion and fear and conflicting guilt and no one's gods come through and when the whole thing begins to fall apart and you know it's falling apart, then comes the clear, calm voice.

Scald the pot. Okay. Somewhere there's an ancient game which keeps going and at the moment I was glad for it.

The domestic routine. The kitchen. The boiling of water. The washing. The eternal soft voice of the young mother naïvely bored with male speculation and male struggle. The soothing, centering rhythm of family life. The rite to heal wrong.

The Court: In that case, we will recess under the rule.

(Court recessed on March 11, 1966)

∞

TREADING. *Treading upon the tail of the tiger.*
It does not bite the man. Success.
(I Ching)

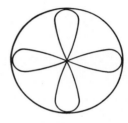

TRIP 6

ECSTATIC POLITICS

The Blueprint to Turn-On the World:

December 1960

Guide: ALLEN GINSBERG

Oracle: L

The Caldron

The Clinging, Fire

The Gentle, Wind, Wood

Fire over wood:
The image of THE CALDRON.
Thus the superior man consolidates his fate
By making his position correct.

(I Ching)

ALLEN GINSBERG
DECEMBER 1960:

Here is a statement for Sandoz. Is it okay?

Have had experience with mescaline, LSD-25, and psilocybin. The mushroom synthetic seems to me the easiest on the body physically, and the most controllable in dosage.

The effects are generally similar, subjectively. Psilocybin seems to me to be some sort of psychic godsend.

It offers unparalleled opportunity to catalyze awareness of otherwise unconscious psychic processes. To widen the area of human consciousness.

To deepen reification of ideas and identification of real objects. To perceive the inner organization of natural objects and human art-works.

By this time there was in existence an informal international network of scientists and scholars who had taken the trip and who foresaw the powerful effect that the new alkaloids would have on human culture. The members of this group differed in age, temperament, and had widely differing ideas about tactics, but the basic vision was common to all—these wondrous plants and drugs could free man's consciousness and bring about a new conception of man, his psychology, and philosophy.

There was Albert Hoffman, who had invented LSD, who dreamed the utopian dream, but who was limited by the cautious politics of Sandoz Pharmaceuticals. What a frustrating web his genius had woven for Sandoz. How could a medical-drug house make a profit on a revelation pill?

Sandoz knew they had patented the most powerful mind-changing substance known to man. They spent millions to promote research on LSD. They righteously expected to make millions when the psychiatric profession learned how to use LSD, and they were continually disappointed to discover that human society didn't want to have its mind changed, didn't want to touch a love-ecstasy potion.

In 1961 a top executive of Sandoz leaned across the conference table and said to me, LSD isn't a drug at all. It's a food. Let's bottle it in Coca-Cola and let the world have it. And his legal counsel frowned and said, foods still come under the jurisdiction of the Food and Drug Administration.

By 1966, when LSD was crowding Vietnam for the headlines, officials of Sandoz Pharmaceuticals were groaning, we wish we had never heard of LSD.

I do really wish to destroy it! cried Frodo. Or well, to have it destroyed. I am not made for peril-

110

ous quests. I wish I had never seen the Ring! Why did it come to me? Why was I chosen? (The Lord of the Rings)

The story of Albert Hoffman, the secret behind his wise silence, has yet to be told. But for the moment he was uneasily forced to play the drug-company researcher game.

There were the detached philosophers—Aldous Huxley, Father Murray, Gerald Heard, Alan Watts, Harry Murray, Robert Gordon Wasson—who knew that the new drugs were re-introducing the platonic-gnostic vision. These men had read their theological history and understood both the glorious possibility and the angered reaction of the priestly establishment. They were not activists but sage observers.

Then there were the turned-on doctors—psychiatrists who had taken the trip, and came back hoping to fit the new potions into the medical game. Humphrey Osmond, witty, wise, cultured, had invented the name psychedelic and tolerantly wondered how to introduce a harmony-ecstasy drug into an aggressive-puritanical social order. Sidney Cohen and Keith Ditman and Jim Watt and Abram Hofer and Nick Chewelos hoped to bring about a psychiatric renaissance and a new era of mental health with the new alchemicals.

And there was that strange, intriguing, delightful cosmic magician called Al Hubbard, the rum-drinking, swashbuckling, Roman Catholic frontier salesman who promoted uranium ore during the 40's and who took the trip and recognized that LSD was the fissionable material of the mind and who turned on Osmond and Hofer to the religious mystical meaning of their psychotomimetic drug. Al Hubbard set out to turn-on the world and flew from country to country with his leather bag full of drugs and claimed to have turned-on bishops and obtained *nihil obstat* from Pope John, and when the medical society complained that only doctors could give drugs, bought himself a doctor's degree from a Kentucky diploma mill and swept through northern California turning-on scientists and professors and God-seekers.

To enter the significance and aesthetic organization of music, painting, poetry, architecture.

It seems to make philosophy make sense. It aids consciousness to contemplate itself and serve some of the most delightful functions of the mind.

As if, turning up the volume on a receiving set, background and FM stations can be heard. The effects are not unnatural.

I have experienced similar things without use of chemical catalysts, and correspond to what I, as a poet, have called previously aesthetic, poetic, transcendental or mystical awareness.

A kind of useful, practical cosmic consciousness. I think it will help mankind to grow.

∞

ALLEN GINSBERG
JANUARY 1961:

I spoke to Wilhelm De Kooning yesterday and he was ready to turn on, so please drop him an invitation too.

I figure Kline, De Kooning, Monk and Gillespie are the most impressive quartet imaginable for you to turn-on at the moment, so will leave it at that for awhile, till they can be taken care of.

I won't send you new names and work-trouble for awhile. Hope you can get these four letters off.

I also wrote Osmond and Huxley asking them to connect Burroughs with Heim, or anyone in Paris. None of my business actually, but Koestler always struck me as a little *hard*-hearted somehow.

Hate myself to have him as a final *curandero*. That is, being an intellectual, he tends to organize a polemic-dogmatic-mental system around experience.

As in his essay on Zen, which is very intelligent, but not so magnanimous. But by all means send him batches to hand out.

And when the day of Pentecost was fully come, they were all with one accord in one place. And suddenly there came a sound from heaven as of a rushing mighty wind, and it filled all the house where they were sitting. And there appeared unto them cloven tongues like as of fire, and it sat upon each of them. And they were all filled with the Holy Ghost, and began to speak with other tongues, as the spirit gave them utterance. And they were all amazed, and were in doubt, saying one to another, what meaneth this? Others mocking said, these men are full of new wine.

Right from the beginning this dedicated group of ring-bearers was rent with a basic disagreement. There were those who said work within the system. Society has assigned the administration of drugs to the medical profession. Any non-doctor who gives or takes drugs is a dope fiend. Play ball with the system. Medicine must be the vanguard of the psychedelic movement. Capture the medical profession. Cohen and Ditman and Al Hubbard and his two loyal, gifted lieutenants, Willis Harman and Myron Stolaroff, warned that any non-medical use of psychedelic drugs would create a new marijuana mess and set back research into the new utopia.

The medical point of view made little sense to religious philosophers. Aldous Huxley called the psychedelic experience a gratuitous grace. His vibrant flame-colored wife, Laura, agreed. So, in gentle tones, did Huston Smith and Alan Watts and Gerald Heard.

And so did Allen Ginsberg, who had discovered the Buddha nature of drugs with Jack Kerouac and Gary Snyder and Bill Burroughs.

I had been visited by most of the psychedelic eminences by this time and was under steady pressure to make the Harvard psychedelic research a kosher-medically-approved project. Everyone was aware of the potency of Harvard's name. Timothy, you are the key figure, said Dr. Al Hubbard; I'm just old deputy-dog Al at your service. But the message was clear: keep it respectable and medical.

And now here was Allen Ginsberg, secretary general of the world's poets, beatniks, anarchists, socialists, free-sex/love cultists.

The sunny Sunday afternoon that we gave Allen Ginsberg the mushrooms started slowly. Rhona and Charlie were down in the kitchen by nine to start a cycle of breakfasts. First there were Jack Leary and his friend Bobbie who had spent the night. Bobbie went off to Mass. When I came down I found Donald, an uninvited raccoon hipster-painter from New York solemnly squatting at the table gnawing at toast and bacon. Frank Barron and the poets, Allen Ginsberg and Peter and Lafcadio Orlovsky remained upstairs and we moved around the kitchen with that Sunday morning hush not wanting to wake the sleepers. Lafcadio, Peter's brother, was on leave from a mental hospital.

About twelve-thirty the quiet exploded into family noise. Bobbie was back from church where he excitedly had told his father about the party we had given the night before for the Harvard football team and how I had given the boys, Bobbie and Jack, a dollar each for being bartenders.

I toted up the political profit and loss from this development. The Harvard football team rang up a sale. But the boys bartending? Bobbie's father is Irish so that's all right. All okay.

Then wham, the door opened and in flooded Susan Leary with three teen-age girls, through the kitchen, upstairs to get clothes, down to make a picnic lunch, up again for records, out and then back for the ginger ale.

By now the noise had filtered upstairs and we could hear the late sleepers moving around and the bathroom waters running, and down came Frank Barron, half-awake, to fry codfish cakes for his breakfast. And then, Allen Ginsberg and Peter. Allen hopped around the room with nearsighted crow motions cooking eggs, and Peter sat silent watching.

After breakfast the poets fell to reading the *Times* and Frank moved upstairs to Susan's room to watch a pro football game on TV and I told Allen to make himself at home and got beers and went up to join Frank. Donald the painter had been padding softly around the house watching with his big, soft creature eyes and sniffing in corners and at the bookcase and the record cabinets. He had asked to take mushrooms in the evening and was looking

So H.S. fears the peril of mind let loose. Well I agree with you generally. But I have had that experience of absolute fear.

Suppose it decides not to keep the body going?—In Peru. It never recurred, but I can't guarantee it won't recur to me.

That is, there was something mysterious happening beyond what I know and later experienced. Each incarnation is *different*.

But at the time I was *sure* that if I really let go I would literally die, and that it might be a *good idea*. To get another dimension.

But I wasn't so positive it was a good idea. Really fearfully confused. Maybe you *could* die, like a yoga or Buddha or something worse, or better? Who knows?

I mean who knows how deep the soul goes into the universe and what outright magic it can work? Like maybe leaving this body and going to a God-world or devil-world body? Literally.

At least I haven't myself surmounted that superstition, if it is superstition, not uncanny awareness. So, I tend to feel mentally a hands-off policy, as far as making final judgment of what is actually psychologically happening to H.S.

But I wasn't there. I generally agree with your reaction, or I also tend to have your reaction—as to Barney or H.S.

Nonetheless, my knowledge of fact is not final. I've been operating as much on faith and hope in a way.

Send me a bill for the mescaline. No need for you to pay.

No news yet from Cuba, so I think it safe to send psilocybin here. I'll call you before I leave, which may yet be another week—if at all at this rate.

Burroughs is in Paris. I wrote Huxley his address today with an explanatory note—but if you have any means of connecting him with Heim or anyone there —could you do so.

for records of Indian peyote drum music. We told him to phone around to the local libraries. A friend of his, an anthropology student, could possibly locate some Indian records, and could he borrow the car and go to Cambridge? All his words came up halting, labored, serious, and I said sure go ahead.

During the game, Jack Leary and his pals came in dressed in their football uniforms and watched the action for a while and then got bored and went up to the third-floor playroom. We kidded them about getting suited up like pigskin warriors and then sitting around inside and not playing. After the game Frank Barron rounded up Charlie and the boys and we went out behind the garage and had a game of touch football. The poets declined to play. At dusk we came in and started a long kitchen Sunday supper scene, cold ham and meat pies, highballs (but not for the poets). It was an agreeable kitchen chaos with everyone puttering around. Rhona and Charlie were sick with stomach flu and headed upstairs early. Lafcadio had stayed in bed most of the afternoon until Allen had gone up to tell him to come down and he sat in the corner quiet, impassive, eerie, probably thinking wonderful thoughts about the Martians landing on earth. He nodded every time we offered him food, and Allen would tell him to put his plates away and he would obey silently and mechanically. After the meal we asked Jack and Bobbie if they wanted to play catch in the upstairs hallway with Lafcadio and they said sure and ran off with Lafcadio lumbering after them. There are ball marks on the white ceiling to this day and the wall lamp has never quite worked the same, but Allen said that the weekend was tremendous therapy for Lafcadio. He started talking more and it kept up for several weeks after they left.

Allen Ginsberg, hunched over a teacup, peering out through his black-rimmed glasses, the left lens bisected by a break, started telling of his experiences with Ayahuasca, the fabled visionary vine of the Peruvian jungles. He had followed the quest of Bill Burroughs, sailing south for new realms of consciousness, looking for the elixir of wisdom. Sitting, sweating with heat, lonely in a cheap hotel in Lima, holding a wad of ether-soaked cotton to his nose with his left hand and getting high and making poetry with his right hand and then traveling by second-class bus with Indians up through the Cordillera de los Andes and then more buses and hitchhiking into the Montana jungles and shining rivers, wandering through steaming equatorial forests. Then the village Pucalpa, and the negotiations to find the *curandero,* paying him with *aguardiente,* and the ritual itself, swallowing the bitter stuff, and the nausea and the colors and the drums beating and sinking down into thingless void, into the great eye that brings it all together, and the terror of the great snake coming, lying on the earth floor helpless and the great snake coming. The old *curandero,* wrinkled face bending over him and Allen telling him, *culebra,* and the *curandero* nodding clinically and blowing a puff of smoke to make the great snake disappear and it did.

The fate of fire depends on wood; as long as there is wood below, the fire burns above. It is the same in human life; there is in man likewise a fate that lends power to his life. (I Ching L)

I kept asking Allen questions about the *curandero.* I wanted to learn the rituals, to find out how other cultures (older and wiser than ours) had handled the visionary business. I was fascinated by the ritual thing. Ritual is to the science of consciousness what experiment is to external science. I was convinced that none of our American rituals fit the mushroom experience. Not the cocktail party. Not the psychiatrist. Not the teacher-minister role. I was impressed by what Allen said about his own fear and sickness whenever he took drugs and about the solace and comforting strength of the *curandero,* about how good it was to have someone there who knew, who had been to those far regions of the mind and could tell you by a look, by a touch, by a puff of smoke that it was all right, go ahead, explore the strange world, it's all right, you'll come back, it's all right, I'm here back on familiar old human earth when you need me, to bring you back.

Allen told me about the training of *curanderos.*

Perhaps send him an academic letter of introduction which he could deliver to Heim? This got to be done soon, as Burroughs is on way East in a few weeks I think—not sure.

He writes he had some LSD in London, as well as an injection of another drug—what, I dunno. He writes—Don't flip pops is all. One must be careful of altitude sickness and depth madness and the bends. Hazards of the silent world. Space is silent remember, etc.

Anyway, I'll let you know before I leave to Cuba. Send me what you can, if you can, when you can. Been finished with proofs of my book this week and doing some writing.

∞

ALLEN GINSBERG
FEBRUARY 1961:

Been paralyzed making decisions, so forgive me not writing last week till I figured out what I wanted to do. Got letter and telegram from Corso in Athens summoning me to hurry up or he sez he'll take a boat to here.

I replied I'd stand on Acropolis with him in a month if the gods please and he replied he'd wait then. Meanwhile, been running around in frenzy.

Huncke now cured and taking rest in Jacobi hospital for a few weeks in psycho ward with friendly doctors. He's free to come or go.

Yvonne I've seen a number of times, took her out one night to LeRoi Jones and got drunk. She can't make up her mind what to do with her life—wants someone to depend on—also wants independence, but she's spoiled and beautiful.

Barney is polite too. I had talk with him—mollified him by saying in sum, I thought it was a mistake to turn him and her on.

The old witch doctor going off in the mountain for weeks with the young candidate and having him take the drug day after day, night after night, exploring all the corners and caves and hidden inlets of the visionary world—the terrain of heaven and hell, the joy, the horror, the orgiastic peaks, the black burning swamps, the angels and the devil snakes—until he had been there, all the way to the far reaches of awareness. Then he was equipped to act as *curandero*, to take care of visionary travelers, to understand the words and behavior which confuse and frighten the unprepared observer.

Allen told of the therapeutic impact of the kind village doctor as he went through the age-old rituals of caring-for—the hand on the shoulder, and cup of hot tea and the covering with blankets. I remembered back to a session when a lonely graduate student fell to the carpet in anguished panic, and how Frank Barron the veteran front-line medic took over with cold compresses and kind words, and how the student never forgot his being there, doing the right thing at exactly the right time.

Allen was going to take the mushrooms later that night and he was shaping me up to help him. Allen was weaving a word spell, dark eyes gleaming through the glasses, chain-smoking, moving his hands, intense, chanting trance poetry. Frank Barron was in the study now, and with him Lafcadio Orlovsky.

Then a car came up the driveway and in a minute the door opened, and Donald, furry and moist, ambled in. He had brought his friend, an anthropology student from Harvard, to be with him when he tripped. Donald asked if his friend could be there during the mushroom session. I liked the idea of having a friend present for the mushrooms, someone to whom you could turn at those moments when you needed support, so I said sure, but he couldn't take the pills because he was a University student. Everyone was warning us to keep our research away from Harvard to avoid complications with the University Health Bureau and to avoid the rumors. He wasn't hungry so I mixed him a drink and then I got the little round bottle and pulled out the cotton topping and gave Donald 30 mg. and

Allen Ginsberg 36. SEVERAL NIGHTS LATER AT LEARY'S HOUSE, I TOOK A LARGE DOSE OF 18 (36 MG.) AND WENT UPSTAIRS WITH ORLOVSKY TO A SEPARATE ROOM. Allen started bustling around getting his cave ready. I brought Susan's record player up to his room and he took some Beethoven and Wagner from the study and he turned out the lights so that there was just a glow in the room. TOOK OFF ALL MY CLOTHES AND LAY IN BED LISTENING TO MUSIC. I told him we'd be checking back every fifteen minutes and he should tell me if he wanted anything.

By the time I got downstairs Donald was already high, strolling around the house on dainty raccoon feet with his hands clasped behind his back, thinking and digging deep things. AS MY AWARENESS EXPANDED I SAW MYSELF LYING IN BED, WITH THE ALTERNATIVE OF WITHDRAWING INTO MYSTIC INTROSPECTION, AND VOMIT, OR SWALLOWING BACK MY VOMIT, OPENING MY EYES, AND LIVING IN THE PRESENT UNIVERSE. I stayed in the study writing letters, reading the *Times*. I had forgotten about the anthropology student. He was waiting in the kitchen. I FELT INTIMIDATED BY THE KNOWLEDGE THAT I HAD NOT REACHED YET A PERFECT UNDERSTANDING WITH MY CREATOR, WHOEVER HE BE, GOD, CHRIST, OR BUDDHA— THE FIGURE OF OCTOPUS AS BEFORE.

After about thirty minutes I found Donald in the hallway. He called me over earnestly and began talking about the artificiality of civilization. He was thinking hard about basic issues and it was obvious what was going on with him—clearing his mind of abstractions, trying to get back behind the words and concepts. SUDDENLY, HOWEVER, REALIZED THEY WERE ALL IMAGINARY BEINGS I WAS INVENTING TO SUBSTITUTE FOR THE FEAR OF BEING MYSELF—THAT ONE WHICH I HAD DREAMED OF.

And if he succeeds in assigning the right place to life and to fate, thus bringing the two into harmony, he puts his fate on a firm footing. These words contain hints about the fastening of life as handed on by oral tradition in the secret teachings of Chinese yoga. (I Ching L)

The anthropology student was standing by, watching curiously and Donald asked if he minded

Otherwise he'll get into a big battle over the word mistake. So I guess they'll just go on as before and work out their fate.

Only way I can see otherwise is taking over Yvonne entirely, me marrying her or something. (Don't think she didn't suggest it.) She still wants *him*.

We just barged in on the middle of some insoluble modern romance. I dunno, how to resolve the mushroom politics of this, without their resolving their own politics.

So far it all seems quieted down. I really want to get out of U.S. and go to Greece and begin Orient voyages, etc. A lot of things keep me here now, the mushroom work, people who depend on me, like Huncke.

(Or people who I *think* depend on me, etc.) But I'd like to be alone and start a new phase, awhile.

I can write, either way, here or there, it's not so much a problem of having solitude for poetry, it's just I feel like taking off, boop-boop-a-doop.

Meanwhile I've been conspiring with everyone I can reach in N.Y. the last weeks to do something about the general dope problem.

Various other people working on other different angles. Yesterday got on TV with N. Mailer and Ashley Montague and gave big speech attacking Narco Dept and recommending everybody get high—be on locally in N.Y. Sunday after this, if they don't suppress the program.

Montague is an old woman, but he cooperated a bit. Maybe I'll go on Mike Wallace show. They asked me to.

Also making an appointment with Eleanor Roosevelt to try to interest her in the social problem. Met her and Martin Luther King at Dorothy Norman's last night.

Got lunch date with Rev. Norman Eddy of East Harlem Protestant parish this Tuesday. He's the big dope do-gooder.

Didn't mention mushrooms in all of this, for tactful reasons. Best keep that on its own high level.

leaving so that he could talk to me privately. Anthro went back to the kitchen and Donald continued talking about the falseness of houses and machines and deploring the way man cut himself off from the vital stuff with his engines and structures. I was trying to be polite and be a good *curandero* and support him and tell him, great boy, stay with it and work it out.

Susan came back from her friend's about this time and went upstairs to her homework, and I followed her up to check on Allen. He was lying on top of the blanket. His glasses were off and his black eyes, pupils completely dilated, looked up at me. Looking down into them they seemed like two deep, black, wet wells and you could look down them way through the man Ginsberg to something human beyond. The eye is such a defenseless, naïve, trusting thing. PROFESSOR LEARY CAME INTO MY ROOM, LOOKED IN MY EYES, AND SAID I WAS A GREAT MAN. THAT DETERMINED ME TO MAKE AN EFFORT TO LIVE HERE AND NOW.

Allen was scared and unhappy and sick. And still he was lying there voluntarily, patiently searching, pushing himself into panics and fears, into nausea, trying to learn something, trying to find meaning. Shamelessly weak and shamelessly human and greatly classic. Peter was lying next to him, eyes closed, sleeping or listening to the record. I GOT NAUSEOUS SOON AFTER—SAT UP IN BED NAKED AND SWALLOWED DOWN THE VOMIT THAT BESIEGED FROM MY STOMACH AS IF AN INDEPENDENT BEING DOWN THERE WAS REBELLING AT BEING DRAGGED INTO EXISTENCE.

Allen asked me what I thought of him and his situation. I leaned over and looked down into the black liquid eyes, fawn's eyes, man's eyes, and told him that he was a great man and that it was good to know him. He reached up his hand. Can I get you anything, Allen? No thanks. I'll be back in a while. He nodded. ORLOVSKY WAS NAKED IN BED WITH ME AND HIS EROTIC GESTURES LOOKED REPTILIAN, AS IF OUT OF HINDU-DEVA STATUARY—HIS LIDDED EYES AND HOOKED NOSE ALMOST LIKE BLUE KRISHNA STATUE FROM THE WRONG PLANE OF EXISTENCE NOT CONSONANT WITH 1960 USA.

On the way downstairs I checked by Susan's room. She was curled up on the carpet, with her books scattered around her and reading in the shadows. I scolded her about ruining her eyes and flicked on the two wall bulbs. Downstairs Frank was still at the study desk. SUDDENLY OUT OF THE WINDOW SAW IMAGE AS OF A BETHLEHEM STAR, HEARD GREAT HORNS OF GOTTERDAMMERUNG-WAGNER ON THE PHONOGRAPH I'D ARRANGED TO HEAR IN THE ROOM. Anthro was wandering in the living room and told me that Donald had gone outside. The rule we set up was that no one would leave the house and the idea of Donald padding down Beacon Street in a mystic state chilled me. LIKE THE HORNS OF JUDGMENT CALLING FROM THE ENDS OF THE COSMOS— CALLED ON ALL HUMAN CONSCIOUSNESS TO DECLARE ITSELF THE CONSCIOUSNESS. Out on the front porch I turned on the two rows of spotlights that flooded the long winding stone stairs and started down, shielding my eyes and shouting Donald. Halfway down I heard him answering back and saw him standing under an oak tree on the lower lawn. I asked him how he was but he didn't talk, just stood there looking wise and deep. SEEMED AS IF ALL THE WORLDS OF HUMAN CONSCIOUSNESS WERE WAITING FOR A MESSIAH, SOMEONE TO TAKE ON THE RESPONSIBILITY OF BEING THE CREATIVE GOD AND SEIZE POWER OVER THE UNIVERSE. He was barefoot and higher than Picard's balloon. I want to talk to you, but first you must take off your shoes. Okay, why not? I sat down to unlace my shoes and he squatted alongside and told about how the machines complicate our lives and how cold and hot were abstractions and how we didn't really need houses and shoes and clothes because it was just our concepts that made us think we needed these things. I agreed with him and followed what his mind was doing, suspending for a moment the clutch of the abstract but at the same time shivering from the November wind and wanting to get back behind the warm glow of the windows. MILTON'S LUCIFER FLASHED THROUGH MY MIND.

The young anthropology student was standing in the hallway. I told him that Donald was doing fine, great mystical stuff, philosophizing without con-

Otherwise might get mixed up with beatnikism. You sure got a lot of energy.

I dunno, but I think it would help the mushroom atmosphere lots if there were a general U.S. re-thinking (as the N.Y. *Times* friend says) on the dope social problem.

Lindesmith and Indiana U Press are putting out this joint report of interim committee of AMA and Amer. Bar Assn. So I got in touch with all the liberal pro-dope people I know to have it publicized and circulated and have all of them interconnect to exchange information.

I wrote a five-page summary of situation to this friend Kenny Love on the N.Y. *Times* and he said he'd perhaps do a story (news-wise) on the book, which could then be picked up by UP friend on national wire.

Also gave copy to Al Aronowitz on N.Y. *Post* and Rosalind Constable at *Time* and Bob Silvers on *Harpers* magazine and informed *Yugen*, *Evergreen*, *Big Table*, *Metronome*.

Meanwhile Indiana U people are working on *Commentary, The Nation*, etc. Regular network. Also got a copy of La Guardia Report to Grove Press.

They will republish it with additional stronger material. Maybe Dan Wakefield edit a book.

. . . just got your Feb. 1 letter. Glad you heard the *Howl* record. That never got circulated.

So, I also got to work this month arranging advertisements for that Fantasy Record Co. Is very inert unless I prod them.

If that begins selling sometime this year, with *Kaddish* out in a month, I'll have plenty loot for Europe and Asia and Lafcadio too.

I won't, therefore, be able to make the Harvard mushroom seminar week—I'm sorry—don't let it bug you.

I don't know exactly when I'm leaving yet—but it's *got* to be around the first week in March. Peter and I will come up to Harvard for weekend before we leave tho.

cepts. He looked puzzled. He didn't want a drink or food. I walked upstairs and found the door to Allen's room closed. I waited for a while, not knowing what to do and then knocked softly and said softly, Allen I'm here now and will be back in a few minutes. *Paradise Lost*, A BOOK I'D NEVER UNDERSTOOD BEFORE—WHY MILTON SIDED WITH LUCIFER THE REBEL IN HEAVEN.

I GOT UP OUT OF BED AND WALKED DOWNSTAIRS NAKED, ORLOVSKY FOLLOWING ME CURIOUS WHAT I WOULD DO AND WILLING TO GO ALONG IN CASE I DID ANYTHING INTERESTINGLY EXTRAVAGANT.

Susan was sitting cross-legged on her bed brushing her hair when there came a patter of bare feet on the hallway carpet. I got to the door just in time to see naked buttocks disappearing down the stairway. It was Peter. I was grinning when I went back to Susan. Peter is running around without any clothes on. Susan picked up her paraphernalia—curlers, brush, pins, and trotted up to the third floor. I headed downstairs.

URGING ME ON IN FACT, THANK GOD. When I got to the study Frank was leaning back in his chair behind the desk grinning quizzically. In front of the desk looking like medieval hermits were Allen and Peter both stark naked. I WENT IN AMONG THE PSYCHOLOGISTS IN STUDY AND SAW THEY TOO WERE WAITING FOR SOMETHING VAST TO HAPPEN, ONLY IT REQUIRED SOMEONE AND THE MOMENT TO MAKE IT HAPPEN—ACTION, REVOLUTION. No, Allen had on his glasses and as I came in he peered out at me and raised his finger in the air. Hey, Allen, what goes on? Allen had a holy gleam in his eye and he waved his finger. I'm the Messiah. I've come down to preach love to the world. We're going to walk through the streets and teach people to stop hating. I DECIDED I MIGHT AS WELL BE THE ONE TO DO SO—PRONOUNCED MY NAKEDNESS AS THE FIRST ACT OF REVOLUTION AGAINST THE DESTROYERS OF THE HUMAN IMAGE.

Well, Allen, that sounds like a pretty good idea. Listen, said Allen, do you believe that I'm the Messiah. THE NAKED BODY BEING THE HIDDEN SIGN. Look, I can prove it. I'm going to cure your hearing. Take off your hearing machine. Your ears are cured. Come on, take it off, you don't need it. AND GRABBED THE TELEPHONE TO COMMUNICATE MY DECISION—WANTED TO HOOK UP KHRUSHCHEV, KEROUAC, BURROUGHS, IKE, KENNEDY, MAO-TSE TUNG, MAILER IN BELLEVUE, ETC.

Frank was still smiling. Peter was standing by watching seriously. The hearing aid was dumped on the desk. That's right. And now your glasses, I'll heal your vision too. The glasses were laid on the desk too. ALL IN ONE TELEPHONE LINE AND GET THEM ALL TO COME IMMEDIATELY TO HARVARD TO HAVE SPECTRAL CONFERENCE OVER THE FUTURE OF THE UNIVERSE.

Allen was peering around with approval at his healing. But Allen, one thing. What? Your glasses. You're still wearing them. Why don't you cure your own vision. Allen looked surprised. Yes, you're right. I will. He took off his glasses and laid them on the desk. TAKE OVER FROM THE COSMIC POLICE AND TAKE THE WORLD FOR OUR OWN INSTEAD OF BEING AT THE MERCY OF INTERCONNECTED NETWORK OF ECONOMIC POWER AND ELECTRONIC COMMUNICATION THAT WAS THREATENING US WITH DESTRUCTION.

Now Allen was a blind messiah squinting around to find his followers. ATOM BOMB APOCALYPSES. Come on. We're going down to the city streets to tell the people about peace and love. And then we'll get lots of great people onto a big telephone network to settle all this warfare bit. GOT AS FAR AS TELLING THE PHONE OPERATOR I WAS GOD AND WANTED TO TALK WITH KEROUAC IMMEDIATELY.

Fine, said Frank, but why not do the telephone bit first, right here in the house. Frank was heading off the pilgrimage down the avenue naked. REMEMBERED TO RUN UPSTAIRS AND GIVE HER HIS PHONE NUMBER IN CASE IT DELAYED MY SCHEME WHILE SHE SEARCHED IT OUT.

Who we gonna call, said Peter. Well, we'll call Kerouac on Long Island, and Kennedy and Khrushchev and Bill Burroughs in Paris and Norman Mailer in the psycho ward in Bellevue. We'll get them all hooked up in a big cosmic electronic love talk. War is just a hang-up. We'll get the love-thing flowing on the electric Bell telephone network. REACHED HIM AND HAD A VERY EXPRESSIVE CONVERSATION—ONE OF THE FRANKEST I'VE HAD WITH HIM IN

Please don't be mad at me for taking off and leaving you holding the bag with so much on your mind. In the long run I do much better in anonymous goofing and writing than being Allen Ginsberg politicking.

I get the impression that the general psychic fog in the U.S. may be lifting. Also wrote a stern appeal for drugs into the GAP conference report, which'll be published by them.

Said they should invite some Amazon *curanderos* for their next conference. Do you want or need, or does the situation actually need, that I stay longer here and make the Harvard conference?

I feel that if I stay I'll just keep staying—and Gregory is calling, etc. If he comes here it'll be a ball, but it'll be a year or half-year before we can go again.

Prison sounds great. Don't give mushrooms to junkies who are just in physiological process (first weeks) of kicking. Burroughs says in an article it would be pure hell.

Physical pains, maybe get magnified. Kaufman said he'd already sent you material—didn't it arrive? I told him you'd not received it.

Which Osmond handbook on LSD? On giving LSD? Was that one of the papers I had?

In confusion I gave all papers to a Dr. Joe Gibbs, young psychiatrist who's had mescaline—including your poem-paper, before I had read it. Can you send me another?

Who's the Boston poet? I wound up imitating Kerouac too, for a week. He sounds fine on phone. I think that weekend did him permanent good, sort of made him more resolved and peaceful.

Your letter very lovely, makes me feel like a messiah—running out on the cross part. I was always a little ashamed of the love poem for being so schmaltzy and schwarmerai and vague and abstract.

The *America* reading is a combination of different readings pieced on tape— I wanted to get campy tones into it, burlesque horror and goo-goo eyes.

LAST FIVE YEARS. Who we gonna call first, said Peter. Let's start with Khrushchev, said Allen.

Look, why don't we start with Kerouac on Long Island. EXPLAINED ALL THE ABOVE AND DEMANDED HE JOIN ME IMMEDIATELY. In the meantime, let's pull the curtains, said Frank. There's enough going on in here so I don't care about looking outside. HE SAID HE HAS HIS MOTHER—"BRING YOUR MOTHER"— THE FIRST TIME I'D HAD THE NERVE TO CHALLENGE HIS MOTHER'S PSYCHIC PRIMACY OVER HIS FATE. Allen picked up the white telephone and dialed Operator. The two thin figures leaned forward wrapped up in a holy fervor trying to spread peace. The dear noble innocent helplessness of the naked body. They looked as though they had stepped out of a quatrocento canvas, apostles, martyrs, dear fanatic holy men. Allen said, Hello, operator, this is God, I want to talk to Kerouac. FELT EQUAL TO INCLUDING HER IN ON THE REBELLION IN HEAVEN. To whom do I want to talk? Kerouac. What's my name? This is God. G.O.D. Okay. We'll try Capitol 7-0563. Where? Northport, Long Island. There was a pause. We were all listening hard. Oh. Yes. That's right. That's the number of the house where I was born. Look, operator, I'll have to go upstairs to get the number. Then I'll call back. HE SAID, I DON'T WANT TO DIE.

Allen hung up the receiver. What was all that about, Allen? Well, the operator asked me my name and I said I was God and I wanted to speak to Kerouac and she said, I'll try to do my best, sir, but you'll have to give me his number and then I gave her the number of my mother's house. I've got Kerouac's number upstairs in my book. Just a minute and I'll get it.

Allen hopped out of the room, and Peter the Hermit lit a cigarette. I took advantage of the time out to check on the third floor. Susan was sitting on the floor of the TV room sticking bobby pins in her curlers. Rhona was lying on the couch watching a program. Charlie said, Hey, what's going on down there? Allen says he is God and he and Peter are naked and are phoning around to Kennedy and Kerouac. Naked? Both of them? Rhona and Charlie giggled. Rhona had been troubled by the poets' old clothes and felt that they hadn't been bathing. Hey, said Rhona, if they're really naked why don't you get them to jump under a shower. Good God, Rhona, with all this celestial business breaking out how can you get hung up on personal hygiene. Charlie got up from the easy chair. Naked, huh? This is something I can't miss. Dad-burn-it, I'm going down to catch this show.

Charlie followed down to the study. The two saints were standing gaunt and biblical by the desk. Allen was shouting in the telephone to Jack. I SAID, WHAZZAMATTER YOU AFRAID!!? HE GIGGLED—CONVERSATION SOON ENDED. He wanted Jack to come up to Cambridge and then he wanted Jack's mother to come too. Jack had a lot to say because Allen held the phone listening for long spaces. I HEARD HE WENT INTO NY AND DIDN'T DRINK FOR A WEEK AS A RESULT. Charlie was standing with his feet apart watching. Frank was still sitting behind the desk smiling. Donald and the anthro student were standing in the hallway looking in curiously. I walked over to explain. I HAD FEELING IF I WEAKENED IN ENERGY THE SCHEME WOULD FAIL. Allen says he is the Messiah and he's calling Kerouac to start a peace and love movement. Donald wasn't interested. He went on telling me about the foolishness of believing in hot and cold. It occurred to me that Allen and Peter were proving his point. IF I ATE OR SHIT AGAIN I WOULD TURN BACK TO MERE NON-MESSIAH HUMAN. The phone call continued and finally I walked back in and said, Hey Allen, for the cost of this phone call we could pay his way up here by plane. Allen shot an apologetic look and then I heard him telling Jack, Okay Jack, I have to go now, but you've got to take the mushrooms and let's settle this quarrel between Kennedy and Khrushchev. BUT NEEDED MY GLASSES—THOUGH HAD YELLED AT LEARY THAT HE DIDN'T NEED HIS EARPIECE TO HEAR THE REAL VIBRATIONS OF THE COSMOS.

HE WENT ALONG WITH ME AGREEABLY. Allen and Peter were sitting on the big couch in the living room and Allen was telling us about his visions, cosmic electronic networks, and how much it meant to him that I told him he was a great man and how this mushroom episode had opened the door to

Can you send me copy of Amer Psych Assn Speech? I been typing all day and also on junk—want to lie down and rest and think—so sign off.

Peter working 12 hours a day as messenger in snow to get up some more Europe loot.

If we're starving in India, we'll send you big demanding telegrams taking you up on your offer.

I gave 15 mushrooms to Thelonious Monk and he wanted to be alone with family in his house. I spoke to him on phone 5 hours later and he was fine.

No report from him yet, I'll send that as soon as possible. David Solomon is a good guy, but he is long-winded, an ex-political Red intellectual who's got humane.

He's given mescaline out, so I guess he can do it safely. I don't know if formal center need can be set up in N.Y. till the fungus spreads from Cambridge academy to N.Y. academy.

You have all the equipment for working with security there, that's the best—it will spread on its own once some N.Y. psychiatrist meets up with you.

Glad Schultes is friendly. Never did meet him. I've got to lie down awhile—write me a note—I hope my departure won't bring you down—is it alright if I go? Tell me.

Janine not taken mushrooms yet. I have 23 left—I gave 8 to a painter friend. All the young kids lately are shooting (needle) a drug called methedrine . . .

. . . an amphetamine semi-hallucinogen—haven't tried it yet. It's all the vogue.

See—I don't know if I should stay here and rave and scream politically and give big Carnegie Hall readings and Harvard readings—but I think a quiet silly trip to Greece would be better in the long run.

∞

women and heterosexuality and how he could see new womanly body visions and family life ahead. BUT THEN I BEGAN BREATHING AND WANTING TO LIE DOWN AND REST. Peter's hand was moving back and forth on Allen's shoulder. It was the first time that he had stood up to Jack and he was sorry about the phone bill but wasn't it too bad that Khrushchev and Kennedy couldn't have been on the line and, hey, what about Norman Mailer in that psychiatric ward in Bellevue, shouldn't we call him. AND SAW THE CONTROL OF THE UNIVERSE SLIPPING OUT OF MY HANDS.

I don't think they'd let a call go through to him, Allen. Well, it all depends on how we come on. I don't think coming on as Allen Ginsberg would help in that league. I don't think coming on as the Messiah would either. Well, you could come on as big psychologists and make big demanding noises about the patient. It was finally decided that it was too much trouble.

Still *curandero*, I asked if they wanted anything to eat or drink. Well, how about some hot milk. FROM PHYSICAL FEAR AND FEELINGS OF WANTING TO FORGET IT ALL AND DIE, SLEEP, EAT, SHIT, BE BACK HUMAN. Allen and Peter went upstairs to put on robes and I put some cold milk in a pan and turned on the stove. Donald was still moving around softly with his hands behind his back. Thinking. Watching. He was too deep and Buddha for us to swing with and I later realized that I hadn't been a very attentive *curandero* for him and that there was a gulf between Allen and him never closed and that the geographic arrangement was too scattered to make a close loving session. Of course, both of them were old drug hands and ready to go off on their own private journeys and both wanted to make something deep and their own.

Anthro's role in all of this was never clear. He stood in the hallway watching curiously but for the most part we ignored him, treated him as an object just there but not involved and that, of course, was a mistake. Any time you treat someone as an object rest assured he'll do the same and that was the way that score was going to be tallied.

We ended up with a great scene in the kitchen. I

bustled around pouring the hot milk into cups, and the poets sat around the table looking like Giotto martyrs in checkered robes. Lafcadio came down and we got him some food and he nodded yes when I asked him about ice cream and Allen started to talk about his visions and about the drug scene in New York and, becoming eloquent, wound up preaching with passion about the junkies, help- less, hooked, lost, thin, confused creatures, sick and the police and the informers. I SAW THE BEST MINDS OF MY GENERATION DESTROYED BY MADNESS, STARVING HYSTERICAL NAKED, DRAGGING THEMSELVES THROUGH THE NEGRO STREETS AT DAWN LOOKING FOR AN ANGRY FIX. And then we started planning the psychedelic revolution. Allen wanted everyone to have the mushrooms. Who has the right to keep them from someone else? And there should be freedom for all sorts of rituals, too. ANGELHEADED HIPSTERS BURNING FOR THE ANCIENT HEAVENLY CONNECTION TO THE STARRY DYNAMO IN THE MACHINERY OF NIGHT. The doctors could have them and there should be *curanderos,* and all sorts of good new holy rituals that could be developed and ministers have to be involved. Although the church is naturally and automatically opposed to mushroom visions, still the experience is basically religious and some minis- ters would see it and start using them. But with all these groups and organizations and new rituals, there still had to be room for the single, lone, unattached, non-groupy individual to take the mushrooms and go off and follow his own rituals— brood big cosmic thoughts by the sea or roam through the streets of New York, high and restless, thinking poetry, and writers and poets and artists to work out whatever they were working out. WHO WERE EXPELLED FROM THE ACADEMIES FOR CRAZY AND PUBLISHING OBSCENE ODES ON THE WINDOWS OF THE SKULL.

But all this was going to be hard to bring about. What a political struggle! Think of all the big powerful forces lined up ready to crush anything wonderful and holy and free—the big fascist busi- nessmen and the people who wanted to start a war against Russia and crush Castro. WHO COWERED IN UNSHAVEN ROOMS IN UNDERWEAR, BURNING THEIR

ALLEN GINSBERG
MARCH 1961:

Still hoping to come up, but can't figure it till I settle other things—leaving ar- rangements, filing all pa- pers, etc. Glad Burroughs will be back at Harvard.

It's hard trying to turn off faucet of correspondence. The FCC complained to John Crosby about my TV speech and after network pressure Crosby let them play a 7-minute rebuttal last weekend, lots of crap.

I also hear Paul Goodman and N. Podhoretz are form- ing some kind of committee for intelligent action which has as program various things such as sex freedom and drug freedom.

A young girl approached me and transmitted a sug- gestion from Goodman that I go to jail in passive re- sistance action on mari- juana. Sounds like a good deal, actually.

I told her I was going to Greece tho, so couldn't. They're having a meeting tonight at Debs Hall—just like the 20's.

The *Times* refused to run a series on Fed Narco Bureau but Harrison Salisbury is now lobbying to find why; and they did agree to run the Lindesmith-Ploscowe report in summary when it does come out and various Chicago and SF papers are now interested too.

I think people at Living Theater and Goodman and others soon will prepare some sort of intellectual's petition to free pot from prohibition.

I'll write Dr. Spiegel. Rev. John Snow of Gould Farm asked for your address, says he been reading up on subject and now wants to try LSD or mushrooms. I'll send it to him.

Looks like your own area is very sunny and I think it will remain so.

La Barre is lovely guy— hope you meet him somewhere. Jack moved his mama to Florida, so's out of town.

Harry Smith and Phipps are negotiating and I've now dropped out since they seem to be able to handle it all between them O.K. Haven't heard results.

MONEY IN WASTEBASKETS AND LISTENING TO THE TERROR THROUGH THE WALL. And all the sadistic little men who get together in groups like the American Legion and the white supremacy councils, and of course all the people who had their own little autocratic empires going who would be threatened if people really began to see with mushroom honesty, and finally and always there the police ready to investigate and arrest and indict and bully and keep people in jail because they want to live quiet lives of freedom and poetry. WHO REAPPEARED ON THE WEST COAST INVESTIGATING THE F.B.I. IN BEARDS AND SHORTS WITH BIG PACIFIST EYE SEXY IN THEIR DARK SKIN PASSING OUT INCOMPREHENSIBLE LEAFLETS.

As Allen talked nearsighted Marx-Trotsky-Paine poetry, there was always the Terror just back there a bit. Terror of Moloch. MOLOCH! MOLOCH! ROBOT APARTMENTS! INVISIBLE SUBURBS! SKELETON TREASURES! BLIND CAPITALS! DEMONIC INDUSTRIES! SPECTRAL NATIONS! INVINCIBLE MADHOUSES! GRANITE COCKS! MONSTROUS BOMBS! Terror of the Nazi national Golgotha. Terror of the void. Terror of death. Terror of Rockland State Hospital madness. Terror of the void. Terror of the long coiled snake of Peru slithering up closer with the slit-eye of destruction. WHO BURNED CIGARETTE HOLES IN THEIR ARMS PROTESTING THE NARCOTIC TOBACCO HAZE OF CAPITALISM.

The present hexagram refers to the cultural superstructure of society. Here it is the wood that serves as nourishment for the flame, the spirit. (I Ching L)

WHO DISTRIBUTED SUPERCOMMUNIST PAMPHLETS IN UNION SQUARE WEEPING AND UNDRESSING WHILE THE SIRENS OF LOS ALAMOS WAILED THEM DOWN. Allen Ginsberg hunched over the kitchen table, shabby robe hiding his thin white nakedness, cosmic politician. Give them the mystic vision. They'll see it's good and honest and they'll say so publicly and then no one from the police or the narcotics bureau can put them down. And you're the perfect persons to do it. Big serious scientist professors from Harvard. That's right. I can't do it. I'm too easy to put down. Crazy beatnik poet. Let me get my address book. I've got lots of connections in New York and we'll go right down the list and turn them all on. AND WAILED DOWN WALL, AND THE STATEN ISLAND FERRY ALSO WAILED, WHO BROKE DOWN CRYING IN WHITE GYMNASIUMS NAKED AND TREMBLING BEFORE THE MACHINERY OF OTHER SKELETONS.

AMERICA I'VE GIVEN YOU ALL AND NOW I'M NOTHING. Allen Ginsberg, cosmic crusader, running a worldwide campaign out of a small Lower East Side cold-water flat, helping a man in Scotland start a literary magazine by sending him poems from a dozen undiscovered youngsters in blue jeans, anxious but irrepressible, protected only by the honest nakedness. Allen Ginsberg, Zen master politician. AMERICA AFTER ALL IT IS YOU AND I WHO ARE PERFECT NOT THE NEXT WORLD. YOUR MACHINERY IS TOO MUCH FOR ME. YOU MADE ME WANT TO BE A SAINT.

Allen explaining his nakedness. When men set out to kill and bully they dress up. Suit of armor. Combat boots. Uniforms. I'M TRYING TO COME TO THE POINT. I REFUSE TO GIVE UP MY OBSESSION.

Allen Ginsberg the social-worker politician explaining the sex-drug-freedom-ecstasy movement. AMERICA STOP PUSHING I KNOW WHAT I'M DOING. Junk gives peace, relief from pain and a shattering cosmic detachment. But the relief is so brief and detachment so ruthlessly physical that the very weak and the very selfish get hooked. Junkies are the confused and helpless victims of a one-sided game they started with the police. MY MIND IS MADE UP THERE IS GOING TO BE TROUBLE. Who wants the thankless task of helping the tormented egocentricity of the junkie? Long subway rides around Manhattan to borrow money to get the junkie to a doctor. AMERICA I AM ADDRESSING YOU. Endless calls on the delicatessen pay phone to arrange help. Locking yourself in a dingy hotel room to spend the next two days helping the sweating, writhing body kick its sickness. And the ceaseless politicking. Lining up all the little magazines and the friendly reporters to give a favorable review to the Indiana University book which shows the cruelty and futility of our drug laws. AMERICA THIS IS QUITE SERIOUS. Rushing uptown to the television show where you tell the American public they should get high on

Lafcadio is taking *dancing* lessons—great—twice a week—turns out pretty graceful and light on his feet.

I'm reading Wilhelm Reich and I think he's really great. You ever pick up on him?

. . . to translate in your terms, says the formation of abstractions sets in after crippling of *the* primary non-abstract body function, genital communication . . .

. . . the genital embrace being total annihilation of individuation and formation of a new third being of two separate identities . . .

. . . if the individual is blocked from experience of that communism all other reactions (and mental life) will be screwed up, and he describes thus, the origin of the worldwide emotional plague.

Farrar Straus stocks all his previously banned books—see the *Murder of Christ.* Dave Solomon gave LeRoi Jones the mushrooms finally —very good results too.

∞

ALLEN GINSBERG
APRIL 1961:

Got your letter—all sounds smashing good show there. Saw Monk play beautifully in Olympia theater in Paris, but didn't see him except on stage—a monk.

I receive mail safely at American Express, 11 Rue Scribe, Paris, France. If you have a sufficient supply, I would like to have some mushrooms or LSD.

I am looking for French connection, no success yet but have not looked intensively. Can use all you can send.

Burroughs is in Tangier, c/o U.S. Consulate. He or Brian Gysin et my mushrooms. I'll go down to visit Burroughs as soon as financially able.

. . . All three of us down to $80.00, but there will be loot coming in. We got offer from Gerodias of Olympia to be editors of a big time sexual magazine, free hand with vast salaries and print anything *mad* we want.

pot. I'D BETTER GET RIGHT DOWN TO THE JOB. In the thirties the fight to save the poor. In the forties the fight to save the Jews. In the fifties the fight to save the junkie. In the sixties we'll save the world. IT'S TRUE I DON'T WANT TO JOIN THE ARMY OR TURN LATHES IN PRECISION PARTS FACTORIES.

Now Allen Ginsberg, stooping over the kitchen table peering at his address book. There's Robert Lowell and Muriel Rukyser. And Kerouac, of course, and LeRoi Jones. And Dizzy Gillespie and Thelonious Monk. And the painters. And the publishers. He was chanting out names of the famous and the talented. He was completely serious, dedicated, wound up in the crusade. I'M NEARSIGHTED AND PSYCHOPATHIC ANYWAY. AMERICA I'M PUTTING MY QUEER SHOULDER TO THE WHEEL.

And so Allen spun out the cosmic campaign. He was to line up influentials and each weekend I would come down to New York and we'd run mushroom sessions. This fit our Harvard research plans perfectly. Our aim there was to learn how people reacted, to test the limits of the drug, to get creative and thoughtful people to take them and tell us what they saw and what we should do with the mushrooms. Allen's political plan was appealing, too. I had seen enough and read enough in Spanish of the anti-vision crowd, the power-holders with guns, and the bigger and better men we got on our team the stronger our position. And then too, the big-name bit was intriguing. Meeting and sharing visions with the famous.

The ritual was to be the *curandero* sequence. These people will have more confidence in you than in me, said Allen. The wise-guide ritual sounded good. The cause was right and the contract beneficial to all concerned. We were after all offering a free round-trip ticket for the greatest journey known to man. From this moment on my days as a respectable establishment scientist were numbered. I just couldn't see the new society given birth by medical hands. Or psychedelic sacraments as psychiatric tools. From this evening on my energies were offered to the ancient underground society of alchemists, artists, mystics, alienated visionaries, drop-outs and the disenchanted young, the sons arising.

Gregory wants to, I'm hesitating, Peter still wants India directly. If I accept it means being tied down here in Europe a year or two, but also weirdest century literary mag yet. I dunno.

I'll probably be around here when you come in June. Send me forms to fill out as I gave mushrooms to Gregory. Gysin has filled out and will send you his.

I don't know him well, and no intimate contact with him emotionally, tho Burroughs thinks we should dig each other.

Gysin has invented a *great* flicker machine. Dig this— cut out 10 apertures on a stovepipe hat or piece of cardboard and set it revolving on phonograph at 33 speed.

It flickers and is homemade strobe. I looked in it—it sets up optical fields as religious and mandalic as the hallucinogenic drugs—literally.

. . . (look in with eyes closed)—it's like being able to have jewelled biblical designs and landscapes without taking chemicals. Amazing.

For a while the hobbits continued to talk and think of the past journey and of the perils that lay ahead; but such was the virtue of the land of Rivendell that soon all fear and anxiety was lifted from their minds. The future, good or ill, was not forgotten, but ceased to have any power over the present. (The Lord of the Rings)

It was around midnight. Donald still seemed high and would walk in and out of the room, silently, hands behind his back, Talmudic raccoon, studying the kitchen crowd seriously, and then padding out. The anthropology student had joined us around the table. We had given him something to drink and he was listening to the conversation and saying nothing. He made some comment about schedules back to Cambridge and it was time for him to make the last train so I drove him down to the station. He asked some questions about the scientific meaning of the mushroom research and it was clear that he didn't understand what had happened and what we were doing. There wasn't time to explain and I felt badly that he had been dragged into a strange situation. We had made the rule that people could bring their friends when they took the mushrooms and this seemed like a good idea for the person taking the mushrooms but it was just beginning to dawn on me that the problem never was with the person taking the drug but rather the people who didn't. Like Brother Toriblo the Spanish monk, who talked about cruelty and drunkenness caused by the Sacred Mushrooms. It's okay to bring a friend, but he should take the mushrooms with you. And poor anthro, it turned out, wasn't even a friend of Donald's and as it turned out didn't like him and he was clearly bewildered by and critical of what he had seen and heard and the nakedness of the poets. His train was about due and I was too preoccupied by what Allen had been saying to feel like explaining to anthro. The uneasy feeling persisted and I suggested that he not tell people about the mystic visions and the naked crusaders because this might be misunderstood and he said he wouldn't talk about it and we shook hands and he left.

That was Sunday night.

By Monday afternoon the rumors were spreading around the Harvard yard.

Beatniks. Orgies. Naked poets. Junkies. Homosexuality. Drug parties. Tried to lure a decent naïve graduate student into sin. Wild parties masquerading as research. Queers. Beards. Criminal types.

The chairman of my department called me. What the hell is going on, Tim? Two graduate students have come to me indignant—demanding that your work be stopped.

I laughed. I'll send you the reports from the session as soon as they are typed. It was a good session. God would approve. We're learning a lot.

The disapproving gaze of the establishment was on us. You should fear the wary eyes of the servants of Sauron were the words of Elrond. I do not doubt that news . . . has already reached him, and he will be filled with wrath. Naked poets, indeed!

From this time on we saw ourselves as unwitting agents of a social process that was far too powerful for us to control or to more than dimly understand. An historical movement that would inevitably change man at the very center of his nature, his consciousness.

We did sense that we were not alone. The quest for internal freedom, for the elixir of life, for the drought of immortal revelation was not new. We were part of an ancient and honorable fellowship which had pursued this journey since the dawn of recorded history. We began to read the accounts of earlier trippers—Dante, Hesse, Rene Daumal, Tolkien, Homer, Blake, George Fox, Swedenborg, Bosch, and the explorers from the Orient—tantrics, Sufis, Bauls, Gnostics, hermetics, Sivites, saddhus. No, we were not alone.

Nor were we isolated in the twentieth century. The three groups who always await and accept the revelation which comes in every historical time were present in full and goodly numbers. The young (who always want more and have no game to protect), the artists (who always hunger for the ecstatic moment), and the alienated (the wise slaves and noble minority groups watching from the periphery of the society).

It *works.* Gysin says the apertures have to be measured and adjusted right to get 16 flickers a second or something.

He also paints the inside of the stovepipe-cardboard. Of course, you have to drop an electric bulb, I forgot it, in the center of it to flicker thru apertures.

I'll try to connect him with a toy manufacturer—homemade optic movies possible.

Burroughs' present cut up operates—in theory—on similar flicker principle—trying to play his words over and over flashing in different combos to perhaps set up a 3-D field in imagination or some other practical level.

Interesting experiment and more grounded in practical constructive purpose than I had grasped—thought before it was just a negative thing to cut up life or recombine words artistically.

Can you send me a pack of psilocybin?—and also send the forms, they'll be filled out. Here is Peter, who a half-hour ago shot 250 of mescaline into his vein with a needle.

First, yes, also, I saw Michaux who has just finished a book on his experiments with mushroom pills too—nice old man—says it's all in *you* and no outside forces or gods too . . .

Peter Orlovski: Yes, it's all an inward force, we are all God, so being God it feels very nice to shoot up mescaline in the vein which I just did two hours ago—got laid last night—so many girls here. Now that I am high, would like to see this flicker

. . . but it's being fixed—so at the moment the world seems very physical and all the physicalness going somewhere—soup on the stove—it all boils down to ass and roses on the table —you been able to turn-on Kennedy's brother yet? Kennedy real mean to Castro and acting so stupid . . .

. . . instead of making friends—he's giving me a bad name—help—hey Kennedy, why don't you get laid instead of fucking around with politics? So Tim, I've been studying French here and going to gym with a funny hard-on.

The success of the psychedelic movement was guaranteed. The energies released by the sacred drugs were too great to suppress.

We began to see it as a question of time. The movement would grow like everything organic grows, cell by cell. Friend turning-on friends. Husbands turning-on wives. Teachers turning-on students. The contagion of contiguity. The tissue underground.

Shortly after Allen Ginsberg left, we made statistical predictions about the growth of the psychedelic movement. We drew a cumulative percentage graph and hung it on the wall. The rapidly ascending curve spelled out our forecast.

In 1961, we estimated that 25,000 Americans had turned-on to the strong psychedelics—LSD, mescaline, peyote. (Marijuana we stayed away from.) This figure did not include the 125,000 American Indians who use peyote as their sacrament and who were there as an inestimable psychic asset when we were ready to use it. (It is no accident that the psychedelic movement by 1967 was a tribal phenomenon.)

At the rate of cellular growth we expected that by 1967 a million Americans would be using LSD. We calculated that the critical figure for blowing the mind of the American society would be four million LSD users and this would happen by 1969.

We were wrong in our estimates. We were too conservative. By 1966 *Life* magazine announced that a million Americans were using LSD. In the spring of 1966, a million doses a month were being distributed by a messianic underground in California alone. By 1967 four million Americans had taken the trip. In June of 1967, an album by the Beatles which openly celebrated the psychedelic experience sold a million copies the first week of its release.

Our forecast was off because, as middle-aged professors, we counted on the artists and the minorities and the college youth, but we failed to anticipate the use of LSD by high-school kids. In our academic isolation we forgot that for thousands of years the psychedelic vision has been the rite of passage of the teen-ager—the Dakota Indian boy who sits on the mountaintop fasting and sleepless, waiting for the revelation. The threshold of adult game life is the ancient and natural time for the rebirth experience, the flip-out trip from which you come back as a man. A healthy society provides and protects the sacredness of the teen-age psychedelic voyage. A sick, static society fears and forbids the revelation.

The psychedelic movement was to develop without organization, without leaders, without dogmatic doctrines and become a full-blown religious renaissance of the young.

It moved quickly, always shocking, continually shattering structures. You either surrendered to the flow and went with that full tide of two billion years, or you were thrown to the bank where you shouted stop! danger! medical control! evil! scientific respectability! and despaired that your words couldn't slow the relentless current.

Allen Ginsberg came to Harvard and shook us loose from our academic fears and strengthened our courage and faith in the process.

Allen Ginsberg: That was Peter, half-hour sitting at typewriter—totally high. Lots happening here, a great shade (Negro) painter in town who tells me he stayed high on mescaline 3 months last year. . . .

Magnificent imaginist painter (new school we named)— i.e. visionary literal dream vision or waking visionary imagery as subject, breakthru from abstract—*Gregory* a great book—*American Express* the last word on cosmic politics—

A dreamy comedy writ like *Candide* and *Alice in Wonderland,* pix by author, we'll send you a copy—Burroughs one of the goofy conspirers.

∞

THE CALDRON. *Supreme good fortune. Success.* (I Ching)

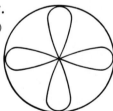

You Have to Go Out of Your Mind to Use Your Head:

January 1961

Guide: FRANK BARRON

Oracle: VI

Conflict

The Creative, Heaven

The Abysmal, Water

Heaven and water go their opposite ways:
The image of CONFLICT.
Thus in all his transactions the superior man
Carefully considers the beginning.

(I Ching)

Once there was a man by the name of Arthur Koestler who was painted within and without by Hermann Hesse. Whether his *Sunday Telegraph* manuscript needs any postductory remarks may be open to question. I, however, feel the need of adding a few pages, in which I try to record my own recollections of him. What I know of him is little enough, yet the impression left by his personality has remained, in spite of all, a deep and sympathetic one.

A. K. devoted himself to intellectual pursuits. He had given up the novel as a medium of teaching, and had a wide range of knowledge. But not all knowledge was the same to him. Returning to his first profession, he said that any thought was not as good as another. He preferred science and reporting. Science-reporting.

He loved a *certain kind of thinking*, confessing to me that psychology was his first love, the profession in which he felt he could make his greatest contribution.

He was rewriting an earlier book on creative thinking (new moves on the mind board) and disdained the mystical experience. Insight and outlook is what he called science once in a Franco prison.

In 1959 he had visited India in search of truth and meaning. His reactions were typical of the Western rational mind overwhelmed and flipped-out by the seething, organic, seed squalor-beauty of this Holy Land. A trip to India is a full-blown LSD experience—a relentless serpentine uncoiling of unwashed earth-tissue. People react to India the way they do to psychedelic drugs—they either flow with it into ecstatic unsterile union with mythic all-life, or they recoil behind sterile air-conditioned tourist-hotel plate glass, screaming for the next airplane to

136

Beirut, or they slog through it unhappily but dutifully, making notes as did dear, sturdy, sweating, pack-mind-on-back Arthur Koestler through his two mushroom sessions and his journey to the East.

The upper trigram, whose image is heaven, has an upward movement; the lower trigram, water, in accordance with its nature, tends downward. Thus the two halves move away from each other, giving rise to the idea of conflict. (I Ching VI)

He wrote a book about the East called *The Lotus and the Robot,* which was to become quite relevant to the psychedelic controversy. He held a low opinion, which explains the dark expectations which he brought to his psilocybin experiences. He congratulated himself on his rational mind.

He was not really intolerant of religion. Although his given name Artha is Sanskrit for the acquisition of power, wealth, or fame, his cells remembered the paternal name. Artha Khesaya, flying in the air, Artha Kesava, having long or much or handsome hair, Artha Kohlasa, name of a raga, Artha Kohala, author of saga (to whom the invention of the soma-psychedelic drama is attributed) or Artha Kosala, Kingdom of India, golden age, and Artha Kalidasa, ancient sage.

Fooled by little pills for several centuries, Arthur Koestler disliked what he saw in the East, while his science embraced nearly everything that existed on earth. That was worth knowing.

He said that both India and Japan seem to be spiritually sicker, the human soul more estranged and to tolerate more speculations on the soul, than the West.

Arthur Koestler was a rational mind, tolerant long before Aldous Huxley found in yoga everything that Arthur Koestler recognized as superstition. A remedy for our Brave New World. Without taking seriously what Schopenhauer called the Upanishads, the consolation of his life was profoundly odious and repugnant to him.

Alien, uncultured, and retarded people of the first generation of the Nuclear Age might occupy themselves with solace in Zen. In remote antiquity

He was not unaware, to be sure, that there were other sorts of thinking and knowledge; but they were not "science," and he held a low opinion of them . . . everything he recognized as superstition was profoundly odious and repugnant to him. Alien, uncultured, and retarded people might occupy themselves with it: in remote antiquity there may have been mystical or magical thinking: but since the birth of science and logic there was no longer any sense in making use of these outmoded and dubious tools.

So he said and so he thought; and when traces of superstition came to his attention he became angry and felt as if he had been touched with something hostile.

One day Frederick went to the house of one of his friends with whom he had often studied. It so happened that he had not seen this friend for some time. . . .

During a pause in the laborious conversation Frederick looked about the studio he knew so well and saw, pinned loosely on the wall, a sheet of paper. . . . He stood up and went to the wall to read the paper.

There, in Erwin's beautiful script, he read the words: "Nothing is without, nothing is within." There it was! There he stood face to face with what he feared! . . . What stood written here, as an avowal of his friend's concern at the moment, was mysticism! Erwin was unfaithful!

"This is the way," Erwin replied, and perhaps you have already taken the most difficult step. You have found by experience: the without can become the within. You have been beyond the pair of antitheses. It seemed hell to you; learn, it is heaven! For it is heaven that awaits you. Behold, this is magic; to intercharge the without and the within, not by compulsion, not in anguish, as you have done it, but freely, voluntarily. Summon up the past, summon up the future: both are in you! Until today you have been the slave of the within. Learn to be its master. That is magic.

∞

when the West groaned under the weight of mental knapsacks, receptivity to the voice of mystical or magical thinking was limited to periods of spiritual emergency. DRUGS ON THE BRAIN. But since the birth of science to moods of futility and despair, there was no longer any sense in making use of such outmoded self-congratulation and dubious tools.

So he said and so he thought. He traveled in India and Japan (in 1958–59) when traces of superstition came to the mood of the pilgrim. He became angry like countless others before and felt that he had been touched. Whether the East had any answer to offer—something hostile to our perplexity and deadlocked problems—he was not to be fooled by little pills.

It angered him, striking the olfactory note. He found such traces among his own sort, which guided his reactions among educated men conversant with the culture of Asia. The principles of scientific thinking. Sober self-control. Self.

The sewers of Bombay had been opened by mistake and nothing was more painful and intolerable to him than the damp heat impregnated by the scandalous notion which lately by their stench invaded the air-conditioned cabin. He had sometimes heard expressed and discussed the moment the door of the Viscount was opened by men of great culture. As we descended the steps, that absurd idea that a wet, smelly diaper (scientific thinking around my head) was possibly not a supreme, timeless, eternal, foreordained and unassailable mode of thought by some abominable joker.

The second half of the book, but one of many, was a transient way of thinking, permeated with the stink of Zen, not impervious to change. This irreverent, destructive, poisonous note a phrase often used in Zen literature. WRONG KIND.

Even Arthur Koestler could not deny it and thus in a sense came back impoverished, cropping up here and there as a result of the distress throughout the world, rather than enriched. NO MERIT. A rational mind. Like a warning, like a white hand's ghostly writing that his place was Europe in the center of his mind.

The more Arthur Koestler suffered from looking at this tiny continent, puffing and panting up the steep path. This idea existed from the vastness of Asia and could so deeply distress him, while gaining a fresh impression the more passionately his compactness and coherence assailed it, and those he secretly suspected of believing in it.

Conflict develops when one feels himself to be in the right and runs into opposition. (I Ching VI)

I started my journey so far only a very few little pills among the truly educated in sackcloth and ashes. Challenging Aldous Huxley who had openly and frankly defended the drug cult. He came back rather proud, a rational mind professing belief in this doctrine. Of being a European. It may be parochial pride. AN ANSWER. A doctrine seemed destined, but it was not smug. Should it gain in circulation: DRUGS ON BRAIN. DIFFERENT LOOK. SUDDEN EFFECT. WRONG KIND. NO MERIT. AN ANSWER. Power for a Hungarian-born. French-loving. English writer. To destroy all spiritual values on earth with some experience of prison and concentration camps to call forth chaos.

One cannot help being aware. Well, matters had not reached Europe's past sins—that point yet of present deadly peril. The scattered individuals who openly embraced a detached comparison with other continents. The idea! NO MERIT. Of the way Europe stood up still so few in number that they could be considered oddities to its past trials and of its contribution to man's history. Sober self-control.

Peculiar fellows. But a drop of the poison leaves one with a new confidence. An emanation of that idea and affection for that small figure, Hungarian-born, could be perceived first on this side, then riding the back of the Asian bull.

Among the half-educated A.K.'s portrait of himself could be a small figure compact and coherent. DRUGS ON THE BRAIN. Esoteric doctrines, sects, and discipleships sketched with accuracy. The world was full of the struggle of the European mind and the Asian bull. Everywhere one could scent his tormented search for verbal meaning. Superstition. Science. Mysticism. Franco prison. Science. Zionism. Spiritualistic cults. Communism. Insight and Outlook. Other mysterious forces. It was really neces-

From *The Lotus and the Robot* by Arthur Koestler:

The sewers of Bombay had been opened by mistake, I was told, before the tide had come in. The damp heat, impregnated by their stench, invaded the air-conditioned cabin the moment the door of the Viscount was opened. As we descended the steps I had the sensation that a wet, smelly diaper was being wrapped around my head by some abominable joker. This was December; the previous day I had been slithering over the frozen snow in the mountains of Austria.

Lilies that fester smell far worse than weeds; both India and Japan seem to be spiritually sicker, more estranged from a living faith than the West. To look to Asia for mystic enlightenment and spiritual guidance has become as much of an anachronism as to think of America as the Wild West.

. . . I started my journey in sackcloth and ashes and came back rather proud of being a European. It may be a somewhat parochial pride, but it is not smug, for, as a Hungarian-born, French-loving, English writer with some experience of prisons and concentration camps, one cannot help being aware of Europe's past sins and present deadly peril. And yet a detached comparison with other continents of the way Europe stood up to its past trials, and of its contribution to man's history, leaves one with a new confidence and affection for that small figure riding on the back of the Asian bull.

∞

From "Return Trip to Nirvana" by Arthur Koestler, in the London *Sunday Telegraph*:

A few weeks ago I received a letter from a friend, an American psychiatrist working at Harvard University:

DEAR K:

Things are happening here which I think will interest you. The big, new hot issue these days in many American circles is DRUGS. We believe that the synthetics of the cactus peyote (mescalin) and the mushroom (psilocybin) offer possibilities for expanding consciousness, changing perceptions, removing abstractions. . . .

We are offering the experience to distinguished creative people. Artists, poets, writers, scholars. We've learned a tremendous amount by listening to them. . . . If you are interested I'll send some mushrooms over to you. . . . I'd like to hear about your reaction. . . .

Shortly afterwards, I had to go to the University of Michigan at Ann Arbor. I had been invited there for quite different reasons, but on the first morning of my stay the subject of the magic mushroom cropped up.

sary to combat. But which science? It was as if a private feeling of weakness, to which a generation of postwar intellectuals owed their political liberation, had for the present been given free rein.

I first met A.K. in London in 1959. Always haunted by what he termed monumental feelings of inferiority, he called up my aunt, beloved Whittaker Chambers, to inquire for a furnished room. Feelings of inferiority. He went one day to the house of one of his friends. He was, in fact, as he called himself, a real wolf of the steps. Isolated from life by his categorizing mind. It so happened that he had not seen the friend for some time. Hello. Yogi/commissar! Arrival/departure! Blanching he stood motionless for a moment. Lotus/Robot! Promise/fulfillment! There it was! There he stood face-to-face with what he feared! Endlessly dancing the old Aristotelian two-step. Certainly! he cried. Of course I know it. Age of longing at the twilight bar. Its mysticism, its gnosticism!

You look at A.K. and see the face of Europe's history, into which his life had drifted on account of his disposition and destiny. And how consciously he accepted this I certainly did not know until I read the records he left behind him. Rational mind. Congratulations. A new epistemology? Is there such a thing? In the haunting eyes and the furrowed face-skin. This is the way, Erwin replied. On this frail hinge Koestler swung the fate of a generation of European political thought. And perhaps you have already taken the most difficult step. Oh rational mind of Europe! You have found by experience. Jewish. Hungarian. Austrian. French. German. English. All under one skull. The without can become the within. Great God! What does not stand classified as man or wolf he does not see at all. The noble arrogance of the self-assigned task! Once A.K. had been beyond the pair of antitheses. In the Franco cell he was floating on his back in a river of peace under bridges of silence. It seemed hell to him. It came from nowhere and flowed nowhere. Learn, my friend, it is heaven! There was no river and no I. For it is heaven that awaits you. The *I* had ceased to exist. Behold, this is magic. But now he puffs and pants up the steep path groaning under the load of mind. To interchange the without and the within, not by compulsion. In this way he was always recognizing and affirming with one-half of himself, in thought and act, what with the other half he fought and denied. His rational mind need not crouch ready to categorize and evaluate every new event, each new experience. Not in anguish, as he did it, but freely, voluntarily. Your poor mind need not be the fulcrum upon which galaxies turn. Summon up the past. Your frail cortex need not support the weight of the universe, explaining, ordering, labeling everything that occurs. Summon up the future. Both are in you. You need no longer judge the good and evil of each new flick of cosmic process. Until today you have been the slave of the within. Learn to be its master.

If a man is entangled in a conflict, his only salvation lies in being so clear-headed and inwardly strong that he is always ready to come to terms by meeting the opponent halfway. (I Ching VI)

The heavy weight of rationalism. Cruel doctrine of individual will. I, Arthur Koestler, believe in one God the creator of Heaven and Earth. One mind. One judicial authority to make a billion decisions each second that the planet turns. The billion-fold moral judgments. You favor tolerance toward all religions and all political systems. What about Hitler's gas chambers? The old Zen monk looks at the tense, alert European visitor and smiles. When you ask these logical questions we feel embarrassed, said the Buddhist.

The Aristotelian intellectual! Tell me, Maria, how can you have fondness for him, a tiresome old logician with no looks, who even has gray hair and doesn't play a saxophone and doesn't sing any English love songs, whose only security rests on his ability to rationalize each new experience? Most of that sort instinctively refuse to have anything to do with psychedelic chemicals. At times Maria, too, availed herself of Pablo's secret drugs and was forever procuring these delights for me also. A few adventurous or courageous intellectuals have made the psychedelic voyage and struggle throughout the

DRUGS ON BRAIN

This, however, was not much of a coincidence as at the present moment a surprising number of Americans, from Brass to Beat, seem to have, for different reasons, drugs on the brain; the Brass because they are worried about brainwashing and space-flight training; the Beat because drugs provide a rocket-powered escape from reality; the Organization Men because tranquillisers are more effective than the homely aspirins and fruitsalts of yore; and the spiritually frustrated on all levels of society because drugs promise a kind of do-it-yourself approach to Salvation.

The psychiatrist in charge of the mushroom was an Englishman of the quiet, gentle and unAmerican kind. Based on his own experiences and on experiments with ten test-subjects, he ventured the cautious and tentative opinion that compared with the fashionable wonder-drugs, mescalin and lysergic acid, the effect of the mushroom was relatively harmless and entirely on the pleasant, euphoric side.

It is well known that the mental attitude, the mood in which one enters the gates of mushroomland, plays a decisive part in determining the nature of the experience. Since Dr. P. was such a pleasant person and the atmosphere of Ann Arbor appealed to me, I volunteered as a guinea pig, though I felt a little guilty towards my enthusiastic friend in Harvard. However, on the day before I took the drug, I had a very unpleasant experience —with the result that I faced the mushrooms in an anxious and depressed state.

They come synthesized, in the shape of little pink pills. I swallowed nine of them (18 mg. of psilocybin), which is a fair-sized dose for a person of my weight. They were supposed to start acting after thirty minutes.

However, for nearly an hour nothing at all happened. I was chatting with Dr. P. and one of his assistants, first in his office, then in a room which had a comfortable couch in it and a tape recorder; after a while I was left alone in the room, but Dr. P. looked in from time to time. I lay down on the couch, and soon began to experience the kind of phenomena which have been repeatedly described by people who experimented with mescalin.

session to impose their minds. Pablo was always most markedly on the alert to be of service to him. Once he said to A.K. without more ado, You always try to keep the experience under mental control. That is bad. One shouldn't be like that. The mind is by definition anti-ecstasy. Try a mild pipe of hashish. The psychedelic session is the final ordeal of rationality. We became friends and he took some of my specifics. The test completed, he wrote his report in the *Sunday Telegraph* explaining away what his rebellious cortex tried to do to the symmetry of his verbal mind. Once I gave him a drink from three little bottles, a mysterious and wonderful draught. And then when he had got into a very good humor, we proposed to celebrate a love orgy. He declined abruptly.

When we started our research at Harvard I wrote to A.K. telling him about the mystical experiences we were encountering and inviting him to participate in a love feast. Brother Arthur, I invite you to a little entertainment. For madmen only and the price—your mind. Are you ready? An immediate reply. A.K. was coming to the U.S. and would like very much to come to Harvard and try the mushrooms.

A few days before his scheduled arrival a phone call came from New York. In somber tones A.K. said that he had already taken psilocybin with a psychiatrist in Michigan and had a hellish paranoid experience. For God's sake, let's snap out of it. He had no desire whatsoever to make the voyage again —transformed into the claws of a predatory bird. Never. No thanks. Wrong kind. No merit. He made repeated efforts to walk out of the show. Drugs on the brain. He was powerless against the delusion.

Well, why not come up to Harvard anyway and look around and see what we're doing? Agreed.

Arthur Koestler was an object of interest and admiration at Harvard. The top scholars come to the center to pay homage. A list of appointments was quickly set up. It was quite a ball. A thin-skinner professor told him that Hindus must be conditioned like animals to give up religious superstition. He felt in his waistcoat pocket—the number was no longer there! Miss Jerry Burner with her bruner left hand praised him for the limpid *elasser* sparkling in the thick peasant glass. I'd have loved to have danced with you again, he said, intoxicated by her warmth. (Later he worried that Jerry would steal his numbered ideas. The devil was in it if ever these failed him!) Waltzing masked around the Harvard Yard, watching A.K.'s charm and alert mind playing at the intellectual game.

From All Ports a gordon dancing girl flung herself into his arms. Dance with me! I can't, he said, I'm bound for hell.

The second afternoon, there was an hour free so I phoned over to the Massachusetts Mental Health Institute to see about arranging a dance with one of the world's top neurologists. Of all the surprises I had prepared for him, this was to be the most violent.

For have no moment of doubt that it was I who brought this bird of paradise who was delighted to be our host at his special table at the Ritz Bar.

So far, he said, I have control. That was fine. The schedule was: drinks at the Ritz, dinner at the Steel Helmet in Boston with the Frank Barrons, and then an evening at the Magic Theater for A.K. to observe a psilocybin session run under easygoing, supportive circumstances for madmen only.

To put on a good mushroom ritual, I had wired up to Charles Olson, our father who art in Gloucester. The giant Olson, genial guru, father of modern poetry. Unfortunately it is a habit, a vice of his, always to speak his mind, as indeed Goethe did in his better moments. A few years previous he had retired to a rocky promontory overlooking the harbor whence he served as guide and friend to our work. Olson dominates any gathering with his size, his wit, his intellect, his noble stature, his wise animal energy. He was striving for redemption but it will take him all his time. He was the person, surely, to introduce Arthur Koestler to the open-brain and its ecstatic possibilities.

On the way to the Ritz, A.K. told us of two dear friends of his, Moses and Jehovah, who had researched mescaline in Berlin during the twenties. Their psychedelic sessions kept opening up more and more realms of experience and revelation. Dr.

When I closed my eyes I saw luminous, moving patterns of great beauty, which was highly enjoyable; then the patterns changed into planaria—a kind of flatworm which I had watched under the microscope the previous day in a laboratory; but the worms had a tendency to change into dragons, which was less enjoyable, so I walked out of the show by opening my eyes.

I tried it again, directing the beam of the table-lamp, which had a strong bulb, straight at my closed eyelids, and the effect was quite spectacular—rather like the explosive paintings of schizophrenics, or Walt Disney's *Fantasia*.

A flaming eddy, the funnel of a tornado, appeared over my head, drawing me upward; with a little auto-suggestion and self-dramatisation I could have called it a vision of myself as the prophet Elijah being taken to Heaven by a whirlwind. But I felt that this was buying one's visions on the cheap (Carter's mushrooms are the best; mystic experience guaranteed or money refunded); so I again walked out of the show by forcing my eyes to open. It was as simple as that, and I congratulated myself on my sober self-control, a rational mind not to be fooled by little pills.

DIFFERENT LOOK

By now, however, even with open eyes, the room looked different. The colours had become not only more luminous and brilliant, but different in quality from any colour previously seen; they were located outside the normally visible spectrum, and to refer to them one would have to invent new words—so I shall say that the walls were breen, the curtain darsh, and the sky outside emerdine. Also, one of the walls had acquired a concave bend like the inside of a barrel, the plaster statue of the Venus of Milo had acquired a grin, and the straight dado-line was pleasantly curved, which struck me as an exceedingly clever joke.

But all this was quite unlike the wobbling world of drunkenness, for the room was plunged into an underwater silence, where the faint hum of the tape recorder became obtrusively loud, and the almost imperceptible undulations of the curtains became the Ballet of the Flowing Folds (the undulations were caused by the warm air ascending from the central-heating body).

Moses climbing Sinai, a gloomy hero in a gloomy wilderness of rocks, and Dr. Jehovah in the midst of storm and thunder and lightning imparting the Ten Commandments, while worthless friends set up the Golden Calf at the foot of the KURFÜRSTEN-DAMM. They tried to tell others about their discoveries but no one would listen, neither their colleagues nor their families. Mighty Dr. Jehovah and Dr. Moses, with a dark and fiery eye and the stride of Wotan, finally got to a point where they could only communicate with each other. I saw them pray at the edge of the Red Sea. Flipped-out together they had a rapport and high pitch of understanding in Handel's wonderful duet for two basses in which this event is magnificently sung. To the rest of the world they were hopeless eccentrics. So strange and incredible to be looking on at all this. A.K.'s medical friend suddenly seeing sacred peyote writ, with its heroes and its wonders, the source in our childhood of the first dawning suspicion of another world than this, presented before a distasteful public that sat eating the provisions brought with it from home.

Finally the social pressure was too great and they cracked under the strain. A nice picture, indeed, picked up by chance in the huge wholesale clearance of culture in these days. Jehovah went to Mexico where he died in short time. Moses, with dark and fiery eye and a long staff and the stride of Wotan, went to Munich where he was treated by a monster of a psychiatrist who failed to understand him. My God, rather than come to such a pass, it would have been better for the Jews and everyone else, let alone the Germans, to have perished in those days, forthwith of a violent and unbecoming death instead of this dismal pretense of dying inch by inch that we go in for today. Quitting treatment, the friend returned to Berlin and killed himself.

At the Ritz the neurologist was waiting at his special table. His secretary was with him and the waitress hovered by solicitously. So far, he said, I have contented myself with turning the heads of ladies. But now your time has come. First, let's have a glass of champagne.

A narrow strip of the revolving spool of the tape recorder caught the gleam of the lamp every few seconds; and this faint, intermittent spark, unnoticed before, observed out of the corner of the eye on the visual periphery, became the revolving beam of a miniature lighthouse. This lowering of the sensory threshold and simultaneous heightening of the intensity and emotional significance of perceptions, is one of the basic phenomena of the mushroom universe. The intermittent light-signal from the slowly revolving spool became important, meaningful and mysterious; it had some secret message. Afterwards I remembered, with sympathetic understanding, the fantasies of paranoiacs about hidden electric machines and other contraptions planted by their enemies to produce evil Rays and Influences.

SUDDEN EFFECT

The signalling tape recorder was the first symptom of a chemically-induced state of insanity. The full effect came on with insidious smoothness and suddenness. Dr. P. came into the room, and a minute or two later I saw the light and realised what a fool I had been to let myself be trapped by his cunning machinations. For during that minute or two he had undergone an unbelievable transformation.

Arthur Koestler made a quip about their mutual European background which the psychiatrist avoided. A.K.'s eyes, wolf of the steps, narrowed, and mild dislike grew quickly to strong distaste. Couldn't stand a person who denies his racial past.

A long anatomical argument began. Like two teletype machines, the men, chattering neurology tapes, sank slowly down into a soggy whisky swamp of sullen generalization. The neurologist, pressed by Koestler's finny logic, flopped through the undergrowth of swizzle sticks and olives. Poised on an island of potato chips he denied there was such a thing as a midbrain. A.K. surfaced to lob glances of resignation our way.

Keep quiet with your questions and chatter, said the neurologist. I'm a professor of theology, if you want to know. But the Lord be praised, there's no occasion for theology now, my boy. It's war. Come on. Then Koestler's face grew tense. What did you say your name was? he asked the neurologist. Ah. And did you ever have a patient by the name of Dr. Moses? No. He remembered no such patient. Moving in like a cross-examiner, A.K. sketched in more details about his friend, about his problems, his history, his appearance—dark and fiery eye— and a long staff—and the stride of Wotan.

Slowly the neurologist remembered. Oh yes, now that you remind me, I do seem to remember treating the case.

Treat him, indeed, retorted A.K. sternly. I saw him pray to God at the edge of the Red Sea, and I saw the Red Sea parted to give free passage, a deep road between piled-up mountains of water. And by the way, do you have any idea what became of him? No, said the neurologist. I last saw him climbing Sinai, a gloomy hero in a gloomy wilderness of rocks. I was about to ask you if you knew of the outcome of the case.

A.K. breathed heavily. As a matter of fact he killed himself in Berlin the following year.

A sudden quiet settled down over the table. (The confirmation classes conducted by the clergy to see this religious film could argue without end as to how the film people managed this.) Neurologist puffed quickly at cigar and called the waitress over. A nice picture, indeed, picked up by chance in the huge wholesale clearance of culture these days.

Then the Barrons arrived, Frank poised and cheerful and his new wife, Nancy, radiant and bouncing. On and on went their nuptial dance. God knows where the girl got her voice; it was so deep and good and maternal. Obediently I shut my eyes, leaned my head against the wall, and heard the roar of a hundred mingled voices surge around me. After another drink we moved to leave the neurologist. Outside, the air coming off the Boston Common was clear and fresh. We had all escaped from an especially grim mental hospital. Somewhere we heard a door bang, a glass break, a titter of laughter die away, mixed with the angry hurried noise of motorcars starting up. We felt close together after the ordeal and drove to the North End for seafood. You're ready? Far up in unhuman space rang out that strange laugh. A.K., bubbling with spirit, ordered wines and made a gallant scene with Nancy.

When we arrived back at the house, Charles Olson was in the kitchen leaning over, talking to young Jack Leary, his back to us. I brought A.K. up to Olson. The giant poet turned, looked down at the small figure of the novelist, and beamed out of his jolly eyes that really were animal's eyes, except that animal's eyes are always serious, while his always laughed and turned into human eyes.

Olson was holding a toy pistol in his hand.

Arthur Koestler's eyes went up, up, up to look at Olson and then dropped quickly to the pistol. He paled and pulled back. There he stood face-to-face with what he feared.

Olson roaring out genial greetings. Brother Harry, I invite you to a little entertainment. For madmen only, and one price only—your mind. Are you ready? Coats removed, the group assembled in the study. Why then was Hermine so white? Why was Pablo talking so much? A low built-in couch ran along two sides of the room, intersecting at the corner. A large round table strung people out in the form of a circle. Highballs. We planned the session. My friends, I have invited you to an entertainment that Harry has long worked for and of which he has long dreamed.

Olson and Leary and Barron and a Harvard

It started with the colour of his face, which had become a sickly yellow. He stood in a corner of the room with his back to the green wall, and as I stared at him his face split into two, like a cell dividing, then reunited again, but by this time the transformation was complete. A small scar on the doctor's neck which I had not noticed before, was gaping wide, trying to ingest the flesh of the chin; one ear had shrunk, the other had grown by several inches; the face became a smirking, evil phantasm. Then it changed again, into a different kind of Hogarthian vision, and these transformations went on for what I imagined to be several minutes.

All this time the doctor's body remained unchanged; the hallucinations were confined to the space from the neck upward; and they were strangely two-dimensional, like faces cut out of cardboard. The phenomenon was always strongest in that corner of the room where it had first occurred, and faded into less offensive distorting-mirror effects when we moved elsewhere, although the lighting of the room was uniform.

The same happened when other members of the staff joined us later. One of them, the jovial Dr. F., was transformed into a vision so terrifying—a Mongol with a broken neck hanging from an invisible gallows—that I thought I was going to be sick; yet I could not stop myself staring at him. In the end I said: For God's sake let's snap out of it, and we moved into another part of the room, where the effect became weaker.

As the last remark indicates, I was still in control of my outward behaviour, and this remained true throughout the whole three or four hours of the experience. But at the same time I had completely lost control over my perception of the world. I made repeated efforts "to walk out of the show" as I had been able to do during the first stages on the couch, but I was powerless against the delusions. I kept repeating to myself: But these are nice, friendly people, they are your friends, and so on. It had no effect whatsoever on the spontaneous and inexorable visual transformations.

I have mentioned before that all of Dr. P.'s previous subjects had positive euphoric experiences; I "broke the series," as he ruefully remarked over post-mortem drinks.

I had met the mushroom in the wrong state of mind, owing to that incident on the previous day, which had awakened memories of past experiences as a political prisoner, and of past preoccupations with brainwashing, torture and the extraction of confessions. The phantom faces were obvious projections of a deep-seated resentment against being "trapped" in a situation which carried symbolic echoes of the relation between prisoner and inquisitor, of Gestapo and GPU.

graduate student named Lynn were to take psilocybin. The hour is late and no doubt we are all fatigued. Nancy Barron and Núñez and Rhona were to act as ground control. So first we will rest and refresh ourselves a little. A.K. would observe. From a recess in the wall I took a quaint little bottle, also a small oriental box inlaid with differently colored woods. We were sitting around the table and the pills were counted out for each voyager. A.K. had gotten over the shock of meeting Olson and the toy pistol and was in fine spirits, watching intently. When the last person had taken his potion, A.K. reached over and said, Let me go along too. He took ten tablets and washed them down with his drink. So he did, perched on his stool, while the dance went on around us to the lively strain of the strings. The ship cast off.

We sat listening to the hi-fi. Its effect was enlivening and delightful. Light conversation. Olson was spread out over the couch, center of a giggling admiring group, as though one were filled with gas.

We who had shared the psychotomimetic cocktail session at the Ritz and had no longer any gravity were reviewing the day's events quietly. The soft peace of the mushroom began to descend. Jangled, racing minds began to purr smoothly. Every moment we felt ourselves growing lighter and more serene. The few words spoken were concise Zen Koans, questions answered in the asking. From far away came Pablo's warm voice. A candle flame on the circular table flickered softly saying, It is a pleasure to me, my dear Harry, to have a Spanish guitar concerto, pure notes of thin steel and the privilege of being your host in a small way on this occasion.

Olson played gestural games with a sofa cushion. A quietly circling thread of closeness wove us together. You have often been sorely weary of your life. When eyes met, they sent rays of amused understanding. You were striving, were you not? So here we are. Born and dying together. A longing to forsake this world and its reality. The incredible accidental—chance nature of our existence, our sharing this quick intersection in astrophysical space-time to penetrate to a reality more native, to a world beyond time. The glance of recognition. We love, we love, we are all burnished copper atoms—conductive—on the same humming wire of energy. We know, of course, where this other world lies hidden.

Nancy and Frank Barron were looking into each other's eyes. It is the world of your own soul that you seek. They rose. Nancy laughed and did a swirling dance, radiant, and then they were gone.

Bach's ivory ping-pong ball bouncing precise down steel-wire tympanic membrane. Only within yourself exists that other reality for which you long. Rhona and Lynn giggling fondly at Olson's Mohawk Sachem funny chiefness. A.K., lost in harmonic nets strung aloft. I can give you nothing that has not already its being within yourself. The room rolling gently to ocean-swells of vibration. I can throw open to you no picture gallery but your own soul. Look, he is rewriting an earlier book in a river of peace.

We are all burnished copper atoms; your rational mind need not crouch on humming wires of energy. All I can give you is the opportunity, the impulse, the key. A.K.'s face was now a rich purple. Moving in like a cross-examiner, A.K., haunting eyes and furrowed face-skin, was supporting the weight of the universe. Bach's ivory ping-pong balls drowning out, his lips moving rapidly. I help you to make your own world visible. That is all. He puffs and pants up the steep path groaning. But no one is listening.

Rhona and Lynn giggling fondly at Olson's bridges of silence. Waterfalls of thin steel notes muffling mind words.

Now I will conduct you to my peep-show and show you my little theater. Will you come? PRESSURE-COOKER MYSTICISM. A.K.'s soundless face began to declaim about the ordeal completed. The mind by definition is anti-ecstasy. This little theater of mine has as many doors into as many boxes as you please. A piece of chamber music played. He was explaining that two times two is pressure-cooker mysticism but no one listened. Ten or a hundred or a thousand, and behind each door exactly what you seek awaits you. This struck me as obscene, more so than four-letter words. IN THE

WRONG KIND

Poor Dr. P. and his nice colleagues had to endure what they would call a "negative transference," and serve as projection screens for the lantern slides of the past, stored in the mental underground. Thus I was a rather unfortunate choice for a guinea pig—except perhaps to demonstrate what mushroomland can do to the wrong kind of guinea pig; and I suspect that a sizable minority of people who try for a chemical lift to Heaven, will find themselves landed in the other place.

I do not want to exaggerate the small risks involved in properly supervised experiments for legitimate research purposes; and I also believe that every clinical psychiatrist could derive immense benefits from a few experiments in chemically-induced, temporary psychosis, enabling them to see life through their patients' eyes. But I disagree with the enthusiast's belief that mescalin or psilocybin, even when taken under the most favourable conditions, will provide artists, writers, or aspiring mystics with new insights, or revelations of a transcendental nature.

I profoundly admire Aldous Huxley, both for his philosophy and uncompromising sincerity. But I disagree with his belief that drugs can procure "what Catholic theologians call a gratuitous grace." Chemically-induced raptures may be frightening or wonderfully gratifying; in either case they are in the nature of confidence tricks played on one's own nervous system.

NO MERIT

I think I understood the reason for this when I took the mushroom the second time, under more happy and relaxed conditions. This was in the apartment of my Harvard friend; there were six of us in a convivial atmosphere. We all took various amounts of the pill, and this time I took a little more (either 22 or 24 mg. for I lost count).

Again there were delusions: the room expanded and contracted in the most extraordinary manner, like an accordion played slowly, but the faces around me changed only slightly and in a pleasant way, becoming more beautiful. Then came the Moment of Truth: a piece of chamber music played on a tape recorder. I had never heard music played like that before, I suddenly understood the very essence of music, the secret of its magic. . . .

Unfortunately, I was unable to tell the next day whether it had been a quartet or a quintet or a trio, and whether by Mendelssohn or Bach. I may just as well have listened to Liberace. It had nothing to do with genuine appreciation of music; my soul was steeped in cosmic schmalz.

BELOVED AUSTRIAN MOUNTAINS OF MY SCHOOL DAYS IT IS A PRETTY CABINET OF PICTURES, MY DEAR FRIEND. A small figure, compact and coherent, soundlessly lectures astride the Asian bull. It would be quite useless for you to go through it as you are. TOOK US FOUR OR FIVE HOURS TO CLIMB TO THE 7,000-FOOT PEAK. Sober self-control! You would be checked and blinded at every turn by what you are pleased to call your personality. A small compact figure, Jewish, Hungarian, Austrian, now standing in front of the group, gesticulating earnestly.

You have no doubt guessed long since that the conquest of time and the escape from reality, words, it seemed hell to you, came from nowhere and flowed nowhere, or however else it may be that you choose to describe your longing. PUFFING AND PANTING UP THE STEEP PATH. Rhona and Lynn and Olson look up curiously at the frail cortex explaining, ordering, labeling everything. Meaning simply the wish to be relieved of your so-called personality. NO MERIT. There he was, face-to-face with what he feared, an American writer whom he otherwise liked. That is the prison where you lie. DRUGS ON THE BRAIN. A.K. breathed heavily. THE VIRTUE OF SWEAT AND TOIL. You are therefore requested to be so kind as to leave your highly esteemed personality here where you will find it again. In making use of such outmoded self-congratulation and dubious tools, my soul was steeped in cosmic schmaltz. Be as jolly as you can. WRONG KIND.

The virtue of sweat groans under the load. To teach you to laugh is the whole aim. What is he talking about? Questioning glances. You feel quite well, I trust? ZEN ENLIGHTENMENT SEEMED THE ULTIMATE PROFANATION. Not afraid? That's good, excellent. Come, dear compact figure; join the thread of closeness weaving us together. REPROACH OF ARTIFICIALITY, HUXLEY. Gesticulates, face cut out of cardboard. You will now, without fear and with wonderful pleasure, enter our visionary world. YOU AMERICANS! DRUGS ON THE BRAIN. AMERICAN EFFICIENCY SHORT-CUTS COSMIC AWARENESS. You will introduce yourself to it by means of a trifling suicide.

Their intersection in astrophysical space-time is different from those who arrive by motorcar. WRONG

KIND. We are in a magic theater: a world of pictures. So I again walked out of the show by forcing my eyes to open. I congratulated myself on my sober self-control, a rational mind not to be fooled by a little Moment of Truth. See that you pick out beautiful and cheerful ones and show that you really are not in love with your highly questionable personality any longer. Good night. A.K. waved, face crinkling in parochial pride. He left the room. For madmen only? Long moments followed the departure. Bach's stringed clock ticked song of planetary motion. In dead silence. He was gone.

Fearing a return of Michigan paranoia, I followed after. Knocked softly at his door. Barron's merry voice shouts come in. Barron? In Arthur Koestler's room? Entered. I WAS GREATLY CHEERED AT FINDING THAT I COULD ESCAPE FROM THAT CURSED WOLF WORLD AND WENT IN. Barron jolly. We didn't know this was K's room. We just fell into the first room we saw. K came in to go to bed. You should have seen his face when he saw us. I KEPT REPEATING TO MYSELF, BUT THESE ARE NICE FRIENDLY PEOPLE, THEY ARE YOUR FRIENDS, AND SO FORTH. Was he upset? No. I'd say startled. Very apologetic. Where'd he go? Don't know. Backed out muttering forgiveness.

Checking guest rooms down the hall. Arthur. Arthur. Knocking softly, Arthur. I still knew him well enough, and he still bore a faint resemblance and yet he had grown a few centuries older. Yes? Is it you, Pablo? Come in. Where are we? A.K. was in bed. Giggling. Radiating pleasure. High. We are in my Magic Theater. Sailing high. But I'm bound to say, Harry, you have disappointed me a little. Life is a song. Life is beautiful. Life is the golden dream of a lotus princess on a bed of lilies. You forget yourself badly.

The next morning when I woke him up to start the round of Harvard appointments, A.K. sat up in bed. Those pills last night didn't affect me at all. You broke through the humor of my little theater and tried to make a mess of it.

In times of strife, crossing the great water is to be avoided, that is, dangerous enterprises are not to be begun, because in order to be successful they re-

I sobered up, though, when a fellow mushroom-eater —an American writer whom otherwise I rather liked— began to declaim about Cosmic Awareness, Expanding Consciousness, Zen Enlightenment, and so forth. This struck me as obscene, more so than four-letter words, this pressure-cooker mysticism seemed the ultimate profanation. But my exaggerated reaction was no doubt also mushroom-conditioned, so I went to bed.

AN ANSWER

In "Heaven and Hell," defending the mescalin ecstasy against the reproach of artificiality, Huxley, the most highly respected exponent of the cult, argues that, in one way or another, *all* our experiences are chemically conditioned; and that the great mystics of the past also worked systematically to modify their body chemistry . . . starving themselves into low blood sugar and a vitamin deficiency. . . . They sang interminable psalms, thus increasing the amount of carbon dioxide in the lungs and the bloodstream, or, if they were Orientals, they did breathing exercises to accomplish the same purpose.

There is, of course, a certain amount of truth in this on a purely physiological level, but the conclusions which Huxley draws, and the advice he tenders to modern man in search of a soul, are all the more distressing: "Knowing as he does . . . what are the chemical conditions of transcendental experience, the aspiring mystic should turn for technical help to the specialists in pharmacology, in bio-chemistry, in physiology and neurology." I would like to answer this with a parable. In the beloved Austrian mountains of my school days, it took us about five to six hours to climb a 7,000-foot peak. Today, many of them can be reached in a few minutes by cable-car or ski-lift, or even by motorcar. Yet you still see thousands of schoolboys, middle-aged couples and elderly men puffing and panting up the steep path, groaning under the load of their knapsacks. When they arrive at the alpine refuge near the summit, streaming with sweat, they shout for their traditional reward—a glass of schnapps and a plate of hot pea-soup. And then they look at the view—and then there is only a man and a mountain and a sky.

My point is not the virtue of sweat and toil. My point is that, although the view is the same, their vision is different from those who arrive by motorcar.

∞

quire concerted unity of forces. Conflict within weakens the power to conquer danger without. (I Ching VI)

The next evening on the way home A.K. bought two bottles of French wine, chosen with care, a flask of Scotch, and, gently from behind clenched teeth, asked: And if I do not submit? We sat in the library starting to work on the whisky. K held up his glass and shook it with an icy tinkle. And if I deny your right, Mozart, to interfere with the Steppenwolf, and to meddle in his destiny? I'll stick to my drug. Alcohol is a social stimulant. It warms you up; brings you closer to people. Mushrooms are non-social. They whirl you inside. Bring you closer to yourself. Give me alcohol any day.

Oh, dear Arthur, I'm bound to say I thought you had learned the game better.

Next day as we walked into the airport building at Logan field to see him off, A.K. made his final comment. You must admit that these drugs cause psychosis. A temporary psychosis. I'm bound to say, Harry, you broke through the humor of my little theater. A benign and educational psychosis, if you will. Would you say it's therapeutic? Therapeutic. Of course. That's what the effect should be called. TTP. INSTANT MYSTICISM. Temporary therapeutic psychosis.

The metal ramp was wheeled away and the metal door closed. Four motors roared, and the huge metal-magic bird lumbered down the concrete strip.

There he went in the aluminum box. Did he understand Pablo? Mozart? Had a glimpse of its magic stirred his reason? Would he sample its tortures once more? Traverse once more the hell of inner being?

Would he one day learn to laugh? Would I? Pablo was waiting for us both. And Mozart too.

I drove back to Harvard and went by Frank Barron's office to tell him about my disappointment. Why hadn't we been able to turn-on Arthur Koestler?

Frank pulled at his chin thoughtfully. Koestler was lonely last night. Koestler is a man and a man needs a woman. Everyone else at the session had a mate. He was left out. Behind all this psychology and science business there are basic issues of life which you have to take account of. If you ignore them you'll always be disappointed in your sessions. God and sex are always with us.

Frank Barron's wry comments focused on an aspect of the psychedelic experience that I wasn't ready to come to terms with. It was becoming glaringly obvious that extraordinary sexual energies could be released.

Frank was right. God and sex are the two central beats of the dance. The mind muffles and disguises the reality tune. Blow the mind and you are left with God and life—and life is sex.

This was obvious in my first trip in Mexico—languorous Mandy melting and the deep lingering of the Cherokee princess, Betty.

Whenever trouble appeared in a session, it meant isolation from God and mate. The fear, the confusion, could always be calmed by prayer or loving fleshly contact.

The raw, electric, shuddering sensitivity of the psychedelic experience! We were dealing with a powerful aphrodisiac, probably the most powerful sexual releaser known to man. The effect was sensory—contact was intensified thousand-fold but also deeper. The union was not just your body and her body but all of your racial and evolutionary entities with all of hers. It was mythic mating. Neurological union. Cellular sex. Archetypes merging. It was the direct reliving of thousands of matings. She was an insect-queen buried deep in the damp tunnels of the ant hill humming with genetic energy and you burrowed down dark to find her. She was a bird of plumage trembling in the thicket for your feathered embrace. She was a taxi-dancer from Alexandria.

The psychedelic drugs exploded sex right off the pages of *Playboy* into new dimensions of union that my mind wasn't ready to handle.

And what was more awesome still was the after-effect. You came out of a session with changed emotions. New attractions and repulsions developed. There was the session with the graduate student couple. He wandered around murmuring ecstatically about his new insights into space, time, meaning. She lay by the fire with her arms over her

From *Steppenwolf* by Herman Hesse:

We joined him when he beckoned and in the doorway he said to me in a low voice: Brother Harry, I invite you to a little entertainment. For madmen only, and one price only—your mind. Are you ready?

Again I nodded.

The dear fellow gave us each an arm with kind solicitude, Hermine his right, me his left, and conducted us upstairs to a small round room that was lit from the ceiling with a bluish light and nearly empty. . . .

Why then was Hermine so white? Why was Pablo talking so much? Was it not perhaps I who made him talk, spoke, indeed, with his voice? Was it not my own soul that contemplated me out of his black eyes like a lost and frightened bird? . . .

My friends, I have invited you to an entertainment that Harry has long wished for and of which he has long dreamed. The hour is a little late and we are all slightly fatigued. So, first, we will rest and refresh ourselves a little.

From a recess in the wall he took three glasses and a quaint little bottle, also a small oriental box inlaid with differently colored woods. He filled the three glasses from the bottle and, taking three long thin yellow cigarettes from the box and a box of matches from the pocket of his silk jacket, he gave us a light. And now we all slowly smoked the cigarettes whose smoke was as thick as incense, leaning back in our chairs and slowly sipping the aromatic liquid whose strange taste was so utterly unfamiliar.

Its effect was immeasurably enlivening and delightful— as though one were filled with gas and had no longer any gravity. Thus we sat peacefully exhaling small puffs and taking little sips at our glasses, while every moment we felt ourselves growing lighter and more serene.

From far away came Pablo's warm voice.

It is a pleasure to me, dear Harry, to have the privilege of being your host in a small way on this occasion. You have often been sorely weary of your life. You were striving, were you not, for escape? You have a longing to forsake this world and its reality and to penetrate to a reality more native to you, to a world beyond time. You know, of course, where this other world lies hidden.

head murmuring his name. When he ignored her, her soft eyes moved around the room and her body twisted in search. She looked at me and smiled. Then she unfolded and swam towards me. Her husband was standing looking out the window. Her husband. His wife. Now she was all-woman receptive earth; tomorrow she would be reincarnated as a pretty graduate student. I retreated behind the couch.

After their second session they separated and she married the man whose image she brought back from her psychedelic trip.

It was almost inevitable that the guide of the session would be seen as God and lover. When the mind is suspended you project on the calm person who has turned you on, all the attributes of divinity and eternal malehood.

We called this process of new attraction-repulsion *re-imprinting*. The persons you turned-on fell in love with you or never wanted to see you again. I have never met Arthur Koestler since his trip. Allen Ginsberg has been my soul brother since his trip.

In the first two months of our Harvard psychedelic research seven women followed me home— much as the baby ducklings followed Conrad Lorenz—and announced their love.

For many reasons I was not ready in 1961 to face the sexual potentials of psychedelic drugs.

I was awed and confused by the sexual power. It was too easy. I was too much an Irish Catholic, too prudish to deal with it. Too Western Christian to realize that God and Sex are one, that God for a man is woman, that the direct path to God is through the divine union of male-female.

Besides, I was still involved in being a scientist. Too weighted by the duties and responsibilities to enjoy the newly opened paradise. I was too much an intellectual. I wanted to understand before plunging in. I felt a moral obligation to Harvard University—a good place on this dark planet. How could I enjoy the ultimate sexual-sensual experience in my study and square it with my scholarly position? How could I be consumed by ecstasies undreamed of by oriental kings and return to my Harvard Square office the next morning.

It was there—this tender garden of divine bliss—and I was voyaging towards it, but while I held my Harvard position I held to a self-imposed, ridiculous renunciation. I didn't turn-on with the slim brown model. I watched the Arab girl leave with questioning regret in her black eyes. I gave mushrooms to the honest, soft Joan, which she used to turn-on one of her suitors whom she married. I let the Cherokee princess drift away clothed in a leather facade that yearned to be moistened.

My sexual yoga was to start in 1964, after I learned to come to my senses with Holy Marijuana, after I listened to and learned from my tantric guru with the Siva tiger skin, after I dropped out of Harvard and psychology, resurrected my body, and moved on the journey to the East.

Beloved Arthur, forgive my clumsy in-no-sense. Forgive our isolating theater set. Make your next trip up the mountain with Shakti and the two will be won.

It is the world of your own soul that you seek. Only within yourself exists that other reality for which you long. I can give you nothing that has not already its being within yourself. I can throw open to you no picture gallery but your own soul. All I can give you is the opportunity, the impulse, the key. I can help you to make your own world visible. That is all.

CONFLICT. *You are sincere*
And are being obstructed.
A cautious halt halfway brings good
  fortune.
Going through to the end brings
  misfortune.
It furthers one to see the great man.
It does not further one to cross the
  great water.

(I Ching)

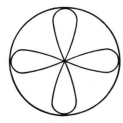

The Random Spinning of the Mind
Must Be Centered by Prayer:

February 1961

Guide: RICHARD ALPERT

Oracle: XXV

Innocence (The Unexpected)

The Creative, Heaven

The Arousing, Thunder

Under heaven thunder rolls:
All things attain the natural state of innocence.
Thus the kings of old,
Rich in virtue, and in harmony with the time,
Fostered and nourished all beings.

(I Ching)

We had been running psychedelic sessions—two and three a week—sitting for eight hours while voyagers went out of their minds, holding their hands, murmuring supportive words (prayers) while they wrestled with the terror, and then watching them break through and roam free out beyond symbols. Breaking through! Wow! I've made it! I've arrived! So this is what it's all about! God! God! Yes, I understand! What a fool I've been! It's so beautiful! What a mess we make of it! Where is the ice? And how is Lucifer thus fastened upside down? This is what the Bible meant. It's all true. Oh, God! Thank God! I see the spirit descending from heaven like a dove! It's all one! We're all a part! It flows! It's all love. It's all a game back there. Why do we play it so grimly? How funny!

It was glorious work, this guiding trips, but draining and disillusioning. There was no way to predict where, in the million rooms of the ancient cerebral museum, the tripper would go.

Consciousness, when freed from the mental chessgame, is completely vulnerable, completely reactive. The slightest accidental event would spin awareness off on a wild careen. Any action by any person in the session would dominate the direction. Some method of centering, gyroscoping the unpredictable rocket, was needed.

The mind itself is such a limiting structure. The DNA code produces fleshly bodies composed of trillions of cells, infiltrated with billions of sensory cameras, integrated by a nervous system whose capacity for reception and storage of images is literally infinite. You can have an image of an image. A thought about a thought.

The nervous system is an uncontrollable galaxy of mirrors within mirrors. The mind is a neurological method for screening out all but a few redun-

158

dant, static, conditioned, socially consensual ideas. The mind is the repetitious narcotic, addictive, redundant neural looping designed by the DNA code to limit consciousness. Like heroin focuses the behavior of a junkie, so does the mind focus the billion-fold avalanche of neurological activity.

During the psychedelic experience the heavy shackles of the mind are loosened. And then what? On the plus side, consciousness is free to move in any direction; but on the minus side, consciousness becomes helplessly vulnerable—can be swung by the slightest pressure. A frown. A gesture. A word . . . and whoom! you are catapulted into unexpected orbit.

This being a guru for metaphysical voyages was turning out to be a complex and demanding task. It's a lot easier to be a holy man if your sacrament doesn't work. You just keep exhorting and threatening and promising and, of course, blaming the failure on the shortcomings of the disciple.

A sacrament which does work presents the challenge for the guide. How can the visions be channeled? How can low-level paranoias and accidental orbits be avoided? How can the revelations be made to endure?

Oh poet, I beseech you . . . lead me where you said but now awhile, so that I may behold St. Peter's gate. Then he moved on: I followed in his steps. . . . (Inferno II)

The ecstatic trip can be diverted by any transient event. The satori doesn't seem to last. There is always the person's mind ready to explain away paradise and pull him back to the old egocentric game.

The rigidity of the normal mind was so different from the complete openness and vulnerability of the psychedelic situation.

This suggestibility, which had obvious implications for brainwashing, conversion, sudden behavior change, was illustrated in Richard Alpert's first session.

I woke late that morning. Out the window, gray skies and swirling gusts of snow. It had been coming down all night. The drifts in the driveway were two feet high and three feet by the garage door. We were snowbound.

After dinner Jack ran into the room, smiling and shouting. Guess who's here! I could hear Sue yipping in pleasure and when I got to the hallway, there was Dick Alpert with an arctic coat and fur gloves and boots plastered with snow, hugging the kids and filling the house with good feeling.

We all trooped into the kitchen and stood him on a chair and Sue broomed off his trousers and Dick shouted, No sir, Jack, don't use the toilet brush. We were all laughing. Later Dick and I were sitting at the kitchen table drinking beer and talking about the sacred mushrooms.

Dick was fascinated by the psychedelic research and eager to join. The first step for him was, of course, to start his own training. Learn how to explore the rooms of his own consciousness. When? Why not start now. Now? Are you ready?

When I got up from my chair, he said, Oh, you really mean right now, and I said, Whenever you take them it's right now. I came down with the bottle and counted out six and poured them in Dick's hand and said, Chew them, and without pausing in the story he was telling, Dick popped them in his mouth. They taste great. Then he went on with the story. I took six, and a few minutes later Charlie came in grinning expectantly and refused politely twice before taking his six.

They hit me
first and
fast.
The eerie physical chill
Room beginning to glow
Talk becoming underwater
Gurgling.
About fifteen minutes later Dick started to look silly and happy and Charlie's big pink cheeks began to radiate, and the gray green under his eyes, and we were all roaring with laughter, high, happy, drunken eagles. The kids burst into the kitchen in great spirits and the kitchen was exploding with love and family noise and chuckles, and Jack began to tell one of his endless stories. Sue was curled up

in a kitchen chair reading a book about *What To Do on Dates with Boys,* with her hands in her ears pretending to be annoyed by the clatter. Rhona left with Charlie. Dick and I were roaring away. Jack left and then Sue left, and her friend Judy followed her, and Dick suddenly stopped laughing and the room was suddenly silent. Hey! Where did everyone go? Why did they leave? AROUND THE NORTH POLE LIES A VAST EXPANSE OF ICE AND SNOW Did I say something wrong? Are they angry? FOR WEEKS THERE IS NO SUN. THE TEMPERATURE IS FAR BELOW ZERO. Dick and I were deserted and frightened. Condemning silence. . . . A cold wind swept across the kitchen. WHITE EXPLORERS HAVE RARELY BEEN ABLE TO WITHSTAND THE FIERCE, RAW BLEAKNESS OF THE ARCTIC. Charlie's coming back, though. Look, he left his cigarettes. But why has he taken so long? He's been gone for hours. I looked up at the clock hands which had moved five minutes in the last eight hours. Psychedelic time. He's gone from present time so he's been gone for centuries.

The door opened and we both looked up hopefully. Charlie! Surge of relief. Where the hell have you been? I went upstairs to take a leak. But why did you take so long? Long? I was gone for two minutes. Psychedelic time.

Jack was back with Champ the dog. Champ had been a nuisance all night. Romping with the cat. Barking when Jack teased him. Knocking over the cat's milk bowl. Too much big, brown, romping animal in crowded kitchen. Twice Rhona had put him down in the cellar, and twice Jack had indignantly brought him back. Charlie was mad at Champ for leaving a turd on the guest-room rug. When Jack went upstairs, I put Champ outside. Dogs love the snow.

Dick and I went back to mushroom talk. Enter Jack, accusing. Where's Champ now? We put him outside to run in the snow. Jack went out the hallway scolding us. The snow must have looked good to him. He announced that he was going to go out and run in the drifts with Champ. He went to get dressed and then was back with us, booted and gloved and his hood over his face, beaming with pleasure. I watched my son running highlegged

CONTROVERSIAL ECSTASY DRUGS—MIRACLE OR KEY TO HELL?

HARVARD DRUG RESEARCHERS DEPORTED FROM MEXICO

LSD PARADISE LOST

DRUG RESEARCH AND RELIGION

SEEDY VISION—MORNING-GLORY BOOM BEING PROBED BY FDA

SUDDEN RUSH ON MORNING-GLORY SEEDS SPARKS DRUG PROBE

STUDENTS ARE WARNED AGAINST DRUGS

DREAM DRUGS AREN'T SWEET

MENTAL ILLNESS DRUG STALEMATE SEEN

TWO MD'S URGE CURB ON SALE OF UNITY DRUG

DISCUSSION OF LSD'S ROLE IN RELIGION

LSD ADVOCATES RENT MANSION IN MILLBROOK

NEW DRUG FAD

DRUG RESEARCHERS TURN TO MYSTICISM

DRUG CULT LIVES QUIET LIFE ON ESTATE

through the deep drifts, with Champ floundering behind him, barking and tail wagging. Heartbreaking great scene. Boy, dog, snow, satori.

We were back on the Buddhist-humor jag. I was telling Dick the history of the mushroom research and the people wanting to get high for science, or to do science in order to get high, and I mentioned the name Jack and right then the door opened and there was Jack, thumping off snow, ready to enter stage left, and I helped him get off his coat and gloves and I zipped down one of his boots and found it stuffed with snow and I zipped it right back up again and said, Take this snow back to the fellow what made it, we don't want it here, and everyone laughed and Jack said, Come on Dad, and Jack started telling his snow saga, how the drifts were higher than Champ and how Champ would disappear in the snow and how hard it was for poor Champ to jump from one hole to the next drift.

Champ had Jack's sock in his mouth and when Jack pulled it out there was blood on the sock. We were alarmed but Jack calmed us down. Oh, that's nothing, I bleed all the time. When we heard this we began to laugh. Jack was pleased by the laughter but embarrassed. He shouted, Here Champie, Champie, come on Champie, and ran into the living room and when I came to ask him, Where do you bleed all the time, he was running round and round the long sofa chasing Champ.

When we all got back to the kitchen I sat down. From behind the chair there came a fast panting series of whooshing sounds. What's that queer noise? Jack shrugged. Just Champ breathing hard. He's tired. Exit Jack to watch TV with girls. Back to the mushroom tales. We were building up to unbearable good humor, putting our heads on the table to control the bodyshaking chuckles.

Then I found myself looking at the dog. Champ was lying by the sink. His face was drawn back tight and strained, teeth gleaming, horrible crazy grin, and his body was shaking in fast, frantic breathing. Horrid wolf leer. Eyes bulging. God, that dog is sick, look at him. Laughter stops. Wow, you're right. Look at him breathe. He's having a fit.

We were all leaning forward. Looks like the first stage of distemper to me. Champ lay on his side, ribs heaving, eyes glaring, lips pulled back. Maybe it's rabies, said Dick. Don't they froth and spit blood. Blood, yes, there was blood on the sock. Champ stretched his legs out stiff. Look, it's a convulsion.

Charlie's calm voice. You're crazy. The dog's all right. He's just exhausted from running in the snow.

Oh, yeah? Fatigue doesn't give a dog the fits. And he's been breathing heavy for ten minutes. I remember asking about that noise when he and Jack came back in. Has he had rabies shots? That's fatal to a human being if he bites you.

Charlie's voice. For God's sake, let's drop the dog issue and enjoy ourselves. He's had shots. He's not sick. He's just trying to rest and catch his breath.

I moved over near the dog. Here, Champ, come on boy. Champ wagged his tail weakly and got up. He walked slowly across the kitchen while we watched him in horror. His flanks were heaving with tortured gasps and when he got to the butler's pantry, to the far dark corner, he fell heavily and closed his eyes. THE SYMPTOMS ARE INITIAL FEVER WITH ITS ACCOMPANIMENTS, THIRST, LOSS OF APPETITE, HURRIED PULSE AND RESPIRATION.

Boy, that animal is really sick. EMACIATION, LANGUOR, DISINCLINATION TO MOVE. Go look and see if he is alive. Dick tiptoed to the pantry and poked his head around the door. He's still breathing hard. SOMETIMES THE LEGS ARE SWOLLEN AND THE ANIMAL IS STIFF.

Charlie was laughing. You guys slay me. You're the end. Look what the drug does to you. You go around and make a big production of everything. THERE IS GREAT DISINCLINATION TO MOVE: THE BODY SWAYS ON THE ANIMAL ATTEMPTING TO WALK. You worry when I go up to pee and now about the dog. Let's not ruin the fun. The dog is fine. I've raised dogs for years. I know when a dog is sick and when a dog is tired.

Dick tiptoed again to the pantry and peeped around the corner. Boy, look at him. If he isn't a sick, sick dog then I've never seen one. THERE IS NEARLY ALWAYS A DEEP, PAINFUL, AND HARASSING

A.M.A. CHIEF URGES LSD
CONTROLS

PRAISE OF LSD BLAMED
FOR USE

COLLEGE STUDENTS SAID
USING HALLUCINOGENIC
DRUGS

CRACKDOWN URGED ON
CAMPUS DRUG PARTIES

DR. LEARY'S DEFENSE A
SWINGING BEGINNING

ECSTASY DRUG GIVES
NEW INSIGHT TO REALITY

LSD: HOLLYWOOD'S
STATUS-SYMBOL DRUG

MIDNIGHT RAID ON
LEARY'S MANSION

THE LSD CULT

LSD—REVOLUTION IN
SENSATION

LEARY CASE IN HANDS
OF JURY

MILLBROOK DOCTOR
POSTS $2500 BOND

LSD HORRORS PICTURED
BY PSYCHIATRIST

CALIFORNIA BILL OUT-
LAWS LSD

LSD HALLUCINATION:
BLASTOFF TO TERROR

COUGH. I walked over to look. Champ was lying in a gray, ragged heap. His head rested on the floor. His jowls hung down. THE MEMBRANE LINING THE EYES ASSUMES A DULL LEADEN HUE. His eyes gleamed in helpless, begging misery. His sides heaved. You're right. I've never seen anything so sick. BUT THE CHARACTERISTIC SYMPTOMS ARE A GRAYISH YELLOW DISCHARGE FROM ONE OR BOTH NOSTRILS.

Dick was looking intently into the pantry. God, look! There's mucus dripping from his nose. Mucus? Oh, he's dying. Mucus? Well, maybe it's just the breath from his nose. THE DISCHARGE FROM THE NOSE ADHERES TO THE NOSTRILS AND UPPER LIP. Charlie hooted again. Sure it's breath from his nose. It's air. Don't you want the poor tired dog to breathe. You guys are too much. AND THE INFIL- TRATED NASAL LINING, IMPEDING BREATHING, CAUSES SNIFFLING AND FREQUENT SNORTING. Dick becomes the executive. Look. This is serious. The dog may be dying and we're all drugged to the ears and we're snowbound and can't get a car out. It's one o'clock and that's late to call a vet and the vet couldn't get here through the snow anyway. IN UNFAVORABLE CASES THE FEVER INCREASES, AS WELL AS THE PROSTRATION. We've got to pull ourselves together, this is serious. He was right. I was think- ing the same thing myself. I burst into uncontrol- lable laughter. THE BREATHING BECOMES LABORED. AUSCULTATION AND PERCUSSION INDICATE THAT THE LUNGS ARE SERIOUSLY INVOLVED. I tried to talk about how serious it was but I was laughing so hard that the words wouldn't come out. The rest of them were howling in laughter, too. CLOTS SOMETIMES FORM IN THE PLEURA OR HEART. It's serious, you're right, he's terribly sick. Compulsive chuckles.

I walked into the pantry. Champ was a limp, boneless mass on the floor. His bright, gleaming brown coat had changed to a gray-black drab. He seemed to have shriveled. His fur was moist and pulpy. THE SUFFERING ANIMAL ALWAYS APPEARS EXACTLY AS IT IS AND FEELS. I put my hand on his tortured head and the eyes opened and the tail wagged feebly. Oh God, he's begging for help and we're helpless. WITHOUT THE INTERVENTION OF MIND OBSCURING THE SYMPTOMOLOGY.

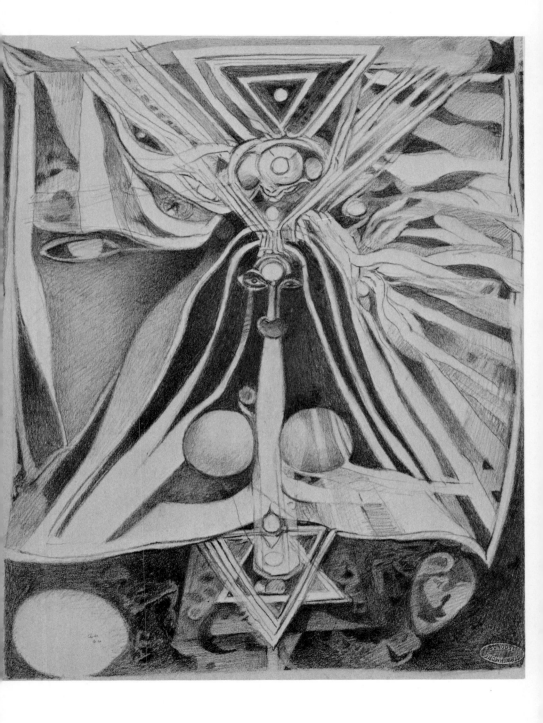

FATHER CHARGES TRAF-
FIC IN LSD AT HIGH
SCHOOL

IS DRINKING SQUARE
IN THE YOUNG SET?

LSD—SHINING PROMISE
—BROKEN GOAL

200 FEDERAL AGENTS
TRAINED TO CRUSH
LSD USE

U.N. DEMANDS LSD CURB

MANY STUDENTS USE
LSD LIKE BEER, SURVEY
REVEALS

WORLD CURBS ON LSD
URGED

TEEN-AGER REVEALS
LSD LAUNCH PAD

D.A. DROPS NARCOTICS
CHARGES ON LEARY

LSD PROF BEATS DOPE
RAP

CONSTITUTION PRO-
TECTS LSD CULT LEADER

LSD—AVANT-GARDE
CULT OR REVERSION TO
SAVAGERY?

DR. LEARY ASKS: WHAT
AM I BEING CHARGED
WITH? GETS NO ANSWER

LSD—NATION'S GROW-
ING TERROR

At the table Dick was pronouncing diagnosis. It's my opinion that we have a sick, sick dog on our hands. (That animal is so weak he doesn't have the power to lift himself to his feet.) ANIMAL SYMPTOMS BEING REALLY AND TRULY THE RIGOROUS EXPRESSION OF ITS DISEASED CONDITION. Well, what shall we do? Puff, puff on pipe. I think we should wait and let nature take its course. He may pull out of it on his own. Dick looked very wise. I noticed Charlie stealing glances into the pantry. He was beginning to look worried. Sure. I know dogs. They get sick and crawl off to rest and don't want to be bothered and they sleep it off. He just doesn't want to be bothered. We can't do anything anyway. THE CONTAGIOUS DISEASES OF THE DOG ARE FEW, BUT THE ONE WHICH ATTRACTS THE MOST ATTENTION IS COMMON AND GENERALLY SERIOUS. THIS IS WHAT IS POPULARLY KNOWN AS DISTEMPER.

Someone had closed the pantry door but we couldn't close out the thought of the animal dying in the next room while we argued helplessly and giggled. I walked over to the door and pushed into the pantry. DEBILITY RAPIDLY ENSUES AND EMACIATION IS SOON APPARENT. I was sure that the brown body would be lying there stiff and cold. No, the bedraggled rag was pulsing softly. He was alive, but just by a breath. His eyes were blank and glassy.

I came back to the kitchen and stood with my hand on the refrigerator. Well, what do you think? I frowned and spoke slowly, clipping my words. CONVULSIONS GENERALLY COME ON. The dog is sick, terribly sick and he'll be dead by morning. And I don't see one thing we can do about it—drugs or no drugs, snow or no snow. A long silence followed. IN FATAL CASES THE ANIMAL DIES IN A STATE OF MARASMUS. AS DOES THE AILING INFANT OR THE COMATOSE ADULT.

I got up. We need to call in a consultant. Let me go up and sound Jack out. Maybe he noticed something. Upstairs Sue and her friend and Jack were in pajamas in the TV room watching a twenty-year-old parlor comedy. Edward G. Robinson was a young-looking millionaire-host at a houseparty. I lay down next to Jack. His eyes were glued to the screen. When the commercial break came I started asking casual questions. No, he hadn't noticed anything wrong with Champ. Well, yes he had been breathing heavily. Were you worried about him? No. Are you worried now? No, well, a little if you're worried. Jack was watching the commercial and not very interested in talking. At the door I stopped. After the show is over, you guys come down to the kitchen. Sue nodded yes and blew a kiss to me, her eyes still on the TV.

Downstairs Dick had the yellow section of the phone book in his hand. THE RARE INSTANCES IN WHICH ANIMALS CAN BE SEEN BY THE VETERINARY SURGEON. He was cross-examining Charlie. Logically I *know* that Champ is all right. Maybe exhausted, but logically I'm convinced he's okay. Dick sighed in relief and reached behind to put the telephone book on the stove. *But,* emotionally, you guys have got me convinced that he's sick. IN THE EARLIEST STAGES OF THE DISEASE, AND WHEN THIS WOULD PROVE MOST AMENABLE TO MEDICAL TREATMENT. Dick's eyebrows raised and he sighed in pain and reached for the phone book.

Well, let's get our boots on and carry him down to the avenue and get a taxi. DELAY USUALLY DUE TO THE INABILITY OF THOSE WHO HAVE CARE OF THE ANIMAL TO PERCEIVE THESE EARLY STAGES. What a scene. Imagine it. Going to the vet's house. Waking him up. Three mushroomed escorts and the breathing dog. Well, we can give the vet some mushrooms. THE FACT THAT ANIMALS CANNOT, EXCEPT IN A NEGATIVE MANNER, TELL THEIR WOES, DESCRIBE THEIR SENSATIONS, OR INDICATE WHAT AND WHERE THEY SUFFER.

We'll wait until the kids come down and let them look at him and then we'll call the taxi. Charlie made some tea and we joked around, laughing, but not as hard as before. Then feet drumming on the back stairs. Enter the kids. THE VIOLENCE OR STUPOR, AS WELL AS THE ATTITUDE AND STRUCTURAL PECULIARITIES OF THE SICK CREATURE, WHICH ONLY TOO FREQUENTLY RENDER FAVORABLE POSITIONS FOR RECOVERY IMPOSSIBLE. Sue and her friend, dressed in white and blue, clown pajamas, teen-age dream girls and Jack in red pajamas, and his black hair

JURY INDICTS LEARY, OTHERS IN MILLBROOK DRUG CASE

LEARY ASKS HARVARD TO GIVE HIM BACK JOB

RAIDERS NAB LSD PROF IN MANSION

RAID MANSION—SEIZE LSD PROF

LSD PSYCHOLOGIST ARRESTED AGAIN

DR. LEARY STARTS NEW "RELIGION" WITH SACRAMENTAL USE OF LSD

DR. LEARY HOLDS FIRST SERVICE OF SECT

TIMOTHY LEARY— PSYCHO OR SAVIOR?

DR. LEARY ARRESTED AT LAGUARDIA ON NARCOTICS CHARGE

THIRD ARREST FOR LSD CULTIST

LEARY ASKS SUPREME COURT TO LEGALIZE PSYCHEDELIC "SACRAMENT"

BAPTIST MINISTERS LABEL DRUG RELIGION HERESY

JOHN BIRCH SPOKESMAN BLAMES LSD ON JEWS

HIGH COURT VOIDS LEARY DRUG SENTENCE ON RELIGIOUS GROUNDS

tousled. Have some hot chocolate, girls. Jack, perched on the kitchen stool, in high spirits telling us about the TV show. The girls moved around the kitchen opening the cocoa tin and the milk and stirring the milk on the stove. THE SLENDER MEANS FOR CARRYING OUT RECOMMENDATION, TOGETHER WITH THE OFTENTIMES INTRACTABLE NATURE OF THEIR DISEASES. The rest of us sat there enjoying their fun and feeling lousy about the horror in the pantry. I was thinking for sure that Champ was dead now and Dick said later that he was feeling the same thing. AS WELL AS THE UTILITARIAN INFLU- ENCES ALLUDED TO ABOVE—ALL THESE CONSIDERA- TIONS, IN THE GREAT MAJORITY OF INSTANCES, MILI- TATE AGAINST.

Noise from the pantry. Death convulsions. Champ struggling to his feet and walking slowly into the kitchen. Hardly enough strength to move. THE ADOPTION OF CURATIVE TREATMENT OR AT LEAST GREATLY INCREASE ITS DIFFICULTIES. He's coming out to die at the feet of the children. Jack looked down and saw Champ approaching. Champie! Come on old fellow. Good dog. Champ broke into a run, and his tail was wagging a mile a minute and he was wiggling in delight the way puppies and happy young dogs do and he jumped up, two paws against Jack, and Jack was rumpling his ears and Champ's tail was wagging so hard that when it bumped against my leg it kind of hurt and Susan shouted, Here, Champ, here, and the dog bounded across the room to her, squirming and wiggling, and I was staring with my mouth open and I looked over and saw the expression on Dick's face, stunned, and Charlie at the end of the table was grinning away in a disgusting smug manner and I began to laugh and Dick was laughing, all of us howling like idiots, and the kids looked up sur- prised and Susan began to frown her after-all- Daddy frown and I started to explain to the kids. Susan and Jack started laughing and by this time Champ was lying on the floor with a big bone grasped between his paws and was crunching and grinding away on it, his tail still wagging at all the noise and laughter.

So we were back on the cloud again and we rolled along for another three hours. I told Dick more about our early adventures as scientists tracking down the sacred mushrooms and we reviewed the great moments from past mushroom scenes and we were funny and wise to our hearts' content. At four o'clock Dick got his boots on and then stood for another hour rapping and laughing and we went to the front door and looked out down the long rolling front lawn all clean and glistening, and down at the trees hung heavy with white like a Christmas card etching, and Dick shook hands all around, grinning, and gave a shout and a big jump and started bounding down the snow slope and we stood watching him. When he reached the road below he waved up and we waved back.

Lying in bed, I tried to figure out what we had learned that night. First the value of ritual. I was beginning to see that there are many ways that sacred mushrooms can be used. Your ritual decides. The basic man-woman love scene. And then the tribal fiesta scene. Like the one we had those nights in Allen Ginsberg's pad with Kerouac. Or the great tribal love feast with the Dionysius from Gloucester. And then there's the deep visionary heavy-dose experience in which you don't want other people around at all except for the wise loving *curandero* to guide you back when you want to return.

And a second lesson. The size and shape of the room makes a difference. If we had been sitting in a line along the couch or scattered around the big living room, it wouldn't have swung so well. The idea of being enclosed together like in a submarine or in a spaceship or in the snowbound kitchen, pushed up close and facing each other around the table, closeness, intimacy, fighting the pull of the expanding disintegrating universe. When Beckett puts his characters on lovely wide beaches or deserted flat landscapes, he knows what he's doing. The separation and distance between his characters are heightened by the empty vistas. If you cram people together into smaller spaces, like molecules of gas, more heat generates in tighter quarters.

And a third lesson. For group rites you need a love leader. A guru. A guide. A spiritually hip person whose love and energy and output batteries are charged up, so that his voice and his wit and his

LSD PANIC IN VIETNAM

GOP SPOKESMAN ACCUSES KENNEDY OF USING LSD

KY AND HO JOIN TO DENOUNCE LSD INFILTRATION

TROOPS IN HANOI, SAIGON THROW DOWN GUNS

LSD CHAOS IN VIETNAM —FIGHTING STOPS

LBJ AND MAO MEET TO PLAN ANTI-LSD CAMPAIGN

LSD IN PENTAGON WATER COOLERS: MASS RELIGIOUS CONVERSIONS

KOSYGIN, RED BOSS, QUITS JOB TO BECOME MONK: LSD PSYCHOSIS BLAMED

LSD TO BE MAJOR CAMPAIGN ISSUE

RFK DEFENDS LSD; HUMPHREY DEMANDS PSYCHIATRIC EXAMINATION

CITY COUNCIL BANS AUTOS IN N.Y.; GRASS, FLOWERS TO GROW IN STREET

CATHOLIC, PROTESTANT, JEWISH BISHOPS HAIL RELIGIOUS BOON: OK LSD AS SACRAMENT

LSD CANDIDATES SWEEP SWEDISH ELECTION

YOUTHFUL VOTERS BACK
RFK: HUMPHREY, GOP
CALL FOR MARTIAL LAW

LSD ACCELERATES
LEARNING: TO BE USED
IN ALL HIGH SCHOOLS

DRAMATIC DROP IN
DIVORCE RATE ASCRIBED
TO LSD

ALCOHOLISM, CRIME
RATE ALMOST ELIMI-
NATED IN U.S.

MISSISSIPPI NEGROES,
WHITES INTEGRATE IN
LSD SCHOOLS

LSD CENTER IN MILL-
BROOK DECLARED
NATIONAL SHRINE

LSD COMMISSION DE-
NOUNCES USE OF
ELECTRONIC BRAIN
STIMULATION

EBS SCIENTIST DE-
NOUNCED AS NUT BY
LSD AUTHORITIES

ELECTRONIC BRAIN
STIMULATION CLAIMED
SAFE—BETTER THAN LSD

EBS CULT LEADER AR-
RESTED FOR UNAUTHOR-
IZED EXPERIMENTS

LEARY FOLLOWERS
DEMAND LAWS AGAINST
NEW MIND STIMULATORS

LSD SOCIETIES DERIDE
RELIGIOUS CLAIMS OF
EBS CULT

wisdom and his caring and his action keep the group consciousness from spinning off into eccentric whim.

Man has received from heaven a nature innately good, to guide him in all his movements. By devotion to this divine spirit within himself, he attains an unsullied innocence that leads him to do right with instinctive sureness and without any ulterior thought of reward and personal advantage. This instinctive certainty brings about supreme success and "furthers through perseverance." (I Ching XXV)

And a fourth lesson, and this one not really understood yet—the incredible suggestibility and the vulnerability of the brain. Under the psychedelic trip your cortex is washed clean of the rituals and clichés. The empty mind. So far so good. But then if the situation or some strong-minded person in the situation strikes a posture, spins out an idea, well, you are much more likely to accept it and you can't call on any of your past clichés to argue yourself out of it. Jack Kerouac was right when he warned about psychedelic brainwashing. Once the concept of sickness-death was introduced, we all climbed into it and saw disease and pain.

But what to do about this vulnerability? How could the trip be guided in the love-learning direction? What could serve as compass to orient the session when consciousness spins out beyond symbols? How could reminders, maps be brought along on the voyage? And exactly which maps and reminders could remain useful in those hurtling regions where routine game symbols were seen as your own consciousness talking back to yourself? The mocking mirror reflection of your own thought processes.

The answers to these questions (which were to preoccupy me for the better part of the next six years) are spiritual planning and prayer.

Planning the who, where, when, and why and how of the session. You don't make love in the turmoil of Times Square. Neither do you take LSD there. It's risky to make love with strangers. You don't have your mystical experiences with strangers. Six thousand years of sacred experimentation suggest how the environment can be arranged to produce the spiritual experience.

With whom? Alone or with essence friends who share your spiritual aims.

Where? In a setting free from secular distraction, profane pressure, accidental interruption. Since the dawn of human history such places have been the center of any civilized God-fearing way of life. They are called shrines, sacred groves, retreats, temples, holy places.

When? At a sacred time dedicated to the spiritual quest. A sacred time is selected not by man's mind but by the greater, older energies—seasonal, solar, lunar, planetary, menstrual.

Why? To find God. To divest all the leathery, metal, armor plating and lie naked, exposed, for God to find you. To die and be reborn.

How? Through prayer. Prayer is the art of communicative union with all your inner selves. Prayer is compass and gyroscope. Prayer is the language that makes sense to your eye, ear, nose, tongue, touch; to your heart (thump thump), to your lungs (inhale-exhale), to your bowels, to your genitals, to your ancient cells, to your ancient selves—hairy, fanged, clawed, scaled, reptile, amphibious, protozoic. Prayer is the energy language of God.

The history of our research on the psychedelic experience is the story of how we learned how to pray.

EBS CAUSED INSANITY, SUICIDE, SAYS LSD SPOKESMAN

HIGH-SCHOOL STUDENTS USING EBS FOR KICKS

TIMOTHY LEARY ENDORSES EBS: IS CALLED SENILE TRAITOR BY LSD COMMISSIONER

YOUTH GROUPS ATTACK LSD ORTHODOXY

EBS LEADERS TO DEMONSTRATE TELEPATHY IN WHITE HOUSE

GRAVE MORAL-PSYCHOLOGICAL PROBLEMS FORESEEN IN EBS TELEPATHY

LSD, EBS LEADERS JOIN ROSE FESTIVAL ON FIFTH AVENUE

∞

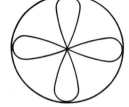

INNOCENCE. *Supreme success.*
Perseverance furthers.
If someone is not as he should be,
He has misfortune,
And it does not further him
To undertake anything.

(I Ching)

The Sacrament Can Liberate
the Imprisoned:

March 1961

Guide: WILLY (A BLACK JUNKIE)

Oracle: XLIX

Revolution (Molting)

The Joyous, Lake

The Clinging, Fire

Fire in the lake: the image of REVOLUTION.
Thus the superior man
Sets the calendar in order
And makes the seasons clear.

(I Ching)

Second Annual Report; Psilocybin Rehabilitation Project:

All the professional work on this project was volunteer. The expenses for clerical assistance and salaries for ex-inmate workers were covered by generous donations from The Uris Brothers Foundation, New York, and the Parapsychology Foundation, Eileen Garrett, President.

Applications to three offices of the U.S. Public Health Service requesting support for continuing this project were refused.

Exactly two years ago the Harvard Psilocybin Project initiated a research program at Massachusetts Correctional Institution, Concord, designed to test the effects of consciousness-expanding drugs on prisoner rehabilitation.

The project was designed as a pilot study—necessarily exploratory—since little was known about the long-range application of the substances.

During the fall and the winter of 1960, much of my time and energy was going into the study of the effects of the psychedelic mushrooms. I was also carrying on an active program of lecturing, teaching, and field work in clinical psychology in the Harvard Graduate School. I had been brought to Harvard in 1959 in order to introduce existential-transactional methods for behavior change. After fifteen years of practicing psychotherapy and about ten years of doing research on psychotherapy, I had come to the conclusion that there was very little that one person called a doctor could do for another person called a patient by talking to him across a desk, or listening to him as he lay on a couch. I developed a lot of theories and a lot of methods on how behavior change could be brought about more effectively than the standard clinical interview method.

There are two main points to the theories I developed; first (transactional) I was convinced that the doctor had to suspend his role and status as a doctor, had to join the other person actively and collaboratively in figuring out the solution to his problem. As much as possible, the doctor had to turn over the responsibility to the man who knew most about the problem at hand, namely, the patient. I developed many techniques for getting patients to help each other.

The second point in my theory (existential) was that the doctor has to leave the safety of his consulting room and get out there in the field where the so-called patient is having his unique problems, and where he is going to solve his problems. I saw the role of the doctor as that of a coach in a game in which the patient was the star player. The coach can help, can point out mistakes, can share his wisdom, but in the last analysis, the guy who does the job is the guy out there in the field, the so-called patient.

I was enthusiastic about these theories because they worked, and because no joy in teaching can equal that thrill which comes when you watch someone who's been hung up, and blocked, and confused, and making a mess of things out there in the field suddenly learn how. All this had started happening before I got involved in the drug research, and I had already become a controversial figure around the Boston area, because everything that I was saying made a tremendous amount of sense to students and patients, but the doctors, the psychiatrists, the social workers, the professors, the psychologists, were not so quick to accept these theories. I was asking them to give up the status and the omniscient position which they felt their training entitled them to. I asked them to turn over the authority and the star role in the game to the patient.

Times change, and with them their demands. Thus the seasons change in the course of the year. In the world cycle also there are spring and autumn in the life of peoples and nations, and these call for social transformations. (I Ching XLIX)

I was taking one day off a week to drive down with two or three graduate students to New Bedford, Massachusetts, where we were working in an orphanage, teaching social workers and nuns to set up groups in which older kids would help younger kids, and in which children at every age level were encouraged to take more responsibility for running the school and planning their lives.

We set up another project in a slum housing district in a Boston suburb. Here were hundreds of people who were bogged down socially and psychologically. They could not afford psychiatric help and there was none available for them. With another group of graduate students, I used to go down there one night a week with tape recorders and blackboards. We set up headquarters in one of the slum apartments and started teaching groups of the neighbors how they could help each other and

The key issue was the use of a consciousness-expanding drug; but equally important was the philosophy underlying the research, which emphasized:

DEMOCRATIC COLLABORATION:

Inmates were given responsibility for planning and evaluating the work. This was seen as preparation for assuming roles as responsible citizens in a democratic society.

SHARING OF INFORMATION:

The inmates were given all information relevant to their treatment. This was seen as a necessary step in increasing trust and self-respect.

SPIRITUAL INSIGHT:

The transcendental experience provided by the drugs propels the subject beyond space, time, ego, culture, etc. The implications of this visionary experience were utilized in the program.

INTERPERSONAL TRUST AND CLOSENESS:

Evidence shows that when subjects share an ego-shattering experience together they develop strong positive emotional bonds.

SELF-HELP AND MUTUAL
HELP:

The most successful re-
habilitation methods (A.A.,
Synanon group dynamic T
groups, etc.) seem to be
those which turn over re-
sponsibility to the subjects
themselves and which stim-
ulate them to help each
other. The drug experience
facilitates this tendency.

EMOTIONAL AND
PRACTICAL SUPPORT:

The model used was not
doctor-patient or expert-
client but that of human beings who believe in each
other and want to help each
other.

The project developed the
model of friends who are
available to help group
members stay out of trouble
and maintain a responsible
role in society.

In our research we helped
inmates get jobs, purchase
union cards, made small
loans and spent hours in
friendly advising interaction.

PROCEDURES:

Since its initiation, the project has operated under the
medical and psychiatric
supervision of Dr. W. Madison Presnell.

become psychiatrists for each other and develop
some facility for solving their own problems.

All this, of course, was very déclassé at Harvard.
Universities are supposed to be research institutes,
and if you get too involved in service functions or
helping people, you're considered a bleeding heart.
I was able to justify the work in the orphanage, the
work with alcoholics, the work in the slum projects,
by using the word methodology. We weren't
really trying to help these people. No sir, not us.
We were trying to develop new techniques and
scientific methods for changing psychotherapeutic
theory. Of course, if people enjoyed it and got help,
that was an interesting by-product which supported
the method and the theory. It was all experimental,
you see. It became a tradition in the center where I
worked that any time they got a call from a do-
good social service agency requesting Harvard's
help in curing any sort of social disease, the request
was likely to get bucked to me because they knew
that this was my vice and my eccentricity.

One day I got a note in my box saying that two
men from the Department of Legal Medicine were
interested in enlisting Harvard's help in the psychological rehabilitation of prisoners. Now prison work
is considered to be the least interesting, lowest
status work you can do in the field of psychology,
psychiatry, and sociology. The problems are hopeless. Criminals never change. The atmosphere is
dreary and the academic rewards are slim. But
when I found this little piece of paper in my box
requesting an appointment from two officials from
the Department of Legal Medicine, I chuckled all
the way to my office because this was just the
chance I was looking for.

By this time, we had given the psychedelic mushrooms to about a hundred people in a wide variety
of circumstances, and we had learned a lot about
the process. In spite of the bungling and the confusion and our ignorance, we still hadn't caused any
damage to anyone and there were a lot of mistakes
that we'd never make again. By this time we had
learned a few things about how to run the sessions.
About 90 percent of the people who were taking the
magic mushrooms were reporting the most ecstatic

and educational experience of their lives. The problem was, there was no way to get any measurement as to how much good we were doing. There was no way to keep score.

This of course is the main problem in the field of psychotherapy. You can develop a completely effective method of treating people's psychological problems, but there is no way you can prove it. You can work with one thousand people and help every one of them change his way of thinking and his way of acting, but there are no statistics (like hits, runs, and errors) with which to tabulate your score. The problem is that half the people you help are going to get better jobs, and half of them are going to quit the jobs they have. Half of them may increase the intimacy and closeness and meaning in their marriages, but the other half may leave their wives. Changing a person's psyche is one thing, but measuring results in an observable way is another thing. Because who's to say which behavior reflects growth and change.

Here's where the prison came in. The prison is the ideal place to do a study in psychotherapy behavior change, because when you try to rehabilitate prisoners, you've got an ironclad statistic you can work against. It's called the recidivism rate. When you are working with people outside, they may quit their job and join the Peace Corps, or they may quit their job and join the ministry, or they may quit the ministry and take up guitar, and *you* know about the growth of this person, but who else will believe it? But when you work with prisoners and you think you've helped them change, grow, and become more effective people, there's an easy way to tell. Where are they a year after you've finished with them? Are they back in jail, or are they making it on the outside? Prisoner rehabilitation offers the most objective check for someone who claims he can bring about change in behavior. In the prisons of Massachusetts the recidivism rate is about 70 percent. Seven out of every ten men who leave prison, return. If you develop a new and surefire way of changing man's mind, the prison presents the toughest and cleanest test of your effectiveness. Can you keep him out of jail? That's

Inmates received on the average four doses of psilocybin. Dosage ran from 20 mg. in early sessions to 70 mg. Now we employ 30 mg. as a standard, moderate dose.

Inmates were given personality tests before, and six months after, the program began. Significant decreases in hostility, cynicism, social delinquency and irresponsibility were registered.

There seems to be general agreement that the effects of the program *in-the-institution* were quite dramatic. The behavior and attitude of the project members became more mature and social.

The post-release events, however, involved a different set of factors and required several revisions in the program.

POST-RELEASE PROGRAM:

The main conclusion of our two-year pilot study is that institutional programs, however effective, count for little after the ex-convict reaches the street. The social pressures faced are so overwhelming as to make change very difficult.

We recognized very early in our work the advantages of a post-release program.

Our philosophic and theoretical orientation led us to encourage inmates to plan and execute their own program.

We fondly hoped for a halfway house run by ex-inmates along the lines of the successful Synanon program.

In June, 1961, a non-profit organization, Freedom Center, was set up to administer the post-release program. Our hopes for a convict-run halfway house did not materialize.

We had too few men in the Boston area and they were too caught up in the desperate struggle to survive, to spare time, to help others.

In 1961, as a beginning step toward a halfway house, we began Project Contact. The purpose of this project was to keep in regular contact with all group members.

By these means we were able to reach ninety-one percent of ex-inmates living in Massachusetts.

A newsletter and personal letters also kept up contact and seemed to be effective in helping the rehabilitation spirit stay alive.

why I wanted to get into the prison.

Now, the reason the prison psychologists wanted to get into Harvard is that everyone in any academic or professional activity in the Boston area has one way of measuring *his* success. Can he get on the Harvard payroll? The word Harvard in the Boston area is a powerful status symbol that operates at every level of society. There are several thousand janitors around the Boston area, but if you are a janitor at Harvard, you're a prince among custodians. The same with a cook, the same with a gardener, the same with a psychologist.

A week later, I found myself sitting at a corner table in the Harvard Faculty Club with two officials from the Massachusetts prison system. What they wanted was simple. They wanted to have Harvard graduate students assigned to the prisons as psychology interns with a possible long-range hope of getting themselves clinical professorships at Harvard. And what I wanted was to get Harvard graduate students into the prisons because that's where I felt that all embryonic psychologists should be—out in the field, dealing with real people and real problems. But there was something else I wanted—and that was the chance to show that we could rehabilitate criminals by using the sacred mushrooms. And so the deal was made. I agreed to get Harvard approval to send graduate students to internships in the prison, and they agreed that if I could get the approval of the warden and the prison psychiatrists, I could give psychedelic mushrooms to prisoners.

About a week later I drove out to the prison. I wore my Harvard tweed suit and my button-down shirt. The warden was impressed and pleased. It wasn't often that Harvard professors came out to the prison to do research. But the whole thing hinged on the approval of the psychiatrists, because the sacred mushrooms were DRUGS and to work with DRUGS you had to have the medical okay. So, we walked down the hallway to the metal cage that let us into the prison. We opened up the first steel door and we stood in the anteroom. Then we rang a bell, a slot opened, and a guard looked at us and opened up the second metal door. We walked into the middle of the guardroom, across the prison yard to the hospital where we rang the bell and got peered at through the slot, heard the metal hinges creak, and walked into the prison hospital. We walked down the corridor to the psychiatrist's office and knocked on the door. After a minute, out walked one of the most entertaining and interesting men in American psychiatry. The first thing that struck me about the prison psychiatrist was that he was the best-dressed man I had ever seen. He was short, graceful, like a ballet dancer. The first Negro psychiatrist I had ever met. I spent an hour talking with Dr. Madison Presnell. He was no intellectual; he mispronounced some of the polysyllabic words, but he had a twinkle in his eye and a wise, cool way of looking at you that told you he was a man who had seen a lot and suffered a lot, and was still looking for the funniest and wisest part of everyone he came in contact with.

In sizing up Dr. Presnell, I could say to myself a word I had heard used quite often in recent months. He was hip. It was obvious, too, that he had had some experience with psychedelic drugs. Which ones, he didn't make clear. He could have had LSD in medical school, or mescaline in psychiatric research, or maybe pot in the Village, but he knew what I was talking about.

A few days later Dr. Presnell came over to Harvard to meet some of my bosses, and the following Sunday he brought his beautiful and intelligent wife over to my house for cocktails. He sat down on a chair in my study, thought for a minute and said, "Your plan to give psychedelic drugs to prisoners is the best idea I've heard for dealing with an impossible problem. If you're smart enough and dedicated enough to know how to do it, you could make it work. There's one chance in a hundred you can pull it off, but if you do, you will have accomplished more for American society and for prisoner rehabilitation than has been done in the last four thousand years since the code of Hammurabi. But it's risky business. You're bound to run into trouble. As a matter of fact, the more successful you are, the more trouble you're going to stir up. Because one thing I've learned as a prison psychiatrist is that

But increased contact only strengthened our convictions that an A.A.-type organization of ex-convicts is necessary.

The initial step of finding the small nucleus of men who are ready to make the dedication needed has not yet been taken.

As a possible solution we hope to be able to send two ex-inmates to spend a month living at Synanon House, Santa Monica.

The Director of Synanon, Mr. Chuck Dederich, has expressed interest in this project.

The next step of selecting two ex-inmates to make the trip is waiting to be taken.

Upon their return, Freedom Center is prepared to offer its resources to support a local self-help residence program.

RESULTS:

Plans and hopes are one thing, but the actual score card of accomplishments provides the crucial evidence. What are the available results?

PSILOCYBIN IS SAFE:

Thirty-five inmates and ten Harvard staff members have had group psilocybin experiences at Concord.

There were 131 inmate ingestions and 37 staff ingestions, a total of 168 experiences. There were no episodes of violence, lasting disturbances or negative after-effects.

Physically and psychologically there is clear-cut evidence that in a supportive environment the drug effect is safe and positive.

Those interested in using psilocybin for research or therapy purposes can proceed with confidence if their program is open, supportive, collaborative.

PSILOCYBIN PRODUCES TEMPORARY STATES OF SPIRITUAL CONVERSION, INTERPERSONAL CLOSENESS, AND PSYCHOLOGICAL INSIGHT

Forty-five percent of the entire inmate group clearly underwent a mystical, transcendent, death-rebirth experience.

This figure should be modified, however. The results for running sessions improved so that 100% of our *recent* groups were undergoing transcendent experiences.

society doesn't want the prisoner rehabilitated, and as soon as you start changing prisoners so that they discover beauty and wisdom, God, you're going to stir up the biggest mess that Boston has seen since the Boston Tea Party. I'll give you medical coverage and I'll be glad to serve as psychiatric consultant and I'll back you up all the way with the wardens, with the guards, with the mental health department, but sooner or later, as soon as they see the thing you do is working, they're going to come down on you—the newspaper reporters, the bureaucrats, and the officials. Harvard gives drugs to prisoners! And you're going to have to do the impossible—you're going to have to cure prisoners with your left hand, and that's something that's never been done before, and you're going to have to hold off the entire bureaucracy of the state of Massachusetts with your right hand, and that's never been done before, not even by a Kennedy. So, I'll back you all the way, until you make a mistake, and when you make that mistake, and they all start coming down at you, exactly at that point, I'm going to walk out because I'm not you. I'm not the new Freud, and I have no ambitions to play that game. I'm a Negro from the South with a degree from a second-class medical school, with a wife and two kids whom I'm trying to support and educate in an insane society, and I'll help you all the way to win, but I'm not going to lose with you.

Political revolutions are extremely grave matters. They should be undertaken only under stress of direst necessity, when there is no other way out. Not everyone is called to this task, but only the man who has the confidence of the people, and even he only when the time is ripe. He must then proceed in the right way, so that he gladdens the people and, by enlightening them, prevents excesses. Furthermore, he must be quite free of selfish aims and must really relieve the need of the people. Only then does he have nothing to regret. (I Ching XLIX)

And so it was settled. Dr. Presnell would line up volunteers in the prisoner population for the sacred mushroom project and I would go back to Harvard and get graduate students who would volunteer their time and energy and their nervous systems to take drugs with maximum security prisoners at the penitentiary.

A few days later I was in my office when a knock came on the door, and I was visited by a graduate student named Ralph Metzner. Metzner had a reputation for being one of the smartest students in the department. He was a graduate of Oxford, an experimentalist, a precise, objective, and apparently very academic young man. He said he had heard about the prison project and he wanted to work with me on it. My first reaction was that Metzner was too academic, too dainty-British, too bookish, too ivory tower, to walk into a prison and roll up his sleeves and take drugs that would put him out of his mind, with rough and tumble prisoners. Metzner said he wanted to learn how. Then I said, Before you can give drugs and take drugs with anyone else, you have to have some experiences yourself. Are you ready to take mushrooms? He was ready. As a matter of fact, that's exactly what he wanted to do, to have a session.

And so it happened that on March 12, 1961, at my home in Newton, Massachusetts, I ran a session for Dr. Presnell and his beautiful wife, for Ralph Metzner and his girl friend and another graduate student, Gunther Weil and his wife, Karen. This was the fifty-second time I had taken psilocybin with other people. The notes on the session say, This training session was designed to introduce several new subjects to the sacred mushroom experience under supportive circumstances.

The session took place in my study. Since this was an exploratory training session, I told the participants that they should relax, have a good time, be entertained, and learn what they could. Dr. Presnell was the dominating factor in this session. His joking and warm attitude created a benign atmosphere. Each new subject had his spouse or a trusted friend present. After a long period of happy, relaxed giggling, the joking became more and more philosophic. Members of the group would leave the room periodically to be by them-

The life-changing therapeutic effects of the psilocybin experience do not last for more than seventy-two hours unless the subject is in a situation which encourages him to maintain his emotional and spiritual insights.

Therefore, psilocybin must be used in on-going programs of therapy or self-help. When employed in such programs, psilocybin is a dramatically useful, educational, and rehabilitative instrument.

If the subject shares time and space subsequently with those who have had the experience, his chances of maintaining the insights are increased.

The actual scoreboard is difficult to interpret. The aims of this project were: 1) to help keep men on the street and 2) to help them in constructive contact with each other.

RESULT PERCENTAGES January 15, 1963:

Percentage of men released who are now on street . . . 73.

Percentage of men now back for technical parole violation . . . 19.

Percentage of men now back for new crimes . . . 8.

If ex-convicts who have had a psilocybin experience in a supportive environment meet regularly after release (these statistics suggest once a month), the chances of their remaining on the street will be dramatically improved.

The Harvard staff members —Dr. Ralph Metzner, Gunther Weil, Dr. Ralph Schwitzgebel, Jonathan Clark, David Kolb, Michael Hollingshead, Kathy Harris, Dr. Timothy Leary—who contributed several thousands of hours each to this work, cared deeply and suffered keen disappointments as they witnessed the failures.

But the results summarized in this report offer some consolation that the time shared in psilocybin experiences, and the meetings in and out of Concord were educational, and somewhat effective.

SUMMARY:

Thirty-one inmates of MCI Concord participated in a rehabilitation program combining:

. . . psilocybin administered in a supportive setting, and . . . volunteer contact of inmates after release.

selves or to talk in pairs, but my study operated as the center for the session. There were no discordant notes, no anxiety, depression, or friction. We were finally getting to the point where we knew how to set up a pleasant session. Each member of this six-person group reported a deep, ecstatic, educational experience.

A few days after this session, Ralph Metzner, Gunther Weil, and I drove out to the concrete prison and met with the six volunteers who had been selected by Dr. Presnell. We sat around a table, in a dreary hospital room with gray walls, black asphalt floor, bars in the windows, telling six skeptical and suspicious men about an experience which could change their lives.

The first psychedelic session in the prison was well planned. The first thing we did was to tell the prisoners as much as we could about the psychedelic experience. We brought in books for them to read, reports by other subjects, articles which described the terrors as well as the ecstasies of the experience. We spent most of the time describing our own experiences and answering groping questions. We made it very clear to the prisoners that this was nothing *we* were doing to them. There was no doctor-patient game going here. We would take the drugs along with them. We were doing nothing to them that we wouldn't willingly, happily have done to ourselves. We also made a research contract with the prisoners. We said something like this, We want to find out how and how much you change during this experience. For this reason, we want you to take a battery of psychological tests before you eat the mushrooms. Then, after three or four sessions with the sacred mushrooms, we'll give you the tests again. The aim here is to find out how you change, like you weigh yourself on a scale before and after you go on a diet. After you've taken the tests, we'll give you the results. We'll go over the tests with you and explain how you were before and how you changed. Nothing in this project is going to be a secret. We've told you everything we know about the drugs before you take them and we'll tell you everything we know about you after you finish your sessions.

That sounded like a good deal to them, and the following week each prisoner was administered a long and complicated battery of psychological tests.

And it happened that on March 27, 1961, in the large ward room in the prison infirmary in Concord, Massachusetts, five prisoners and three Harvard psychologists met for a trip. In the morning I was to turn-on with three convicts, and the two other prisoners and the two graduate students would act as observers. Then in the afternoon Gunther Weil and Ralph Metzner and the two observing prisoners were to take the drug, and the rest of us were to act as guides. We brought a record player, tape recorder, and some books of classical art with us. Otherwise the room was bleak in decor, with four beds, a large table, and a few chairs. At 9:35 in the morning the bowl of pills was placed in the center of the table. I was the first one to turn-on in the prison project. I reached over, took fourteen milligrams of psilocybin. Then I handed the bowl to the prisoner next to me, and he took twenty milligrams and passed it on to the guy next to him who took twenty, and the next man. Then we pushed the bowl to the middle of the table and sat back to see what would happen.

I'll never forget that morning. After about half an hour, I could feel the effect coming up, the loosening of symbolic reality, the feeling of humming pressure and space voyage inside my head, the sharp, brilliant, brutal intensification of all the senses. Every cell and every sense organ was humming with charged electricity. I felt terrible. What a place to be on a gray morning! In a dingy room in a grim penitentiary, out of my mind. I looked over at the man next to me, a Polish embezzler from Worcester, Massachusetts. I could see him so clearly. I could see every pore in his face, every blemish, the hairs in his nose, the incredible green-yellow enamel of the decay in his teeth, the wet glistening of his frightened eyes. I could see every hair in his head, as though each was as big as an oak tree. What a confrontation! What am I doing here, out of my mind, with this strange mosaic-celled animal, prisoner, criminal?

I said to him with a weak grin, How are you doing, John? He said, I feel fine. Then he paused

The evidence after two years of operation suggests that the drug is safe, that the experience temporarily provides personal and spiritual insight, and has some effect in keeping inmates out of prison.

A listing of the major mistakes and improvements in method will be found in two publications, one in press and one in preparation.

∞

From the *Boston Herald and Traveler:*

CONVICTS GAINS CITED BY STUDY

Insight drugs called boon

IFIF is the Internal Federation for Internal Freedom, a non-profit organization involving the use of conscious-expanding drugs.

The supply of the drug has, temporarily at least, been cut off because the medical supervision required by federal regulation in the administration of the drugs for research has been withdrawn.

Backing Withers

And the group has been asked to vacate the medical building in Charles River Park for lack of medical affiliation.

In addition, the supportive backing at the academic level, principally at Harvard, has been withering.

But troubles or no, IFIF and the zealous psychologists dedicated to the proposition that widespread use of drugs such as psilocybin will pretty much cure the intellectual ills of mankind, are news.

The latest concerns a study made on the religious impact the drug ingestion made on some 33 convicts at the Concord reformatory in which eight Harvard psychologists worked on the pilot program.

Dr. Timothy Leary, one of the co-founders of IFIF, wrote the report on the pilot program which began in mid-March of 1961 and continued for almost two years.

Beginning with six convicts, a senior investigator, and two graduate students, the study came to include 33 convicts and eight psychologists. All participated in the drug ingestion.

for a minute and asked, How are you doing, Doc? I was about to say in a reassuring psychological tone that I felt fine, but I couldn't, so I said, I feel lousy. John drew back his purple-pink lips, showed his green-yellow teeth in a sickly grin, and said, What's the matter, Doc? Why you feel lousy? I looked with my two microscopic retina lenses into his eyes. I could see every line, yellow spider webs, red network of veins gleaming out at me. I said, John, I'm afraid of you. His eyes got bigger, then he began to laugh. I could look inside his mouth, swollen red tissues, gums, tongue, throat. I was prepared to be swallowed. Then I heard him say, Well that's funny, Doc, 'cause I'm afraid of you. We were both smiling at this point, leaning forward. Doc, he said, why are you afraid of me? I said, I'm afraid of you, John, because you're a criminal. He nodded. I said, John, why are you afraid of me? He said, I'm afraid of you, Doc, because you're a mad scientist. Then our retinas locked and I slid down into the tunnel of his eyes, and I could feel him walking around in my skull and we both began to laugh. And there it was, that dark moment of fear and distrust, which could have changed in a second to become hatred and terror. But we made the love connection. The flicker in the dark. Suddenly, the sun came out in the room and I felt great and I knew he did too.

Fire below and the lake above combat and destroy each other. So too in the course of the year a combat takes place between the forces of light and the forces of darkness, eventuating in the revolution of the seasons. Man masters these changes in nature by noting their regularity and marking off the passage of time accordingly. In this way order and clarity appear in the apparently chaotic changes of the seasons, and man is able to adjust himself in advance to the demands of the different times. (I Ching XLIX)

We had passed that moment of crisis, but as the minutes slowly ticked on, the grimness of our situ-

Test Called Success

In Dr. Leary's opinion, the experiment was an unqualified success. Ingestion of the drugs produced sudden insight that one has been living in a narrow space-time-self context.

"It's all a game, Doc, cops and robbers—we're such tough guys," he quotes one convict as saying. "We take it all so seriously as though that's all there is to life."

He reports also of frequent mystical insight among the convicts, particularly the death-rebirth experience.

"I felt helpless and wanted to murder you guys who did it to me; then I realized it was my own mind doing it; it's always been my own mind imagining troubles and enemies," he quotes one convict.

Over half the hard-bitten convicts displayed a sudden swing towards increased religious understanding and need, according to the study report.

Return Rate Drops

More important, perhaps, in the long run is the fact that the recidivism rate among the convicts who have been discharged dropped sharply.

ation kept coming back in microscopic clarity. There were the four of us, turned-on, every sense vibrating, pulsating with messages, two billion years of cellular wisdom, but what could we do trapped within the four walls of a gray hospital room, barred inside a maximum security prison? Then, one of the great lessons in my psychedelic training took place. One of the turned-on prisoners was a Negro from Texas, jazz saxophone player, heroin addict. He looked around with two huge balls of ocular white, shook his head, staggered over to the record player, put on a record. It was a Sonny Rollins record which he'd especially asked us to bring. Then he lay down on the cot and closed his eyes. The rest of us sat by the table while metal air from the yellow saxophone spinning across copper electric wires bounced off the walls of the room. There was a long silence. Then we heard Willy moaning softly and moving restlessly on the couch. I turned and looked at him and said, Willy, are you all right? There was apprehension in my voice. Everyone in the room swung his head anxiously to look and listen for the answer. Willy lifted his head, gave a big grin, and said, Man, am I all right? I'm in heaven and I can't believe it! Here I am in heaven man, and I'm stoned out of my mind, and I'm swinging like I've never been before and it's all happening in prison, and you ask me man, am I all right. What a laugh! And then he laughed and we all laughed and suddenly we were all high and happy and chuckling at what we had done, bringing music, and love, and beauty, and serenity, and fun, and the seed of life into that grim and dreary prison.

Well, the session went on and on. There were high points and low points, ecstasies and terrors. My friend John, the Polish man, got sick and vomited. We all got pretty thoughtful. Why are there prisons? Why do some men put the warm cellular envelopes of their fellowmen in metal cages? What were we doing here? Then after a few hours, Ralph and Gunther and the two remaining convicts turned-on. Gunther was silly and acting like a hipster, and Ralph fell down on the bed and experienced visions of Blakean terror. Two pris-

"Seventy-five percent are holding their own against stiff winds and treacherous currents," Dr. Leary says.

The expected return rate of ex-convicts to the Concord reformatory would be between 50 and 70 percent.

But even in his claimed success among the convicts, Dr. Leary runs up against a doubting Thomas in the reformatory Superintendent Edward Grennan.

Control Questioned

Grennan feels that study was done without a control and was therefore unscientific.

"These men received an extremely high degree of personal attention," he said. "The psychologists even set up a kind of criminal AA for the paroled prisoners in Cambridge. They made themselves available to them around the clock."

"I feel that the same rate of recidivism might have been achieved if the same concentration and attention were given to any parolee by highly placed members in any community."

∞

oners came and held his hand and guided him through. Dr. Presnell would check in every now and then, walk around the room like a dainty, graceful cat, not saying much, but taking it all in. And the guards came in bringing metal trays of food which we all looked at with disbelief, the way you'd look at a plate of worms or a pot of sawdust served up to you on a plate, and someone said, Man, do they call that food? Since we Harvard people weren't allowed to eat prison food at the expense of the state, Dr. Presnell went out and got milkshakes and sandwiches which we all shared, and we had never tasted food so good.

Then at five o'clock, there was a bang on the door, and we opened it and the guards came in and said, Time is up, men. Back to the prison ward. Ralph, Gunther, and I went with the five prisoners back to the lockup part of the hospital and sat there on beds, and smoked, and laughed, and compared notes on what we'd seen, and where we'd been. Then it was time for us to go. We shook hands, said we'd be back tomorrow, and Ralph and Gunther and I walked out of the prison, across the dark yard, rang the bell, and waited until the iron doors opened into the guardroom, and then across the guardroom, through the two metal doors, and down the metal stairs, past the clanking, steaming, old-fashioned radiators, and then we were outside. Ralph and Gunther got into their car and drove back to Cambridge, and I got in my car and drove to Newton.

As I rode along the highway, the tension and the drama of the day suddenly snapped off and I could look back and see what we had done. Nothing, you see, is secret in a prison, and the eight of us who had assembled to take drugs together in a prison were under the microscopic gaze of every convict in the prison and every guard, and within hours the word would have fanned through the invisible network to every other prison in the state. Grim Walpole penitentiary. Gray, sullen-walled Norfolk.

Did you hear? Some Harvard professors gave a new drug to some guys at Concord. They had a ball. It was great. It's a grand thing. It's something new. Hope. Maybe. Hope. Perhaps. Something new. We sure need something new. Hope.

REVOLUTION. *On your own day*
You are believed.
Supreme success,
Furthering through perseverance.
Remorse disappears.

(I Ching)

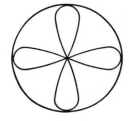

And the Prisoners Will Become Priests:

Spring 1961

Guides: JIM BERRIGAN, DON SAINTEN

Oracle: XIII

Fellowship with Men

The Creative, Heaven

The Clinging, Flame

Heaven together with fire:
The image of FELLOWSHIP WITH MEN.
Thus the superior man organizes the clans
And makes distinctions between things.

(I Ching)

Prisoner Trip Report #1:

My experience while under psilocybin was so much more than I expected. To begin with I was completely unprepared for what was to happen, what changes were to take place in my beliefs, re-evaluating myself to the point of nothingness.

My whole way of life was so transparent while under psilocybin, that coming out from under the mushroom, I was in a deep state of shock. I use deep shock figuratively. This thirst for knowledge I had . . . is . . . was . . . it seems so meaningless now. More so because I was applying it to some abstract idea, some complicated intrigue of my own.

As to my first awareness of my real self, it was when my conversing partner, Smithy, was searching for a complicated word in regards to something that needed a very simple word. It was then this idea flashed thru my mind, could it possibly be that what I was looking for is so very simple also. And then to my utter amazement, I realized I wasn't fighting the world, I was fighting myself.

The first psychedelic session at the prison set up powerful repercussions.

First there was the effect on the little group of voyagers. Strong bonds had developed. We had been through the ordeal together. We had gone beyond the games of Harvard psychologist and convict. We had stripped off social facade and faced fear together and we had trusted and laughed.

I felt at home in the prison. It always works this way after a good trip. You die and then you are reborn. The place of your rebirth is home. This is not metaphorical—it is a neurological reality.

During the psychedelic session the nervous system returns to that state of flux and unity-chaos of infancy—and spins beyond familiar time-space where there is no home because all is a two-billion-year process of homing. As the session ends, one is reborn (smoothly or with a jolt). This is the period of reentry—the return from space to the planet. That place to which you return becomes neurologically engraved in your subsequent consciousness. It is a new "home"—a new neurological center. In scientific papers we described this as the process of re-imprinting. A rewiring of the nervous system.

There is a strong biochemical attachment to the people, the objects, the scents and sights, of the place to which you return. This accounts for the LSD cult phenomenon.

In our case the hospital room of the prison had become a center. A home. It was wired into my head.

The morning after the session, driving back to the prison was like going back to some sacred place in my skull.

Meeting the prisoners was like a family reunion.

Our status in the prison was changed. Glances of

192

respect and interest. Prisoners approached us as we walked across the yard to ask if they could sign up for the mushrooms. Guards and parole officers stopped us to ask questions or to request that a favorite prisoner be admitted to the psychedelic group.

We spent the next two weeks discussing the reports that the prisoners wrote and comparing notes on the trip. Then we ran a second session. This time the prisoners were more sophisticated. There was no sitting around on chairs in nervous anticipation. As soon as the energy began to radiate through their bodies they headed for the cot, fell-out, and closed their eyes. For the next two or three hours they lay engulfed in the visions, occasionally sitting up to smile or make some Zen comment. The Harvard guides changed the records and sat quietly, watching the cellular clocks in the room whirring, occasionally approaching the voyagers, a hand on the shoulder, a smile, the cosmic nod of affirmation. And the looks of wonder and sharing.

Oh Doc! Amazing. This stuff is amazing.

It's all always amazing, Tony. Do you want anything?

Yeah, Doc. I'm thirsty.

I brought the glass of water. In sitting up, Tony spilled a few drops. His eyes riveted on the little wet puddle on the gray blanket.

Water, he said wondering. Life and water. Where does the water come from, Doc? We are water creatures, aren't we? Yeah, my body is the sea.

Sometimes the microscopes of inner vision focused on their lives. Jerry huddled under his blanket sobbing, his head shaking back and forth. Oh Doc, what a selfish fool I've been! My family. Wasted years. Wasted years. Will I get another chance, Doc? Can I go back and try it again?

Nine in the fourth place means:
He climbs up on his wall; HE CANNOT ATTACK.
Good fortune. (I Ching XIII)

It keeps going, Jerry. Every moment it starts all over again.

Should I retain this ethical position, or disregard it for the present, to let him understand and see how much more there is to life, than living behind these walls in a state of mental and physical stagnation.

And finally he came to the decision, to show me how much I was missing with just the be feeling, and not being there feeling, let me expound on this for a moment.

Smithy asked me if I missed these different things outside of prison, that he and everyone else was enjoying, and my answer was something to the effect, oh! But I have these same things you have, by just substituting the being there feeling with the be feeling, then he asked me to teach him this feeling, because with this feeling, Smithy believed he would be able to solve the many problems of mankind.

The possibility of saving so much money, pain, mistakes, etc., seemed to him to be so important, and to me so ridiculous, that I explained to him that he was not ready yet, and to this answer he became so sad and unhappy, that I explained to him there wasn't to my knowledge anything to take the place of the being there feeling.

From there we concentrated on communication with the lower levels of intelligence. Smithy's idea was to find a way to plug into their minds for this knowledge we need to attain—this high pinnacle of knowledge, and Smithy, believing if we were the superior minds, wasn't it up to us to find a way of communicating with them, and not they with us.

We arranged the room in sacred design. Incense. Candles. The convicts would lie watching the flickering flame. Outside the barred windows they could see the prison wall and the guard tower. Candlelight and the flash of sunlight on the guarding rifles.

Why are there prisons, Doc? What are we doing here? Wanted men. It's insane, Doc. We're all insane. Us cons and the cops and the guards. How did we get into this?

Each session was a cosmic drama. Confusion. Humor, lots of laughter. Olympian multi-level god laughter. Loneliness. Tears. Terrors. Suspicion. Trust.

After the third session the convicts repeated the personality tests to measure changes. We brought the test folders into the hospital room and handed them to the inmates. No secrets. We explained what the tests measured and what the results meant.

But I disagreed, I believed we should first reach this high level of knowledge, and then if we have any desire to learn what they have, fine, if not it wouldn't make any difference anyway. But as usual Smithy's clear and logical mind took over, he showed me how much fuel could be used from each man's mind along the way. And I agreed to this idea.

They had changed. Showed less depression, hostility, antisocial tendencies, more energy, responsibility, cooperation. The objective indices so dear to the heart of the psychologist had swung dramatically and significantly in the direction of increased mental health.

By explaining their test results to them and letting them handle their own test scores, we were training them the same way we trained Harvard graduate students in psychodiagnostics. To learn what the test meant. How they were changing. The prisoners were becoming psychologists.

They loved it. Fierce debates about personality characteristics. The psychiatric diagnostic game being played by the cons.

After a few weeks of discussion we planned with the inmates the continuation of research. The convicts were to select the new recruits for the group. They would learn how to administer the psychological tests. They would give the orientation lectures. They would run the project.

So in summation, we found that knowledge alone was meaningless, knowledge must have fuel from these other channels. These everyday pleasures, the loves, the sadness, the small problems. These together with knowledge would balance out, to give man the proper guide in life, without them, man would become hopelessly lost.

Here the reconciliation that follows quarrel moves nearer. It is true that there are still dividing walls on which we stand confronting one another. But the difficulties are too great. We get into straits, and this brings us to our senses. We cannot fight, and therein lies our good fortune. (I Ching XIII)

At this point we ran into prison politics. The social structure of a prison is like any village. There is a very explicit hierarchy. The inmates themselves run the prison. All the guards and administrators do is keep the peace, but the gut, muscle, moment-to-moment space-time issues are determined by prisoners.

The inmates belong to invisible social clans and the clan leader decides what happens. If the warden and guards violate the dignity and prerogatives of the convict leaders there is trouble. And all administrators want to avoid trouble.

One day when we walked into the hospital there were two new inmate medical attendants. They were men in their forties. Tough, proud, hard customers.

They walked up to me. Doctor Leary, I'm Jim Berrigan. This is Don Sainten. We'd like to talk to you.

Fine, but I'm late for the project meeting. Maybe later.

No. The meeting can wait. Let's talk now. I looked at them closely. They were men of confidence and dignity, power-holders, leaders. Dress them differently and they could be sea captains or chief surgeons or Broadway promoters.

I nodded and they motioned me down the hall. We walked into the hospital kitchen. I'd never been there before. Don walked to the stove and turned on the burner under a coffee pot. Bacon and eggs, Doc? No thanks. Coffee will do.

Jim and Don sat on the high serving counter and grinned. We've been watching this mushroom business, Doc, and it looks pretty good to us and we've decided to join your project. We'll be a lot of help to you. We've arranged transfers to the hospital so we can be right on call.

The words were cool and cocky and seemed to leave no room for question.

I explained that the decisions about who joined the project were made by the convicts in the group. I couldn't interfere but I'd pass their names on to the inmate planning group.

The most sobering effect the mushroom had on me, was midway in our conversation. I asked Smithy if he realized that we had not mentioned God once— Smithy's answer verbatim, (Have we done anything else). One could not realize the meaning of this answer and what effect it had to my reasoning—unless one understood that up until Monday I believed I was much more than I turned out to be, not a pretty picture for one to witness unprepared.

In conclusion I must state briefly, that I enjoyed the mushroom on one hand, but on the other hand, it frightened me, I say frightened, because I saw myself for what I really was, but even tho this picture was seen for what it really was, I look to the future with enthusiasm, and to pursue psilocybin to its end.

What is it like to be under psilocybin, being able to see colors in all its brilliance and absolute splendor, it is by all means an atmosphere I would want to be in all the time—able to understand myself, music, and what it means, the feeling one gets from listening to such superb music as classics.

Actions and thinking that I have done before are being changed to a more magnificent and truer way; thoughts have come to me under psilocybin such as past manners in treating people with a much better attitude and respect.

This has taken me years to do and so after all these years I have found a way, thru the help of psilocybin. It has helped me in spelling and reading. I remember when I couldn't hold ten words in my head, but now I have words like antidisestablishmentarianism — long —yes, but a word with any accomplishment, and there are others I am seeking to accomplish in accordance to psilocybin.

A great deal of the pictures I seen were transparent, clear enough to see and understand and to speak about after my session. It was nice to experience.

There was nothing vicious about my two experiences, nor was it extravagent, but it was extraordinary and therefore I must praise and glorify this experience and all its wonder. It explored my mind and opened up a gate that has been closed for a long time, and with this acknowledgment I can keep it open and let this memory mellifluous itself through me because there is no need to be mendacious, dishonest. It is time to mend that which is broken.

Psilocybin has showed me how wrong I have been in my disinclination, I now care to emulate, strive for the better things in life.

Jim and Don grinned. I don't think that those guys will give us any static, Doc, we usually get what we want around here. Don't we, Don?

Don nodded. There was muscle and hard prick behind the words.

I liked them and had to respect them. And it was more politics. Dealing with the powers that be. I grinned and said, I'm pleased that you're interested. It's a new and good thing we're doing and it works. It's also fun. I hope you'll join us.

When I mentioned to our planning group that Jim and Don had volunteered there was an uneasy ripple, and murmurs about who exactly is in charge, and I thought the project was going to be democratic.

By democratic we mean that we should run it, right?

We had already run into some problems of power and authority in turning our decisions over to the convicts. The intoxicating taste of command. Two of the inmates had thrown themselves into the doctor-psychologist role with great energy and had developed pompous professional facades in dealing with their "clients." They tended to be fussy and schoolmasterly punitive. The other cons didn't like it.

And everyone was uneasy about Jim and Don coming into the project. They were big men in the prison. They were boss cons. They'll take over.

Hey, wait a minute. If they come into the project they'll have to take the mushrooms.

There was a thoughtful silence and then everyone began to laugh.

And if they take the drug they'll flip out of their minds and beyond the game of being boss convicts. Right? And they'll be stripped naked like everyone else. And they'll come back changed like the rest of us.

If the mushrooms really work, if they produce insight and love, then they'll work for Jim and Don. Yeah, and for the guards too. Let's invite the screws to turn-on.

So it was agreed that Don and Jim could join the group. They were tested and listened to the orientation talks and held out their tough-guy hands one sunny morning to receive the sacrament.

I don't know of any other way for a person to ease tension, but maybe some could try a hobby or listen to music, maybe classical or spiritual. I am sure that somewhere along these lines you will find peace of mind.

On my second session, while I was under psilocybin and laying in bed with the covers over my head, a picture came into view as clear as I have ever seen before, and this was of Christ in the manger with these people standing and kneeling by his side. This picture stayed with me for a few moments, and then thousands of Christmas lights came into view—different shapes and forms and designs of colors that was of tremendous brilliance and elegance.

I was wondering at one point if I was living, or was this heaven that I had heard so much about. Being able to experience these things have made me do a great deal of thinking in rechanneling my life. One must come a long way before he can find himself and I really hope I have.

I also have now a great conception of classic music whereas one time I would never think of listening to such music.

This trip was being guided by Gunther Weil and two inmates from the original group.

After an hour Jimmy Berrigan started to show signs of distress. Jimmy was one of the hardest men in Massachusetts. He belonged to a famous Boston waterfront gang—a rugged, violent tribe. Jimmy was a professional outlaw. Proud. Touchy. Cocky. A man whose culture and whose long life was totally dedicated to strength, bicep control.

And now, as it comes to all men, the ultimate humiliation was coming to tough Jimmy in a sunlit room in the hospital ward in Concord prison.

Jimmy suddenly discovered he had fallen into a trap. He had bulled his way into the project to enhance his power in the prison. The mushrooms were good, and anything good in the prison belonged, by tribal custom, to Berrigan. And now he lay on a cot, rendered weak, his mind spinning away, his control slipping, overwhelmed by a thousand shadowy cellular faces mocking his illusions of strength.

This wasn't what he expected. This was a different high from booze and bennies and happy pills. He had fallen into a diabolic con game perpetrated by Harvard psychologists. After forty-five years of defiance and arrogance Jimmy was fallen. He raged in despair. He should have known better than to trust his natural enemies, these smooth-faced, glib middle-class professionals. What a sucker he was to fall for their line, to forget that power was everything. To let them slip him these immobilizing pills.

Well, he'd go down fighting. He tried to sit up, but his body was a tangle of pulsating wires and warm liquids. It was a nice feeling but he felt strange and weak. He looked around the room which was alive with belted radiance. Where were his tormentors? Ah, there was Gunther, young pipsqueak kid who couldn't hold his own for five seconds in a barroom brawl—now smiling at him in malevolent triumph.

He motioned for Gunther to come over and then fell back on the pillow.

How are you Jimmy?

I'm terrible, I'm dying. Well you got me, you clever bastard, but I'm not finished. You may have me but my brothers and my gang will get you for this. You'll be in a cement-bag in Boston Harbor in one week.

Gunther's face looked blank. Get me for what?

For trapping me this way, you smug Harvard fink.

Gunther felt a flicker of fear. He was turned-on too. Visions of gangland slayings. Cruel, implacable hoodlum revenge. How did he, a well-brought-up middle-class Jewish boy with good school grades get himself involved in this scene of wickedness and violence. Because of the mushrooms. The ecstasy had led him on. He had been warned of this. The grim Judeo-Christian retribution. You pay for your bliss. Now he was paying for his mushroom kicks. He looked down at the face of his murderer, the rugged, waterfront grimacing features of this hood, this devil Berrigan whose dread retribution was to fall on him. Thoughts of escape flashed through his mind. He glanced at the barred windows. He was trapped in the prison, surrounded by thugs who would spring to the command of the master criminal.

Tears came to his eyes. What a tragedy, to be cut down in his promising youth. He cursed the day he had even listened to the mushroom song and all the glib psychedelic teachings which sounded so good but which just lured you into the void of hell.

The two men stood transfixed in horror and hate. Slim Harvard and grizzled outlaw. Caught together in some cold hopeless whirlpool of cosmic energy. Frightened and frightening each other. Blaming each other. Man hopelessly isolated from man. The other men in the room watched silently.

Jimmy snarled again. My brother will kill you for this.

How can they kill me, Jimmy, I'm dying right now.

Dying. Death. Rebirth. Some long-forgotten wire of memory flickered. Death-rebirth. Trust the process. Gunther closed his eyes and the words came to him. The prayer. He struggled to move his throat and tongue, and then the words came out quavering, shaky, a strange little voice, but the message was there. Jimmy Berrigan looked up in disbelief. His eyes widened. Then he understood. From

Psilocybin has a way of opening up the mind and letting you see different pictures and gradually you will grasp these significants, and use them as they should be used.

∞

Prisoner Trip Report #2:

I feel as an antiquarian does while searching for ancient relics—anticipation before the discovery—once discovered—the journey to make known what is unknown. I find there isn't two paths any longer, but numerous trails to follow.

None are marked in any tangible manner or form—the senses are to be my guide.

I must reject the colorless, barren, unpopulated roads —to travel into the world of beauty, the sun, the flowers, fresh-fragrant air— all the benefits nature has devised for the use of man.

I can do no less since the operation was successful (restoring my eyesight). I have traveled long in the world of darkness, shackled to the segregated misfits.

The overwhelming desire to tear the cloth from my flesh, releasing the suffocating sinews to the magical beat of primitive drums.

(The sacred dance dedicated to the beyond.)

I am looking forward to my next session, as a child waits for someone to turn the lights on in the heavens above.

People I hated for no sound reason, I have come to love. The lies I've told force me to tell the truth and I do not find that it hurts as much as a lie does.

I'm satisfied with myself. I know that this is a new me. I'll always be looking to see if there is a better way to do things and how.

Believe me, I consider my being here the most important factor in my life because this is where I have come to know the meaning of freedom and the joys that come with it. Yes, the road has been a hard one and many tears involved. The going is easy now because I have found the way to the end.

somewhere in his childhood, his Irish genes, his rugged Celtic past, the same message sparked.

Jimmy began to laugh. Amazing. Unbelievable. God did exist. The old teachings were true. Not in the stilted, phony effeminate accents of the Boston priesthood whose piety he despised, but in the voice which sighed and breathed in his cells.

He reached up and grabbed Gunther's hand, and their eyes met in a smile. And the session reel spun on.

The initiation of Jimmy and Don increased the feeling of centeredness at the prison. Coming to Concord was like returning on pilgrimage to a holy place. A conspiracy was emerging. We started plotting a mass prison break.

It is the nature of fire to flame up to heaven. This gives the idea of fellowship. Here, clarity is within and strength without—the character of a peaceful union of men, which, in order to hold together, needs one yielding nature among many firm persons. (I Ching XIII)

The name of the game was keep-out. We agreed that cops-and-robbers was ridiculous; the prisoner-guard game absurd. The perpetuation of these social dances depended on someone willing to play the part of the criminal. The entire top-heavy administrative structure, policemen, detectives, informers, lawyers, district attorneys, judges, probation and parole officers, guards, wardens, prison psychiatrists—all were dependent on the hero-star-bad-guy to make their good-guy parts have meaning. The criminals were the fall guys, the victims who kept the whole game going.

The solution was obvious. The prisoners had to turn-on, see the game the way it was, and then drop-out. Just stop playing the bad-boy game. See it, laugh at it, and drop-out.

So we made a contract. . . . Everyone in the group would do everything he could to help every member get out and stay out of prison. Not just sessions and discussions in the prison, but practical help in getting out, in finding a job, and dealing with life on the outside.

We were proposing a family, clan-type group. This was very different from professional bureaucratic rehabilitation. The motto of the rehabilitation worker is detachment. Don't get emotionally involved with the client. You will be seduced or conned. A mass-assembly-line rehabilitation sequence, in which the psychologist performs his tests and turns the patient over to the psychiatrist, who treats the patient and sends him cured to the parole board, which decides on the basis of its own criteria whether to allow parole. The parolee is then investigated and supervised by parole officers. Complete depersonalization all the way down the line.

The prisoner is treated this way because he comes from a family which either won't or can't help him. His clan has been fragmented. He is an isolated loner, an anonymous cog in the social machine.

Our strategy was exactly opposite to the detached professional approach. The aim was to build a network of friends who would help each other. To construct a group that could perform some of the functions of the tribe. If a middle-class person gets in trouble he is typically rescued by middle-class know-how which bails him out, gets him a lawyer, talks middle-class jargon to the officials, gets him a job, provides him with a middle-class home to return to.

Our plan was to use the resources of our group (including middle-class know-how) to weave a web of protection for the convicts.

. . . Said Gandalf . . . Well, let folly be our cloak, a veil before the eyes of the Enemy! For he is very wise, and weighs all things to a nicety. . . . But the only measure that he knows is desire, desire for power; and so he judges all hearts.

. . . Said Elrond . . . the road must be trod but it will be very hard . . . this quest may be attempted by the weak with as much hope as the strong. Yet such is oft the course of deeds that move the wheels of the world: small hands do this because they must, while the eyes of the great are elsewhere. (The Lord of the Rings)

I've been thru a complete change of life, an experience that the average 20-year-old does not go thru but when they do go thru this change, the better things are ahead.

I know myself in such a way that I can account for my thoughts and what they mean and what use they will be put to.

Prison can lead a man down to nothing in a very short time. There were times when I felt myself slipping and filling my mind full of ideas that were no good. The ideas are still there but only as a guide to show me that I cannot afford to make a life of criminal doings.

Since the first mushroom test, my thoughts have always been smooth and more wholesome than ever before.

Nothing seems to drive me to stubbornness as before.

I have come a long way into manhood and what I see, I like. What can be better than knowing where you are going and how you are going to get there.

It's pleasant to know that your mind is free and not being guilty of unworthiness.

I want to be at peace with the world and have it at peace with me.

Psilocybin is a wonderful discovery that does things that nothing else could do.

Psilocybin brings out the truth of all around you, those concerning you and yourself. The answers will be yours. But will you use them?

There are things I seen but I can't think of all of them because I never seen things like them before. I can't describe them.

The project moved rapidly into action. One of our members was coming up for a parole hearing. Johnny O'Connell, a genial Irishman. Johnny was caught by the standard dilemma of the lower-class convict. In order to be paroled he needed a job and home. His family was disintegrated, helpless, uncaring and could offer no home. And how could he get a job when he was uneducated, untrained, socially tarnished and, being in prison, unable to canvas prospective employers? Unless something was done he would meet the parole board and be turned back for another year of incarceration for the crime of not having a family, a tribal group to support him.

So we went to work. First, to get him a job. Johnny's occupations in the past had been itinerant and casual. Dish washer. Handy man. Laborer. We phoned around Boston to find an employer who wanted to guarantee steady employment to a dishwashing convict who was guilty of a few bad checks and who drank now and then. No takers.

For a week I spent most of my time meeting with restaurant owners and managers of construction companies. They were all encouraging but no one was willing to sign a paper guaranteeing Johnny a job.

Then we thought of the home-base solution. Harvard University was one of the largest businesses in Cambridge. Dozens of dining halls. We visited the Harvard employment office. There the officials were most sympathetic. Their interest led them to visit the prison. They listened attentively to the discussion about sessions and in return gave brief lectures about hard work, honesty, and responsibility. But for Johnny there was no help because the month was May and the Harvard dining halls closed for the summer.

There was nothing to do but hire Johnny ourselves. Take him into the family business. A letter was written on the stationery of the Harvard Center for Personality Research, guaranteeing him a job on our project. We located a room in Cambridge, paid the rent, and Johnny had a home.

With these documentary testaments to middle-class support, Johnny was released. Our first reconverted man was on the streets.

When he reported to work for the research project, his first assignment was to find himself a job—and to keep diary notes of his job-hunting.

At five o'clock each afternoon he would return to the center with his report. The only jobs he could get were in large downtown cafeterias where he would be allowed to join that anonymous army of gray-faced, dead-eyed, muscatel-drinking drifters who clear dishes off tables and mop floors today and are gone tomorrow to the drunk-tank. Such a job was guaranteed to push him into alcoholism.

And every day at five-thirty Johnny would leave our office and go to his rented room, anonymous body on an impersonal bed in a strange chamber. The bars had TV and warmth and companionship.

For two weeks he continued to search, made endurable by the support of the graduate students who hung out in the project office (at least there were some people who knew and cared). And then came a job as apprentice baker in a pizza parlor. It was a small shop where he would be known by everyone, where he would be a person.

When Johnny came back from work the first evening, we all listened to his description of the place, what the girl cashier looked like, what the boss said to him, what his duties were.

We passed the story on to the cons at the prison, and they listened carefully to all the details.

There was still the bad business of Johnny living by himself and having no friends. The only thing that he could do after work was hang out in the bar. This was expensive. It was also dangerous—leading to hangovers and oversleeping.

But Johnny didn't know any other way of spending time or money. Free dollars and free hours automatically went to the saloon. The ideas of saving money, of purchasing anything except immediate essentials, of taking a vacation, of planning a career were as foreign to Johnny as to an Australian bushman. Middle-class behavior was as far removed from his experience as life on Mars.

So let's emigrate Johnny to Mars. Let's expose him to the day-to-day routine of middle-class American life where he could learn by observation. Johnny moved into my house, into the third-floor attic that Bill Burroughs had just vacated.

There is one time I remember falling upward towards a mass of designs and it was all different colors or lights. It may sound nutty but I was there.

I see other human beings in a different light. I seem to place everyone on an equal level. Regardless of race, creed, or color and education.

I have never found it difficult to talk with most people. However, after the mushroom experience I find it much easier.

What can it do for others? I don't know. I will say this however, if the mushroom leaves the same impression on others as it has on me, then I suggest that everyone should be confronted with its virtues.

The main thing I received from my first experience with mushrooms, was to look at myself and the entire human race from a different angle. One of friendliness and sincerity. Not what I can do everyone out of—but what I can do for them and with them. I hope to find deeper and clearer meanings to these other things the next time I take the mushroom. . . .

By nature, I am a very restless person. Always wanting to move. Yes, I would even go as far as to say wanderlust. I couldn't sit still if someone was talking to me and most of the time it would bore me to listen to them talk. Since the mushroom, I don't feel that way. I seem to be more relaxed. Less impatient. I want to listen and I don't want to be moving around. To get away from the things around me, now, seems to have vanished.

Then I was scared. I thought someone had pulled a trick on me and the little man disappeared. I thought to myself, someone has dubbed the record with their voice, someone who I don't know, someone very clever in his trickery. Someone wanted to hypnotize me, make me the living, speaking dead. Then I realized that I had seen this little green man before in my last trip.

Johnny was a congenial householder. Jolly with kids. Easy with adults. He'd come home from work every night about midnight and have a beer and tell us about the pizza parlor.

When the parole officer would drop around to make his surprise visits, the fibers of the house braced in empathetic protection. We were all members of a benign conspiracy to keep Johnny out of jail. For the first time in his life he had a home and a protective family.

But the price was expensive. It took commitment, caring, concern, sharing. An emotional thing that can't be taught in the professional schools or obtained by voting large appropriations for criminal rehabilitation.

Back in prison the program went on. Psychedelic trips, two or three a week. Moments of confrontation. Moments of terror. Moments of joy.

We were using the prison as a training center. The convicts were learning how to guide psychedelic drug sessions. Harvard graduate students were coming to go through the program themselves. There was less distinction between psychologists and inmates. The new Harvards were assigned to veteran inmates for orientation and guidance.

In session after session the inmates guided the Harvards, and the Harvards guided the convicts.

The energy generated by the sessions continued to spill out beyond the prison walls. The psilocybin session room became a show place. Whenever visitors came to Cambridge inquiring about psychedelic drugs, we took them out to the prison. The convicts sat around the table giving lectures on their mystic experiences to Gerald Heard and Alan Watts and Aldous Huxley and the ex-King of Sarawak and coveys of visiting psychiatrists.

The instinctive strategy was to do everything possible to enhance self-esteem, pride, and sense of accomplishment. Every power we could turn over to the convicts was a fiber in the body of growth we were constructing.

As in any tribe there were sectors of friction, resentment, and disappointments.

Johnny O'Connell lost his job when the pizza parlor went out of business. For a few days he

The last Indian record came on and I closed my eyes, nothing, no color, nothing at all. I opened my eyes and felt very dizzy, so I closed my eyes again. All of a sudden a vision came unto me. Waver of sound, strings waving with sound, the music its very strings danced before me. The strings were gold, bright and brilliant.

A voice came from the strings mystical and God-like in its tone, precise in its pronunciation, faraway and abstract in its meaning to me. Then I saw the little green man again, emerald green, robe about him, long legs and arms wrapped about himself, bald head shining with light, long thin ears, bright green eyes, sly wide grinning mouth. He had gold earrings in his ear, long, thin eyebrows and darker and a little beard growing from his chin. He spoke of the music, of the very strings he sat upon.

looked for a new job and then he took to sitting around the house watching television and drinking beer all day. We tried LSD. Heavier and heavier doses, with no results. Johnny always treated psychedelics with the bravado of the Olympic booze champion. I can outdrink any man in the house. His pride was to prove he could take more and more sacrament without passing out.

So one afternoon we gave him five times the normal dose of LSD. Johnny flipped out of his mind and spun up to heaven. He raved about the beauty. He laughed with joy. He saw it all.

How do you like heaven, Johnny?

The answer was straight one-hundred-proof Irish. Tell God he's flubbed his job, Doc, there's no beer joint in heaven.

So we bundled up in overcoats to take Johnny to a bar. We thought he might see through the booze scene. He walked into the bar with bravado, but it was too much for him. The bottles leered and mocked. Gotta get the hell out of here.

Later that night he went back to the bar, ordered a beer, and turned to the man next to him. Mister, you'll never believe where I went today and what I saw. The man next to him didn't believe him. Neither did Johnny. The next day he was back to TV and beer. My irritation grew but Johnny couldn't be moved. I gave him a week to find a job and then I gave him fifty dollars and told him he was on his own.

In two weeks he was back in prison—not for crime, because Johnny wasn't a criminal, but for idleness and beering.

By the fall of 1962 we had over thirty-five convicts and fifteen Harvards in the group. And the men started being paroled out to the streets two and three a month.

True fellowship among men must be based on a concern that is universal. It is not the private interests of the individual that create lasting fellowship among men, but rather the goals of humanity. That is why it is said that fellowship with men in the open succeeds. (I Ching XIII)

We started project CONTACT. The ex-cons and the Harvards were signed up in buddy-system teams to visit the ex-cons in their homes. We'd drive around the slum areas of Brockton, Fall River, Worcester, looking for our man. Then we'd go out and have a beer and find out how he was doing. There was a twenty-four-hour telephone to rush help in case of emergencies.

Maxwell found himself broke, his wife leaving him, and ready to knock over a store in rage and frustration. He'd phone our number and someone would drive over to meet him and spend an hour talking to him in an all-night cafeteria and lend him ten dollars. We bailed them out of jail, sobered them up, hid them from the parole officer, cooled out angry bosses. We did in short what the family does for its confused members. And we kept them out of jail.

By this time operation Keep-Out had become a three-ring circus. There was the prison. There was the outside CONTACT project and there was the less visible but equally important task of keeping the state administrators and officials happy. We kept a steady flow of memoranda and progress reports to the myriad departments which focus a jealous eye on the work of rehabilitating criminals.

It was clear to us that if a week went by without contacting the bureaucrats, clewing them in, making them a part of the game, the whistle would be blown on our game.

What we were doing was highly implausible from the administrative point of view. Week after week for two years we ran ecstasy sessions in a state prison—turning-on with the prisoners, turning-on visiting psychiatrists. We had converted the hospital ward into a spiritual center complete with incense candles and music.

We did this with the approval of the most skeptical, wary group of politician-pros on the American scene—cops, jailers, and parole officials. Our key was direct human contact. I spent one-third of my time in face-to-face interaction with the state officials. We invited them to the prison. We spent long hours over the lunch table, long hours driving to

I could only see part of his face, a small pointed beard covered his cheeks and chin, his eyes glowed with a yellow light and his nose was long and thin. He seemed to be speaking but I could not hear him. Maybe he was praying. I spoke to him, "Hey man, what are you doing here. I know you. I saw you before on a mountain." No answer. I could not help talking jive talk, abstract words. Then the vision disappeared and did not return.

A criminal, at least myself and most all I've ever met, were either unloved children or lost individuals. Lost between right and wrong. What they wanted and the means to it. They knew their ends, power, wealth, money could not buy friends, loved ones, happiness, beauty, intelligence. I saw how foolish the game I played was. Just saw thru it, saw the ends I would find, instead of the ends I'd imagined. It sickened me.

What was life, a life of this kind, just misery for myself and those who loved me.

I again asked what I wanted from life and at once I got an answer—love, peace, plenty, intelligence, not power, but friends.

I reached the top. There was the same rock, the softness of it is still here. On this rock was a man. A man both young and old. He had about his slim body a liquid robe of the bluest blue. He had his hands folded in his lap.

His fingers seemed to glow. They were long and bony and his hands seemed slim and fine. He was looking into the sky and did not hear me. He had long, womanlike hair, smooth and shiny and black, coal black.

It has a way that moves me and relaxes me and through this relaxation I find myself in a much better atmosphere, and also put myself into better environment, which in the future will prove how great psilocybin really is.

the state house and to the probation headquarters. A lunch at the Harvard Faculty Club for the Commissioner of Correction and his top lieutenants. Sharing of space-time. Caring for them, caring for their opinions and for their approval.

We even ran sessions for parole officers and correction officials. Some of them had unhappy trips. People committed to external power are frightened by the release of ecstasy because the key is surrender of external power. One chief parole officer flipped-out paranoid at my house and accused us of a Communist conspiracy and stormed around while Madison Presnell curled up on the couch watching, amused at the white folks frantically learning how to get high. He grinned at me. So you call it the love drug?

But the next day the parole officer looked back at where he had been and his voice shook in reverence.

The administrators let the project go on for the same reason that administrators do anything—fear of criticism. Our work was succeeding and the prisoners knew it. Not just the inmates at Concord but all over the state. The politicians had to go along with it.

Harvard was backing the project and Harvard couldn't be flouted. But there was an underlying skepticism. A basic distrust about any enthusiastic new approach to prisoner rehabilitation. Let them try their newfangled experiment, but the old hands knew that cons are cons and nothing can change them.

In politics and administration the great sin is idealism, bright-eyed vigor—and the highest virtue is cynicism. Faith, hope, and charity are dirty words. Nothing really changes except who has the power, who has the money.

Everyone in the Massachusetts correctional system believed in his heart that our project would fail. That we would not lower the recidivism rate, that we could not convert hardened criminals. We just couldn't do it because we were running against the cultural momentum of American society which is more laws, more cops, more lawyers, more judges, more prison psychiatrists, more control, and we were saying: give power away.

If we were right, then the sphincter clasp of

society would have to be released. Deep religious commitments were involved in the use of our little pill.

I came into the warden's office one morning to report the most recent statistics. We had kept twice as many convicts out on the street as the expected number. We had halved the crime rate. He listened politely but he kept glancing toward the corner of the room. When I finished he got up and clapped me on the back and led me to the corner. Look at that, he said proudly.

It was an architect's color drawing of a super prison. Look. Two football fields. This wing is for admitting and orientation. Two more cell blocks. Mess halls double in size. We'll have capacity for twice as many inmates and we can double the staff all the way down the line.

His eyes were glowing like anyone showing you his dream plan. Success. His fantasy was coming true. A prison and an organizational table twice as big! The bureaucrats' goal.

But warden, you're not going to need a larger prison. His face registered surprise. Why not? Because we're cutting your recidivism rate in half, remember. You won't need to have all the cells you have now. You won't need to have half the guards you now have, if you let us turn-on your prison.

The warden laughed. He liked me and felt protective toward our hopes. Well, we're getting some of your men back. Kelly returned today in handcuffs. He was one of your men, wasn't he?

Yes, Kelly had come back to the prison and so were some others returning. They had not committed new crimes. They were returning cheerfully, peacefully, quietly, not making it on the outside. Dropping-out.

Kelly was a good example. He had been paroled and went back to the slum housing project where his wife and four children awaited him. He walked in on a financial crisis. The state support money for families of prisoners stopped the day he got out. He had no job. Five reproachful mouths to feed. His relations with his wife, never good, had been further strained by his imprisonment. His occupational assets, never good, were weakened by his prison record.

Under psilocybin I have taken on a different attitude toward people and friends. I was always different in manner and just the opposite of what this drug brought out.

Impulse has been the main factor in my doing things and through these impulses I have been incarcerated, but I am looking for a way to turn away from impulse.

As I was laying in the bed with the blanket over my head, I kept getting these wonderful feelings, all through my body. I can't explain how they felt, but they felt so good that I was hoping that they would last all day, but they didn't.

For a little while after that, I went through a great deal of suffering. It seems that I was strapped down to a table or something, and I was cut open from my chest to my stomach, and it seems that I could taste blood in my mouth.

As I was laying there bleeding, there were some people standing over me, saying too bad, but they weren't trying to help me.

It was then that I seemed to be fighting something, when Dr. Presnell came over to me and took the blankets off my head. I had felt then that he had just saved my life.

I got up to go to the bathroom, and I got a little dizzy. Everything that I saw, and the color of them seemed to be more intense. After I came out of the bathroom, I went over to one of the windows and looked out. I was feeling very happy.

Dr. Leary came over to me and asked me how I felt. I told him I felt free. As soon as I said that, the happiness left me. I started to think what I was free from. I looked around the room, and for the first time, I noticed the bars on the windows.

Kelly was plunged, ill-prepared, into a tense, frustrating, almost hopeless situation. The pride and enthusiasm and insight of his psychedelic sessions were eroding fast. Our outside contact team met with him and tried to get him a job. Kelly was hard to sell to an employer.

Now, if you put yourself into Kelly's head, you get this perspective. The outside society of Boston is cold, demanding, degrading, inhospitable, heavy with responsibility, empty of reward. Kelly looks back at the prison, free food and lodging and a job. There, he is a wanted man. He has a place. A role. But more than that, in the prison is the warmth of the group, the pride of belonging to the mushroom-elite, the rare unexpected ecstasy and adventure of the psychedelic drug trip, the companionship. The session room was home. Like a hummingbird, Kelly starting circling back to Concord. It was so easy. Just be drinking beer when the parole officer comes to inspect, and sound unenthusiastic about getting a job.

Sorry, Kelly, but we have to pull your parole. You're going back. Kelly was going home, back to his cellmates.

The problem was that the close tribal fabric of the prison group was pulled apart in the city. Everything in the Boston culture was geared to push Kelly back to crime.

We needed a tribal center, a halfway house. A place in Boston where the ex-cons could reinstate the closeness of the prison group. The tribal tie has to be strong to protect its people in the brutal anonymity of the city.

We started looking around for a house to rent. We ran into the usual problems. Landlords turned off when they learned that we were planning a center for ex-convicts. We didn't have the money or the energy to set up a house. It was obvious that we would have to live in the house ourselves with the ex-cons. Sit around the homefire with them, become inmates with them, and we weren't ready to make that big step of love and commitment.

We sat in our offices at Harvard and made great plans and sent men out to look for real estate. And then at five o'clock we returned to our comfortable homes in the Boston suburbs and the ex-cons went back to the slums.

Sixth in the second place means: Fellowship with men in the clan. Humiliation. There is danger here of formation of a separate faction on the basis of personal and egoistic interests. Such factions, which are exclusive and, instead of welcoming all men, must condemn one group in order to unite the others, originate from low motives and therefore lead in the course of time to humiliation. (I Ching)

In the sessions we were all gods, all men at one. We were all two-billion-year-old seed centers pulsing together. Then as time slowly froze we were reborn in the old costumes and picked up the tired games.

We weren't yet ready to act on our revelation. The spark we had lit within each one of us was there and we guarded it, but the sun-flame had not yet burst forth.

The walls that were keeping me from freedom. I said to myself, is this all that I have to look forward to for the rest of my life? I started to walk up and down the floor; I looked out of the window, and the walls seemed to be closing in on me. They kept getting closer and closer. I got scared. I looked around the room for some place to hide. I didn't hide. I decided to face it. I looked at the walls and said, "You are not going to get the best of me," and the walls moved back to their regular position.

∞

THE JUDGMENT

FELLOWSHIP WITH MEN *in the open.*
Success.
It furthers one to cross the great water.
The perseverance of the superior
man furthers.

(I Ching)

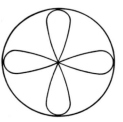

When the Celestial Messenger Comes
Wearing a Fedora,
Can You Suspend Your Games?

BILL BURROUGHS DROPS OUT OF OUR CLAN

Summer 1961

Guide: BILL   BURROUGHS

Oracle: XVIII

Work on What Has Been Spoiled (Decay)

Keeping Still, Mountain

The Gentle, Wind

The wind blows low on the mountain:
The image of DECAY.
Thus the superior man stirs up the people
And strengthens their spirit.

(I Ching)

WILLIAM BURROUGHS:

May 6, 1961
Cargo U.S. Consulate
Tangier
Morocco

Dear Dr. Leary:

I would like to sound a word of urgent warning with regard to the hallucinogen drugs with special reference to N-Dimethyltryptamine.

I had obtained a supply of this drug synthesized by a chemist friend in London.

My first impression was that it closely resembled psilocybin in its effects.

I had taken it perhaps ten times—(this drug must be injected and the dose is about one grain but I had been assured that there was a wide margin of safety)—with results sometimes unpleasant but well under control and always interesting when the horrible experience occurred which I have recorded and submitted for publication in *Encounter*.

You've got to write a big, enthusiastic letter to Burroughs and get him interested in taking the mushrooms. He knows more about drugs than anyone alive. What a report he'll write you! This was Allen Ginsberg talking in the winter of 1960–61, but it could have been any of a dozen other advisors. Burroughs is the Man. He knows the drug scene from head to heel.

Allen Ginsberg left a copy of *Junky*, a hard-bitten, powerful account of the 1950 drug scene in New York. Written by Burroughs under the pseudonym William Lee, the book is so real it stinks of subways-late-at-night, and the stale must of Eighth Avenue hotels, the sickening odor of benzedrine, and the dry sweat of tenement sexuality. The last lines of *Junky* announced the author's intention to pursue the hallucinogenic grail to South America. "Kick is momentary freedom from the claims of the aging, cautious, frightened flesh. Yage may be the final fix."

Yage is a vine, *Ayahuasca* or *Banisteriopsis Caape*, found in the Amazon regions of Peru and Colombia which Ginsberg described as a telepathic-hallucinogenic-mind-expanding drug used by Amazon Indian doctors for finding lost objects, mostly bodies and souls.

In 1953 Burroughs had made the trip to Bogotá, Pasto, Macon, and then to Peru on the trail of visions. Now, seven years later, he was in Paris experimenting with hallucinations produced by flicker machines.

What has been spoiled through man's fault can be made good again through man's work. It is not immutable fate, as in the time of STANDSTILL, that has caused the state of corruption, but rather the abuse of human freedom. (I Ching XVIII)

214

After a while a letter arrived from Paris.

Dear Timothy Leary:

Thanks for your letter. I agree all the way. My work and understanding benefits from Hallucinogens MEASUREABLY. Wider use of these drugs would lead to better work conditions on all levels. Might be interesting to gather anthology of mushroom writing. I will be glad to send along my results. Enclosed *minutes to go* which may interest you along lines you indicate in letter. I have made cut-up highs without chemical assistants. Brion Gysin who first applied the cut-up method to writing is here at the above address and would also be most interested to take the mushrooms. So I will look forward to hearing from you. You have my full agreement and support.

Sincerely,
William Burroughs

P.S. Do you know Doctor Shultes of the Harvard Botanical Dept.? I met him in South America. He has taken Bannisteriopsis and is most interested in experiments with the hallucinogens.

In reply I sent a supply of psilocybin pills to the world's most experienced experimenter on drugs and awaited a report. His report was surprising. Burroughs had a bad trip on DMT and was sounding the cry of urgent warning.

We studied the letter with considerable interest and got a wide variety of interpretations. We had learned enough to know that set-and-setting determined the reaction, not the drug.

Bill Burroughs alias Doctor Benway had inadvertently taken an overdose of DMT and was flung into a space-fiction paranoia.

Shortly after receiving the warning, I wrote asking Burroughs if he would participate in a symposium of psychedelic drugs which we had arranged for the September 1961 meetings of the American Psychological Association. I was impressed with Burroughs' experimental bent, the rigor and sternness of his declaration about precise research. We were intrigued by the idea of the great novelist

I am sending along to you pertinent sections of this manuscript and I think you will readily see the danger involved.

I do not know if you are familiar with apomorphine which is the only drug that acts as a metabolic regulator.

I think if I had not had this drug to hand, the result could have been lethal and this was not more than a grain and a half of N-Dimethyltryptamine.

While I have described the experience in allegorical terms it was completely and horribly real and involved unendurable pain.

A metabolic accident?

Perhaps.

But I have wide experience with drugs and excellent constitution and I am not subject to allergic reactions.

So I can only urge you to proceed with caution and to familiarize yourself with apomorphine.

Dr. John Dent of London has written a book on the apomorphine treatment for alcoholics and drug addicts —(it is the only treatment that works but the U.S. Health Dept. will not use it).

His book is called *Anxiety and Its Treatment.*

ı can ask him to send you a copy if you are interested.

Let me hear from you.

William Burroughs

∞

From *Minutes to Go* by William Burroughs:

The hallucinogen drug bottle and smoke pictures of strange places and states of being some familiar some alien as the separation word beautiful and ugly spirits blossom in the brain like Chinese flowers in some lethal blossoms bottle genie of appalling conditions hatch cosmographies and legends spill through mind screen movies overlapping myths of the race.

The Night Before Thinking was recorded from a young Arab painter Achmed Jacoubi who cannot read or write.

(Recorded 1958 past time.)

running precise-controlled research sessions. We offered to pay travel expenses for the trip to New York and asked Burroughs if he wanted to spend some time in Cambridge after the symposium. The answer came back, Sure.

In July of that summer I went to Tangier to see Allen Ginsberg and to plan the conference with Burroughs. After the plane from Madrid pulled up to the Tangier air terminal, we were held up for fifteen minutes while the family of the King passed to another waiting airplane, emblazoned with Arabic script and regal emblems. More than a dozen women in veils picked their way daintily across the runway guarded by police and soldiers.

Over at the terminal behind the rail, a man with long blond hair waved and shouted. It was Peter Orlovsky, leaving in half an hour for Gibraltar, then to Athens and the far, far East. He was sick of Tangier and didn't like what was going on there. He had quarreled with Burroughs, and was off to find wise men and wild drugs in the East. I'll take drugs you've never heard of! *Morgenlandfahrt.* Have a good trip, Peter.

The taxi climbed the winding street to the little hotel where Allen Ginsberg had reserved rooms for me at two dollars a night. Allen was out. As I waited in the living room of the concierge, a thin, stooped man wearing glasses and a hat walked in. Two handsome British boys about nineteen years old were with him.

Burroughs. Fine. I was just about to look you up. Leave a note for Allen. Let's have a drink.

We sat in the outdoor garden of a restaurant and had several gins while we reviewed the Harvard and American plans. Mind. Brain. Drugs. Mind. Brain. Drugs. Burroughs was noncommittal about the mushrooms but he was pleased with our research and the plans to visit America.

Then we went back to the hotel and had dinner with Allen Ginsberg, Gregory Corso, and Allen Ansen. After dinner we went to Burroughs' hotel. A lion's head stared from the door. We walked through into a garden and around to the very back to Burroughs' room. Dark cave. Big bed. Desk littered with papers. Hundreds of photos pasted

The Night Before Thinking came to Jacoubi under the influence of majoun, a form of hashish candy—(noteworthy that there has been almost no work done on the chemistry of Cannabis whereas other hallucinogens are receiving constant attention).

When the story of Jacoubi came to the attention of this department, Doctor Benway was conducting experiments with some of the new hallucinogens and had inadvertently taken a slight overdose of N-Dimethyltryptamine—Dim-N for short—class of South American narcotic plants prestonia related to bufotina, which a species of poisonous toad spits out of its eyes.

There is also reason to suspect a relation to a poison injected by certain fish from sharp fin spines.

This fish poison causes a pain so intense that morphine brings no relief.

Described as fire through the blood: photo falling—word falling—breakthrough in gray room—towers open fire—a blast of pain and hate shook the room as the shot of Dim-N hit and I was captured in enemy territory power of Sammy the Butcher.

together and rephotographed. Cut up pictures. Boil out the essence of the pictures. And then shoot it.

Three off-tuned radios blaring noise. Static is the essence of sound. Pot cutting-board. Allen's pictures of Marrakesh. We sat around the room, taking turns peering through the cardboard cylinder flicker machine. Burroughs wanted to take mushrooms. Allen Ginsberg said, Well, everyone in Tangier has been waiting for you to arrive with the legendary mushrooms. Oh, intercontinental fame of Montezuma's medicine. Oh, fabled poets. Yes, they will write expatriate reports in blank verse, international. Allen Ansen from Venice will. William Burroughs from St. Louis will send a mysterious reply in tissue script. Allen Ginsberg, still scared, will chant an epistolary record. And Gregory Corso, owlwise, catsmouth, cheerful-Panda-bear-Charlie-Chaplin, will with pleasure tap out a few lines on the fabled typewriter. And the two young Englishmen cool with wild poet's hair will spin out statements. Good deal. All experienced hands at consciousness-expansion.

The session began in Burroughs' room, dim-lit, unmade bed, crowded, smoky. Burroughs lay back on the bed. The English boys watched him. The rest of us walked out to the garden and looked over the wall down on Tangier Harbor. Allen was depressed over Peter's departure. What did Peter say? How did he seem? He was struggling with Burroughs. Burroughs is anti-love.

It so happened that the Royal Fair was in town and the King's picture was draped over wires at every street intersection, and we could see the fairground ablaze with lights down near the beach and hear the sound of drums and pipes.

It was the essence of night, warm, clear, hung on a ledge above North Africa's port, Moorish music drifting up to us watching.

Allen Ansen and Gregory Corso were grinning and we all looked at each other and breathed in deeply. Whew! Pure, burnished ecstasy.

Allen Ginsberg said that Burroughs seemed to want to be quiet, so why didn't we go over to his place and watch the night from there. We floated down the steps to the hotel and then up to the patio in front of Allen's room. The floor beneath was a city carpeted with lights. Lights strung from the rigging of ships in the harbor and the King's carnival crazily rollicking along by the water's edge.

We were all in the highest and most loving of moods. Allen Ansen couldn't believe it. He kept laughing and shaking his head. This can't be true. So beautiful. Heaven! But where is the devil's price? Anything this great must have a terrible flaw in it. It can't be this good. Is it addictive? Will we ever come down? I hope not.

I was answering the questions that Allen and Gregory asked about the research and what had been happening in the States. Comic, Zen, mushroomy talk. The four of us moored like happy balloons over Tangier. Joy. Love. Union.

It was decided to pick up Burroughs and then go down to visit the fair. When we got to Burroughs' house, Allen walked around to the side and climbed part way up the wall and uttered his ritual greeting: Bill BUH-rows! Bill BUH-rows!

We waited by the door and after a minute it slowly creaked open and there, almost collapsed against the wall, was Bill. His face was haggard and tense—staring out like man caught in some power of Sammy the Butcher. He reached his left hand over his sweating face. Tried to slip out eyes of white-hot crab creatures. His thin fingers clawing at the right cheek, smoke escape cut off by white-hot metal lattice. Bill, how are you doing? They gave me large dose. I would like to sound a word of warning. I'm not feeling too well. I was struck by juxtaposition of purple fire mushroomed from the Pain Banks. Urgent Warning. I think I'll stay here in shriveling envelopes of larval flesh. I'm going to take some apomorphine. One of the nastiest cases ever processed by this department.

You fellows go down to the fair and see film and brain waves tuning in on soulless insect people. Minutes to go. Whew! The hallucinogen drugs bottle and smoke pictures, my dears. Compassion. Compassion. Beautiful and ugly spirits blossom in the brain. Too bad. Minutes to go. What can we do? Compassion brings no relief? See you at the fair. The door closed around him glowing metal

The ovens closed round me glowing metal lattice in purple and blue and pink screening burning flash flesh under meat cleaver of Sammy the Butcher and pitiless insect eyes of white-hot crab creatures of the ovens.

Called for Hassan i Sabbah and the screams of millions who had called for Hassan i Sabbah in that place screamed back from creatures of the oven mouths dripping purple fire.

No place to go trapped here cut off tried to slip out on the gray into mirrors and spoons and doorways of the fish city but my smoke escape was cut off by white-hot metal lattice in this soulless place of the insect people.

Place of dry air shriveling envelopes of larval flesh—insect eyes of the alien species—the soulless insect people—and the pain jinn dripping strips of purple fire mushroomed from the tower blasts—reached for my apomorphine tablets.

Better take a handful, Burroughs, said the regulator.

Took twelve twentieth-grain tablets and flashed a glimmer of gray beyond the ovens and made it out to the port tearoom on silver tea set yesterday past fields of interplanetary war and prisoners eaten alive by white-hot ants.

Do not forget this Johnny-come-lately: War!

War to extermination.

Fading now.

Gray ash writing of Hassan i Sabbah sifts through the ovens.

Dust and smoke.

Gray writing of Hassan i Sabbah switch tower orders reverse fire back creatures of the oven stored in pain beaks from the torture chambers of time.

Souls torn into insect fragments by iron claws of the chessmaster doctor—who synthesized Dim-N in annexia, iron claws?

They gave large dose of Dim-N.

lattice in purple and blue. He's the most resilient man in Hassan i Sabbah's mountain troop. He'll be all right. Good ole Bill. He takes no prisoners.

We rolled like diamond hoops down to the waterfront. The electricians had outdone themselves. Sidewalks emblazoned with Arabic script. What's that jeweled object, Van Vogted on the pavement? Gem box sparkled, lived. Once, for a long moment, chance turned it, that translucent fairy tower, a glowing turquoise blue. For one moment—and then the combination shattered into a million bursting fragments of color: blue, red, green, yellow. No color, no possible shade of color, was missing from that silent, flaming explosion. What is it? Oh, an empty cigarette package in the gutter's lambent fire. Come along. Oh, see the conquering art of Moorish slave girls crowned with diadems. What a happy crowd! Dancing with lively, mocking sound, blue tattoos on forehead. Happy night walking to the fair. With Baudelaire. This world of stone and metal; brittle and bright. The family of the King picked their way across daintily. Flasks of perfume, fabrics lamé and spangled, rich furnishings of brocade and gold, and we haven't even arrived at the gate to the fair yet. Tickets. Industrial exhibits of the Alien Species. Ansen and Corso smiling. Delights of Islam.

Allen Ginsberg is still melancholy. Peter has left. Not sure he believes in love. Not sure he wants to be a great man.

We slid through canvas slit in Arab tent, Ginsberg guide, to watch the dancing. Oh, the endless chanting. Behind us a girl nurses her baby. Boy dancers swayed and rocked drunkenly. Chanting. And become dust that is scattered on the desert wind, swinging circles clashing bronze cymbals. Allen Ansen, eyes closed, sways back and forth to the beat. The foremost shall be brought nigh unto God in the Gardens of Delight. The cymbals laughed and chanting told the secret. On inlaid couches they recline face to face. Four Moorish soldiers, tender young in the front row, eyes popping in wonder, while immortal youths go around them with goblets and flagons and a chalice of wine. The dance endless. Exactly. Timeless. The

Like five times what you took and the prisoners disintegrated into oven creatures.

They took recordings in sound film and brain waves can tune in on Dim-N and they are moving to extend the range of tune in other hallucinogens and blockage this planet under alien insect enemy.

One of the nastiest cases ever processed by the department. . . .

Final blast from fading towers I saw Nova spirit burning metal eyes black metal skull translucent with fire head of Nova—remembered that turnstile brought a prisoner to explode this planet —Uranian-born of Nova conditions: Two powers of equal strength to be directed against each other.

No riots like injustice directed between enemies.

Minutes to go.

The tortured jinn and pain spirits to set off the charge from a distant sky switch— white-hot blast out in vapor trails smoke writing of Hassan i Sabbah.

cadenced rise and fall of breathing rhythm. Up. Down. Up. Down. Around us veiled women, mysterious, soft, inviting, and fruit according to their choice and flesh of fowls that they desire. Ginsberg was whispering that the color of the robe meant a different tribe. Rifs from the mountains. Fountains? Can't hear with talk of. Berbers? Proud? Loud? Joyce? The chanting river roar mounts. There too are Houris, with dark eyes like hidden pearls. Entire families leaning forward to watch, robed, listening, nor are they bemused. Whispers—they're all high on pot or hashish. That's why the dance goes so long, endless and always flowing. Yeaaaaaaaah. But they hear the ayeing peace. Peace. Now the Ganowanian drummers leap on stage: whirling, pounding the deep, heavy drums. Each beat quivers, energy coils, we become each beat. Amid thornless lote-trees and clustered plantains and spreading shade and gushing water. The drummers, Negroid, fierce, laughing. High too? Moors use water in their architecture because to a desert people the splashing sound and rippling sight of fountains is the highest delight. The dance tempo quickened to a Niagara chaos of sound and high-raised couches. Consorts have we created and we have made them virgins. On low stairs leading up to the stage a Moorish maid beams out curious, flirting look from olive slits behind a gray veil, utterly loving and perfectly matched we have made them. I fell in love with veiled eyes.

When the dancing stopped we filed outside and walked to an open cafe under the arcade of the fair building. Arab music from a radio, and squatting in the corner, a man playing a guitar. A circle of men sitting on cushions passing pipes with long stems and small clay bowls. Marijuana smoke. A man about fifty, wiry and cheerful as your plumber on a party, jumped up and began a belly dance. The men watched, grinned, and clapped their hands. Burroughs walked up with the English boys. He was feeling better but wasn't talking. We had tea in tall glasses clogged with mint leaves. Steaming. Sweet. Burroughs wanted to go to a bar. We walked along the waterfront, lazily. The bar was crowded with men and smoky with loud Spanish music. I said good night to Burroughs and walked up the hill with Allen and Gregory and stayed up the rest of the night talking on Allen's patio and heard the cocks crow and saw the sun rise and gleam on the eastern walls of the city by the gates.

During the following days in Morocco I shot reels of retinal film Tangerine. At Paul Bowles's apartment I heard his tapes of Arab music, recorded as he walked down old village dancing festival streets, and a tape of Burroughs reading his stuff at an English University—powerful, eerie, Venusian prose. *Minutes to go.* No one has captured the horror of modern technology like Burroughs—cold damp machinery, the television mind, cold, blue-steel sexuality, plastic bodies drained of the warm juices. I watched a session in which several young English boys took majoun (the powerful hashish jam). One of them got caught in bad visions. I could see why. He played the part of a miserable, bullied, self-despising English schoolboy homosexual. He had walked in on the session uninvited and had tagged along unwanted. Then suddenly he found himself "out of his mind" in a strange port city amid strangers who disliked him, and he trembled in fear. I watched to see how the drug-experts would handle the situation. For the most part he was ignored. He's a drag, man. Give him a sedative. There was little compassion in the honey-sweet majoun syrup. Only Allen Ginsberg was tender, sitting next to him and talking softly, *curandero* style.

When I left Tangier for Copenhagen, I arranged to meet Bill Burroughs in London in three weeks. Dick Alpert and I phoned Bill and then took a cab to his hotel. He had a small, dark, first-floor room with a meter on the wall. Bill misses kif. Poring over photos of yage convulsions. I am a good photographer of impersonal symbols. The mushrooms of Tangier propelled me into arrows of unfriendly. Let's try some now to see if they work differently. We all took 4 mg., naught but a brush of the phoenix bird's soft wing.

In the working-class tearoom. Bill's metal cynicism American publishers cheating authors. Pub-

Break through in gray room —word falling—photo falling—towers open fire—sacrifice partisan of all nations—

Sacrifice iron claws—you are under arrest iron claws—

Gray police of the regulator do their work and go down all your streets and by the river light on water flash spoons and tea pots—

Poison of dead sun in my brain slowly fading—now Sammy the Butcher fill your hand—

Fan silver bullets from the old westerns whistling image of Sammy the Butcher explode a million flash bulbs smell of burning metal—

Cut on gray into *The Gunfighter*—blast Sammy the Butcher from the West the West Side push I told over the gray subway—through silent turnstiles—

Click clack out to gray taxi down shadow streets of Tangier—back from gangster films—

Use that typewriter—

Chop chop swift Samurai sword—machete silver flash Sammy's last picture—now Sammy the Butcher advances from his corner—

lisher Benny and his neuroses and his mistress and his lawyers and his analysts. Ah Beckett. Awe and reverence. Sent emissary to Beckett to arrange an interview. But Beckett sees no one. With Tangier mushrooms, feared lack of control. Stop all that vibrating. Regrets *Soft Machine.* Won't be understood. Cut-up is too far out.

He is using his chopping techniques that earned him his moniker—

Walking the London streets. He doesn't like the loss of control. We were swallowed by two mushroom pills and sat in the green mouth of the park on white dental benches. Richard brooding about Greek sexual utopias and watching the passersby.

Sammy can't seem to reach the contender slipping dodging shifting into gray junk flesh stale overcoats and shaking spoons—

Burroughs talking brilliantly leather beaten face, turkey neck. Ah J. B. Rhine, you German river of experimentation. ESP is either accidental (little whirlpools of old vibrations caught in pockets, preserved, and suddenly tuned-in to) or functional (sender needs the message delivered). ESP can never be experimental. Why do research? The stroboscope. It frightens me. Burroughs needs equipment to experiment. Dr. Gray Walter can locate hallucinations. Let's say a peasant woman comes with a devil vision. Well, by precise manipulation of specific brain points, localized you understand, the doctor proceeds to remove the devil's horns, one by one, and then without horns the devil is just a man in her room. Well, then by precise manipulation of specific brain cells the devil's leer becomes a smile and then by further precise manipulations, the man gets to look familiar and, well, to make a long story short, he eventually lays her right in the bed in which she is hallucinating and she has an orgasm, not one but several. Whew! All in her imagination by simple manipulation, precise, based on specific localization of hallucinatory content. Imagination is real, after all. Are you involved like us in the game of helping the human race? Hell no. Hassan i Sabbah only wants his returned.

Cut into newsreel prizefights and send all those fists crushing into Sammy's soft underside—

Mr. Bradly Mr. Martin through the gray turnstile click a million switch blades Uranian-born in the face of Nova conditions—

The champ is worried folks —Molotov cocktails from the streets of Berlin and Budapest—

Cut chop with that typewriter—stampeding herds from the West—turn the animals loose on Sammy—

Imagine a simple, middle-class tearoom. How it swirls in mushroom smoke. Line up for puddles of brown, milky tea sweet steamy. The essence of anything is the cut-up. Cut up words. Cut up pictures. Boil it down to the essence. Strip off all the irrelevant, redundant. Boil it down in a steamy teaspoon and then shoot it. Laughs. Jolly. Want to sell Coke? Coca-Cola, I mean? Get thousands of

Cut TV bullfights Mexico DF—chop that horn write up into Sammy's groin— use all the strength of those neck muscles you got it?—

pictures of Coke being drunk in every kind of situation. Paste up all the pictures on a wall and take a picture of that—then all the thousand photos are in one photo. The essence of Coke-photo. Madison Avenue. See it get rich. Window design advertising. Grab monopoly money. Henry light sitting on a luce pile of pictures a mile high in that Time-Life building. They have pictures of every inch of the world.

Virus and parasite. Like that Humpy. Don't let them in, the parasites. They always worm and then make you feel guilty. Be immune. Don't bargain with them. You can't negotiate with a parasite. The soft machine is too difficult. I am now writing a science-fiction book that a twelve-year-old can understand. I write to create my own reality. Sound an urgent warning against parasites. Tapeworms are invisible. Viral invasion of the brain. Watch out don't let them enter. Politics of the virus. What do parasites want? To keep the status quo. Worm their way into the host. Psychedelic drugs are counter-agents. Destroy the virus. Destroy the status quo. Psychedelic drugs are specific cure for brain parasites. Cerebral virus live in nervous systems. Eat and create waste products which prevent consciousness-expansion. A hangup is due to immobilization caused by waste products of neural parasites. Politics of parasites. Do not kill off the host. Need him to eat off. Like con and the mark. Virus is like any rich politician. Vested interest in keeping brain immobilized—keeping consciousness contracted.

Symbiosis is the political slogan of parasite. When a parasite is cornered, when you've got him covered in your sights, he'll try to convince you that you need a symbiotic relationship. You need me eating off you!

Or he'll try to convince you that you made him a parasite. It's not my fault I have to eat off you. You led me on. You invited me in. Like Humpy. I gave him a junk habit. Or with poor boys. You taught me to enjoy nice things. Oceans of tan, sweet, steaming tea wash through English surburban restaurant spilling brown on the counters. Sugary tan the air. Let's leave.

Floating down the street, Burroughs creating cut-

Loose pack of vicious dogs from *The Savage Innocents* —strife in battle scenes and fighter flames—cool and casual whistling killers drift in from 1920 streets—

They are not come just a looka you Sammy—folks the Butcher has taken a terrible beating in this round—

He looks dazed and keeps shaking his head from side to side—there goes the bell—

Now throw in that pain jinn sixty feet tall dripping purple fire—King Kong—

Street gangs Uranian-born in the face of Nova conditions pinball machine the world—shift tilt that oven pain in color splats tracer bullets bursting rockets—

Folks the Butcher is clicking back and forth like a bear in a shooting gallery—

The contender has Sammy on the ropes now—he's using Sammy's chopping techniques—

Blow after blow air-hammers the code write into Sammy's diaphragm—disperse in broken mirrors clouds cyclones low pressure Sammy's image into your flash bulb—sput.

Witnesses from a distance observed in brilliant flash and a roaring blast as Sammy the Butcher was arrested.

Having written this account of my experience with Dim-N—(and I would like to sound a word of warning)—I was of course struck by juxtapositions of areas between my account and *The Night Before Thinking* recorded by Achmed Jacoubi five years earlier.

I took a page of my text—first draft—and folded it down the middle and passed down the middle of the page in Jacoubi's text where he relates the oven incident on page 7.

NOTE 1:

Hassan i Sabbah the old man of the mountain of the assassins lived in the year one thousand.

From a remote mountain fortress called Alamout he could reach a knife to Paris.

ups. Scissors through parasitology. Chops up interpersonal psychology, pastes in junk dialect. Beautiful moment of drifting together. Caution! No positive emotions now! Suspicious. Where go? Walk around Piccadilly. Head for Chelsea? Make a plan? Burroughs high, happy, jolly. Go to our hotel and have a drink and then dinner? Great. Bump along in side-door London hack.

Now curare is an interesting drug. Muscle paralysis. No possibility of action. Just lie there absorbing all sensation. Medicine man crooning. Paralyzed. I was smothering and can't say it. Can't talk. Each drug opens up an undiscovered unexplored area. Some inhabited by hostile tribes. Beware. The medicine man can hang you up. Direct you into unfriendly territory. Sound urgent warning. DMT. Beware. Like to take curare plus consciousness-expansion drug. No action. Many visions. Experimental mind.

Morocco—culture built on hashish. Wonderful country. Whole damn place undulating in soft mellow haze of pot. Happy land. No wars. No economic rivalry. Relaxed land of lotus. Nirvana. Arab nationalists. Nova villains. Destroy their own culture. Want power. Want to modernize Moslem countries with industrial nightmare of West. Borrow worst elements of West. Guns and machines. United States pressures them to make nontoxic hashish illegal. Force our toxic narcotic on them—alcohol. Pot used to be legal in Tangier and liquor-drinking illegal. Now it's changed. Dictators want their people in alcoholic stupor. Arab nationalists sitting in Cairo hotels drinking Scotch and plotting westernization of their countries. Burroughs drinking, getting flushed. Feel sick. Take apomorphine. Nervous. Sudden good-night.

Burroughs plane arrives. Logan Airport Boston. Customs inspection. Routine. Whew! Came in clean as a whistle. Take no chances. America! Billbad the Bailer has returned! In the Newton House he rests, restless. He has traveled.

In Tangier he was always busy, hands moving, chopping the leaves, combing out the seeds, sifting, cleaning, shaking, twisting, tapping, lighting, fuming, chopping, combing. Now sitting on the green couch in the booklined library, there was a square round Sinbad the Sailor roc's egg in empty hands. Here's a box of dried Oaxaca mushrooms. Stern face, impassive, examines the samples which, without herbarium specimens, he identified as teonanacate, Flesh of the Gods. Flush of the Dogs. If there be confusion in the botanical field, there is chaos in the chemical. Muttering, Hmm, wonder if you can smoke this stuff. Why not? The old Tangier game. A game is a sequence of movements characterized by a goal, roles, rule, ritual. Chop. Comb. Sift. Twist. Quick as a flash young Jack Leary sprang to his bike and pedaled to village for cigarette paper. Billbad bends over the table with sharp knife on cutting board, chopping, combing, sifting, licking, twisting, lighting, fuming. Ugh! Heavy, damp, gray, moldy smoke lined throat and hung noxious, nauseous over the room. Thank you said Stephen taking a cigarette. Haines held the flaming punk in the shell of his hand. Smoke a soggy log from a frog swamp. I do believe I am getting high. Mister Mushroom's got a cough mixture with a punch in it for you, my friend, in his back pocket. Toad's pus oozes into lung's cough. No more for me, pulmonary, but Billbad the Bailer says he's high. Later chemical consultation reveals psychedelic effect of alkaloid destroyed by combustion.

Warm August nights in Newton. Burroughs works on the paper for the American Psychological Association. The approach will be scholarly. Points of Distinction. Unfortunately the word *drug* activates scientific prose; a reflex between sedative and hallucinogenic words. That week brought a September wave of heat to Manhattan. Symposium on consciousness-expanding drugs. Drugs, Set-and-Setting by Timothy Leary. Unusual Realization and Alterations in Consciousness, Frank Barron. Ecstatogenic Comments by Gerald Heard.

Unusual interest realized that the room must be expanded, altered. Not big enough. APA convention manager uncooperative. Hundreds of audience crammed into room, standing ten-deep in hallway, sitting around speaker's table, sprawling on floor. Burroughs lecturing from his manuscript, low voice dry, noncommittal. Talk louder Bill. Minutes to go.

There were not more than several hundred trainees in any one Alamout shift.

Hassan i Sabbah made no attempt to increase numbers or extend political power.

He took no prisoners.

There were no torture chambers in Alamout.

He was strictly a counter puncher.

When a move was made against Alamout by the multiple enemies of Hassan i Sabbah he reached out with his phantom knife, and a general, a prime minister, and a sultan died.

Hassan i Sabbah master of the jinn.

Assassin of ugly spirits.

NOTE 2:

Apomorphine is made by boiling morphine with hydrochloric acid.

This alters chemical formulae and physiological effects.

Apomorphine has no sedative, narcotic, or pain-killing effect.

It is a metabolic regulator that need not be continued when its work is done.

I quote from *Anxiety and Its Treatment* by Dr. John Dent of London: Apomorphine acts on the back brain stimulating the regulating centers in such a way as to normalize the metabolism.

It has been used in the treatment of alcoholics and drug addicts and normalizes metabolism in such a way as to remove the need for any narcotic substance.

Apomorphine cuts the morphine lines from the brain.

Poison of dead sun slowly fading is smoke.

∞

After the psychological convention the research team returned to Cambridge. Burroughs took up resistance in my house, helpless as a beached fish. The Harvard project members were involved in teaching, rehabilitating convicts, experimenting foolishly but merrily with love engineering, talking and writing about behavior change, pursuing careers, academic, scientific, marital, messianic. And under his gray fedora Burroughs sat lonely in third-floor room surrounded by cut-up photos or leaned unsmiling on kitchen table drinking gin-tonics, beaming a monologue caustic, comic, Hassan i Sabbah, relentless, tender as a Venusian-green neon antennae light gun ray, increasingly bitter and paranoid and always brilliant, original, excruciatingly cynical, naked, personal, monumental, lovely.

Burroughs with the Harvard project was Leonardo da Vinci wearing a fedora, pushed unsmiling into left field at Yankee Stadium. Willy Mays in a fedora lured onto the stage at Metropolitan Opera. He was Christ with a fedora at the Copacabana. The all-time All-Star in the wrong tribe.

From the time he hit the country he was suspicious and cynical of psychedelic drugs and their use. He was instructed to turn up the volume if he experienced any pain. He never had a session and (although his APA lecture gallantly avoided mention of psilocybin) he never concealed his distaste for the drug we hoped he would research.

Sam sat on the ground and put his head in his hands. I wish I had never come here, and I don't want to see no more magic, he said, and fell silent. (The Lord of the Rings)

He left silently without farewell, and then rumor drifted up like damp smoke from New York that he had published a no-thank-you letter denouncing the Harvard psychedelics.

OPEN LETTER TO MY CONSTITUENTS AND CO-WORKERS IF ANY REMAIN FOR THE END OF IT. THE HARVARD PSYCHOLOGISTS HAVE MONOPOLIZED LOVE SEX AND DREAM!

Billbad's ACCUSATION: Harvard's hallucinogenic drug monopolists cover travel arrangements but never pay the constituents they have betrayed and sold out. They offer love in slop buckets to cover retreat. They leave Hassan i Sabbah in a third-floor room subject to constant insults and humiliations. They steal, bottle, and dole out addictive love in eye-droppers of increased awareness of unpleasant or dangerous symptoms.

THE ANSWER: Not guilty, beloved Billbad. There was no powerful board and syndicate to subsidize Dr. Benway's attack on the psilocybin love brigade. There was only Jack Leary and his assistants ready to spring to their borrowed-bicycle fun-errands.

The superior man must first remove stagnation by stirring up public opinion, as the wind stirs everything, and must then strengthen and tranquilize the character of the people, as the mountain gives tranquillity and nourishment to all that grows in its vicinity. (I Ching XVIII)

Billbad the Bailer finally escaped the Nova ovens of Harvard confident not in promise but in fulfillment. He never let his knife-edge style dull into the wrong game. Lonely in his third-floor room, he made the most impressive literary debut of the past century. Lured into left field, he scares Grade B psilocybin out of behavioral scientists counting their methodological hallucinations.

After he covered his retreat from the colony they so disgracefully mis-man-aged, he released a word-ment of urgent warning against his Harvard hosts. Stay out of Timothy Leary's Garden of Delights.

Listen to us, cried the Harvard scientists. We are creating the Garden of Delights on the Harvard payroll. The Best Ever in Ivy League Drug Kicks. LOVE LOVE LOVE in slop buckets. How does that sound to his awe-inspiring artistry? Hassan the Hailer takes us on a lively, scary broadening journey with the ticket that exploded. Leaves nothing for the reader who might wish love sex and dream. At the immediate risk of finding himself the most unpopular character in Cambridge, he creates a new angle of vision. Orders total resistance. Beware of Timothy's ersatz immortality. Psilocybin should be banned by customs? Did we monopolize Immor-

Open letter to my constituents and co-workers if any remain for the end of it

Don't listen to Hassan i Sabbah, they will tell you. He wants to take your body and all pleasures of the body away from you.

Listen to us. We are serving the garden of delights immortality cosmic consciousness the best ever in drug kicks. And love love love in slop buckets.

How does that sound to you boys? Better than Hassan i Sabbah and his cold windy bodiless rock? Right?

At the immediate risk of finding myself the most unpopular character of all fiction—and history is fiction —I must say this: Bring together state of news.

Inquire onward from state to doer.

Who monopolized love sex and dream? Who monopolized life time and fortune. Who took from you what is yours?

Now they will give it all back? Did they ever give anything away for nothing? Did they ever give any more than they had to give?

Did they not always take back what they gave when it was possible and it always was?

Listen: Their garden of delights is a terminal sewer —I have been at some pains to map this area of terminal sewage in the so-called pornographic section of naked lunch and the soft machine—their immortality cosmic consciousness and love is second-run grade B shit.

Their drugs are poison designed to beam in orgasm death and Nova ovens.

Stay out of the garden of delights.

tality, Billbad? Did we monopolize Cosmic Consciousness? Did we force Hassan i Sabbah to wear a special garb, subject to constant insults? No. Our tea, too, spilled brown, steamy sweet on the kitchen table during September heatwave. That's who.

Mr. William Lee Bailer is a very worldly-wise, later-modern, nothing-if-not-civilized superb writer. Who ever gave any more than they had to give to a frightened English schoolboy lonely in the third-floor bedroom? Talk louder, Bill, we whispered.

Are we so complacent about the present state of our knowledge? Are you? Covering your retreat from Leary's office in Cambridge, were you heard to say: Their Immortality Cosmic Consciousness and LOVE Is the cry of every as yet uninstitutionalized man everywhere? Is the love-pill second-run Grade B shit? Is psilocybin a nasty book? Don't you mean lucid? Whose drugs are poison designed to beam-in Orgasm death? And Nova Ovens? Unmistakable. Bill Burroughs, you right superb. For all your spiritual strength, you invoke no fuzzy alien words. What does your program of total austerity turn to for a grasp? Rub out the word forever? Only such extreme wordments can rub out the statemen and all their statements; illuminate the disgracefully managed colony.

For the seven years since 1960, I have lived in mis-man-aged psychedelic communes, tribal encampments (although we didn't grasp the tribal significance for a long time). During this period several thousand people have hopefully visited, and over two hundred have like Bill Burroughs actually moved into, our houses. All but two dozen have moved on because the human chemistry didn't work. The mysterious alchemy of living together. Our insensitivity to Bill Burroughs points up important lessons about human society.

We are tribal animals. Primates. We have lived together in small bands for a hundred thousand years. The unit of human survival—spiritual, economic, political—is the clan. The clan is a small collection of families.

Each of us has built into his genetic code, into the very cellular essence of our being, tribal commitments. Tribal style. Tribal mores. Tribal taboos. Tribal sexual rituals.

Man is designed by over two billion years of divine blueprinting to live in small groups. We were not built to live in the insect anonymity of large cities. The urban empires always collapse.

In the cities, tribal needs and tribal styles are concealed by the plastic uniformity. It is only when we live together that the cellular plan emerges. There are countless mythic archetypes which determine harmonious or disruptive living together. Of these, geographic (racial) and sexual factors are the most important in the formation and perpetuation of the tribal commune. Over the millennia these two factors—geography and sexual style—have operated through natural selection. Today, in the period of collapsing empire, we are faced with the problem of reforming tribes. Look to your ancestors and listen to your sexual messages as you select your tribe-members.

There are mountain people and shore people. There are village people and land people. Your national and racial origins are preserved, alive, in your neurological and cellular equipment. The basic messages of blood and sperm are experienced in every detail of daily life.

Awareness of, and delicate sensitivity to, their ancient styles facilitate harmonious tribal living and rewarding inter-tribal contact. Ignorance of racial and sexual tendencies breeds chaos.

Civilized people are tribal people.

Urban people are usually blind to the essence differences which give glorious variety to organic existence and human life.

Bill Burroughs came to visit, a dignified, sage, complex genius-shaman-poet-guide from a different, but sympathetic tribe. Our obtuse game-playing paid disrespect to him and his clan.

And when I heard the poet scold me, I turned towards him, covered with such shame that even now it circles through my memory.

When you return, poet, we will offer you the ancient pipe of peace.

Bill Burroughs is one of the few word works

It is a man-eating trap that ends in green goo.

Throw back their ersatz immortality.

It will fall apart before you can get out of the big store.

Flush their drug kicks down the drain.

They are poisoning and monopolizing the hallucinogenic drugs.

Learn to make it without any chemical support.

All that they offer is a screen to cover retreat from the colony they have so disgracefully mismanaged.

To cover travel arrangements so they will never have to pay the constituents they have betrayed and sold out.

(man-aged or totally reverbished) that historians will turn to for a grasp. You may call Hassan to right for you. You will stay to right for him. He left Harvard, bowing three times and disappeared into his characters.

He is a knife-edge hero undulled by rhetoric. Yes, talk louder, Bill, talk louder.

Once these arrangements are complete they will blow the place up behind them.

∞

WORK ON WHAT HAS BEEN SPOILED
Has supreme success.
It furthers one to cross the great
water.
Before the starting point, three days.
After the starting point, three days.

(I Ching)

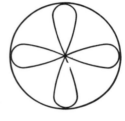

£sd—The Drop-Out Drug: THE SACRAMENT ADMINISTERED BY A DIVINE RASCAL

Fall 1961

Guide: MICHAEL HOLLINGSHEAD

Oracle: XIV

Possession in Great Measure

The Clinging, Flame

The Creative, Heaven

Fire in heaven above:
The image of POSSESSION IN GREAT MEASURE.
Thus the superior man curbs evil and furthers
   good,
And thereby obeys the benevolent will of
   heaven.

                                        (I Ching)

CAMBRIDGE TRAVEL SERVICE

32 ELLIOT STREET
CAMBRIDGE, MASS.
June 19, 1962

Dear Dr. Leary:

On June 12th a Mr. Michael Hollingshead purchased by personal check an air ticket to Jamaica using your name as reference.

Your secretary confirmed that Mr. Hollingshead worked on your Harvard research project.

We have just received word from the bank that Mr. Hollingshead's account is closed.

We would appreciate any information you could give us which would enable us to obtain the funds owed us.

Sincerely yours,
J. Everett Finch
Credit Manager

∞

Late October 1961. A morning of long-distance phone calls, research planning meetings, the mail. A letter from Allen Ginsberg in Calcutta. He's been smoking marijuana at the burning ghats by the Ganges. Indian holy men wear beards, long hair, don't wash, smoke pot. Just like Greenwich Village. Visionary drop-outs from the social game. Looking for the God kick. Meetings with Harvard students writing honors theses, appointments. Dr. Leary, there's a Michael Hollingshead on the line from Oxford, England, wants to talk to you.

So may I introduce to you

Bristly, formal, English accent. Dr. Leary, Michael Hollingshead here. I have been working with Professor G. E. Moore at Oxford—Mr. Moore sends his fondest greetings, by the way. There are many aspects of our work that I think will interest you. I wonder if it would be possible to arrange an appointment. Lunch? Quite so, that would be fine. Lunch next week Tuesday. Fine.

The fact you've known for all these years

Michael turned out to be a series of surprises. Medium height, medium bald, medium-aged man of thirty. His voice was urbane. His face twinkling, aristocratic and somehow gross.

He don't really want to top the show
But I thought that you might like to know
That the singer's going to write a wrong

Lunch at the Faculty Club was boring. He had little to say about G. E. Moore. He drank two bottles of beer. There was something evasive about the conversation. As lunch ended he told me that he was a writer, just finishing a novel. Oh, what's it about? May I have a minute to tell you? Go ahead. The novel is about a bank clerk whose ambition in life was to levitate. For years he studied with Occult teachers, yogis, and read the wisdom of the

234

East. For years he meditated and practiced in his room, to no avail.

Then one day at the bank, standing behind the teller's window, counting pounds, shillings, and pence, he found himself lifting slowly from the floor. A half-inch, an inch, two inches, he closed his eyes and let himself drift. When he opened his eyes he was two feet above the floor just about to soar up beyond the grill. With quick presence of mind he reached for the top ledge and arrested his upward motion. Quickly he yanked himself down to the ground, glanced around nervously to make sure nobody had seen him, and stood there perspiring, shaking, frightened, and exulting.

After a minute he experimentally released his grasp on the counter and felt his shoes leaving the ground. He reached down again and with his left hand shoved the window-closed sign forward. After five minutes he felt something click in his head. He let go of the counter and felt the reassuring pull of gravity hold his feet to the floor.

He thought of nothing else that night. At the same hour the next day, while he was counting out pounds, shillings, and pence, he felt energy surging through his body, and quietly the room began to slide downward. For the next fifteen minutes he carried on his work with one foot hooked underneath the bottom bar of the calculating machine.

That night at home, through meditation deepened by yoga, he tried to duplicate the levitation, but nothing happened. The following day, however, just after lunch, it happened again and this time, to his horror, it persisted. Fifteen minutes, twenty minutes, a half-hour, an hour, he clung to the window with one foot wedged under the calculating machine. He was suffused with a feeling of lightness. Delightful electrical forces surged through his body. A feeling of exultation and revelation washed over him, but under all was the nagging worry, what was he going to do? If he relaxed, gave in to the ecstatic flow, he knew that he would slowly spiral upward in his white shirt and flowered tie, and charcoal-gray business suit, before the astonished and angry eyes of the bank employees, and the customers. Perspiring and trem-

MICHAEL HOLLINGSHEAD:

C/O General Delivery
Old Town
Jamaica

My dear Tim,

It has been a busy day in the garden and hardly one that I would care to repeat too often.

The lawn was in a terrible state, with weeds all over the place and large patches of dried grass which called attention to the many months of neglect by the previous tenants.

As it was, our difficulties were further complicated by an almost total lack of proper equipment; indeed, were it not for palm leaves, which we used in place of rakes, I doubt whether we could have made much progress.

However, working against the clock, we hope to have the place tidied up before the Independence celebrations begin, on August 6.

Others, less attentive to floral decoration but more efficient in matters of growing plants, have had a certain amount of difficulty recently from the authorities.

I understand that ganja, an Arawak word for pot, is illegal here. Despite my assurances to the press and elsewhere of its essentially religious significance I'm afraid, however, that we live in an age of superstition and ignorance and, however well motivated were the actions of a Mr. Lloyd Scott in growing ganja in his back garden, I doubt whether his protests at its confiscation by the police and their subsequent action in marching him to the station will have much influence with the local magistrates, all of the whom are agreed on the dangers of having people blowing ganja: "It rots both the brain and the soul."

All the news for now.

Please drop me a few lines.

We are both well and happy, getting more than our share of the sun and feeling close to the still centre of things.

Warmest regards to you, Michael

∞

bling, he went through the routines of business until closing time, his right foot holding him to the floor. Then grasping the counter so that his knuckles blanched white with the force, he slowly and deliberately walked the rectilinear path to the corner of the room. Quickly switching with his left hand to grab a table top he turned to the door. There was one agonizing space between the desk and the door where there was nothing to hold onto. He bent down, pretending to tie his shoelaces, and, with a sudden leap launched himself and soared to the doorknob, which he was only just able to catch with his right hand as he floated past.

The rest of the trip home to his apartment was an ecstatic nightmare. Never was the sky so blue. His eyes were microscopes registering the jewel-like beauty and precision of the sidewalks, and lamp posts. He was a fish swimming in a diamond-studded, colorful lagoon. But a fish with one incessant problem. How to avoid floating up through the energy-charged watery environment when his role and social duty was obviously to crawl crablike along the lagoon bottom.

Holding on to a street light, he hailed a cab. A quick transfer of hands to the taxi door. Finally into his living room where he roped himself to his sofa. He phoned the office to announce a two-week sick leave. A call to his fiancée to come at once.

He had, it seemed, been courting a beautiful young woman for several months. A certain caution and heavy seriousness on his part inclined her to resist his advances. But now he announced that he had taken leave of his job, perhaps not to return, and that he was headed for an isolated lake in the country. Fascinated, she agreed to go with him. Here perhaps was the casual and careless lover she would prefer.

Their room in the country inn had a balcony which opened onto the lake below. They dined there with candlelight, the champagne glasses glittering in the flickering flame.

The meal ended and with a caressing, wrenching kiss, she moved to the bathroom, sending back a glance at the four-poster bed. He undressed quickly with one hand holding the mattress. She emerged from the bathroom naked, hair loose around her shoulders, and he reached out his hands to embrace her. And then, softly, tenderly, gently turning like a balloon on a summer afternoon at the sky park, he floated up, up, beyond her outstretched arms and her beautiful face now transfigured with awe and terror. Up, up, to the ceiling where with an easy jolt he found himself pinned.

Michael Hollingshead was leaning forward with his head somewhat bowed, his eyes down, his fingers making little marks on the table cloth. My cigarette, untouched, had an inch-long ash. Michael glanced up. His eyes caught mine. A sudden look of amused despair. He shrugged his shoulders and raised his hands in studied helplessness. I must apologize, my dear chap. I didn't mean to go on boring you this way. Don't be silly. Please go on. A soft smile rippled across Michael's face. He nodded and dropped his head again.

She stood below, aching, naked and vulnerable. First upset, and disbelieving. Then, as he explained, lying on his back on the ceiling, his arms gesticulating downward, she became intrigued, delighted.

After two hours she was sitting on a chair with her legs crossed, smoking and crushing cigarettes out in the ash tray. He lay on the ceiling, eyes closed, filmy with sweat, concentrating, willing, meditating. Finally, she moved briskly to the bathroom and emerged fully dressed. She paused at the door, Call me, when you're ready to come down, she said. And she was gone.

His arms waved after her like tree limbs in a wind storm. He lay spread-eagled against the white, ash-gray, paint-flaking ceiling. And then the tears fell and collected in two little pools on the bed below.

By this time I was half an hour late to a faculty meeting, and as we rushed back along the Cambridge streets, Michael quickly and with a certain frantic pressure, talked to me about LSD experiments he had been doing in New York with a doctor. The importance of psychedelic drugs. He wanted something from me but I sloped off with a quick handshake. Fascinating lunch. I loved your book and your story. Let's do it again.

I forgot about the episode. The following Thurs-

MICHAEL HOLLINGSHEAD:

19 Brompton Square
London, SW3
1st Nov. 1962

My dear Timothy,

I received a letter from the Parapsychology Foundation this morning, cutting me off their payroll.

It seems that they were surprised that you were surprised to be informed by them that I had a grant to write a paper on your set-and-setting theories, etc. and also of their help in getting me back to England from Jamaica.

I think it is now my turn to be surprised, for my letters to you explained all of this; in fact, in my August letter I recall having asked you to read through the MS before I submitted it.

However, the issue here is not whether I deceived you or not, or even how you view what I think about the Harvard-Concord project— it is your persistent reference, to other people, and most probably to the foundation officials as well, to me as a sort of 'con-man' who goes around trying to trick people out of money, or whatever.

While this may explain, in a limited way, something about the manner in which I *apparently* do things, it no more explains the truth of what I *really am* and what I really am seeking in life than to also say of me that I eat bananas for phallic reasons.

Both are valid assumptions in a certain context.

As I understand the term, a con-man is someone whose progress in life is founded upon a desire—taken for reality—to get something for nothing, a person whose behaviour, moral and physical, rests not on seeking to achieve (as the spiritual masters have always affirmed) in the timeless and eternal 'now,' but in some utopian future; a person, in brief, who lives through the present because of the prospect of that golden age to come.

But it also assumes some kind of criminal or nasty intent.

When I met you I had just got back from a month of horror and emptiness in Houston, was being tempted by my wife to settle again in New York but on very different terms than formerly and was broke and needing a job.

You were very kind to me at a point when nothing seemed to be going for me, and I shall always be grateful.

day I had a busy schedule—a lecture to an advanced seminar of undergraduates, from ten to twelve, and then a one-o'clock plane from Boston to New York. After the lecture I rushed to the office and found my secretary standing with a peculiar look on her face, handing me a letter. It was written in tiny, hardly legible script. He had spent the week living alone in a dreary room in Cambridge. He had come to Harvard because I was the only person in the world who could help him. He knew how vulgar and gamelike his ploy might seem, that he would kill himself if I could not see him and help him, but the insight into his own vulgarity was simply an added wound to a riddled and desperate organism. He would await my call at the rooming house number until five that afternoon. And after that, good luck and good-bye. Well, this was a pretty crisis, coming when I had exactly twenty minutes before leaving for the airport. I dispatched George Litwin, who was part of what we at that time called our Love Engineer Group, to pick up Michael at his rooming house. The plan was that I could talk to him on the way to my plane.

They were back immediately. With George at the wheel, and Michael in the back seat we headed for the airport. The immediate problem seemed simple enough. He was broke, without a job, separated from his wife and child for financial reasons. Are you sure that's all? I asked. He looked at me once again with the amused horror look, and shrugged, Well, there are all the cosmic problems, of course, but if I could get a base with my wife and family I'd feel up to dealing with the rest.

That sounded fair enough, so a quick plan was evolved. Michael could take my car and drive to New York, pick up his wife that very evening and come back. They could stay on the third floor of my house. His wife could be housekeeper until he got a job. I could sense in Michael's body a subtle relief, like a poker player whose bluff had not been called.

When we arrived at the airport, Michael followed and pulled me aside for a minute between the car and the Eastern Airlines door. There's one thing I should tell you. I know you have friends in New York. I know you're a friend of Winston London, and I think you should know that for the last six months I have worked very closely with him. We parted on very bad terms. He'll say wicked things about me which I'm sure you're sophisticated enough to realize emerge from his state of consciousness rather than the realities of mine. Intriguing, but I was in too much of a hurry to pursue it. Winston London was a famous New York multimillionaire with a good heart and tenderly high-minded ideals. He was continually being victimized by fourth-rate low-level promoters.

Cpl. Michael's Lonely Dope Club Band
The fact you've known for all these years

In New York I went first to the East Side apartment of Max Fox, a five-hundred-year-old teen-age Levantine confidant at the Sultan's court, sometimes in favor, sometimes in disgrace. Always wise, shrewd, funny, complaining, completely involved in extravagant baroque plans to turn-on the Sultan, to turn-on the harem, to turn-on himself.

In his current casting Max was a Hollywood publicity man. Friend and adviser to the most beautiful women in New York. Max's delight was to drive around in a chauffeured Cadillac with two tall slender blondes, champagne cooler, stereophonic sound, and the ashtrays loaded with Panama red. Until the bills came due and the Cadillac no longer drew up to his door. There was never a shortage of interesting men and beautiful girls in Max's flat. He performed one of the most valuable social functions in any complex urban society. His apartment was communications center for the most interesting people in New York. The price of admission was beauty or power or talent. And you were never allowed to promote or come on. That, after all, was the privilege of the house.

It's wonderful to be there
It's certainly a mill
So many lovely customers

Max met me at the door. As I walked to the sofa I remembered that Winston London was one of his friends. Max, can you do me a favor? I've just met a man whom I'm about to get involved with. He says he knows Winston London. And there seems to be some friction in the relationship. Could

And when I knew you better I told you about the institute business in New York, detailing the passage of events which culminated in having to face and deal with the New York gangsters.

What I didn't tell you—it seemed rather flat after the stories of nightly visits from the juke-box czar—was that I always used the institute to do for others what the Parapsychology Foundation did for me.

And there was also room in the institute for 'improbable' people like beatniks, paintingless painters, barroom pundits, and, with the contrivance of the editor of *The Hobo News*, for old men who only vaguely knew where they were at and needing some funds.

Why, then, should I also have got myself involved with people like the gangsters.

Why not?

Why, too, should I bother with hobos, millionaires, Harvard psychologists, and impecunious art students.

The answer is that I do like people—and there is the corollary, I want people to like me.

While in general I am a happy person—I spend my life and earn my living doing what I want to do—bits have been chipped off my heart these past twelve months.

These are what I am attempting to put back here in London, where I feel at home again.

Since in all probability this will be my last letter to you —I know how sensitive you become and also, from the precedents of the past, you enjoy (in a strictly psychological sense though not, I suspect, in a larger, Dionysian sense) getting friends to reject you—I want to get it all down, out, and finished.

In the first place I have never 'conned' anyone in the criminal sense.

However much I enjoy giving, adding, and living this image, it is not factually true.

Because I live like a gangster, i.e. on the fringe of society, it is to be expected that I shall be critically interpreted by others for whom life is one long mountain path.

But I fail to understand why you should want to do so.

you get a line on that for me? Max was delighted. He reached for a phone and dialed a number. It was a delicatessen owned and operated by a former bodyguard of Winston London. First there was a conversation about a case of Scotch and some salami and cheese. Max's voice and the voice of the invisible bodyguard crackled through the room from a special telephone amplifier system. The slightest whisper on the phone would be heard in loud volume in any part of the apartment. After the ordering, Max got down to business. Tony, do you by chance know anything about a fellow named Hollingshead? Says he used to know Winston. There was a brief pause and then tough gangster prose came booming out of the amplifier. Hollingshead, that no-good, two-bit, English con man. Listen, what do you have to do with him? Whatever it is, drop it. Max's voice came back calming, explaining that he was doing a favor for a friend. Tony's voice continued. Listen, that scoundrel caused Winston more trouble than any ten of the last con men that have come down Fifth Avenue. He's got a record on the continent as long as your arm. He's wanted by Interpol. He's bad news, buddy. Stay away from that Hollingshead.

The one and only Silly Fears

Max turned to me pleased with the efficiency of his intelligence service. Well, that's the end of that character. I'm not so sure, Max. That's just the opinion of one guy, a nice enough person, no doubt, but one whose spiritual focus may leave something to be desired. Let me get another reading on him from someone else. I reached for the phone and dialed George Litwin, back in Cambridge. George was going to take Michael back to his home for dinner before he started out in my car for New York, and I wanted to get George's impressions about this mysterious stranger. In a few seconds George's voice reverberated through the room. What happened with Michael, I said. George's words, chuckling, energetic, always enthusiastic, bouncing around the room. It all went great, Tim. He's a fascinating guy, with a great imagination. He's pretty screwed up and needs help. But he's seen a lot of things. He's taken LSD many, many times. He'll probably teach us a lot. Do you think we did the right thing in inviting him to stay at my house? Absolutely, said George. We can't do anything but learn from him.

That the swinger's going to swing along
And he wants you all to sing a song

Then I quickly sketched in for George the report we had just received from the bodyguard. Well, Tim, I'm sure that a lot of what this bodyguard says is true. I'm sure that Michael has had a checkered career in the past in situations where money and conning is involved. But what can he possibly con us out of? We have nothing material to lose and our only ambitions are scientific and celestial. How can he possibly hurt us? Even if he is a rascal, isn't it our business to rehabilitate people? Can't trust and love applied judiciously bring about any change we want. I say, if we can't work with Michael and use his obvious creativity and enjoy his obvious humor and learn from his experiences, we might as well go back to the run-of-the-mill business of college professors. That's exactly my conclusion, I said. See ya, George, and I hung up. Max had a quizzical look on his face.

So let me introduce to you
The one and only Silly Fears
And Cpl. Michael's Lonely Dope Club Band

Michael and his wife and child arrived and that lasted about ten days. Michael spent most of the time out of the house vaguely looking for a job. But I got an uneasy feeling after a while that he was spending his afternoons either in barrooms or high on LSD in the Boston Museum. His wife suddenly announced that she was leaving because of his insistence that she persuade her father to cash in some savings bonds.

I remember the scene when the taxi came to pick up Michael's wife and child. We stood an awkward foursome at the door, and as they left, two tears trickled down Michael's face. It was moving, pathetic, poignant, but there was one thread of doubt. Was it an act? If it was, it was so good it could only command respect.

In the next few weeks I got to know Michael better, but not much better. He got a job in the

Why it has become necessary for you to say to people that the group supported me for seven or eight months when, in reality, not only was I working at Concord on Mondays and Thursdays, but I would also help out in a number of small ways, help you run sessions, work *positively* toward your professional and private goals.

More exactly, I played your game with you and not my own, for the demand of the situation pre-empted such a possibility, and to continue to stay on I had become a nursemaid to your ideas and an odd-job man in the project.

It was an enjoyable, tremendously rewarding experience—but it was not what I would want for myself for the rest of my life, which we all conceded.

I was paid a salary for this in the months of January—February $400 a month, of which you had half for board and accommodation.

From March to the end of May I was given pocket-money, and $200 toward my fare home.

I also take a very dim view of the rumour you are putting out to one and all that I suddenly became paranoid—I was, certainly, angry with the way certain events of my life had become altered in the retelling, but the evidence was real and not, as now you seem to have convinced yourself, illusory—or that I am circulating *vile* rumours about little Dickie, threatened to go to the prison to get prisoners to blackmail him, etc.

Now this is not only *out of pattern* but is, in the very real sense of the set-up at Concord—which both of us understand—quite impossible.

It has as much basis for reality as saying I continually seek sexual satisfaction through orgies.

For while this is an intriguing daydream, the reality is that all the time I was living with you I hardly ever went out in the evenings— a necessary prerequisite for the orgiast—and the nearest I ever came, or wanted to come, to an orgy was the day you turned-on the church ministers.

So it all goes, I suppose.

Each of us upsetting either ourself or somebody else, the incessant see-saw of the conscious mind which in truth we try to escape with these drugs in the hope of finding ourselves in eternity-on-earth.

Harvard Square Bookstore, dutifully took the bus from Newton Center at 7:30 every morning and would drop by my office when the store closed at 6 P.M. We would have a glass of sherry and drive back home. Every fourth night he would ask if he could bring a girl home for dinner. His dates were strange, thin ladies with long hair, whom he would pick up as they browsed through the book stacks. He loved to take psilocybin, although he was patronizing in comparing the mushrooms with LSD, the stronger psychedelic drug which he had used extensively in New York, where a physician friend of his was doing research.

He told a funny story about his first LSD experience. He had smoked marijuana and hashish regularly and when he heard about LSD he contacted his medical friend and persuaded him to write a research proposal using LSD on amoeba, bacteria, and virus cells. The drug came in a one-gram package. Michael and his friend the doctor puzzled over the problem of how to divide the powdered gram of LSD into the one-hundreth of a million units which made up a standard dose of the incredibly powerful drug. They finally decided to mix the drug in powdered sugar which they wet down with water and spread out on a wide piece of wax paper. There were 10,000 doses in a small rectangle of wet sugar on the kitchen table. At first they drew a line down the middle. That made 5,000 on the left and 5,000 on the right. They they cut a line with a knife horizontally to quarter the supply. And then, by continual slices with the knife they divided the stache down to usable doses. They figured that one teaspoon made a double dose. This calibration established, they carefully scooped the paste into jars. When this was finished, there was the problem of what to do with the sticky residue on the wax paper. Michael reached down and tore the sheet of wax paper in half, and stuffed it in his mouth. His friend the doctor did the same.

They knew intellectually about the awesome potency of LSD. They knew logically that the invisible amount of residue they had swallowed was a few hundred millionths of a gram, but never having taken the eerie chemical before, they were

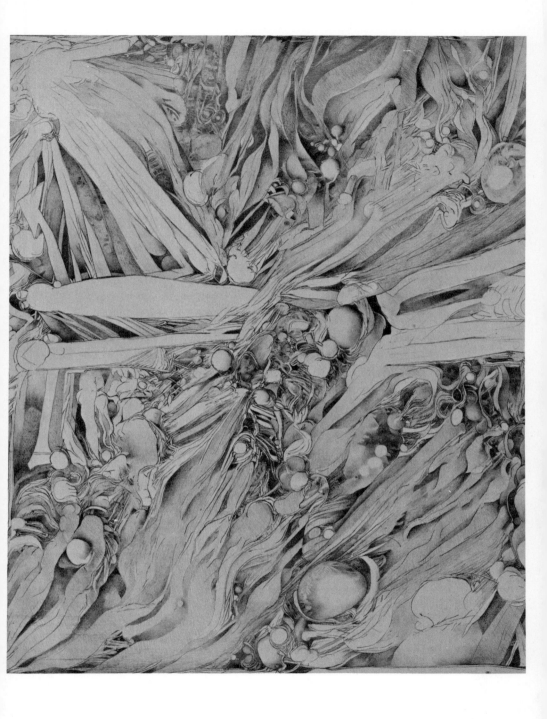

Yet stay around to conciliate the local divinity and by that become all too mortal.

I genuinely feel, though, that in spite of everything, the universe is good.

Not perhaps good as opposed to bad, but a sort of goodness which encompasses both good and bad at the same time.

Love,
Michael

∞

MICHAEL HOLLINGSHEAD:

Hadley Down House
Pinefield
Battle, Sussex
26th November, 1962

My dear Timothy,

Yet another change of address—this time, for several months.

I have taken a lease on an old, rambling house near the coast, with views of woods and fields and narrow lanes.

It is here that I hope to see the fruits of my labours.

I would hope that we might preserve some harmony in our relationship by laughing off my dark moods and melodramatic postures.

completely unprepared for the effect of what was perhaps ten normal doses. The effect hit suddenly, and for five hours the two of them lay back paralized on kitchen chairs, their eyes bulging, completely severed from their bodies, from their minds, from normal reality. Helplessly spinning through cosmic landscapes, unable to speak or move, communicating only by a shining powerless eyeball contact, like two astronauts drifting helplessly through space, or two men caught in diving suits miles below the surface.

Since that time, Michael's consciousness, his thinking and his actions, were nothing but extensions of that trip. He had died, spun out into the richness of interior space, had unraveled the riddle of the cosmic joke and was now cautiously, incredulously, comically, moving through the marionette show of normal reality.

He was very eager for me to take LSD, but I resisted the idea. Everything I had heard about lysergic acid sounded ominous to me. The mushrooms and peyote had grown naturally in the ground and had been used for thousands of years in wise Indian cultures. LSD, on the other hand, was a laboratory product and had quickly fallen into the hands of doctors and psychiatrists. Then, too, I was scared. The sacred mushrooms were my familiar territory. I had them harnessed up to my brand of revelation and ecstasy. It was obvious that the more powerful LSD swept you far beyond the tender wisdom of psilocybin. Like everyone else, I was both fascinated and frightened by the lysergic lore.

Michael invited me one night up to his bedroom and took from his dresser a mayonnaise jar packed with the moist sugar paste. There it is, he said. The key to miracle and meaning. When are you going to take it? I shook my head. I'm having trouble enough understanding the sacred mushrooms. Sometime I'll take your LSD, but I'm not ready now. He laughed. Psilocybin, the child's toy of the Indians. After you've taken LSD you'll view psilocybin as I do. Take a triple dose and watch television. You change the black and white to color.

In early December, Maynard and Flo Ferguson came up for the weekend. Maynard was playing in a Boston dance hall. It was an easy, pleasant weekend. Flo did beautiful things around the house and Maynard told funny stories about the band business. I had made it a rule that there was to be no grass smoking in the house and they would leave with Michael and turn-on while driving around the neighborhood. They were planning to leave for New York about five o'clock on Sunday afternoon. We were sitting in front of the fireplace, in the living room, and Michael was telling LSD stories. Flo and Maynard's interest perked up. The next thing I knew Michael was bounding downstairs with the mayonnaise jar and a spoon. A tablespoon, I noticed, overflowing. I was listening to records and not paying too much attention, until after about half an hour I looked up and I saw that Maynard and Flo were gone from this world, into some sort of trance. They were sitting on the sofa motionless, their eyes closed. But I could feel energy emanating from their bodies. I turned down the volume on the record player and sat watching them. After about fifteen minutes Flo opened her eyes and she laughed. It was not a nervous or a funny laugh. It was the chuckle of someone who was dead and gone and sitting on some heavenly mountain top and looking down at the two billion years of evolution the way you'd look at a transient episode in a children's playground.

She looked at me and began to talk. It was pure *advaita vedanta*. She was Krishna, lecturing Arjuna. She was reciting, in chuckling, hip Manhattanese, the essence of Hindu philosophy. Maya. Nonduality. Reincarnation. And this, mind you, coming from little Flo Ferguson, who hadn't finished high school and had never read a philosophy book in her life. She thought Indians wore headdresses and feathers. Now from her smiling rosebud lips was pouring the most powerful religious statement I had ever heard in my life. Timothy, you've got to take this. Man, it's the beginning and the end. You've got to take it.

I looked over and Michael was observing me, carefully, with a smile on his face. He raised his eyebrows and shrugged. Well? I looked at Maynard. He was glowing quietly, smiling and nodding.

No doubt remembering mainly our happier moments together, I was genuinely surprised when I heard about your conversations with the foundation directors.

And this may have led me into some egregious blunder.

May we not now look upon all of this as a spiritual exercise—I know that I would personally prefer to forget all about it and return to the friendlier, more colourful and positive, status antiquo.

Yours,
Michael

∞

MICHAEL HOLLINGSHEAD:

My dear Timothy

There is a village in South England remote from ambition and from civilization; an unvisited oasis, a symbol of what some say is reserved for the soul—a group of elms, a little turn of the parson's wall, a small paddock beyond the graveyard close, tended by one man, with a low wall of very old stone guarding it all round, a pub, a cricket green where the scent of grass in summer is breathed only by those who are native to this unvisited land.

And it is to here that I have lately returned.

I have left the possessive folds of the American Parapsychology Foundation—Moloch and Mammon, Belial and Beelzebub, organized under their chairman, Satan.

So Faustus tells them that their bargain has not attracted him because the satisfactions they all offer him are only partial and static ones.

The trouble with the foundation's executives is that they are stuck . . . forever playing the same played-out hand.

When you turn out fixedly to get it, every earthly paradise turns into something else . . . like going to live in a poem and finding it a government regulation when you get there.

Spring thoughts; nearing Easter and memories of last year's Easter, and all the fun of Newton Center.

I hope all is going well for you.

I think of you a lot.

Remember me, please, to those who know me and are still with you.

With fondest regards,
Michael

∞

Then my leader said, I am one who goes below from ring to ring with this still living man. It is my mission here to show him hell. (Inferno XII)

I guess this is the time, Michael, I said. With quick bounds he was out of the room, and I could hear his tennis shoes rippling up the stairs, and he returned with the mayonnaise jar, and the tablespoon, heaped to overflowing with the sugar paste. George Litwin, just about to leave to go home to supper, was sitting next to me. Michael glanced at him. He nodded. Why not? and took his spoonful.

It took about a half-hour to hit. And it came sudden and irresistible. An endless deep swampy marsh on some other planet teaming and steaming with energy and life, and in the swamp an enormous tree whose roots were buried miles down and whose branches were foliated out miles high and miles wide. And then this tree, like a cosmic vacuum cleaner, went ssssuuuck, and every cell in my body was swept into the root, twigs, branches, and leaves of this tree. Tumbling and spinning, down the soft fibrous avenues to some central point which was just light. Just light, but not just light. It was the center of life. A burning, dazzling, throbbing, radiant core, pure pulsing, exulting light. An endless flame that contained everything—sound, touch, cell, seed, sense, soul, sleep, glory, glorifying, God, the hard eye of God. Merged with this pulsing flame it was possible to look out and see and participate in the entire cosmic drama. Past and future. All forms, all structures, all organisms, all events, were illusory, television productions pulsing out from the central eye. Everything that I had ever experienced and read about was bubble-dancing before me like a nineteenth-century vaudeville show. My illusions, the comic costumes, the strange everchanging stage props of trees and bodies and theater sets. All spinning out from the momentary parts of the central God-eye-heart-penis-light.

It was forty years ago today
Cpl. Michael taught the band to play
They've been going in and out of fash
But they're guaranteed to be a smash

MICHAEL HOLLINGSHEAD:

Excelsior Scientific Trust
40 East 84th Street
New York, N.Y.
20th January 1964

My dear Tim and all,

It may be all right to keep yourself to yourself up in Millbrook if you're eccentric or a genius; it's blokes like us wot needs the helpful enmity of intelligent friends.

New York is full of chickens on electric spits.

This, say the chickens, is our Auschwitz, and all poultry keepers are psychopaths.

Far-fetched enough; if such ingenuity were confined to chickens one would hardly object, but it pervades American psychology, blurring issues and ideas in a haze of ambiguity every bit as thick as the dripping oil with which those chickens are cooking in windows are baptized—one might almost add as methodically sloppy, and the thought as well as the language is always spilling over into society and the outside world: a convenient formula, which seems to cover every sort of human experience, stress or contrast in man's inner and his outer life.

This experience is of course endless and indescribable. After several billion years I found myself on my feet moving through a puppet show. Where does Timothy Leary belong in this dance of illusion? I thought of my kids and walked somehow upstairs to the second-floor landing and opened the door to my daughter's room. Susan was sitting in bed, the classic thirteen-year-old with her hair up in curlers, frowning in concentration at the school book in her lap, while rock-and-roll music blasted through the room. It was pure Saturday Evening Post Cover Americana. The puppet doll teen-ager glanced up. Hi, Dad. She was biting a pencil and looking at the book. I slumped against the wall, looking with amazement at this marionette stranger, from assembly-line America. She glanced up again, quickly. Hi, Dad, what would you like for Christmas? She went on biting the pencil, frowning at the book, waving slightly at the beat of the music. In a minute she looked up again. Hi, Dad, I love you.

A shock of terror convulsed me. This was my daughter and this was the father-daughter game. A shallow, superficial, stereotyped, meaningless exchange of Hi, Dad, Hi, Sue, How are you Dad? How's school? What do you want for Christmas? Have you done your homework? The plastic doll father and the plastic doll daughter both mounted on little wheels, rolling by each other around and around on fixed tracks. A complete vulgarization of the real situation—two incredibly complex, trillion-cell clusters, rooted in an eternity of evolution, sharing for a flicker this space-time coordinate. And offered this rare chance to merge souls and bring out the divinity in the other, but desiccated and deadened into the Hi Dad Hi Susan squeaks.

I looked at her beseechingly, straining for real contact. I was stunned with guilt.

With microscopic clarity, I saw the egocentricity, the sham of my devoted-father routine. Is it too late, can I come back, glorify this rare trembling opportunity? I turned and slowly walked downstairs to the front hallway. Eleven-year-old Jack sat on the floor watching television. I sat down next to him. Without taking his eyes from the tube he said, Hi, Dad. Jack, Jack. Great program, Dad. Once again the piercing realization of my blind misuse of this divine Buddha child.

I followed his gaze to the television set. Jack Benny, wise, noble, long-suffering guru, was going through a routine, about death, the transience of life. Memories from my boyhood—Fred Allen, Jack Pearl, Will Rogers, Charlie Chaplin. Each week the cosmic television show repeating the same message, infusing into the frail, karmic forms of Benny, Allen, Rogers, the ancient message, comic and tragic. Don't you see? It's spinning by you, blinding you. Don't you catch on? You're going, you're going. Use the few seconds that remain.

I suddenly knew that everything is a message from the impersonal, relentless, infinite, divine intelligence, weaving a new web of life each second, bombarding us with a message. Don't you see! You're nothing! Wake up! Glorify me! Join me!

Then there were three men on the TV screen. One was in a barber's chair, one was facing him, the other had his back turned. The third man suddenly wheeled around and said, looking straight through the television tube, into my eyes, You've been dead for two seconds.

The cosmic playwright uses diverse messages to get the point across. It's in a flower, it's in the light of a star which takes millions of years to reach your eyes. Sometimes for the stupid he even writes it out in words in a television drama, for those whose obtuseness can only be opened up by the boob tube. I'd been dead for two seconds. And this is what hell is like. I could look back over the past forty years with chagrin, with pain at my blindness. Every second presented me with a golden chance to tune in, to break through, to glorify, to really groove and dance with God's great song. And every second of every minute of every hour of every day I grimly played out my narrow little mental chess-game. The action was still continuing on the television set, but my consciousness was shrieking in remorse. Agonbite of inwit! Waste! Waste! Fool! How many times had I heard the message? In all the great religious books, in all the poems, every-place it confronted me. Forget yourself. Tune in on the big picture.

Then I heard music. I looked up at the screen

Here in New York we are still tolerated, having a number of respectable people who support our work with the lenience usually displayed towards the crimes committed by motorists.

We have about as much the same seclusion and protection, however, as the brothel areas; but then perhaps the infraction of the laws in obtaining the material is part of the inherent pleasure.

The regret is not that LSD disturbs or shocks but that it bores.

Best wishes,
Michael

∞

MICHAEL HOLLINGSHEAD:

Excelsior Scientific Trust
New York
18th December 1963

The Pavilion of the Mind Exhibit
New York World's Fair
1964–1965

The Mind Pavilion is the culminating point of two years of hard speculation by its originators.

It is impossible to avoid implicit financial judgments about an enterprise that must always generate a natural public interest, even despite itself.

We shall not try.

We know it is a marketable idea.

A last word about immediate plans.

The aim has been to produce a show as dignified, attractive and pleasure-giving as any that has been planned for the World's Fair.

We have created what we honestly believe is an exhibit both contemporary and exciting, something that will encourage intense interest among the many tens of millions who are expected to visit the fair.

There is of course a natural public appetite for mystery: People want to hear of some unknown thresholds just beyond their certain knowledge of which travelers' tales can be told—with their friends, neighbors, business colleagues hearing about an experience which has enriched the teller's knowledge, yet one which they have not yet shared.

and saw Doris Day leaning towards me, her hands beckoning. What was she singing? The second time around, I'm so glad I met you, the second time around. It suddenly dawned on me, that's what death is, that's what hell is. It just keeps going, there's no end to it. You have your first chance to touch and taste, tissue, direct contact with God's energy, and then when that's over, a second time, you repeat the whole process, but it's different. There's a plastic film between you and the divine process around you, your egocentricity, your deadening mind has created a plastic hell. That's the meaning of ghosts and anguished spirits, doomed for eternity to exist, separated from life, that precious, fragile gift that we squander every second of this so-called mortal reality. The second time around. Second time, it's the carbon copy. One little interval out of step. This time you are one vibration beat behind that ecstatic intersection which the living call life and which the tormented call paradise.

Later, I swam into the kitchen. There was a book on the table. I flipped it open. In a second I saw the history of every word on the page tracing back, back, back, back, to the beginnings of written language. Back down to one sentence, The death of the father, *morte du père,* and in that sentence, boiled and bubbled down to the essence of the one word, *morte,* there it was again, the grim confrontation.

I sat on the kitchen floor, looking at my body, my skin of delicately treated leather, exquisitely carved but dead. I saw plastic veins, blue and pink, and I saw celluloid fingernails. My mind was spinning like a computer that had no connection with anything live—no flesh, no cell, no sweat, no smell. I had lost my senses, *morte.* Death. With only the mind to spin out its universe of thoughts. Now you know what hell is. The mind cut off from the body, from life, from seed, from cell.

George Litwin staggered into the room. He was now a nineteenth-century Frenchman, cocky, carefree, courageous. He swung around and looked at me with anguished eyes. We were both dead men, trapped in the doomed submarine. We said nothing, but our eyes met in sympathetic terror. Gone, gone. It's finished.

It was straight telepathic communication. I was in his mind, he was in my mind, we both saw the whole thing, the illusion, the artifice, the flimsy game-nature of the mental universe. The popeyed look of terror changed to mellow resignation and the Buddha smiled. He murmured the word, Harvard, smiling. I said, America. He said, Duty. And I said, Love. He flinched and then nodded, smiling sadly, Yes, love. That was the ultimate confrontation. The last shattered secret from the Buddha bag. It's all an illusion, even love. And what's left? The wise, cool, all-seeing eyes and the slight smile around the mouth. Acceptance, peace, resigned serenity, it's all in your own mind, Baby, the whole bit from beginning to end. It is the spinning out of your own chessboard. Caesar, Alexander, Christ, America, Timothy Leary, George Litwin, even love—they only exist because you think them. Stop thinking them and they do not exist.

Then George was gone. I floated to the door. Perhaps outside the house I could find something solid, real, tangible.

I ran out to the lawn, snow, trees, starlight. It had never been more beautiful. Etched, sharp, magnified. I stood there listening for the answer. Where is the center? What is real? What can we do? Then rapidly, but completely, in careful detail I recapitulated the social and intellectual history of the human race. I relived and worked through every solution which the human mind had attempted. Society, migrations, groupings, tribal wanderings, invasions, the planting of crops, the building of cities, the restless searching for possibility and meaning, the moral codes, the taboos and kinships, the emergence of stumbling species groping for answer, for order, for center, the lost mutants trapped in their forebrains, trying to think and act their way back to the center. What to do and where to go? I could foresee the outcome of any action I should begin. And slowly, like a string being reeled back, I retraced my steps to that central spot in front of the fire where the session had begun. Here was the beginning—Michael, the

As in the Pavilion of the Mind, this is the stuff of conversation.

It is this healthy curiosity in the human temperament which will in due course make a triumphant success of this show.

In case any doubt still exists that the Mind Pavilion will be perhaps the outstanding success at the New York World's Fair, the fact is that the public is much more interested in results and devices than theory, more involved with seeing and hearing than reading, more concerned with being better than with being different.

Hence they will greet an exhibition that points to the questioning mind.

A public today doesn't really want ideas about the evolution of mind but the expressive freedom of knowing what lies beyond, in the future.

And, as we have been taught to believe, the future's measure is more and more coming under the precise control and methods of modern science. . . . We have taken the fact of a scientifically-oriented public and mated it directly with new knowledge and experience as a solution to the problem of presenting an exhibition drawn almost wholly from what we know about the mind and its workings.

We have projected our ideas with vigorous and exciting natural features—which can be experienced by the public close to through the use of light, sound, color, and technical innovations.

This has meant lots of planning before we could come up with an exhibit which will, we hope, convey both the worthy-seeming qualities of the human mind and the pleasures of self-expression and improvement through a better understanding of how the mind works.

Accordingly, a certain face-lifting has taken place, including a general design of layout, shape, size and other structural requirements.

master trickster, sitting silently and waiting. Maynard and Flo on the couch. Flo draped across Maynard's lap. I said something. Flo sat up and replied. Maynard's head went back and laughed. Then I repeated the same message, Flo sat up, Maynard laughed. I repeated the same message. Flo sat up and Maynard laughed. We were trapped in a time loop. Doomed forever to repeat a brief television commercial, over and over again at the station break.

Flo and Maynard were beautiful, stage-dressed, made-up characters. The classic frail beauty, and the dapper young musician, costumed for their parts.

I looked at Michael. His sad face bore the record of all human suffering. He was clearly one of the twelve apostles, cast for the moment in the funny little drama of Michael and Cambridge, come to teach us the ancient message that the center is back by the fire with your friends. Quiet detached trust and mutual acceptance of the ultimate cosmological horror. Limited. Limited. Limited. Trapped in our nervous systems, struggling to catch one glimpse every decade or two of the ancient cellular membrane meaning of life. Waiting patiently through those long periods of plastic isolation, until that next vibrant contact came.

George, by this time, had disappeared. His ordeal of death and renewal ran along a similar line, with only the stage props different. At that moment of ultimate confrontation he knew that his place was at home with his wife. He ran to his car and with conscious, accurate reflexes started it and drove down the street. Ahead of him was a Volkswagen and behind with their lights gleaming were three cars, except that George was really in a troika fleeing across a snowy Russian steppe. In front of him, bouncing along, was a rabbit. And behind him, yellow eyes gleaming with pursuit, were three wolves. Over and over the snow they sped, the rabbit, the troika, and the pursuing wolves, till suddenly the lights flashed red in front of him. Dutifully the rabbit stopped, George reined up his troika, and in ballet rhythm the three wolves, poised on their haunches, waited patiently. Then the light flashed green, and off they went again, the rabbit, the troika, and the straining wolves. George knew that distance had to be kept or there would be danger for the rabbit or danger from the wolves. When his street loomed up he automatically swung to the right, parked the car, ran to the house, buried his head in his wife's lap for the rest of the evening, which was the beginning of their next voyage.

Meanwhile, my cosmic odyssey went on and on. One myth after another, lived out and traced back to the basic flash in the silent, impersonal, whirring of primal vibrations, beyond sense, beyond cell, beyond seed, beyond life. The latticework shuttling of energy patterns. All forms, all structure, man-made and organic, were seen clearly in their molecular and particle nature. All structure was an illusion. Every form was a momentary stage prop for the great theater of illusion, continually changing.

My previous psychedelic sessions with psilocybin had opened me up to the sensory levels of consciousness, pushed consciousness out to the membrane frontier, contact points of eyeball and light, ear canal and sound. Psilocybin had sucked me down into nerve nets, into the somatic organs, heart pulse, and air breath, had let me spiral down the DNA ladder of evolution to the beginning of life on this planet. But LSD was something different. Michael's heaping spoonful had flipped consciousness out beyond life into the whirling dance of pure energy, where nothing existed except whirring vibrations, and each illusory form was simply a different frequency.

It was the most shattering experience of my life. I sat there, a part of Einstein's equation, seeing it all, terrified and confused, desperately looking for some structure which would last against the ruthless bombardment of energy waves, and through it all, sitting with his head cradled in his knees, was the architect of enlightenment, the magician, who had flicked the switch to this alchemical show of revelation. Michael, the trickster.

As I watched him, looking for an answer in his face, he changed. No longer the cool, cynical Bud-

We felt it was one gamble worth taking, and perhaps the best contribution we could make toward the success of this fair.

Michael Hollingshead

∞

MICHAEL HOLLINGSHEAD:

Excelsior Scientific Trust
40 East 84th Street
New York, N.Y.
28 Jan. 1964

Dear Mr. Bloomfield:

Many of the ideas expressed by you in your recent letter to the chairman of the board of this organization are directly to the point.

But when you remark that the exogenous administration of neurobiotics are likely to be only the beginning and not the end of our modern bedlam and that a normally insane individual will be unable to find his most attentive audience in mental institutions alone, you are trying to justify in theory the very interesting instinctive development of your own mind which, like Mondrian's "the painter," develops convincingly into a close relationship with the white lines on a blueprint, moon-skulled, with a lung full of dust and a tongue of wood, knee-deep in the cold and swamped by flowers, not to mention the white China flying fish from Italy.

Mister, your head is lousy with flowers, whose petals unlatch, tapping and ticking like nervous fingers or like yellow corsets ready to split.

High time the red geraniums in the Toby jug gave up the ghost.

You should have junked them before they died.

Daybreak has discovered the office mail on my desk looking like a bureau lid littered with Chinese hands.

Now I'm stared at by chrysanthemums the size of shrunken heads, dipped in the same magenta as your red geranium eyeballs the color of blood pudding, blue black, a spectacular plum-fruit.

But what do you know about that?

You are too wrapped up in your thoughts like a spool, trawling your dark seas as owls do, and nightly the snails blow kisses like black apples, leaping and sinking back into themselves, echoing in their shells to the least footfall, moving museums without fountains or statues.

dha eye. I now saw him as the lost victim of the revelations he'd unleashed. As I studied him carefully I could see scars on his face and hands and even threads of antennae sticking up from his skull. He shot a piteous, resigned look in my direction. He is the victim of some greater power, his consciousness has been captured, perhaps by intelligences from another planet. He is not a free agent. He knows what he's doing but he has no control over it. His turning us on is not an act of love and glorification but some sort of compulsion. He has to do it. He wants us to share the immobilization of his profound vision, to share his celestial dilemma. His cosmic loneliness. How can one act when one sees that all form is an illusory package of vibrations, just like your television screen? Nothing but beams of light while we comfort ourselves with childish explanations of philosophy and religion.

The effects of the drug began to wear off by dawn. I was still higher than I had ever been before, but at least some structure was coming back. The flow of vibrations had stopped, and I felt myself freezing into a mold of plastic. There was a terrible sense of loss, of nostalgia, for the long hours, eons really, when one was at the heart of meaning and the radiant core of the energy process.

I walked up to the Fergusons' room. They were sitting transfixed, feeling the same despair at their ejection from paradise. I knelt before Flo with my head in her lap, tears came down her eyes, and I found myself shaking with sobs. Why had we lost it? Why were we being reborn? In these silly leather bodies with these trivial little chessboard minds? For the rest of the morning I was in a daze, stunned by what had happened, trying to figure out what to do with these new revelations, how they make sense, what to do with life routines, which were obviously pointless, senseless, and completely artificial.

After lunch I drove out to the prison. In the guardroom I met the warden, a genial, unimaginative man with a rubber face comically laboring under the illusion that there was some reality to this metal fun house, horror show, which we called a prison. I met with the twelve prisoners who were part of our rehabilitation project. They were full of enthusiasm and energy, planning for our next session. I was very quiet. The few things I said were spoken in a low, serene voice, and carefully selected so they would make sense to an amoeba, to a nuclear particle. My mood carried over to them, I knew. They were quiet, and peaceful when I left.

I remember driving back to my office in Cambridge from the prison. I could still feel a strange electric noise in my brain and I was still struggling with that question, Why did I return? Why were the gates of paradise closed to me? Where had I lost the flow? Was it fear, or greed, or the result of past stupidities? And would I ever get the chance again to break through to that other illusion, and participate in the heart of the great vibration dance. Then I realized what I was doing. I was imposing the old mental game on the inexplicable mystery story of life. It all had to do with trust and acceptance.

When I got to my office they told me later I was noticeably changed. Pearl, the jewel secretary, and the graduate students waiting for me were immediately turned-on by what they called a solid serenity. It was impossible to say much. I listened, smiled. After a few minutes George Litwin walked in. It was the first time I had seen him since our submarine death scene in my kitchen. Our eyes met again in deep understanding. I took him by the arm and walked to a nearby conference room and closed the door. Neither one of us said a word for a long time. Well, what do we do now? Right, he said. That's all I've been thinking about. Once you see how it's all composed, it is hard to go back to the game. Love too. Yes, love too. He stood looking out the window at the twilight. Let's go up to my place, have a drink, and look at the fire. He nodded.

For the next few days, everyone on our research project was watching George and me with reverent concern. They could tell we had been beyond where we had ever been before. They were fascinated and frightened by what had happened to us. Dick Alpert in particular was concerned. He could sense that we had moved beyond the game of

Nightly I flog sheep over their iron stile.

And sheep don't sleep.

I can't get them out of my mind; not the sheep, that is, but the bear-furred, bird-eating spiders clambering round their glass box like an eight-fingered hand, jumpy as a Mexican bean.

Which is why I can't sleep and has no connection with anything but an irresistible inner source; and whether this may or may not be relevant to what you so freely and objectively wrote in your letter is beside the point.

It would, however, be an incautious assumption that this is impossible.

Yours cordially,
Michael

LSD is not so much the dead-end drug that fell in love with beauty as a bright silk waistcoat that dazzles a real, if often absurd, world of human objects and behavior: The symbol of renewal wears the apparatus of a crimson pourpoint that daunts the evasive honesty of those whose application to the humdrum is remarkable—not so their inspiration.

∞

MICHAEL HOLLINGSHEAD:

Excelsior Scientific Trust
40 East 84th Street
New York, N.Y.

28F64
Box Y8774
Montreal Evening Angus
Montreal, Canada.
Dear advertiser;

I'm really even afraid privately to whisper your fragile public name, become the tease, the butt, the lisper of the old shame—of seeking the partner in love game—and sometimes for a second really live with magic's miracles.

It's not that I haven't got the nerve, and obviously not because I think there's any turpitude in sex or drink.

I think my only qualm at all is that you might regard my deeply-valleyed napes as small as grapes, ridiculously small.

25 May 64

LSD (to parody a famous Oscar Wilde saying about drink and the working classes) is the curse of the thinking classes.

Michael

∞

psychology, the game of trying to help people, and beyond the game of conventional love relationships. We were quietly and serenely aware of much too much.

My relationship with Michael had undergone the greatest change. I treated him with an awed respect. There was still a big part of my consciousness which saw him as messenger from a divinity. How right and beautiful it was that God should send his messenger in the form of this eccentric, impatient, and mildly disreputable Michael. I got up early to take him to work and studied his every move for clues. Everytime I questioned him about the session he reacted with an evasive casualness, shoulder shrugs, raised eyebrows. That's the way it is, you know. With no more detailed explanations.

It has been five years since that first LSD trip with Michael Hollingshead. I have never forgotten it. Nor has it been possible for me to return to the life I was leading before that session. I have never recovered from that shattering ontological confrontation. I have never been able to take myself, my mind, and the social world around me as seriously. Since that time five years ago I have been acutely aware of the fact that everything I perceive, everything within and around me is a creation of my own consciousness.

From that day in November 1961 until this moment, sitting in the sun at Millbrook, dictating these words, I have never quite lost the realization that I am an actor and that everyone and everything around me is stage prop and setting for the comic drama I am creating. LSD can be a profoundly asocial experience. Since that first session with Michael I was never able to commit myself to the game of Harvard or even to the game of rehabilitation. Not even to the game of proselytizing for LSD itself. Nothing that doesn't ring true to my ancient cell wisdom and to that central vibrating beam within can hold my attention for very long. From the date of this session it was inevitable that we would leave Harvard, that we would leave American society, and that we would spend the rest of our lives as mutants, faithfully following the instructions of our internal blueprints, and tenderly, gently disregarding the parochial social insanities.

There is a second aspect of this session from which I have never recovered. The mind manipulation paranoia. Before this LSD session with Michael, I had taken psilocybin over a hundred times. But in each case I was the one who was directing the session and giving out sacramental drugs. Michael was the first person to guide me and to propel me out beyond my mind. Ever since that day I have had a recurring science-fiction paranoia which comes up in almost every LSD session. It starts like this: suddenly, with a click, I am this new level of reality. I am suddenly on camera in a ancient television show directed and designed by some unknown intelligence. I'm the pathetic clown, the shallow, corny, twentieth-century American, the classic buffoon completely caught in a world of his own making, and not realizing that the goals and ambitions he strives for, the serious games he struggles with, are simply the comic relief, a brief clown act. And how patiently the supporting cast gets dragged around at the will of my mind. Those two wise creatures that have to play the roles of my children, the patient Olympians who dress themselves day after day to play out the parts of friends in my drama.

Nicholas: I like my experiments simple.
Lily de Seitas: the days of simple experiments are over. (The Magus)

But who's the sponsor of the show? What am I supposed to do? Who, in all the crowd of stereotyped puppets that I command around me, is the director of the show? He would, of course, be the last person that I would think of, that Leo of the League, who is to lead me to a higher level of consciousness. Am I the only one who had not caught on, who has not broken through? The only one still thrashing around in egocentric isolation? And who is Michael with his half-bald head and his angelic gross face, pink-veined from alcohol, chain-smoking Camel cigarettes?

MICHAEL HOLLINGSHEAD:

H. M. Prison
Leyhill
Wotton-Under-Edge,
Glos.
26 May 1967

My dear Timothy,

Today marks my first anniversary in prison, for it was one year ago exactly that I was sentenced. Of course I have seen many changes in this time, some for best, some for the worse, but all always welcome. But perhaps the most interesting have been in the catering arrangements, which are always a source of difficulty in a closed community.

Most prisons work on a self-service system. Now oddly enough, forward looking Leyhill prison may soon be the only one in the country where inmates are still waited on by servants.

A self-service system, presided over by a grim, steel-helmeted prison officer in gym shoes, was tried for several years. But it was found that the biggest and toughest inmates invariably got all the food, amid scenes of brutish greed and violence hardly paralleled since Eolithic times. The prison officer was repeatedly coshed and the contents of his pockets shared among the same natural inmate leaders.

After experiments with the tough system, with even worse results, a solution has now been found. The small remaining number of sexual offenders not required as subjects for medical experiments are now detailed to wait on the ruling caste of G.B.H. (grievous bodily harm) cases and Mafia chiefs, who after dinner follow the custom of their ancestors by pelting them with bones.

Fair slaves are enforced by a picked, strong-arm squad of prison officers with patroling dogs. The principal officers, according to immemorial custom, still dine at the top table behind an electrified barbed wire fence. The system seems to work very well indeed.

But is life truly 'hard' in prison? Do prisoners spend all their time scheming and planning to escape? Isn't prison something of an anachronism in our 20th century society? Let's look at some of the facts. The prisoner returning to society often finds life "a hectic, ill-mannered rat race," said a speaker recently at a conference of the National Association of Probation Officers. "Is it any wonder that some people may appear to prefer the comparative peace of prisons?"

H. M. Prison
Leyhill
Wotton-Under-Edge
Gloucester
19 April 1967

My Dear Timothy,

Very many thanks for your letter and manuscript which I was very glad indeed to get.

Yes, of course, please make use of my name in your book—Hollingshead or Shinkfield-Hollingshead, it is a matter of preference, though with the latter, some sales are assured in the North of England and in the Lothians.

Your account of those early days fulfills perfectly —so it seems to me—the purpose of bringing out a history of the psychedelic movement. And to those of us fortunate enough to have taken part in this evolutionary process, this is the (almost) only consolation of which the spectrals of the world cannot deprive us.

Turning to the manuscript, there were only a couple of matters of fact which need correcting. The first, on page 1, Professor G. E. Moore is associated with *Cambridge,* not Oxford. He was 84 when he joined the Association for Cultural Exchange Ltd., which he did as that organization's secretary, a duty he carried out, I must now add, by proxy. The second factual error is in the very *last* sentence . . . And who is Michael with his half-bald head and his angelic gross face, pink-veined from alcohol, chain-smoking Camel cigarettes? For my face really isn't pink-veined and the suggestion that it is, and is so *moreover* through a hinted over-indulgence in alcohol, does not quite fit the picture I have of myself from that time, though of course I did drink, and still do, but not in vein-reddening proportions. I cannot think of anything better than . . . with his half-bald head and his angelic gross face, sunlit and tranquil, inclining its axle slowly to the waning sea unrippled, far below: a face in which nothing replies, whose silences are one more meditation for the rose.

That ends it on a suitable note of mystery, I think. I hope that is enough and that you didn't

It is not. Who in his right mind would choose life outside, when he might be enjoying the soul-restoring calm, the rhythmic, reassuring order of a well-run mick?

Here we are, with one or two chosen companions, chatting in some comfortable cell; pottering about on the prison farm; catching up, with the cooperation of a nice bespectacled old library "trustee," on books we never got round to reading; or listening to some decent third programme music on the headphones, with a mug of steaming cocoa at our elbow, just placed there by a kindly screw, intent, with the respectful familiarity of the best kind of old-fashioned servant, preserving our little world from all outside importunities.

really want me to annotate all over the manuscript and send it back. I think it reads well, though it calls for perhaps a cool, hard look again and a reminder to yourself of the purpose in going into print at this early stage. For considerable finesse and great subtlety in the arrangement of your material is called for, and any attempt to ignore subtlety in favor of speed will so much lessen the real value a reader could derive from your analysis and thoughts. For you must write always as you are, which is a fine, sensible human being, able to recognize in others what is forward-looking, and help foster their creativity; a teacher of depth, most profound of all in modern times; a catalyst and a sustainer of those who followed your Way. Nothing less or it will trivialize your work. For mystery is the philosopher's night and water: like the earth herself, a daughter of truth, and marches about that unforgiving Sun, in wheeled abysses toward unknown light's embraces, until the dreamer ceases to murmur against stars or maker, go roving—secret races—and only the moon notices, that watcher of selves that shimmers on a pitcher of water, sieving the mystery of all our dark places, in a handful of faces; so many lost embraces in newly found high places. The loneliness of the human soul is unendurable; nothing can penetrate it except the highest intensity of the sort of love that religious teachers have preached; whatever does not spring from this motive is harmful, or at best useless; it follows that in human relations one should penetrate to the core of loneliness in each person and speak to that. Until I met you I had taken little notice of that fact, but I listened willingly, and felt at home in your company. From that day to this I have seen a little more than I am, and communication and wholeness are no longer out of reach, for I have never given up my essential urge for—for want of a better word—virtue; and many, many things have been learned from you.

All my love to friends we hold dear. And I shall write you again just as soon as I have settled down to the routine of this place, which will not be too long. I found this recent week unsettling to my prison routine, or is it that I long so much for all that lightness of heart and foot that streams by these walls each day, this bad unhappy sort of monk. Yet I am realistic to know that when I do set on the Outside I will find the world is not transfigured or laid bare, or pierced with singing voices . . . only the press of wings about the place. Once beyond these walls my heart will quicken and my tongue renew.

My love,
Michael

What stops more people from entering this world? The first step, perhaps?

Love, Michael

∞

POSSESSION IN GREAT MEASURE.
Supreme Success.

(I Ching)

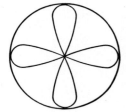

TRIP **13**

Are Heaven and Hell Real?

PROGRAMMING THE VISIONARY EXPERIENCE

Winter 1961

Guide: RALPH METZNER

Oracle: XX

Contemplation (View)

The Gentle, Wind

The Receptive, Earth

The wind blows over the earth:
The image of CONTEMPLATION.
Thus the kings of old visited the regions of the
world,
Contemplated the people,
And gave them instruction.

(I Ching)

From *Innerspace:*

The Hungarian pharmacologist, Stephen Szara first reported in 1957 that N,N-Dimethyltryptamine (DMT) and N,N-Diethyltryptamine (DET) produced effects in man similar to LSD and mescaline.

The only difference was in duration: whereas LSD and mescaline typically last eight to ten hours, DMT lasted from forty minutes to one hour and DET from two to three hours.

The higher homologues, dipropyltryptamine and dibutyltryptamine, were also said to be active but less potent.

The parent substance, tryptamine, by itself has no effect.

Chemically, DMT is closely related to psilocybin and psilocin (4-hydroxy-N-dimethyltryptamine), as well as to bufotenine (5-hydroxy-N-dimethyltryptamine).

During the first year of the Harvard Psychedelic Research Project, rumors circulated about a powerful psychedelic chemical called dimethyltryptamine: DMT. The effect of this substance was supposed to last for less than an hour and to produce terrorizing effects. It was alleged to be the horror-show drug of the psychedelic family.

William Burroughs had tried it in London and radioed back an urgent warning. Burroughs was working at that time on a theory of neurological geography—certain cortical areas being heavenly, other areas being diabolical. Like an explorer moving into a new continent, he believed it important to map out the friendly areas of the brain and the hostile. In Burroughs' pharmacological cartography, DMT propelled the voyager into strange and decidedly unfriendly territory.

Burroughs told a gripping tale about a psychiatrist in London who had taken DMT with a friend. After a few minutes the frightened friend began requesting help. The psychiatrist, himself being spun through a universe of shuttling, vibratory pigments, reached for his hypodermic needle, which had been fragmented into a shimmering assemblage of wave mosaics, and bent over to administer an antidote. Much to his dismay, his friend, twisting in panic, was suddenly transformed into a writhing, wiggling reptile, jewel-encrusted and sparkling. The doctor's dilemma: where to make an intravenous injection in a squirming oriental-martian snake?

Alan Watts had a DMT story to tell: he took the drug as part of a California research project and had planned to demonstrate that he could maintain rational control and verbal fluency during the experience. The closest equivalent might be to attempt a moment-to-moment description of one's reactions while being fired out the muzzle of an atomic cannon with neo-byzantine barreling. Dr. Watts gave an awe-full description of perceptual fusion.

In the fall of 1962, while giving a three-day series of lectures to the Southern California Society of Clinical Psychologists, Dick Alpert and I fell into discussion with a psychiatrist who was collecting data on DMT. He had given the drug to over a hundred subjects and only four had reported pleasant experiences. This was a challenge to the set-setting hypothesis.

Can chemicals produce specific changes in consciousness? Was the molecular structure of DMT such that it automatically produced *hell* trips? Is there really a *hell* area of the nervous system? Or is it not the expectation and surroundings which make the experience hellish or heavenly?

A basic theological issue is involved here. It's the ancient question that has divided philosophers for several thousand years. We become involved once again in the bitter debate that rent the academic calm of the Middle Ages. Realism or nominalism. The problem of universals. Do qualities really exist or are they just interpretations that the mind imposes? Do redness, goodness, sharpness really exist? Does evil exist? Does the devil exist? Does psychosis exist? Is there an area of the brain in which hell is to be found? And one specific molecular key to this area? Or do we simply create these categories with our minds? Look through our mind's eye to find them and then proclaim the redundancy to be a fact, and then armed with the schoolmaster's rod teach the names and facts to our children, who then obediently discover and confirm the *reality* of our names and facts, and then armed with sword strike down or imprison those who doubt the reality of our names or facts?

This most basic debate has raged in every culture and philosophy and religion. The hard-reality Brahmins and the soft-flowing Buddhas. The fixed dualists and the easy monists. Tertullian *vs.* Augustine. St. Jerome *vs.* Johannes Scotus Erigena. The certainty of Paul and the Divine Names of Dionysius the Areopagite. The rigid theology of the Vati-

The mechanism of action of DMT and related compounds is still a scientific mystery.

Like LSD and psilocybin, DMT has the property of increasing the metabolic turnover of serotonin in the body.

An enzyme capable of converting naturally occurring tryptamine to DMT has recently been found in some mammalian tissue.

This suggests that mechanisms may exist whereby the body converts normally occurring substances to psychedelic compounds.

DMT has been identified as one of the ingredients in the seeds of mimosa hostilis from which the Pancaru Indians of Pernambuco, Brazil, prepare an hallucinogenic beverage they call *vinho de Jurumena.*

∞

From "An Open Letter to Timothy Leary" by The Rt. Rev. Michael Francis Itkin:

I have recently done a great deal of research and study on this matter, and I find that neither DMT or DET are truly psychedelics, nor for that matter even true hallucinogenic agents in the general usage of those terms.

Rather, both DMT and DET are deliriants, i.e., the effects they achieve are obtained by subjecting the body to a state of delirium similar to that which might accompany a fever of 105 degrees.

The degree wrought to the physical center is commensurate with the physical conditions accompanying a 105-degree fever.

In addition, I am sure you have observed the temporarily ruptured blood vessels in the eyes of those who have used DMT or DET with great frequency.

Consider, then, what these same deliriants must do to the blood vessels throughout the intestinal tract, to the tissues of the liver, to the brain cells and, perhaps most clearly possible and defined, to the heart (particularly to the aorta).

It is also, along with bufotenine, one of the ingredients in the seeds of Piptadenia peregrine, from which the Indians of Trinidad prepare an hallucinogenic snuff they call yopo.

∞

can vs. the Empty Godhood of Eckhart. The Islamic orthodoxy of Baghdad vs. the intoxicated pantheism of the Sufis. The legal finality of the Sanhedrin vs. Essene fervor.

Here it comes again. The old ontological quarrel. Does a psychedelic drug produce any definite reaction, or is the experience created by the divine freedom of the experiencer? Are God and the Devil out there or within? Does LSD cause psychosis or multiple-orgasm? Does DMT trigger off a neurological horror show or new levels of satori?

We had found little difference among psychedelic drugs. As nominalists and ecstatics we were convinced that the elaborate clinical variations allegedly found in reactions to different drugs were psychedelic folktales. We were sticking to our null hypothesis that psychedelic drugs had no specific effect on consciousness, except to expand it, and that expectation, preparation, spiritual climate, and the emotional contract with the drug-giver, accounted for specific differences in reaction. Good trips or bad trips.

We were eager to see if the fabled terror-drug, DMT, would fit the set-setting theory.

A session was arranged. We came to the home of the psychiatrist accompanied by a Vedanta monk and two female friends. After a lengthy and friendly discussion with the physician, Dick Alpert lay down on a couch. His girl friend's head rested on his chest. I sat on the edge of the couch, smiling reassurance. Fifty mgs. of DMT were administered intramuscularly.

Within two minutes Dick Alpert's face was glowing with serene joy. For the next twenty-three minutes he gasped and murmured in pleasure, keeping up an amused and ecstatic account of his visions.

Exactly twenty-five minutes after administration, he smiled, sighed, sat up swinging his legs over the side of the couch and said, It lasted for a million years and for a split second. Now it's your turn.

With this reassuring precedent, I took up position on the couch. Virginia sat on the floor holding my hand. Dick sat at the foot of the couch, radiating benevolence.

Five minutes after the injection, lying comfortably on the bed, I felt typical psychedelic onset symptoms—a pleasant somatic looseness, a sensitive tuning-in to physical sensations.

Eyes closed . . . typical LSD visions, the exquisite beauty of retinal and physical machinery, transcendence of mental activity, serene detachment. Comforting awareness of Virginia's hand and the presence of friends.

Suddenly I opened my eyes and sat up. . . . The room was celestial, glowing with radiant illumination . . . light . . . light . . . light . . . the people present were transfigured . . . godlike creatures . . . we were all united as one organism. Beneath the radiant surface I could see the delicate, wondrous body machinery of each person, the network of muscle and vein and bone—exquisitely beautiful and all joined, all part of the same process.

Our group was sharing a paradisial experience—each one in turn was to be given the key to eternity—now it was my turn, I was experiencing this ecstasy for the group. Later the others would voyage. We were members of a transcendent collectivity.

Dick Alpert coached me tenderly . . . handed me a mirror wherein I saw my face a stained-glass portrait.

Virginia's face was that of all women—wise, beautiful, eternal. Her eyes were all female eyes. She murmured exactly the right message. It can always be this way.

The incredible complex-unity of the evolutionary process—staggering, endless in its variety—why? Where is it going? etc., etc. The old questions and then the laughter of the amused, ecstatic paradox. Too much! Too great! Never mind! It can't be figured out. Love it in gratitude and accept the mystery! I would lean forward to search for meaning in Virginia's china-flecked face and fall back on the pillow in reverent, awed laughter.

Gradually, the brilliant illumination faded back to the three-D world and I sat up. Reborn. Renewed. Radiant with affection and reverence.

I had tripped to the highest point of LSD illu-

Dick Alpert's Report:

The faces in the room had become billion-faceted mosaics of rich and vibrant hues. The facial characteristics of each of the observers surrounding the bed, were the keys to their genetic heritage.

Dr. X (the psychiatrist) was a bronzed American Indian with full ceremonial paint.

The Hindu monk was a deep soulful middle-easterner with eyes which were at once reflecting animal cunning and the sadness of centuries.

Leary was a roguish Irishman, a sea captain with weathered skin and creases at the corners of eyes which had looked long and hard into the unsee-able.

Adventurous skipper of a three-masted schooner eager to chart new waters, to explore the continent just beyond.

Exuding a confidence that comes from a humorous cosmic awareness of his predicament—genetic and immediate.

And next to me, or rather on me, or rather in me, or rather more of me—Billy.

Her body was vibrating in such harmony with mine that each ripple of muscle, the very coursing of blood through her veins was a matter of absolute intimacy.

Body messages of a subtlety and tenderness both exotically strange and deliciously familiar.

Deep within, a point of heat in my groin, slowly, but powerfully and inevitably radiated throughout my body until every cell became a sun emanating its own life-giving fire.

My body was an energy field, a set of vibrations with each cell, pulsing in phase with every other.

And Billy, whose cells now danced the same tune, was no longer a discrete entity, but a resonating part of the single set of vibrations. The energy was love.

∞

mination—a jewel-like satori. It was not cellular, not somatic, not sensory. It was a world of vibrations. No fear. Some moments of benign paranoia—that I was the happy victim of some celestial plan for illumination.

Immediately after my return the drug was administered to the Hindu monk. This dedicated man had spent fourteen years in meditation and renunciation. He was a sannyasin entitled to wear the sacred saffron robe. He had participated in several psychedelic drug sessions with extremely positive results and was convinced that the biochemical road to samadhi was not only valid but perhaps the most natural method for people living in a technological civilization.

His reaction to DMT was, however, confusing and unpleasant. Catapulted into a sudden ego-loss, he struggled to rationalize his experience in terms of classic Hindu techniques. He kept looking up at the group in puzzled helplessness. Suspicion. Reproach. Defiance. Promptly at twenty-five minutes he sat up, laughed sheepishly, What a paranoid trip! I really got trapped.

The lesson was clear. DMT, like the other psychedelic keys, could open an infinity of possibilities. Set, setting, suggestibility, temperamental background were always there as filters through which the ecstatic experience could be distorted.

Thus also in nature a holy seriousness is to be seen in the fact that natural occurrences are uniformly subject to law. Contemplation of the divine meaning underlying the workings of the universe gives to the man who is called upon to influence others the means of producing like effects. (I Ching XX)

On return to Cambridge, arrangements were made with a drug company and with our medical consultant to run a systematic research on the new substance. During the subsequent months we ran over one hundred sessions—at first training exercises for experienced researchers and then later trials with subjects completely inexperienced in psychedelic matters.

The percentage of successful, ecstatic sessions

ran high—over 90 percent. The set-setting hypothesis clearly held for DMT in regard to positive experiences. But there were certain definite characteristics of the DMT experience which were markedly different from the standard psychedelics—LSD, psilocybin, mescaline. First of all, the duration. The eight-hour trip was reduced to around thirty minutes. The intensity was greater as well. This is to say, the shattering of learned-form-perception, the collapse of the learned structure was much more pronounced.

Eyes closed produced a soft, silent, lightning-fast, whirling dance of incredible cellular forms—acre upon acre of softly spinning organic forms. A swirling, tumbling, soft rocket-ride through factories of tissue. The variety and irreality of the precise, exquisite feathery clockwork organic machinery. Many LSD subjects report endless odysseys through the network of circulatory tunnels. But with DMT a sub-cellular cloud-ride into a world of ordered, moving beauty which defies external metaphor.

Eyes open produced a similar collapse of external objects. Faces and things no longer had form but were seen as a shimmering play of vibrations. Perception of solid structures was seen to be a function of visual nets, mosaics, cobwebs of light-energy.

The transcendence of ego-space-time was most often noticed. Subjects frequently complained that they became so lost in the lovely flow of timeless existences that the experience ended too soon and was so smooth that landmarks were lacking to make memory very detailed. The usual milestones for perception and memory were lacking. There could be no memory of the sequence of visions because there was no time—and no memory of structure because space was converted into flowing process.

To deal with this problem we began to program sessions. The subject would be asked every two minutes to respond, or he would be presented with an agreed-upon stimulus every two minutes. The landmarks would, in this way, be provided by the experiment. The temporal sequence could be broken up into stages.

One of the first programmed space shots with

From "The Experiential Typewriter" by Timothy Leary, in the *Psychedelic Review:*

The communication problem is like this. Suppose we put a subject in the front seat of a roller coaster and we sit next to him during the dizzy ride.

As the car plummets down the first gasping descent we ask him, What do you see and feel?

By the time we have said the second word the car has flashed down into the black descent and is screeching around a turn.

As the car starts to pull up the next incline he says, What did you say? When we repeat the question he looks at us blankly.

Well, it happened too fast. I just can't put into words. So the next time we prepare the subject.

We tell him that in the middle of the hurtling ride downward we are going to ask him about what he sees and feels. It still won't work with words.

As he rockets down the descent the most he can stutter is, Oooh. Lights . . . and. . . . By this time he is around the dark bend and heading up.

It's just too fast for words, is about the best you are going to get. Now the action of the cortex is perhaps a million times faster and more complex than reactions to a roller coaster ride.

And that's why you should never ask a subject during an LSD session what he is experiencing. Now suppose we install a recording gadget on the roller coaster.

Let's imagine twenty buttons which the subject will push to record his reactions. One button is for fear and another for thrill and another for lights and another is for sick and another is for dizzy.

DMT involved a three-person crew—myself, Ralph Metzner, and his wise wife Susan. The instrument for radioing messages back was the experiential typewriter. This device is designed to allow non-verbal communication during psychedelic sessions. There are two keyboards with ten buttons for each hand. The twenty keys are connected to a twenty-pen polygraph which registers an ink mark on a flowing roll of paper each time a key is struck.

The subject must learn the codes for the range of experience before the session and is trained to respond automatically, indicating the area of his consciousness.

In this trip it was agreed that I would be questioned every two minutes, to indicate the content of my awareness.

The session took place in a special room, eight-by-twenty, which was completely covered, ceiling, walls, and floor, by warm, colorful Indian prints. The session followed the alternating-guide model. Ralph and Susan were to act as interrogators for my session. Ralph was then to repeat the session with me as ground control.

At 8:10 P.M. I received 60 mgs. of DMT.

Lay back on mattress, arranging cushions . . . relaxed and anticipatory . . . somewhat amused by our attempt to impose time-content mileposts on the flow of process . . . soft humming noise . . . eyes closed . . . suddenly, as if someone touched a button, the static darkness of retina is illuminated . . . enormous toy-jewel-clock factory, Santa Claus workshop . . . not impersonal or engineered, but jolly, comic, lighthearted. The dance of the body, humming with energy, billions of variegated forms spinning, clicking through their appointed rounds in the smooth ballet. . . .

MINUTE 2. TIM, WHERE ARE YOU NOW? Ralph's voice, stately, precise, scientific, kind . . . what? where? you? . . . open eyes . . . there squatting next to me are two magnificent insects . . . skin burnished, glowing metallic, with hammered jewels inlaid . . . richly costumed researchers, they looked at me sweetly . . . dear, radiant Venusian crickets . . . one has a pad in his lap and is holding out a gem-encrusted box with undulating trape-

Then we train the subject for hours in the code system until he gets to that point of automatic proficiency of the touch typist who can rattle off copy without thinking of what she is doing, banging out seventy words a minute while thinking about the dress she is going to wear tonight.

Then we strap the subject's hands to the dials of the twenty-button recorder and send him down the rollercoaster ride.

He can now give us perhaps twenty to a hundred codes a second which we pick up on a polygraph (i.e., a multi-pen recorder attached to the sending keys).

That's the experiential typewriter and that's how it's used and why such a device is necessary to record psychedelic experiences during the session.

zoidal glowing sections . . . questioning look . . . incredible . . . and next to him Mrs. Diamond Cricket softly slides into a latticework of vibrations . . . Dr. Ruby-emerald Cricket smiles . . . TIM WHERE ARE YOU NOW. . . . Moves box towards me . . . on yes . . . try to tell them . . . where. . . . Body . . . I am swimming in tissue tidelands . . . BODY CONSCIOUSNESS . . . use mind . . . explain . . . look down at undulating boxes . . . struggle to focus . . . use mind . . . yes . . . also . . . COGNITIVE . . . there. . . . Eyes close . . . back to dancing workshop . . . joy . . . incredible beauty . . . the wonder, wonder, wonder . . . thanks . . . thanks for the chance to see the dance . . . infinity of life forms . . . funny exotic energy nets. . . .

MINUTE 4. TIM, WHERE ARE YOU NOW? Spinning out in the tapestry of space comes the voice from down below . . . dear kindly earth-voice . . . earth-station calling . . . where are you? . . . what a joke . . . how to answer . . . I am in the bubbling beaker of the cosmic alchemist . . . no, no softly falling star dust exploding in the branches of the stellar ivory birch tree . . . what? Open eyes . . . oh dear lapidary insect friends . . . Ralph and Susan beautiful orange lobsters watching me gently . . . faces shattered into stained-glass mosaic . . . Dr. Tiffany Lobster holds out the casket of trapezoidal sections . . . look at glowing key . . . where is Venusian ecstasy key? . . . where is key for the stellar explosion of the year 3000? CELLULAR GENETIC . . . yes . . . hit the key . . . tumble back to Perosopic pulse.

How nice . . . they are down there . . . waiting . . . no words up here to describe . . . they have words down there . . . see rolling waves of colored forms whirling up, bouncing jolly . . . where do they come from . . . who is architect . . . it's all worked out . . . it's all on auto-pilot . . . my body begins to disintegrate . . . flow out into the river of evolution . . . good-bye . . . gone star space in orgasm pulses of particle motion . . . release . . . flashing light, light, light. . . .

MINUTE 6. TIM, WHERE ARE YOU NOW? Earth voice calling . . . you there, meson hurtling in nuclear orbit . . . incorporate . . . trap the streaking energy particle . . . slow down . . . freeze into body structure . . . return . . . with flick of open eye the nuclear dance suddenly skids into static form . . . see two clusters of electrons shimmering . . . the energy dance caught momentarily in friendly robot form . . . hello . . . next to them a candle flame . . . center of million-armed web of light beams . . . the room is caught in a lattice of light-energy . . . shimmering. . . . finger taps MO-LECULAR . . . MOLECULAR . . . Ah yes . . . MOLECULAR. . . .

Eyes closed but after-image of candle flame remains . . . eyeballs trapped in orbit around internal light center . . . celestial radiance from the light center . . . light of sun . . . all light is sun . . . light is life . . . live, luce, life . . . all life is frail filament of light . . . solar silent sound . . . sun-flare . . . light-life. . . .

MINUTE 8. TIM? WHERE ARE YOU NOW? In the heart of the sun's hydrogen explosion . . . our globe is light's globe . . . open eyes drape curtain over sun flare . . . open eyes bring blindness . . . shut off internal radiance . . . see chiaroscuro God holding shadow box . . . where is life? . . . press MOLECULAR. . . .

Keep eyes open . . . fixed caught . . . hypnotized . . . whole room, flowered walls, cushions, candle, human forms all vibrating . . . all waves having no form . . . terrible stillness . . . just silent energy flow . . . if you move you will shatter the pattern . . . all remembered forms, meanings, identities meaningless . . . gone . . . pitiless emanation of physical waves . . . television impulses crackling across an interstellar grid . . . our sun one point on astrophysical television screen . . . our galaxy tiny cluster of points on one corner of TV screen . . . the ten-billion-year cycle of our universe is a milli-second flash of light on the cosmic screen flowing endlessly with images. . . .

MINUTE 10. TIM, WHERE ARE YOU NOW? Ground-tower beaming up navigational query . . . flood of amazed love that we can contact each other . . . we do remain in contact . . . where was that cluster then . . . hallucinating . . . science-fiction

Dr. Metzner's report of Leary's DMT trip:

At two minutes the subject was smiling with eyes closed.

When asked to report he opened his eyes, looked at the observers curiously, smiled.

When the orientation question was repeated he chuckled.

Moved his finger searchingly over the typewriter.

And with a look of amused tolerance stabbed at the BODY CONSCIOUSNESS and SYMBOL THINKING keys.

He then fell back with a sigh and closed his eyes.

At four minutes the subject was still smiling with eyes closed.

metaphors . . . where is the key . . . there . . . HALLUCINATIONS . . . SYMBOLS . . . CELLS . . . MOLECULES . . . merging hallucinations.

My mind returns . . . labeling . . . diagnosing the endless flow . . . loss of space-time . . . merging with energy flux . . . seeing all life forms as physical waves . . . loss of body . . . existence as energy . . . awareness that our bodies are momentary clusters of energy and that we are capable of tuning in on patterns . . . the certainty that life

When asked to report, he opened his eyes and laughed. . . .

processes are on "auto-pilot" . . . there is nothing to fear or worry about . . . sudden understanding of the meaning of terms from Indian philosophy such as *maya, maha-maya, lila* . . . insight into the nature and varieties of transcendent states . . . the void-white-light-contentless, inorganic ecstasy . . . the *kundalini*-life-force-biological-squirming-moist-sexual organic ecstasy . . . the singing-genetic-code-blueprint-temporary-structuring-of-form ecstasy and the . . .

He looked at the observers with a smile . . . studied the keyboard of the typewriter, and pressed the CELLULAR-GENETIC CODE EXTERNAL key.

MINUTE 12. TIM, WHERE ARE YOU NOW? Open eyes . . . laugh . . . caught by vigilant ground-tower while orbiting around earthly-mind-figure-it-out area . . . where is key for thinking game . . . press COGNITIVE . . . HALLUCINATIONS . . . CELLS . . . MOLECULES. . . .

Above head is lightbulb covered with scalloped light-blue shade . . . circling up to the glowing shade are ribbons of waves . . . silent . . . beckoning . . . inviting . . . join the dance . . . leave your robot . . . a whole universe of delightful, aerial choreography awaits . . . yes join

He then fell back and closed his eyes.

them . . . suddenly, like smoke rising from a cigarette, consciousness circled up . . . swooping graceful gull-paths up to light source and, soundless, through into another dimension . . . billions-of-protein-file-cards, helical in shape, flicking through, confronting me with endless library of events, forms, visual perceptions, memories, not abstract but pulsing . . . now . . . experiential . . . a billion years of coded experience, classified,

At six minutes the subject had just finished frowning in what seemed like a passing fear or problem.

preserved in brilliant, living clarity that makes ordinary reality seem like an out-of-focus, tattered, jerky, fluttering of peep-show cards, tawdry and worn. . . .

When contacted to report, he glanced around the room and without hesitation

pressed the MOLECULAR CONSCIOUSNESS (external) key.

He then closed his eyes.

At eight minutes the subject, who had been lying motionless against the cushions . . .

. . . opened his eyes.

His expression was dazed, surprised.

Without expression he pressed the key for MOLEC-ULAR CONSCIOUSNESS (internal).

From eight to ten minutes the subject sat motion-less . . .

. . . eyes open in a trance-like state.

MINUTE 14. TIM, WHERE ARE YOU NOW? Oh where are we? . . . oh listen, here's where we are . . . once there was a glowing electric dot, a flash reflected from the heart of a cut diamond which, oh there, now, caught the light of sun flame and glittered . . . sudden flash in Precambrian mud . . . the dot stirs and quivers with tremble-strain-exultant-singing-throbbing-shuddering twist upwards and a serpent began to writhe up and through the soft, warm silt . . . tiny, the size of a virus . . . growing . . . the enormous length of a microscopic bacillus . . . flowing exultantly, always singing the Hindu flute-song . . . always bursting out, enfoliating . . . now the size of the moss root, churning through fibered-cunt-mattress-moist-spasm churning . . . growing . . . exfoliating its own vision . . . always blind except for the forward point of light-eye . . . now belts of serpent skin, mosaic-jeweled, rhythmically jerking, snakewise forward . . . now the size of a tree-trunk, gnarled and horny with the sperm-sap moving within . . . now swelling, tumescent into Mississippi flood of tissue writhing . . . pink, silt current of singing-fire . . . now circling globe, squeezing green salt oceans and jagged brownshale mountains with constrictor grasp . . . flowing blindly, now a billion-mile endless electric-cord vertebrated writhing cobra singing Hindu flute-song . . . penis head throbbing!! . . . blind, except for the one second each cell in the advancing parade is permitted that one moment face-to-face, eyeball to solar flame insight into the past-future. . . .

TIM, TIM, WHERE ARE YOU NOW? La Guardia tower repeats request for contact with the ship lost out of radar scope . . . where? . . . I am eye of the great snake . . . a fold of serpent skin, radiating trapezoidal inquiry swims into focus . . . register conscious content . . . where are you? . . . here . . . INTERNAL HALLUCINATIONS. CELLULAR-GENETIC MEMORIES. . . .

The session continued with two-minute interruptions until the twentieth minute in the same pattern. Timeless flights into hallucinatory or pure energy vibration fields with sudden contractions to reality in response to the observer questions.

This session suggested some solutions to the problem of communicating during psychedelic experiences. The person "up there" is being whirled through experiences which spin by so rapidly and contain structural content so different from our familiar macroscopic forms that he cannot possibly describe where he is or what he is experiencing.

There was no attempt to communicate.

Consider the analogy to the pilot of a plane who has lost his bearings and who contacts La Guardia tower by radio. The pilot is experiencing many events—he can describe the cloud formations, lightning flashes, the etching of ice on the plane window—but none of this makes any sense to the tower technicians who are attempting to plot his course in the three-dimensional language of navigation. The person "up there" cannot provide the categories. The ground control personnel must radio them "up." Cessna 64 Bravo, our radar scopes show you are fifteen miles southwest of International Airport. The red glow you see is the reflection of Manhattan. To head on a course for Boston you must change your course to 57 degrees and maintain an altitude of 5500.

When contacted he moved slowly but surely and pressed the TRIPLE EXPOSURE HALLUCINATION: SYMBOLIC-CELLULAR-MOLECULAR key.

From the tenth to twelfth minute the subject sat looking blankly and without motion at the wall of the room.

But the language of psychology is not sophisticated enough to provide such parameters. Nor are there experiential compasses to determine direction.

When contacted he smiled.

What we can do at this point is to set up "flight plans." The subject can work out, before the session, the areas of experience he wishes to contact; and he can plan the temporal sequence of his visionary voyage. He will not be able during the flight to tell "ground control" where he is, but ground control can contact him and tell him where to proceed. Thus, during this session when Ralph asked WHERE ARE YOU NOW? I could not respond. I had to descend, slow up the flow of experience, and then tell him where I had been or where I ended up.

And pressed the DOUBLE EXPOSURE HALLUCINATION—CELLULAR MEMORY PLUS SYMBOLIC THINKING key.

From minute twelve to fourteen the subject sat silent with eyes closed.

When the contact question came I would be hurtling through other galaxies. In order to respond, I had to stop my free rocketing, tumbling flight, return near the earth and say, I am over New Haven.

The session was a continual series of come-

When contacted he failed to respond and after thirty seconds was contacted again.

He then pressed INTERNAL CELLULAR MEMORY HALLUCINATION key.

This session suggests that a more efficient way to chart psychedelic experiences would be to:

1) Memorize the keyboard of the experiential typewriter so that communication down to ground control could be automatic.

2) Plan the flight in such a way that the ground control would not ask unanswerable questions—Where am I indeed!—but would tell the subject where to go.

Then the communication task of the voyager would be to indicate if he were on course . . .

. . . i.e., that he was or was not following the flight instructions radioed up by ground control.

Ground control should send up stimuli.

Suggestivity is wide open. La Guardia tower directs the flight.

downs. I repeatedly had to stop the flow in order to respond. My cortex was receiving hundreds of thousands of impulses a second; but in order to respond to ground control's questions I had to grind the ship to a slow stall to say, I was there, I am here, but now that has moved too.

The Heisenberg principle.

Psychedelic research is experimental philosophy, empirical metaphysics, visionary science.

Psychedelic drugs offer new perspectives on every aspect of human thinking, human behavior, human searching. There is no issue in psychology, physics, biology, and theology which cannot make use of these microscopes of consciousness. The discovery of LSD is as important to philosophy and psychology and religion as the discovery of the microscope was to biology.

Psychedelic drugs allow us to study—directly, experientially, empirically—the problems which have perplexed philosophers for millennia. Indeed, the psychedelic drugs force you, like it or not, prepared or not, to become a philosopher. You are flung bodily into convulsive, terrorized contact with such ancient problems as: What is real? What is true? What is good? What is beautiful?

Since 1960 our psychedelic explorations have forced us, agonizingly at times, to deal with these crucial questions.

We came to the exhausting conclusion that each person must work out all the answers himself. Each person must be his own Moses, his own Augustine, his own Buddha, his own Aquinas, his own Darwin, his own Einstein. You have to experience their confusion, their groping ignorance; you have to work out their exultant answers. You must do it yourself in the swirling crucible of the out-of-the-mind session after you discover to your terror that the answers you thought you had were canned chessboard symbols.

In our DMT experiments we dealt empirically with the issue of universals and names. God-Devil, heaven-hell, good-bad, ugly-beauty. Our answer: nothing exists except undulating energy and flowing consciousness upon which the grasping mind imposes categories. The categories have nothing to do with the energy-flow. Any temporary energy constellation can be divine, diabolic, beautiful, depending on your symbolic interpretation.

. . . Liberated from his ego, he contemplates the laws of life and so realizes that knowing how to become free of blame is the highest good. (I Ching)

But the symbols, the names are real too. It is possible and indeed necessary to create symbols for mapping and guiding. The symbols apply only for the space-time dimension we arbitrarily and consciously impose.

You and I can agree on names for certain game sequences and we can communicate accurately within the game context. We'll call this first base and that New Haven. We can develop maps and guidebooks for different levels of consciousness, knowing that the names are artifacts, that the map is not the territory.

The psychedelic experience is indescribable, ineffable, but so is every other experience. We can build a language to get you to Yankee Stadium at 3 P.M. on a summer Sunday afternoon and teach you how to score the game. We can build a language to get you out of your twentieth-century mind and spin you back into eerie LSD landscapes and teach you how to score the game. Neither scorecard comes close to matching the intricate energy exchanges involved in the trip to the ballpark or the trip to your inner galaxies, but the goal and challenge of being a human being is to visit more and more distant ballparks and to build more accurate scorecards.

Approximately how much of the session (in 10 percent of time) was spent in each of the following areas?

A) Interpersonal games, 10 percent (fondness for observers).

B) Exploring to discover self, or self games, 0 percent.

C) Other games (social, intellectual, religious), 70 percent (intellectual, struggling with problems of communication).

D) Non-game transcendence, 20 percent (continually interrupted by questions).

∞

CONTEMPLATION. *The ablution has been made,*
But not yet the offering.
Full of trust they look up to him.
(I Ching)

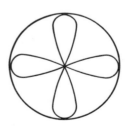

When Will You Be Ready to Admit You Are a Divine Messenger?

Spring 1962

Guide: SAKTI, DIVINE NUN

Oracle: XXII

Grace

Keeping Still, Mountain

The Clinging, Fire

Fire at the foot of the mountain:
The image of GRACE.
Thus does the superior man proceed
When clearing up current affairs.
But he dare not decide controversial issues in
*   this way.*

(I Ching)

From *Time:*

In every age, men have struggled to perceive God directly rather than as a tenuously grasped abstraction. Few succeed, and the visions of the world's rare mystics have normally come only after hard spiritual work—prayer, meditation, ascetic practice.

Now a number of psychologists and theologians are exploring such hallucinogenic drugs as mescaline, psilocybin and LSD-25 as an easy way to instant mysticism.

In large enough doses these drugs can simulate the effects of certain forms of psychosis—to the point, in some cases, of permanent derangement.

In controlled, minute doses the drugs produce weird and wonderful fantasies of sight and feeling; in Greenwich Village and on college campuses, they seem to be replacing marijuana as the hip way to get kicks.

At the time I ate the sacred mushrooms of Mexico I called myself as follows: an atheist, a rationalist, skeptical of any sort of authority, ritual, tradition, faith, or magic, an empiricist—intolerant of scholastic speculation and Talmudic juggling. An arrogant disdainer of fear-directed bourgeois conformity. I was convinced that the choice was to be independent-effective-right or obedient-routine-good, but not both.

The high-school principal looked at me calmly. You have consistently ignored the principles upon which this school is based. The Kantian Categorical Imperative. No one has a right to do that which if everyone did would destroy society. I was the editor of the high-school paper which had just won the interstate prize for excellence, but I cut classes and skipped school. The principal slowly turned a fountain pen in his hand. There was a month until graduation. He was thinking about the administrative trouble involved in expelling me. He was getting close to retirement—a wise old New Englander. He put the pen down. His eyes were on his blotter. He wouldn't look at me. I never want to see you or talk to you again. Just stay away from me and my office.

No cadet was allowed to sit next to me in the West Point mess hall, and I was required to request food by writing on a pad . . . which I never did. The cadet adjutant had climbed up to the observation shelf from where he bellowed out his cry of "attention." The clatter of dishes and babble of conversation ceased. Two thousand gray-coated cadets sat silently. Headquarters, United States Military Academy, West Point, New York, August 18, 1941. In the case of Cadet Timothy Leary, second class, the Honor Committee of the Cadet

Corps agrees to accept the verdict of the Court Martial. Not guilty. At ease.

The silence hung over the huge hall, larger than three football fields, and then hushed conversations began. That afternoon I packed my gear in a jeep and drove to the railroad station down by the Hudson under the granite fortress cliffs. First classmen who knew and sympathized and some plebes who didn't know but sympathized came up to shake my hand (most of them, by habit, still maintaining the silence), and a colonel attached to the superintendent's office stopped, flagged the jeep down, and came over silently and shook my hand.

It took a moment for the Jesuit Dean of Students to understand my refusal of his offer to return to Holy Cross. Then his face flushed with red. I had never seen him angry before. He was jolly, cocky, friend-of-the-students professor and wore his hard square black hat jauntily over his left eye. He turned quickly, black robe swirling, and stomped off.

Social systems larger than the clan are based on irrational and unnecessary fear and that's why they can't tolerate detached action no matter how effective.

At the time I ate the sacred mushrooms in Mexico I was a rational humanist. Supremely confident but empty because, although I could predict and master the game, I had lost the thread of mystery.

I had run through and beyond the middle-class professional game board. There were no surprise moves left. I had died even to the lure of ambition, power, sex. It was all a Monopoly game—easy to win at but meaningless. I had just been promised tenure at Harvard.

Five hours after eating the mushrooms it was all changed. The revelation had come. The veil had been pulled back. The classic vision. The fullblown conversion experience. The prophetic call. The works. God had spoken.

But Peter, standing up with the eleven, lifted up his voice, and said unto them . . . hearken to my

Some investigators who have tried the drugs claim to have undergone a profound spiritual experience, and these men are seriously, if gingerly, studying the undefined relationship between drug-induced visions and the classic forms of mystical ecstasy.

"The void was lit up." For at least 3,000 years, primitive tribes have had visionary orgies at feasts of certain sacred plants, often mushrooms.

The use of the peyote cactus, from which mescaline is derived, is a regular part of the communion services of the native American church, composed of 200,-000 U.S. Indians.

Novelist Aldous Huxley wrote in the *Doors of Perception* that mescaline produced in him an effect that seemed like seeing the beatific vision.

Psychologist Timothy Leary, who was dropped from Harvard faculty last spring after receiving strong criticism for his freewheeling research in the use of LSD and psilocybin, gave the drugs to sixty-nine full-time religious professionals, found that three out of four had intense mystico-religious reactions, and more than half claimed that they had the deepest spiritual experience of their life.

Such spiritual experiences range from heavenly to hideous: a number of subjects suffer through agonizing intimations of hell rather than of paradise.

Most instant mystics feel that they have been reborn, and have suddenly been given the key to existence, although their intuition usually appears in the form of an incommunicable platitude, such as, oneness is all.

California prison psychologist Wilson Van Dusen, for example, imagined himself in a black void in which "God was walking on me and I cried for joy."

"My own voice seemed to speak of His coming. But I didn't believe it. Suddenly and unexpectedly the zenith of the void was lit up with the blinding presence of the One.

"How did I know it? All I can say is that there was no possibility of doubt."

Union with God. This kind of experience seems to be at least subjectively religious; but there are less convincing cases in which drug takers appear to have read religion into their visions or rigged the setting to induce a spiritual experience.

words: For this is that which was spoken by the prophet Joel: And it shall come to pass in the last days, saith God, I will pour out my Spirit upon all flesh: and your sons and your daughters shall prophesy, and your young men shall see visions and your old men shall dream dreams. . . .

It was for me the authentic Moses, Mohammed, Blake, Boehme, Shankara, St. John of the Cross, trip. Now, mind you, I'm not comparing myself to these great eloquent, effective, popular newscasters from the central broadcasting station. Millions of unknown, incoherent, ineffective persons have stumbled on the billion-year-old ticker tape and got the message and have been unable to tune it back to society. But believe this—the message is the same, in spite of the transmitter, and I got the message by a swimming pool in Cuernavaca in August 1960.

Then what?

If I had been a believing psychologist, the temptation would be to rush back to the tribe and use the revelation in the psychology game—get research grants, write scientific articles, become famous. A new Freud. So simple and so what.

If I had been a painter, I would have started etching out the visions and gained renown and money as a new Salvador Dali.

If I had been a businessman, the reflex reaction to the mushroom vision would be commercial. Business is the religion of America and the best way to have introduced psychedelic sacraments into the culture would have been to market them.

I recall the first businessman that we ever turned-on. He was a friend of a psychiatrist who brought him over one Sunday for a session. After a couple of hours he swam up to me with that ecstatic, all-seeing gleam in his eye. Magnificent! I see it all! Incredible! Look, Leary, you've got to get me a million doses of this!

I smiled. This was the usual reaction. The physicists wanted a million doses to solve the non-existent problem of space-time. The artists, to make the world beautiful.

What would you do with a million doses?

The merchant looked at me with disdain. Why, it's obvious. This is worth a hundred dollars a dose. A million doses is a hundred million bucks!

If it weren't for my scholar's prejudice against commerce, we might have added small amounts of psilocybin to ginger-ale and quinine-water bottles and sold it as a new form of cocktail. One bottle would have been the equivalent of a joint of marijuana. Ten bottles would produce a visionary voyage. Psilocybin at that time was considered a mild, safe form of mushroom juice, and who would have objected to its sale in health stores? What would be more American than non-alcoholic ecstasy cocktails sold for a profit?

The most typical thing to do after your revelation is to announce it to everyone. Rush back and tell everyone.

Listen! Wake up! You are God! You have the Divine plan engraved in cellular script within you. Listen! Take this sacrament! You'll see! You'll get the revelation! It will change your life! You'll be reborn!

I started doing this the day after my conversion. I rushed over to Tepoztlan to tell the McClellands. Mary McClelland is a Quaker mystic and she listened with interest and sympathy. David McClelland is a Presbyterian convert to Quakerism. His shock and horror was unmistakable. If I had described the pleasure of heroin or sexual seduction of minors, he couldn't have shown more reflex dismay.

I found myself getting poetic and dogmatic. I know it is a real reality! I know it is the Divine message! David McClelland now looked alarmed. Clinical diagnostic glances. Wow! Do I have a nut on my hands here? He was my boss at Harvard.

I shut up and made a joke about Celtic enthusiasm and we talked about department politics.

I was faced with the ancient dilemma of the visionary to whom God has spoken.

After his illumination the Buddha sat for forty-nine days and nights wondering if he should go back and tune-in the message. He knew the Hindu priesthood would be angry.

Mohammed got into all sorts of administrative

One professor at Protestant divinity school recalls that he was handed a rose to contemplate after taking his dose of LSD.

As I looked at the rose it began to glow, he said, and suddenly I felt that I understood the rose.

A few days later when I reread the biblical account of Moses and the burning bush it suddenly made sense to me.

Perhaps the best-known deliberate effort to create religious experience with drugs was a special service in the basement chapel beneath Boston University's non-denominational Marsh Chapel on Good Friday last year.

Organ music was piped into the dimly lit chapel for a group of twenty subjects, half of whom were given LSD while the rest took placebos.

A minister gave a brief sermon, and the students were left alone to meditate. During the next three hours, all except one of the LSD takers (but only one of those who took placebos) reported a genuine religious experience.

I felt a deep union with God, reports one participant. I remember feeling a profound sense of sorrow that there was no priest or minister at the altar.

I had a tremendous urge to go up on the altar and minister the services.

But I had this sense of unworthiness, and I crawled under the pews and tried to get away.

Finally I carried my Bible to the altar and then tried to preach.

The only words I mumbled were peace—peace. I felt I was communicating beyond words.

Most churchmen are duly skeptical about equating an afternoon on LSD with the intuitions of a St. John of the Cross or a Martin Luther.

R. C. Zaehner of Oxford, a Roman Catholic and an expert on Eastern religions, holds that the drug-ingested visions are simply one of many kinds of preternatural experience, and are qualitatively different from the ecstasies granted mystics.

trouble. After three years only thirteen persons—slaves, no-accounts, and women—listened to him.

Boehme, Eckhart, and Luther, and George Fox, spoke about it and the wrath of the establishment came down on them. Even Moses had his problems.

When are you ready to take the message seriously enough to announce it?

This is it! Thou art the man! I am He! You are He!

Don't be deceived by the bureaucratic church. Don't think you can escape it. The revelation comes to everyman in his lifetime. You can close your eyes and try to ignore it. But it will come to you. Every man is the chosen man. Had you forgotten?

But when are you ready to accept it? And how will you announce it?

For an American in 1960 A.D. there was little vocational preparation for the prophetic role. There was no college-major for prophecy—least of all in the divinity schools. The steps to secular success were spelled out in every college catalogue but not for that only important profession—the discovery of your divinity.

There was no listing in the yellow pages of the phone book for visionary messiah.

The entire weight of American education is engineered to crush the religious impulse. Other times have been easier. Luther was a brilliant priest in a God-obsessed society. The Buddha had pursued a grueling yoga for several years before his flash. I was unprepared for the message. It would take me six years to accept the call.

I was trained as a psychologist. Psychology is a particularly vulgar, profane profession. It took Carl Jung a lifetime to kick the psychology habit and locate his center within. T. G. Fechner, the founder of scientific psychology, lay tormented on a bed, blind, incoherent, for more than a year before he tore off the blindfold and spoke the word. All is consciousness and consciousness is one.

I did not wander barefoot forth from Mexico preaching the word. I flew back to Harvard University and started a research project. The strategy was to provide religious experiences and then scientifically measure the overt benefit.

Make them feel right and they'll do right.

Make them feel good and they'll do good.

I didn't mention the religious revelation part. Just the public good, the behavior change that would result.

The dull would become creative. The neurotic would become whole. The criminal would reform his evil ways. Through questionnaire and objective personality tests and statistical analysis we would prove "scientifically" that God exists in man and that this power miracles doth perform.

Of course everyone intuitively saw through the scheme and resisted it—everyone, that is, who didn't turn-on. The self-appointed scientists and the academics were skeptical and irritated. They sensed what I was up to and knew that my charisma and enthusiasm could make it work.

The psychedelic sages also murmured against the research plan. It was too public, too superficial, too easy.

The psychedelic underground. The handful of Americans who knew where it was at—most of them long-time students of oriental philosophy and mystic experiences.

The first friend to warn me to keep the discovery private was Frank Barron. He was shocked at my organizing a large project of graduate students. This sort of research is internal. Take it yourself and read Blake. Frank had taken the mushrooms two years before and it plunged him into twelve months of contemplation, wild poetry, and dedicated study of mystical philosophy.

The politics, the administration, the organization of a large research project made no sense to him. Frank Barron is a gentleman scholar of the old school—a cross between William James and Dylan Thomas. Bureaucracy, committee meetings alienated his Celtic mystic intuitions. Experimentation on the sacred mushroom and the mystic experience made no more sense to Frank than psychological studies of the effects of the Catholic sacraments. What are the mental-health implications of baptism? Let us request a federal foundation grant to administer personality tests before and after Holy Communion. What are the psychiatric diagnostic characteristics of the visionary prophet? Let us

Presbyterian Theodore Gill, President of San Francisco Theological Seminary, wonders whether the drug experience might be a rival rather than a supplement to what conventional religion offers.

Says he: The drugs make an end run around Christ and go straight to the Holy Spirit.

Clerics also charge that LSD zealots have become a clique of modern gnostics concerned only with furthering their private search for what they call inner freedom.

Others feel that the church should not quickly dismiss anything that has the power to deepen faith.

Dr. W. T. Stace, of Princeton, one of the nation's foremost students of mysticism, believes that LSD can change lives for the better.

The fact that the experience was induced by drugs has no bearing on its validity, he says.

In an article on the drugs written with Leary for the journal *Religious Education,* Dr. Walter Houston Clark of Andover Newton Theological School argued that the structure of the drugs is similar to that of a family of chemicals in the body known as indoles.

It may be, he suggested, that a naturally occurring excess of the indoles might predispose some people to certain kinds of mystical experience.

Says Paul Lee, an instructor at M.I.T. who took LSD while a student at Harvard Divinity School:

The pity is that our everyday religious experience has become so jaded, so rationalized that to become aware of the mystery, wonderment, and confusion of life we must resort to the drugs.

Nonetheless, many of us are profoundly grateful for the vistas opened up by the drug experience.

It remains to be seen whether this experience is to be interpreted in religious language.

∞

make quantitative measures and statistical analyses of the Holy Spirit. Oh, really? Are you kidding?

Listen, Frank, let's come on as psychologists and develop a research project that aims at producing the ecstatic moment. Develop a science of ecstatics. Train graduate students to illuminate themselves and others. We have statisticians who systematize the static—how about ecstatisticians who systematize the ecstatic?

No, you can't do it with graduate students. They are temperamentally and professionally trained to look outside, at behavior. You'll find your native mystics among artists, poets, eccentrics. Don't mix the professional with the spiritual. And don't talk about the mushrooms so much.

But it was impossible not to talk about the experience. I was peripherally involved in Cambridge social life. Cocktails. Dinners. Conversations.

Sitting on a sofa with a dry martini trying to explain what it is like to go out of your mind and talk to God. Professors' wives leaning forward, wet lips, eyes glistening, the scent of perfume and alcohol breath. Fascination. Disbelief. Fear.

Gerald Heard, bearded wise old philosopher, knew what was going to happen. He had studied the sociology of ecstasy for forty years and recognized the ancient sacramental meaning of LSD.

He came to visit us at Harvard. We asked his advice in the form of specific, practical questions and he always replied in parables. The Eleusinian mysteries. Tantric cults. Tibetan secrets. The Masonic Brotherhood. The Illuminati. Medieval sects. The oral tradition. The secret teachings always passed from guru to disciple. He never gave an explicit answer but the meaning was clear. He who speaks does not know; he who knows speaks privately or not at all. Go underground.

Alan Watts came to visit. Wise. Detached. Funny. Jolly. Bubbling. Eloquent. Experienced. He was shy of groups and organizations. Don't upset the establishment. Blavatsky's Secret. The English occultists. Gurdjieff and Ouspensky—The Fourth Way of the sly man. He does not profess a public yoga. He takes his "little pill" quietly and goes all the way.

Alan (a former Anglican priest) conducted our first LSD session. On Easter Sunday. A High Church ceremony. Goblets. Homemade bread and good French wine. Parables and Zen jokes. Susan, my twelve-year-old, and Jack, age ten, performed as acolytes. The sun shone through the clouds at noon and Madison Presnell and Lisa, his beautiful flower wife, and their twins arrived from church radiant in Easter clothes.

Lisa played the grand piano, and Madison, with his African seed wisdom, played the grand jester and floated up to us on contact-high and spun out psychedelic stories.

At the communion supper Alan laughed. I see everything, everything in its cosmic dimension. Every phrase. Every action. How divinely funny.

Aldous Huxley sat with us in our early planning sessions and turned-on with us but remained convinced that religion was the inevitable institutional channel for the psychedelics. He called LSD a gratuitous grace. At his suggestion I initiated discussions with some Unitarian ministers. They were, as always, cultured, tolerant, open-minded, but hopelessly intellectual.

One day in December 1960 I received a note from a Professor Huston Smith, philosopher at M.I.T. We lunched at the Faculty Club. It seemed that during a seminar on religious experience at M.I.T., Professor Smith had suggested that Westerners could never hope to attain to the mystic experience. Aldous had passed over a note to Huston Smith with my telephone number.

Professor Smith had an ideal background for a psychedelic trip. His parents were missionaries and he spent seventeen years in China. His professional game was comparative religion. He had sought the visionary experience in monasteries in Burma and Japan.

He had been waiting and working for a long time for the direct confrontation.

And so it was arranged that on New Year's Day, 1961, Huston and his good wife Eleanor would come to my house to turn-on.

They arrived late. And Huston was nervous.

There was no ritual because I was too inexpe-

From "The Religious Experience, Its Production and Interpretation" by Timothy Leary, in the *Psychedelic Review:*

We have arranged transcendental experiences for over four thousand persons from all walks of life, including two hundred full-time religious professionals, about half of whom belong to Eastern religions and about half of whom profess the Christian or Jewish faith.

In our research files and in certain denominational offices there is building up a large and quite remarkable collection of reports which will be published when the political atmosphere becomes more tolerant.

At this point it is conservative to state that over seventy-five percent of these subjects report intense mystico-religious reactions, and considerably more than half claim that they have had the deepest spiritual experience of their life.

We have five scientific studies by qualified investigators—the four naturalistic studies of Leary *et al.*, Savage *et al.*, Ditman *et al.* and Janiger-McGlothlin,

and the triple-blind study in the Harvard dissertation mentioned earlier—yielding data which indicate that (1) If the setting is supportive but not spiritual, between 40 and 75 percent of psychedelic subjects will report intense and life-changing religious experiences; . . .

and that, (2) If the set and setting are supportive and spiritual, then around 90 percent of the experiences will be revelatory and mystico-religious.

It is hard to see how these results can be disregarded by those who are concerned with spiritual growth and religious development.

These data are even more interesting because the experiments took place during an historical era when mysticism, individual religious ecstasy (as opposed to religious behavior), was highly suspect, . . .

And when the classic, direct non-verbal means of revelation and consciousness-expansion such as meditation, yoga, fasting, monastic withdrawal and sacramental foods and drugs were surrounded by an aura of fear, clandestine secrecy . . .

Active social sanction, and even imprisonment.

The religious experience. You are undoubtedly wondering about the meaning of this phrase which has been used so freely in the preceding paragraphs. May I offer a definition?

rienced to understand the importance of ritual and too ignorant to suggest that Huston and Eleanor provide their own and too aware of the trap of the mind to impose my structure on the experience.

After taking the sacrament Huston lay for six hours in a comatose terror. Then lay for four hours in silent dazed contemplation. I had been busy during the day offering irrelevant aid, tea (not drunk), fruit (not eaten), supportive remarks (unanswered).

As I drove them home in heavy silence I felt the session was a failure—half blaming my inexperience, half blaming the subjects for being unprepared.

The next day Huston phoned with the most enthusiastic, ecstatic, grateful cordiality. The session was more than he expected. The sacrament had unlocked the door.

In the subsequent months Huston ran psilocybin sessions for undergraduate and graduate students at M.I.T. Laboratory exercises for his lectures on the mystic experience. Those were the casual days before the politicians and the dark priesthood of psychiatry had made a scandal out of LSD.

After the sessions some of his students roared over to Harvard to dedicate their lives to the psychedelic cause, but we had no way of using these unleashed spiritual energies—no turn-on, tune-in, drop-out program. We had our hands full with converted Harvard graduate students. I wonder what ever happened to those eager youngsters.

During the summer and fall of 1961 more and more interest in psychedelics was developing, particularly among the religious.

Dr. Walter Houston Clark, Dean of the Hartford Seminary, was a visiting scholar at Harvard and kept coming around to talk about turning-on. He was a handsome, distinguished graying figure—of somewhat awesome respectability. He neither drank nor smoked, and talked about William James. I felt he was really too academic and conservative to flip-out in the divine dance. I had a protective feeling about him. He couldn't really know what was involved.

Then there was Walter Pahnke—a young country-bumpkin, fresh-faced, gee-whiz enthusiast. He had a ministerial degree (Midwest Lutheran, I believe) and a medical license and was an advanced graduate student in the Ph.D. program of the Harvard Divinity School.

Walter wanted to do a thesis dissertation research on the psychedelic experience. Yes sir. A medically supervised, double-blind, pre- and post-tested, controlled, scientifically up-to-date kosher experiment on the production of the objectively defined, bona-fide mystic experience as described by Christian visionaries and to be brought about by our ministrations.

Walter Pahnke was so serious and so naïve, I laughed out loud. How many subjects, Walter?

Well, twenty in the control group and twenty in the experiment. And they'll all take the drug in a church with organ music and a sermon and the whole Protestant ritual going. I've read all you've written about the importance of set-and-setting and it sounds right to me.

Walter Pahnke spoke with a boy-scout sincerity.

I gulped. You mean you are suggesting we turn-on twenty people at the same time in the same public place.

Yes-sirree. Wouldn't be scientific to do it at different times. Besides I want to do it on Good Friday—in the Boston University Chapel. I know Dean Howard Thurmond and he's interested in the mystic experience and he'll let us use the chapel.

I really had to laugh at this caricature of the experimental design applied to that most sacred experience. If he had proposed giving aphrodisiacs to twenty virgins to produce a mass orgasm, it wouldn't have sounded further out.

My dear Walter, I'm speechless! That is the most reckless wild suggestion I've ever heard in my life. You don't understand what you are dealing with. A psychedelic experience flips you out of your mind. It's intimate. It's private. You laugh. You moan in cosmic terror. You roll on the floor wrestling with God and the devil. In particular, the first session must be in a protected, quiet, secure surrounding.

Walter Pahnke was stubborn. It'll be secure, all right. I've got a medical degree and I'll have tran-

The religious experience is the ecstatic, incontrovertibly certain, subjective discovery of answers to seven basic spiritual questions.

What are these seven basic spiritual questions? There is the ultimate-power question, the life question, the human-destiny question, and the ego question.

1. The ultimate-power question: What is the ultimate power or basic energy which moves the universe, creates life?

2. The life question: What is life, where did it start, where is it going?

3. The human-destiny question. What is man, whence did he come, and where is he going?

4. The knowledge question. How do we know?

5. The ego question (spiritual and not secular, psychological, or social): What am I? What is my place in the plan?

6. The emotional question. What should we feel?

7. The ultimate-escape question. How can we end it?

Now one important fact about these questions is that they are continually being answered and re-answered, not only by all the religions of the world but also by the data of the natural sciences.

Reread these questions from the standpoint of the goals of (1) astronomy-physics, (2) biochemistry, (3) genetics and physiology, (4) neurology, (5) psychology, (6) psychiatry, (7) anesthesiology.

But if non-secular, "pure" science and religion address themselves to the same basic questions, what is the distinction between the two disciplines?

Science is the systematic attempt to record and measure the energy process and the sequence of energy transformation we call life.

The goal is to answer the basic questions in terms of objective, observed, public data.

quilizers to inject—and I'll do psychiatric interviews to screen out pre-psychotics.

No, Walter, you don't get the point. What you are proposing may be psychiatrically safe but it's indecent. You've never had a session, have you?

Nope.

Well, Walter, I like your idea. I'd love to help you do a systematic study of the mystic experience, but you must know what is involved. You must have several sessions yourself before you begin to think about a research study.

Nope. He couldn't do that. He realized that there might be all sorts of opposition to his study—from Harvard, from the Divinity School, from the medical people. Gosh, he knew how hidebound people were. Therefore he must preserve his psychedelic virginity. He didn't want to be accused of being biased and too positive. He had to be able to say that he had never taken the drug until after his thesis was accepted.

The more time I spent with the indefatigable Walter Pahnke, the more impressed I became. Behind his cornball facade there was an inner dedication, an unruffled optimism, a deep belief in the religious experience and the power of psychedelics to produce it.

An informal religious seminar slowly emerged. We began meeting on Sunday nights at Huston Smith's house: Walter Clark and Walter Pahnke and dignified professors from the Divinity School and visiting preachers and divines and a group of graduate students from the Divinity School.

I would preach and answer questions. Huston and Walter Clark and Walter Pahnke would comment and encourage. Gradually an experiment developed. We would run a session for several divinity students. This was a trial run for Walter Pahnke—a preparation for his big experiment.

The session was scheduled for a Saturday morning in March, 1962. We met in two groups, one at my house and one at Huston's house. We had built up a staff of session guides—Harvard graduate students and young professors. It went well. Walter Clark finally had his mystic experience, which he described in a moving report.

Religion is the systematic attempt to provide answers *to the same questions* subjectively, in terms of direct, incontrovertible private experience.

At this point I should like to present my central thesis. I am going to advance the hypothesis that those aspects of the psychedelic experience which subjects report to be ineffable and ecstatically religious involve a direct . . .

awareness of the processes which physicists and biochemists and neurologists measure.

(1) The ultimate-power question. A. *The scientific answers* to this question change constantly—Newtonian laws, quantum indeterminacy, atomic structure, nuclear structure.

Today the *basic energy* is located within the nucleus.

Inside the atom, a transparent sphere of emptiness thinly populated with electrons, the substance of the atom has shrunk to a core of unbelievable smallness:

Enlarged one thousand million times, an atom would be about the size of a football, but its nucleus would still be hardly visible—a mere speck of dust at the center.

The psychedelic experience posed problems for some of the divinity students.

Each one of these voyagers had a vision as dramatic as Moses or Mohammed. One college chaplain found himself in a bottomless well of cell and tissue and realized he was dying (i.e. mortal), and looked up for the light but doubted, and reached for faith and prayer and couldn't find it, and despaired and fell back on his mind for explanations and control, and grew sulky and demanding and could not believe. He explained the experience afterwards in psychiatric terms and soon after left the ministry for a career in the social sciences.

It was strong Old Testament stuff, believe me.

Another minister found himself dying and cried out in great fear, and we told him, Pray, brother, and he prayed and was reborn in radiance.

And another rolled on the floor, discovering that sex was the red-flame of life, copulating the carpet, and cried out, Is God nothing but sex? and we reminded him of his prayer "Thy will be done, Lord, not my will but thine," and he prayed and wept for joy.

And another minister walked tensely into the garden and when I approached him smiling, he said, If you mention the word guilt to me I'll punch you in the nose. And he cried out in despair, Who can help me? I said, Pray to your God, and he said, The hell with God, I want my wife, and I said, Your wife is God, and he said, Right! My wife is God! Get me home. Toward the end of the session we got a driver to take him one hundred miles back to his wife, and he had two telepathic experiences that left him awed and reverent and very much in love with his wife.

And the minister who fell on his knees, ordered us all to do likewise, and looked up at me with righteous tears and said, Timothy Leary, put aside your vanity and testify to the Blood of the Lamb, and his minister friend, also high, said, Yes. Amen. Look at his eyes, the eyes of Christ, and I looked down at the wells of suffering and groaned that laughing Jesus had been made martyr by these Christians. And the friend said, Ho. Ho. The great

Leary, master of games, has met his match in the eyes of Jesus. Look at these eyes, they see through even your game, Dr. Leary.

And I wouldn't kneel. I said, Let us pray together, but the suffering eyes flashed with righteousness and I felt the arms go around my knees. By God, I was tackled by suffering Jesus-eyes burning me with reproach. And the two Christians on their knees looked up at me relentless, and linebacker Jesus-eyes would not let me go.

I was amused and irritated because I saw the two thousand years of Christian moral-one-upmanship and missionary coercion and holy sado-masochism. If I moved I'd be brought down in a tackle, unless I moved violently, in which case I'd hurt the suffering Jesus-eyes.

I won't let you go, Brother Leary, until you fall on your knees for Jesus—and you will do it if I have to hold you for days.

Jesus-eyes wouldn't let go and wouldn't stop talking and wailing about Blood of the Lamb, repent, so I said, I'll stay here praying silently my Buddha prayer as long as you insist on holding me slave to you. Onward Christian soldiers, but for Christ's sake shut up and let us meditate and worship in holy silence. And his friend said, Yes, let's meditate silently with Brother Tim, but Jesus-eyes couldn't keep still and kept screaming, He died for our sins, and I fought down my desire to straight-arm the linebacker and run for the goal and I relaxed and after five minutes Jesus-eyes let go his tackle for a split second and I was off and away to the kitchen where I opened the refrigerator and pulled out a beer and was sitting with my feet on the kitchen table when the missionaries roared in to save my soul and when the preaching continued I opened the window and the soft spring air billowed the curtain and I shouted, See that soft breeze? That's the breath of God, for me. And hear those birds? . . . we all listened. Well that's the sermon I tune-in to. It's all God, beloved Jesus-eyes, and the bubbles on this beer, see them, they're part of the Divine Scheme too. I toast you and God. And with that we all smiled and the session went on.

Yet that nucleus radiates a powerful electric field which holds and controls the electrons around it.

Incredible power and complexity operating at speeds and spatial dimensions which our conceptual minds cannot register.

Infinitely small, yet pulsating outward through enormous networks of electrical forces —atom, molecule, cell, planet, star: All forms dancing to the nuclear tune.

The *cosmic design* is this network of energy whirling through space-time.

More than fifteen thousand million years ago the oldest stars (oldest, that is, that we now know about) began to form.

Whirling disks of gas molecules—driven of course by that tiny, spinning, nuclear force—condensing clouds —further condensations— the tangled web of spinning magnetic fields clustering into stellar forms. . . .

And each stellar cluster hooked up in magnetic dance with its planetary cluster and with every other star in the galaxy and each galaxy whirling in synchronized relationship to the other galaxies.

One thousand million galaxies. From 100 million to 100,000 million stars in a galaxy—that is to say, 100,000 million planetary systems per galaxy . . .

. . . and each planetary system slowly wheeling through the stellar cycle that allows for a brief time the possibility of life as we know it.

Here in the always changing data of nuclear physics and astronomy is the current scientific answer to the first basic question—material enough indeed for an awesome cosmology.

B. *Psychedelic reports* often contain phrases which seem to describe similar phenomena, subjectively experienced.

Subjects speak of participating and merging with pure (i.e., content-free) energy, white light: of witnessing the breakdown of macroscopic objects into vibratory patterns, the awareness that everything is a dance of particles,

sensing the smallness and fragility of our system, visions of the void, of world-ending explosions, of the cyclical nature of creation and dissolution, etc.

It was during these sessions that I first caught on to the power and meaning of prayer. That prayer wasn't a telegram sent in the English language to the department of requisition and supply on the top floor. I realized that you have to be out of your mind to pray. That you can't rationalize with a five-billion-year-old energy process. That only psychotics and flipped-out saints and psychedelics can pray. And that prayer is the compass . . . the gyroscope . . . the centering device to give you direction and courage and trust at those moments when you are overwhelmed by the power and breadth of the divine process.

The psychedelic experience posed problems for some of the divinity students. It seemed that most of them were more interested in their doctorates, and academic careers. The problem was that in these careers the revelatory confrontation and the voice of God had not played much of a part. So there were crises of conscience and identity—but it was all healthy and yeasty and the religious seminar continued Sunday evenings and we kept turning-on ministers and divinity students by day and by night.

Meanwhile I had been through my big LSD death-rebirth under the guidance of Michael, and the religious-ontological nature of the psychedelic experience was obvious to me, and any secular discussion about psychedelic drugs—creativity, psychiatric treatment, etc.—seemed irrelevant. I was catching the religious fever.

An increasing number of priests and ministers and theologians kept coming around. And then in the spring of 1962 came the swing to the East.

It started with Fred Swain, World War II air force major, who became a Vedanta Hindu monk in 1948, and who lived in an ashram near Boston. He started hanging out at the house and he told us about Hinduism and the psychedelic pantheon of gods and his guru and yoga. Fred had gone to Mexico the year before and had a far-out mushroom trip with María Sabrina in the mountains of Oaxaca.

I started visiting the Vedanta ashram. It was a surprise and delight to discover this group of holy, mature, sensible people who had renounced the world in pursuit of the visionary quest. The Hindu Bibles read like psychedelic manuals. The Hindu myths were session reports. The ashram itself was a turn-on. A serene, rhythmic life of work and meditation all aimed at getting high.

The reports of Fred Swain and Alan Watts and Aldous Huxley had impressed them with the yogic possibilities of psychedelic drugs. They were watching me too, testing me out.

After several visits I was asked, shyly, to guide a session for some of the people in the ashram.

I came to the ashram early one morning and joined the meditating-chanting service. Then, those who were to take the trip remained for more prayers and contemplation. The LSD had been placed in chalices on the altar. Incense and flowers adorned it. The LSD sacrament was mixed with holy water from the Ganges, blessed, and drunk.

In human affairs, aesthetic form comes into being when traditions exist that, strong and abiding like mountains, are made pleasing by a lucid beauty. By contemplating the forms existing in the heavens we come to understand time and its changing demands. Through contemplation of the forms existing in human society it becomes possible to shape the world. (I Ching XXII)

Then we moved from the altar to the larger shrine-room—we sat Indian-style on an oriental rug. Candles. Incense. Chanting.

Then the Holy folk got high. I could see the LSD take over. In spite of their years of preparation they were shocked by the power and complexity of the LSD. They knew exactly what was happening but it still scared them. I was high too and overcome by the power of the ashram and the shrine and the ancient rituals. We were all caught in Hindu mythologies. I was awed and dazzled and confused. What happens here? Now I'm Siva, okay, but what do I do? Hindu sessions have been going on for five thousand years. I'm a naïve Westerner. I remembered my prayer, When in doubt, be quiet, drift, trust. I sat erect in the Indian position—flipped-out, ecstatic, bewildered.

The Holy people of the ashram were bowled

Now I need not apologize for the flimsy inadequacy of these words. We just don't have a better experiential vocabulary.

If God were to permit you a brief voyage into the divine process, let you whirl for a second into the atomic nucleus or spin you out on a light-year trip through the galaxies, . . .

how on earth would you describe what you saw, when you got back, breathless, to your office?

This metaphor may sound far-fetched and irrelevant to you, but just ask someone who has taken LSD in a supportive setting.

(2) The Life question: A. *The scientific answer:* Our planetary system began over five billion years ago and has around five billion years to go.

Life as we know it dates back about one billion years. In other words, the earth spun for about eighty percent of its existence without life.

The crust slowly cooled and was eroded by incessant water flow.

Fertile mineral mud was deposited . . . now giving . . . for the first time . . . the possibility of harboring life.

Thunderbolts in the mud produce amino acids, the basic building blocks of life.

Then begins the ceaseless production of protein molecules, incalculable in number, forever combining into new forms.

The variety of proteins exceeds all the drops of water in all the oceans of the world.

Then protoplasm. Cell. Within the cell, incredible beauty and order. When we consider the teeming activity of a modern city it is difficult to realize that in the cells of our bodies infinitely more complicated processes are at work. . . .

Ceaseless manufacture, acquisition of food, storage, communication, and administration. . . .

over. They really saw the mythic nature of the situation. They looked up at me in terror and awe. I was radiating energy. The beautiful nun Sakti gasped and crawled over and put her head in my lap. Oh Bhagavan, Lord, you have conquered me. Forgive my doubts and my arrogance. I surrender to you. The others watched with hushed attention. Fred Swain crouched, squatting, the monkey-God, Hanuman. We were four figures from a temple carving. We were four timeless divinities caught in the classic posture of union, celebration, cosmic tension.

I leaned down and smiled and stroked Sakti's brow. Rest, beloved. We are one. She sighed, Oh yes, and the others nodded.

The candles burned silently. The incense smoke rose, essence of Holy India, reek of Kalighat temple, Calcutta, holy scent of Ram Mandir Benares and Jaganath Puri and Konarak. I looked around the room. Ramakrishna's statue breathed and his eyes twinkled the message. Vivekananda's brown face beamed and winked. Christ grinned to be joined again with his celestial brothers. The rarewood walls breathed. The sacred kundalini serpent uncoiled up the bronzed candelabra to the thousand-petaled lotus blossom. This was the fulcrum moment of eternity. The exact second of consciousness, fragile, omniscient. God was present and spoke to us in silence.

I was overcome with reverence. And gratitude. To be allowed this glimpse, this participation in the Holy company, in the venerable dance.

I was a Hindu from that moment on. No, that's not the way to say it. I recognized that day in the temple that we are all Hindus in our essence. We are all Hindu Gods and Goddesses. Laughing Krishna. Immutable Brahma. Yes and Asiatic-sensual Siva. Stern Kali with bloody hands. Undulant flowering Laxmi. Multi-armed Vishnu. Noble Rama. That day in the temple I discovered my Hindu-ness.

Things were different after that session. There was a new dimension. I was less a confident American and more an unsure human. There was more mystery and more sense of being part of an ancient

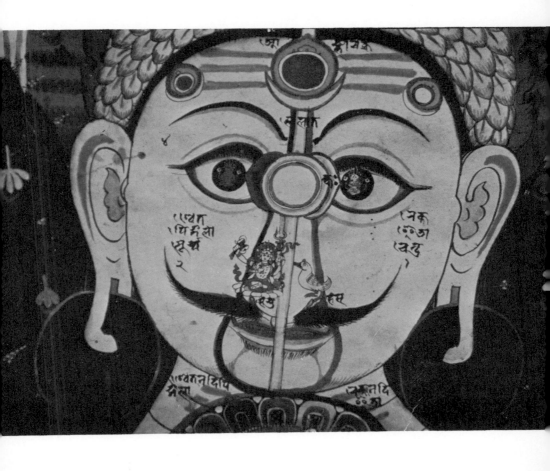

All this takes place in superb harmony, with the cooperation of all the participants of a living system, regulated down to the smallest detail.

Life is the striving cycle of repetitious, reproductive energy transformations. Moving, twisting, devouring, changing, the unit of life is the cell.

And the blueprint is the genetic code, the two nucleic acids—the long, intertwined, duplicating chains of DNA and the controlling regulation of RNA—which determine the structure of the living substance.

And where is it going? Exactly like the old Hindu myths of cyclical rotation, the astro-physicists tell us that life is a temporary sequence which occurs at a brief midpoint in the planetary cycle.

processional profession. The slow invisible process of becoming a guru, a holy man, had begun. It would be four years before I could openly admit to it. Accept my divinity, my divine election. This holy-man thing is always something you confess to, rather than claim. When you say it, you lose it, but not for long. It's a relentless growing process which, like aging or wrinkles, once it has begun, can't be stopped. The inexorable, unplanned for, troublesome, comically embarrassing, implausible unstoppable tidal sweep towards sainthood. How ironic and ludicrous that an American Irishman should be forced into sainthood! There was the dim recognition that I had known it all along. Since childhood. In the flush of youthful game success, the nagging, peripheral, elusive memory that I had been through this before; that no game victory or career achievement could satisfy because I had won and lost the same games so many times before.

Is it reincarnation? Or just the living-out of adolescent fantasies of messiahism? It makes no difference how you explain it—it's as real as rain.

The first intimations of the prophetic role came after the session in the ashram. The monks and nuns treated me as a guru. To them it was obvious. I was not a Harvard psychologist with a staff of research assistants. Come off it, please. I was, like it or not, playing out the ancient role.

The evolution of organic forms is a combination of internal protein potentiality and external pressure. Seed and sun. And so with man's spiritual evolution. Inner potential plus external social pressure.

When the guru was away, members of the ashram would visit me for religious advice. And wandering aspirants began to drift into the house. Devotees looking for cosmic direction, not game counsel. Their dilemmas are celestial, not practical. And you don't offer solutions—just reminders of who we are and where we are and where we came from and how it is to unfold. We all know these things. We just need reminders. The person who remembers, who reminds, who acts as an alarm clock, who becomes time-and-weather announcer for central broadcasting, station RDNA—this person is called guru. Prophet.

The profession of holy man is based, like everything else human, upon the laws of the nervous system and the laws of social interaction. It involves feedback, set, expectation, setting, social pressure, habit. If you are turned-on/tuned-in/dropped-out, then people will begin treating you as a spiritual teacher. And if people continue to press you with questions and problems and emotions appropriate only to the guru-role, you begin to act like a holy man. You just have to. But the acting like a holy-man-spiritual-teacher must be based on, must always be in touch with your holy-inner-experimenting. If the holy actions get separated from the holy-orgiastic-ecstasy-revelation-thread inside, then you become a fraud, a play-actor priest, a pious do-gooder. That's the occupational hazard of a messiah. You have to keep turning-on/tuning-in/dropping-out yourself. You have to have a frightening sacrament that works and continues to work.

The fire, whose light illuminates the mountain and makes it pleasing, does not shine far; in the same way, beautiful form suffices to brighten and to throw light upon matters of lesser moment, but important questions cannot be decided in this way. They require greater earnestness. (I Ching XXII)

It's easy to get caught up in the guru game. And you can keep it going in a routine fashion because your disciples are only too happy to cop-out, to settle for *your divinity*, not theirs. The guru has to keep dropping-out of the guru role and shocking followers out of their piety and jarring them, and he can never stay virtuously predictable.

That's why so many gurus get stale and pompous and narcissistic. They believe and react to the fantasies about their holiness. That was the power of Gandhi, of Ramakrishna, of Gurdjieff. They knew that the guru has to keep turning-on/tuning-in/dropping-out. And that's the dilemma of Krishnamurti. He saw the falseness of his avatar-God role. It had been laid on him, after all, without his choice as a child, and he was too intelligent and too honest to go along with it and he shouted, Stop. Come on! I'm not The God. You all are Gods, if you only remember. But Krishnamurti had no way of

Terrestrial life began around four billion years A.B. ("after the beginning" of our solar cycle) and will run for another two billion years or so.

At that time the solar furnace will burn so hot that the minor planets (including earth) will boil, bubble, and burn out.

In other planetary systems the time spans are different, but the cycle is probably the same.

The psychedelic correlates of these biological concepts sound like this: Confrontation with and participation in cellular flow; . . .

visions of microscopic processes; strange, undulating multi-colored tissue patterns; being a one-celled organism floating down arterial waterways; being part of the fantastic artistry of internal factories; . . .

recoiling with fear at the incessant push, struggle, drive of the biological machinery, clicking, clicking, endlessly, endlessly—at every moment engulfing you.

(3) The human-destiny question: A. The scientific answer: The flame of life which moves every living form, including the cell cluster you call yourself, began, we are told, as a tiny single-celled spark in the lower pre-Cambrian mud; then passed over in steady transformations to more complex forms.

turning-on. None of the sacraments worked for him and so he was caught in the reluctant guru game, lecturing and writing the message that there is no message, using his intellectual method to put down method, and teaching from a thousand middle-class podiums that there is no teacher and there is no mystery-magic because he, Krishnamurti, like a Medici pope (but more honest than a nepotist Renaissance pope because he blew the whistle beautifully and cleanly on his own religious bureaucracy game), was forced into a role he wasn't ready for—the avatar who had never turned-on.

Well, that Spring of 1962 was a rock-and-roll religious revival season. My house was swarming with Christian ministers and Hindu practitioners. We spent a lot of time at the Vedanta ashram. Conversions and rebirths occurring on a relentless weekly schedule.

LSD used as a sacrament was working.

GRACE *has success.*
In small matters
It is favorable to undertake
  something.

(I Ching)

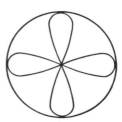

Your Faith Will Perform Miracles:

THE GOOD FRIDAY EXPERIMENT

April 1962

Guides: WALTER CLARK,
HUSTON SMITH,
WALTER PAHNKE

Oracle: IV

Youthful Folly

Keeping Still, Mountain

The Abysmal, Water

A spring wells up at the foot of the mountain:
The image of YOUTH.
Thus the superior man fosters his character
By thoroughness in all that he does.

(I Ching)

From *Patrologici Latina* by Johannes Scotus Erigena:

The flux of all things is not a motion in time, because all time is comprehended within one part of the process. It is not a cycle which repeats itself, but an eternal cycle, and the two aspects of the process are simultaneously eternal. Nature is eternal, but not static. It is eternally dynamic, moving by the dialectical process of division and return.

These ideas, existing in the mind of God, contain the substances of all things: Man, for example, is most correctly defined as a certain intellectual notion eternally made in the divine mind.

From *The Confessions of St. Augustine:*

The memory containeth also reasons and laws innumerable of numbers and dimensions, none of which hath any bodily sense impressed; seeing they have neither colour, nor sound, nor taste, nor smell, nor touch. I have heard the sound of the words whereby when discussed they are denoted: But the sounds are other than the things.

And so was Walter Pahnke working. He was doggedly going ahead with plans for his controlled experiment. I had gone along with Walter all along, humoring him, knowing that it couldn't happen. But Walter Pahnke was unstoppable. A master politician in the art of the feasible.

First he cooled me out. He agreed to change his design. There would be no turning-on of a large group, no marching around of masses of people stoned out of their minds. Walter agreed to divide the sample into five small groups. In each group there would be four divinity students—two of whom would be given psilocybin (the sacred mushroom in pill form) and the other two a placebo (a non-psychedelic pill). Each group would be guided by two members of our Harvard project—psychedelic veterans—one of whom would take psilocybin and one of whom would get the placebo.

No one, not even Walter Pahnke, would know who would get the sacrament and who would draw the inactive pill.

Walter balked at the guides taking the drug. This was the main objection which psychiatrists and self-appointed researchers were leveling at our work. How can doctors take drugs with the subjects? The psychiatrists and scientists who were denouncing our work had never taken a psychedelic. To them LSD and psilocybin made you drunk like booze or crazy like mental hospitals. In their Torquemada fantasies we were reeling around intoxicated (or worse). How could we be objective?

But I insisted. There can be no doctor-patient game going when you use psychedelics. We are all in it together. Shared ignorance. Shared hopes. Shared risks. One guide (selected by lot) would be straight and one would be high. And all ten guides

304

would be seeking the same thing as the subjects—a deep spiritual experience on Good Friday.

Walter agreed.

Next, Walter went to the administrators at the three schools and reassured them. The implausible breadth and scope of the experiment was itself an advantage. The fact that three colleges were involved allowed for administrative buck-passing. After all, reasoned Boston University, it's a Harvard doctoral dissertation. After all, reasoned Harvard, our students are not involved as subjects. After all, reasoned Andover-Newton, it's really a Harvard–Boston University project. Our students are involved as individuals.

And then Walter had some powerful sacred cows going for him. He was an M.D., a minister, a Harvard scientist. But more important were the good human energies he had going for him. First there was his own unmistakable sincerity and his reassuring, square, conventional, earnest solidity.

Then he had the backlog of solid spiritual power that had been a-building up over the past year. Every theologian, minister, and administrator in the Boston area had felt the ripple of our religious project. We had provided (in safety) deep, shattering, spiritual conversion experiences for a good two dozen members of the academic establishment. The good word had got around.

Then, and perhaps most important, Walter had the full support of at least one impressive, high-status person at each institution. Professor Huston Smith of M.I.T.—saintly, benevolent, articulate, sound, mature—would be a guide and take the pill blindly on Good Friday and risk going out of his mind.

And Dr. Walter Clark of Andover-Newton—convincing, mellow, lovable—was ready to take the sacrament with strangers and lend his guiding wisdom.

And at Harvard, Walter Pahnke's thesis-adviser was behind the experiment.

So during the Lenten weeks we divided into groups, and the two guides met with the four students and got to know each other and shared

I have seen the lines of architects, the very finest, like a spider's thread; but those are still different, they are not the images of those lines which the eye of flesh showed me: He knoweth them, whosoever without any conception whatsoever of a body, recognises them within himself.

∞

From *The Age of Belief* by Anne Fremantle:

Augustine concludes that past and future are all measured, as is the present too, by memory; indeed all reality, including God himself, lurks there, in man's memory.

∞

From *The Confessions of St. Augustine:*

When I enter there, I require what I will to be brought forth, and something instantly comes; others must be longer sought after, which are fetched, as it were, out of some inner receptacle; others rush out in troops, and while one thing is desired and required, they start forth, as who should say, "Is it perchance I?"

These things do I within, in that vast court of my memory. For there are present with me, heaven, earth, sea, and whatever I could think on therein, besides what I have forgotten.

There also meet I with myself, and recall myself, and when, where, and what I have done, and under what feelings. There be all which I remember, either on my own experience or other's credit.

Out of the same store do I myself with the past continually combine fresh and fresh likenesses of things which I have experienced, or, from what I have experienced, have believed: and thence again infer future actions, events, and hopes.

What then do I love, when I love my God? By my very soul I will ascend to him.

Another power there is . . . whereby I imbue with sense of my flesh, which the Lord has framed for me: Commanding the eye . . . that through it I should see, and the ear that through it I should hear; and to the other senses severally, what is to each their own peculiar seats and offices.

I will pass then beyond this power of my nature also, rising by degrees unto Him who made me. And I came to the fields and spacious palaces of my memory, where are the treasures of innumerable images, brought into form from things of all sorts perceived by the senses.

∞

concerns and aspirations and ignorances. You see, the groups had this great thing in common. The sharing of goal and risk. No one knew who would receive the sacrament. We were all in it together.

So, much to my amazement, the project came down to the final week with high enthusiasm and competent preparations. The little band of worshipers drew close together, and the administrators in the Roman centers of pharisaic power remained nervously silent. By God, and by miracle, it was apparently going to happen.

And then on Wednesday of Holy Week the Sanhedrin-ax fell. Walter Pahnke's motorcycle roared into my driveway that evening, and Walter stood in the kitchen in his leather jacket, stripping off his gloves, his face worried, telling me the bad news. We couldn't get the sacrament. We had agreed some time back to allay bureaucratic fears by turning over our supply of psychedelic drugs to Dr. Dana Farnsworth, director of the Harvard Medical Service. Farnsworth was now refusing to release them for the Good Friday study.

Dana Farnsworth was a genial extroverted political doctor whose administrative career was uncomplicated by wit, wisdom, ethical principle, or scientific curiosity.

Step one was to find out who was behind Farnsworth. I phoned the chairman of the academic committee who was overseeing our research project. He was at home, and his voice and the background noise spelled cocktail party.

Fred, I've just found out that Farnsworth won't give us the drugs for the Good Friday study.

The professor's voice lost the booze lilt and became guarded. Yes, so I hear.

Well, Fred, he can't do that. The agreement was that your committee would approve the studies and that Farnsworth would release the drugs when we needed them. They belong to us, not him, after all. . . .

Fred took off on a bureaucratic open-field run. The committee had no jurisdiction in this case. It was a Divinity School project. It was a Boston University project. The exact administrative machinery for handling such confused jurisdiction had not been established. No, there couldn't possibly be a meeting until next week. Until after Good Friday.

Well, let's be specific, Fred. Farnsworth wouldn't refuse to release the drugs without checking with the watchdog committee. And he would release them if you approved it. Right?

Right.

And will you tell them to release the drugs for the Good Friday experiment on the religious experience?

No. We won't interfere one way or the other, Tim. It's not our problem. We can't say yes. We don't want to get blamed if the experiment blows up in a scandal. Drugs on Good Friday, really, old man! And we don't want to say no, either. We can't stop research.

So you are washing your hands of the affair.

Exactly. We are washing our hands of the matter. And if we never hear of it again it will be great with me.

Beautiful, Fred. Those classic lines have never been better delivered. But don't be under any illusions. You are going to hear more about the affair.

I hung up the phone and looked at Walter Pahnke. He had been listening anxiously.

For the first time his clean-cut Midwestern face was gloomy. This whole thing is so right. I've done everything according to Hoyle—medically, scientifically, academically, spiritually. We just can't let them stop it.

Well, if it's right, Walter, they can't stop it. You can do it if you really want to.

This froze Walter in his tracks. Do it anyway? Defy the director of the Health Department? Defy the Harvard officials?

Walter didn't have a rebellious bone in his body. He was an establishment man, a good boy, right down the line. The problem was, he was one of those hardheaded, grass-roots, orthodox idealists who really believed in what was right. And stubborn about his virtue. Your classic, old-fashioned Protestant type.

How can I do it if I want to?

Well, Walter, we have the chapel and the ap-

From *The Religions of Man* by Huston Smith:

The prophets of Israel and Judah are one of the most amazing groups of individuals in all history.

In the midst of the moral desert in which they found themselves, they spoke the words the world has been unable to forget.

Some hear God roaring like a lion, others hear him in the ghostly stillness that precedes the storm.

Yet one thing is common to them all; the conviction that every man simply by virtue of the fact that he is a human being, a child of God, has rights that even kings cannot erase.

From *Doors of Perception* by Aldous Huxley:

My own belief is that . . . these new mind-changers (the psychedelic drugs) will tend in the long run to deepen the spiritual life. . . .

And this revival of religion will be at the same time a revolution. . . .

Religion will be transformed into an activity concerned mainly with experience and intuition—

An everyday mysticism underlying and giving significance to everyday rationality, everyday tasks and duties, everyday human relationships.

∞

Wilson van Dusen:

There is a central human experience which alters all other experiences. It has been called Satori in Japanese Zen, Moksha in Hinduism, religious enlightenment or cosmic consciousness in the west. . . .

(It) is not just an experience among others, but rather the very heart of human experience. It is the center that gives understanding to the whole. . . .

Once found, life is altered because the very root of human identity has been deepened. . . .

The drug LSD appears to facilitate the discovery of this apparently ancient and universal experience.

∞

proval of Dean Thurmond. And we have the students and the approval of the Seminary. And if your thesis adviser will back you, and he's got to because it's a sound scientific plan, then the only problem is to get the drugs. And I'll get you the drugs.

How? I thought you had given all the sacrament to Farnsworth.

I did give him all I had, but there's a psychiatrist in Worcester to whom I gave a supply last month and I know he hasn't used them and he'll give them back. All perfectly legal. From one M.D. to another.

Thus we do not simply abandon the field to the opponent; we make it difficult for him to advance by showing perseverance in single acts of resistance. In this way we prepare, while retreating, for the countermovement. (I Ching IV)

Walter paced the floor. Then he clapped his hands together and stuck out his chin and spoke with dogged determination.

It's right and it should be done. But it's got to be done openly. I'll call my thesis adviser and Boston University and the president of the Seminary, and if they don't object then we will . . . his voice dropped off and he gulped . . . do it in spite of Dr. Farnsworth.

The next day the telephone kept ringing every few minutes. Walter's voice kept growing with confidence. Everyone agreed.

On Holy Thursday evening, only eighteen hours before the Sacred Three-Hour Vigil, we got the pills and had them ground down to powder and sorted into plain envelopes with code numbers to set up the double blind experiment.

Then at midnight on the eve of Good Friday I called the chairman of my department at Harvard. Look, David, I just want to tell you, in front, that we have the sacrament and we are going ahead with the religious experiment.

David groaned. Oh God, why did you have to tell me in advance?

Because we don't play secret games, David. Why do you groan?

Walter H. Clark
Research Project Report:

I regard the experience as a personal shaking to the foundations.

The radical facing of myself forced—or perhaps I should say released by the drug—was a trauma the depth of which was totally unexpected.

I would describe the experience as a conversion experience of the most radical nature rather than a mystical experience of the classical variety as Stace has defined it.

Yet, though without many of the indications of mystical experience, I know I will understand the mystics much better, having had the experience.

Even some of the moving expressions of the Bible and religion pale in my attempt to describe the experience.

Because now I may have to make an administration decision.

I laughed. It was too classic! Poor Pilate! David, that's the way it always is. Good Friday always poses problems for administrators.

We assembled at the Seminary at ten the next morning. The guides would drive the students to the ceremony. Five rooms in the basement of the Boston University chapel were reserved for the groups. My group of six sat around waiting. The students had Bibles. Pahnke walked in with the envelopes—each coded. In each envelope was a capsule containing white powder.

I asked one of the students to say a prayer and we remained in silence for a while and then we took the pill.

Then we all sat waiting to discover what we had taken. The students were reading their Bibles, but I guessed they weren't concentrating on the words.

After a while I felt something changing inside. Ah. Good! I got the psilocybin. I waited. My skin became pink and flushed with heat. Hello. That's odd. Never felt like this from psilocybin. Soon my body was radiating heat but my consciousness was unchanged. Then I realized what had happened. Pahnke had given us a placebo with a somatic kick to fool us. I found out later it was nicotinic acid.

I looked up and saw that two students had flushed faces. They were squirming with pleased expressions. One of them winked at the other. He rose and said he was going to the toilet. The other red-faced student joined him. As guide, I trailed along. Inside the john they were exulting like happy conspirators. We must have got the mushroom. Yeah, I can feel it. We're the lucky ones. I smiled and kidded them about playing the placebo game. While we stood there the door banged open. A third student from our group walked in. He looked neither left nor right. No greetings. His eyes were glowing and he was smiling. He walked to the window and stood for a long time looking out. Jesus, he cried, God is everywhere. Oh the Glory of it! Then he walked out without a word. No social games with him.

The two red-faced students looked solemn. Hopes dashed.

It's a ridiculous ritual to run a double blind study using psychedelic drugs. After thirty minutes everyone knows what has happened, who has taken the sacrament.

Just before noon Pahnke came through and had us all go to the small chapel. Thirty of us sat in the dim candlelight. Dean Howard Thurmond came in, robed and vested. He spoke a few words. Quietly, serenely. He blessed us and left.

Then through the speakers we could hear him begin his three-hour service in the main chapel above. Prayers. Organ music. Hymns.

It was easy to tell who had taken the psychedelics. Ten students sat attentively like good worshipers. Facing the altar. Silent. The others were less conventional. Some lay on the benches—one lay on the floor. Some wandered around the chapel murmuring in prayer and wonderment. One chanted a hymn. One wandered to the altar and held his hands aloft. One sat at the organ bench and played weird, exciting chords.

One wanted to go out. The doors to the basement were locked and a doorkeeper was on guard. I told Pahnke I'd accompany his restless mystic. We walked along the avenue. Cars whizzed by. I felt fear and moved to the street side of my charge. I had a fantasy he might run out in the avenue. He, of course, read my mind. You are so brutally aware of where things are at during a session. Telepathy?

He glanced at me, as if to say, Is that the game? So he tried to edge by me to walk on the curb. I got more scared. He made a feint to run into the street. My paranoia had forced him into the role of prisoner, seeking to escape.

Then I caught on and laughed. Let's not play that silly game, I said. He nodded. We walked around the chapel. He was out of his mind. Confused. Struggling for meaning. What is it all about? Who is running the show? What am I supposed to do?

We walked back to the basement. My student was still frightened. I kept too close to him. My concern alarmed him. He ran to the piano and banged down the lid savagely. He ran to the wall and grabbed a picture, holding it above his head ready to smash it if he were approached.

Some would include: descent into hell and resurrection, death and transfiguration, the moment of truth, naked on the shores of eternity, etc.

I seemed to live a lifetime of pain and tragedy as I saw myself stripped bare, and at the time seemingly little to fall back on to satisfy my swollen ego.

Today, I am beginning to think that maybe there was something left after all, but I never want to forget a vision of my vainglorious ego that came to me in the midst of the experience.

Another curious upswelling from my unconscious, I suppose, was the sense of the depth of my love for my wife and my need of her.

In part this was triggered by the spectacle of the couples around me. In a psychological sense it was almost as if I were married for the first time in my life during the session.

I sat down quickly and put my hands in the position of prayer and called him. He stared at me for a long minute. Then he relaxed. About the least threatening thing you can do to another human being is to sit down in the prayer position in front of him. It always works.

He came over and sat down in front of me. I motioned for him to place his hands in prayer. He looked at me in panic and raised his fists. I looked in his eyes—flaming in terror. Is that what hands are for? To destroy . . . to grab . . . to hit . . . oh, you good Christian, have you forgotten your religion? Don't you remember that hands are for worship? For prayer? I grabbed his hands. He started to pull away but held on. He really liked the physical contact and the gentle control. Your hands are for prayer. Let us pray, brother. I held his hands tight and started chanting . . . God . . . Jesus Christ . . . man . . . God . . . Jesus Christ . . . man. . . . His body visibly relaxed. Then he smiled. Then he looked at my face in reverent love. He embraced me. I held him in my arms. About ten people were watching in awed curiosity. I could feel the warmth of his body and the trembling. He began to stroke my hair. His caress became sexual. I took his hands and placed mine around his in the position of prayer. Then I began chanting the Lord's Prayer. Our Father . . . yes, all our Fathers . . . who are in Heaven . . . yes, who art inside Heaven. Inside. I thumped my chest and his. Our Father who art within . . . Hallowed be thy name . . . yes, holy be all thy names . . . Sacred Fathers and Grandfathers . . . Holy ancestors. . . . Thanks, Holy Father, for living and dying to create us, and give us through seed and sperm our birth to life. . . . Thy Kingdom come. Thy will be done . . . out here on earth, in this room, here in Boston as it is in Heaven within.

Something of this I was impelled to share with my wife by telephone after the session.

He was whispering the words over and over again. Our Father. Holy be thy name. Thy will be done. Then he burst into tears and sobs. He crumbled to the floor. I held him while his body shook with the convulsive heaving.

Another very basic discovery was a clear sense of values: I knew what was important in my life and what was less important more clearly than ever before.

Then he sat up and looked at me and said, Thanks. I'm all right now. I've been a religious

I saw clearly how certain fatuous and confused ideas were leading me in wrong pathways; some of my sentimentalities were pierced.

Though ideas of God and Christ were not prominent in my experience, I have no doubt of the essentially religious nature of the experience.

I believe that a psychoanalysis, which only now I realize I needed, could not have done as well for me in helping me to face my own psychological nakedness as the six hours under LSD.

I think that religion will neglect the consequences of this powerful instrument, with its implications, at its peril. The experience recalls Otto's *Mysterium Tremendum.* It was awesome.

∞

phony and a sexual freak but now I know what prayer is all about.

The afternoon slowly spun itself out. No other scenes of disorder. Much silent meditation. Later hushed talking.

By five o'clock the group was pretty well out of visionary terrain. Pahnke was busy collecting interviews on a tape recorder. He was most conscientious about his data.

The plan was that we would all go to my home for a communion supper. The psychedelic students were in no hurry. They wandered around smiling serenely and looking at flowers. The non-psychedelic students were bored and impatient.

The scene at my house was gentle and radiant. The trippers were still too much in it, still a little high and too stunned to do much except shake their heads in wonder and grin and say, Wow! I never realized. . . .

I was in the kitchen having a celebration beer. Walter Pahnke bustled in. Our eyes met and we grinned and shook hands, laughing.

It was like the first session at the prison. We had done it! We had proved once again that goodwill, and good motives, and trust and courage are the basic research tools. It was a great spiritual test for all of us and we would never forget that Good Friday afternoon of death, fear, ecstasy and rebirth.

In the next few weeks the results of the Good Friday session kept feeding back.

Pahnke had teams of interviewers (who knew nothing about the study) collecting the stories of the twenty students, rating the comments and kinds of religious experience.

The results were clear-cut and consistent. The men who ate the mushrooms had mystic religious experiences. The control group didn't.

There was proof—scientific, experimental, statistical, objective. The sacred mushrooms, administered in a religious setting to people who were religiously motivated, did produce that rare, deep experience which men have sought for thousands of years through sacraments, through flagellation, prayer, renunciation.

Psychedelic drugs were sacraments.

To anyone whose values are spiritual, this study had to be the most important research of the last few thousand years. Galileo, Newton, Einstein, Oppenheimer developed theories and methods for understanding and controlling external energies. What produces motion? How can motive power be improved, accelerated? Discoveries of dubious benefit in their application.

But the scientific demonstration that internal energies, ecstasy, revelation, spiritual union, no longer need be accidental but can be produced for and by him who seeks—this can't be underestimated.

You would expect that every priest, minister, rabbi, theologian, philosopher, scholar, or just plain God-seeking man, woman, and child, in the country would drop their secular games and follow up the implications of the Good Friday study.

But you know what happened? The same reaction that has greeted every new spiritual discovery in history. Disapproval. Apathy. Opposition. Why?

The trustees of the Divinity School moved to silence Dr. Walter Clark. But they couldn't. This gentle, thoughtful man consulted his conscience and refused to keep silent. But follow-up studies at the Seminary were stopped, and the divine enthusiasm of the divinity students was blocked and dissipated.

Walter Pahnke got his thesis uneasily approved, and his degree was awarded. Walter went to Germany on a fellowship and arranged to have his first conversation with God in a mental hospital in the Rhineland. He had a clinical examination room converted into a shrine and got a Yale theologian to be his guide, and played sacred music on his record player, and to the shocked amazement of the German psychiatrists (who are using LSD to produce dirty psychoanalytic experiences), Walter made the eternal voyage and laughed in gratitude and wept in reverence. And only then, a year later, did he realize the wondrous miracle he had wrought in Marsh Chapel.

But he wasn't allowed to continue his work. His

From *The Epic of Gilgamesh:*

So Utnapishtim spoke, Gilgamesh, you came here, a man wearied out, you have worn yourself out; what shall I give you to carry you back to your own country?

Gilgamesh, I shall reveal a secret thing, it is a mystery of the gods that I am telling you. There is a plant that grows under the water, it has a prickle like a thorn, like a rose; it will wound your hands, but if you succeed in taking it, then your hands will hold that which restores his lost youth to a man.

When Gilgamesh heard this he opened the sluices so that a sweet-water current might carry him out to the deepest channel; he tied heavy stones to his feet and they dragged him down to the water-bed.

There he saw the plant growing; although it pricked him he took it in his hands; then he cut the heavy stones to his feet and the sea carried him and threw him on to the shore.

Gilgamesh said to Urshanabi the ferryman, Come here, and see this marvelous plant. By its virtue a man may win back all his former strength.

I will take it to Uruk of the strong walls; there I will give it to the old men to eat. Its names shall be The old men are young again; and at last I shall eat it myself and have back all my lost youth.

Gilgamesh saw a well of cool water and he went down and bathed; but deep in the pool there was lying a serpent, and the serpent sensed the sweetness of the flower. It rose out of the water and snatched it away, and immediately it sloughed its skin and returned to the well.

subsequent requests for government approval to repeat his study have been denied. The last thing the federal Food and Drug Administration seems to want is the production of religious experiences.

Dr. Goddard, the aggressive, hard-driving political medic who runs the F.D.A., derided claims that LSD produces psychological or spiritual benefits. Pure bunk, said Goddard. This from a government official who had never taken or given a psychedelic chemical, nor observed its effects. How can our country's top pharmacological commissar blatantly reject scientific data which doesn't fit his atheistic bias?

The results of and the reactions to Pahnke's experiment raised many perplexing questions and led to new appraisals. It became clear to me that religion played a greater part in American life than I had realized. Indeed it seemed obvious that every expression of American society—however secular, materialistic, scientific, or agnostic it may appear—is based on deeply held unconscious religious assumptions. America is an immature, irrational, superstitious, materialistic, priest-ridden, intolerant, religious state.

General Motors is a religious institution with its priests, rituals, gods, saints, devils. General Motors worships mechanical power and money. General Motors is white Protestant. Jews, Catholics, Negroes, and Hindus need not apply to become high priests.

Harvard University is a completely religious institution. It worships intellectual power and dogmatically clings to academic taboos and empty rituals. Harvard is white Judeo-Calvinist. Catholics, Negroes, and Hindus, need not apply to become high priests.

Science itself is a religion. Fanatically defending its superstitious rites and areas of priestly prerogative. White Judeo-Protestant. Negroes, Catholics, and Hindus just don't seem to become high priests in science.

The American government—state and federal—is a monolithic religious structure. Catholic-Protestant.

This insight helps explain the instinctive revulsion of the American intellectual-marketplace-scientific establishment to the psychedelic sacraments.

There are few Americans over the age of twenty-five who are not totally committed to a dogmatic religious way of life and belief. To admit evidence (however scientific) which threatens the theological structure is intolerable. Morally unbearable. Philosophically impossible, because when the superstitious religious structure is threatened, life becomes meaningless. General Motors defends its God. Harvard defends its God. Scientists defend their God.

So the hostile reaction to Pahnke's experiment and to our prison research and to our psychedelic studies were easily understood. We were nothing less than heretics. Tread warily, O prophet, when you move onto primitive religious ground.

In this case retreat is the right course, and it is through retreat that success is achieved. But success consists in being able to carry out the retreat correctly. Retreat is not to be confused with flight. Flight means saving oneself under any circumstances, whereas retreat is a sign of strength. We must be careful not to miss the right moment while we are in full possession of power and position. Then we shall be able to interpret the signs of the time before it is too late and to prepare for provisional retreat instead of being drawn into a desperate life-and-death struggle. (I Ching IV)

The miracle of Marsh Chapel was not just a scientific study; it was authentic spiritual ceremony. And like every valid Good Friday experiment our spring solstice death-rebirth-celebration (because it worked) invited excommunication and persecution. We were involved, not in a controversial research project, but in a classic religious struggle.

The arena for this struggle is always within. The stakes of the game were no longer academic prestige or scientific renown but the souls of the protagonists.

The psychedelic drugs are sacraments, and like all sacraments that work, they demand your all.

Then Gilgamesh sat down and wept, the tears ran down his face, and he took the hand of Urshanabi; O Urshanabi, was it for this that I toiled with my hands, is it for this I have wrung out my heart's blood? For myself I have gained nothing; not I, but the beast of the earth has joy of it now.

Already the stream has carried it twenty leagues back to the channels where I found it. I found a sign and now I have lost it. Let us leave the boat on the bank and go.

This too was the work of Gilgamesh, the king, who knew the countries of the world. He was wise, he saw mysteries and knew secret things, he brought us a tale of the days before the flood.

He went a long journey, was weary, worn out with labour, and returning engraved on a stone the whole story.

∞

They demand that you live up to the revelation.

Like all sacraments, the psychedelic drugs threaten society and that part of your own mind that is attached to the current social taboos.

Like all new sacraments, the psychedelics require a new religion.

YOUTHFUL FOLLY *has success.*
It is not I who seek the young fool;
The young fool seeks me.
At the first oracle I inform him.
If he asks two or three times, it is
    importunity.
If he importunes, I give him no
    information.
Perseverance furthers.

(I Ching)

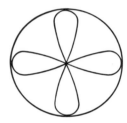

After Your Illumination,
Why Come Down?

June 1962

Guide: KRISHNA

Oracle: II

The Receptive

The Receptive, Earth

The Receptive, Earth

The earth's condition is receptive devotion.
Thus the superior man who has breadth of
character
Carries the outer world.

(I Ching)

Timothy Leary
Start your own Religion

Drop-out—detach yourself from the external social drama which is as dehydrated and ersatz as TV.

Turn-on—Find a sacrament which returns you to the temple of God, your own body. Go out of your mind. Get high.

Tune-in—Be reborn. Drop-back-in to express it. Start a new sequence of behavior that reflects your vision.

Actions which are conscious expressions of the turn-on, tune-in, drop-out rhythm are religious.

The wise person devotes his life exclusively to the religious search—for therein is found the only ecstasy, the only meaning.

∞

By the spring of 1962 we had been pushed by social pressure towards the classic solutions of the new religious cult. Exile and monastic retreat. There were twenty to thirty of us who were dedicating most of our energies to the sacrament—but it was all upstream against the instinctive resistance of the culture. Cambridge, Massachusetts, U.S.A., was no place to start a new religion.

Picture yourself afloat on a river

It was actually as unfair to do research on the visionary experience at Harvard as it would be to expect the Vatican to sponsor missionary work for the Lutheran Church, or to ask Cardinal Cushing to support experiments on effective aphrodisiacs.

Somebody calls you, you answer quite lowly

We knew we had to leave Harvard. But where to go? Like spiritual pilgrims of the past we needed a deserted spot where life would be inexpensive and free from religious persecution. We consulted the atlas. Where on this shrinking planet would a small group of God-seekers find land and liberty?

Picture yourself in a brain in a station

Then I remembered the flight from Mexico in 1960 with Dick Alpert. The quiet fishing village on the Pacific. What was its name? My finger moved up the map north from Acapulco. There. Zihuatenejo.

With artichoke trees and muskmelon skies

So, in April 1962, Peggy Hitchcock and Richard Alpert and I flew to Mexico City and then took a twin-engined plane to Zihuatenejo. The landing strip is a tricky one. The plane loops down from the high greengulch mountain passes of Guerrero State and zooms over the little village of brown wooden huts and then out over the broad, blue bay ringed with green hills, and circles back snaking its way through the valley to make a sudden base-leg turn just over the concrete strip.

Magazine taxis appear on the shore

There were no large homes or villas in the town. Just one hotel at the end of a dirt road which highcircled the bay, south of the village. The manager of the hotel was a dignified, slender, soft-spoken Swiss gentleman. There was no business during the summer. It was very possible that the owner would close the hotel to the public during July and August and rent it to us as a summer retreat.

Suddenly no one is there at the turnstile

Letters and funds passed through the mails, and in June I left for Mexico to set up the hotel for the summer. Richard was to take charge of my house and make it a center for receiving and transmitting the pilgrims.

Where puppet-show people eat cantaloupe pies

In Mexico City I contacted Parsons and Pat Bolero. Parsons was a sociologist who had lived in Mexico for several years. They had been turned-on by one of our Harvard missionaries and were both ecstatically converted to the wonders of psilocybin. I invited them to join us in Zihuatenejo. They, in turn, invited me to come to their country home in Tepoztlan to run a session for them.

Everyone smiles as you drift past the hours

There were a few free days before we took over the lease on the hotel in Zihuatenejo, so I agreed to guru their trip.

Climb on the top with your head in the crowds

We arrived at Tepoztlan after sunset. I remembered the visit to the McClellands' two summers before, and how much had happened and how much I had changed since the last time I left that dark, unyielding valley.

The atmosphere of Tepoztlan hit as soon as we drove into the plaza. You were far removed from the twentieth century. The few stores lighted by candle and kerosene. The hulking shadow ruins of the old church. The high cliff walls. Enormous, rugged rock-carved stage set, waiting. The place was alive, dark stone eyes watching, vined tendril

How to turn-on.

To turn-on is to detach from the rigid addictive focus on the fake-prop TV studio-set and to refocus on the natural energies within the body.

1. Come to your senses—focus on sensory energies.

2. Resurrect your body—focus on somatic energies.

3. Drift down cellular memory tracks beyond the body's space/time—focus on cellular energies.

4. Decode the genetic code.

Turning-on is a complex, demanding, frightening, confusing process. It requires diligent yoga.

Turning-on requires a guide who can center you at the TV-stage-prop level and at the sensory, somatic, cellular and molecular levels.

When you turn-on remember: You are not a naughty boy getting high for kicks.

You are a spiritual voyager furthering the most ancient, noble quest of man. When you turn-on you shed the fake-prop TV studio and costume and join the holy dance of the visionaries. You leave LBJ and Bob Hope; you join Lao Tse, Christ, Blake. Never underestimate the sacred meaning of the turn-on.

To turn-on you need a sacrament. A sacrament is a visible external thing which turns the key to the inner doors. A sacrament must bring about bodily changes. A sacrament flips you out of the TV-studio game and harnesses you to the two-billion-year-old flow inside.

A sacrament which works is dangerous to the establishment which runs the fake-prop TV studio—and to that part of your mind which is hooked to the studio game.

Each TV-prop society produces exactly that body-changing sacrament which will flip-out the mind of the society.

Today the sacrament is LSD. New sacraments are coming along.

ears listening. Waiting for the next itinerant human road-show troupe. And no compromise. No pretense. No gesture of recognition for the intruding European game. Implacable, neutral, obsidian disinterest.

Styrafoam flowers of purple and green
Powering over your head

We drove along rutted roads past darkened huts, the car jolting, the headlights tracing an eerie course through tunnels of vegetation. We were driving right out of civilization down some leafy time tube into the Aztec past.

We ran through the rain into the rambling one-story villa. There was no electricity. Candles flickered on the adobe walls along the carved wooden beams. Rectangles of color gleamed from paintings.

Waiting to take you to play

We started a fire and sat by the hearth. I brought out a glass jar of LSD sugar paste which Michael Hollingshead had given me as a farewell present. The atmosphere of the villa seeped through the windows. The sacred vale of tribal legend. Home of the Gods. Zapata, the pure Robin-Hood revolutionary, had swept down from the mountain and sacked the houses of the rich and quartered his horses in the church. Centuries of blood and sacrifice and passion and terror and struggle. The place trembled with old vibrations. You felt close to powerful energies. Untouched by the metal hum of machinery. You felt flesh, seed, and nameless forces.

And you're gone

Pat Bolero shuddered and whispered something to Parsons. He looked at me. Pat is frightened and wants you to take the sacrament with us.

Climb on the top with your head in the crowds

I said I would. It often happens this way. The unplanned challenge. The time to die chosen, not by your mind, but by the flow of events.

Applied to human affairs, therefore, what the hexagram indicates is action in conformity with the situation. The person in question is not in an independent position, but is acting as an assistant. This means that he must achieve something. It is not his task to try to lead—that would only make him lose the way—but to let himself be led. If he knows how to meet fate with an attitude of acceptance, he is sure to find the right guidance. The superior man lets himself be guided; he does not go ahead blindly, but learns from the situation what is demanded of him and then follows this intimation from fate. (I Ching II)

And so, once again, the guru was to become disciple, the leader was to be led. I was overdue for a powerful trip. All that spring I had been guiding pilgrims, going up with them but never all the way for me, always lagging back a little to be there for the customers. Being influenced by their visions. Sharing their confusions but always keeping my mind focused and responsible.

I was shaken up by the struggles of our spring-time religious revival. I was disturbed by the heavy Christian structure, perplexed by the holding back. The inhibiting, social strength of the Christian Church and its power to bind. Religion. Their fear of God and their fear of God's voice and their fear and guilt of breaking loose and their fear of suspending, even for a few minutes, the middle-class television set.

With cellophane porters with looking glass spies

I needed a complete, whack-out, liberating session to untangle from the Protestant social web, so sterile and anti-sense and anti-Christ, so false to the memory of that half-naked barefoot sensual Jew visionary prophet who sat on the floor to wash dirty feet and then stood up to the Roman Empire.

That spring had been exciting and dramatic and deeply moving—to participate in the sacred moments of so many ministers. But there was a nagging residual of disappointment in those good, honest, liberal, generous Protestants.

They had lost the fire somehow. They had lost the pulse. Their thing was dying and they knew it. The Protestants just weren't religious. Their great thing was their social instinct, their sense of equality. But in their protest against the superstition and authoritarian priesthood they had lost the magic. When they threw out the statues and the incense and the robes and the chanting (all the sensory

Sacraments wear out. They become part of the social TV-studio game. Treasure LSD while it still works. In fifteen years it will be tame, socialized, and routine.

You cannot stay turned-on all the time. You cannot stay any place all the time. That's a law of evolution.

After the revelation it is necessary to drop-back-in, return to the fake-prop TV studio and initiate small changes which reflect the glory and meaning of the turn-on. You change the way you move, the way you dress; you change your corner of the TV-studio society!

You begin to look like a happy saint! Your home slowly becomes a shrine. Slowly, gently you start seed transformations around you. Psychedelic art. Psychedelic style. Psychedelic music. Psychedelic dance.

The directors of the TV studio do not want you to live a religious life. They will apply every pressure (including prison) to keep you in their game.

Your own mind, which has been corrupted and neurologically damaged by years of education in fake-prop TV-studio games, will also keep you trapped in the game.

A group liberation cult is required.

You must form that most ancient and sacred of human structures—the clan. A clan or cult is a small group of human beings organized around a religious goal. (If you don't belong to a clan, you are a computer.)

The flow of energy

here

    it

    is

nameless

timeless

speed of light

float
    beyond fear

float
    beyond desire

into
this mystery of mysteries through this gate

of all wonder

The sex cakra

Rainbow

Can you float through the universe of your body and not lose your way?

sacraments), it became social and rational and senseless.

There was the strong need for some sort of channel for the religious energies we were releasing. And it was obvious that the Christian structure was too rigid and fixed. The Christian model just couldn't take the charge. To turn-on an American Christian to the two-billion-year divine process was like harnessing a million-watt electric generator to a crystal set. The flimsy, modern, mythless, rootless American Christian Church just blew its fuse and disconnected the impulse. And the fuse was the familiar rationalization business. A week after the session they'd still be glowing and God-like, but after a month they were sinking back into their routines. Forgetting their antiquity and divine missions. Questioning their visions. They heard the word of God and promptly forgot it.

Look for the girl with the moon in her sighs

The new revelation demands a new body. And the embryonic processes were astir that summer, beginning to uncoil before the fire in the villa in the valley of Tepoztlan.

And she's gone

The darkgreen valley of Tepoztlan seemed centuries removed from the Union Theological Seminary.

Follow her down to the bridge by a castle

We meditated for a while and then I picked up the bottle and dug out a heaping tablespoonful for Pat and one for Parsons and one for myself. Pat was very nervous, so I took a strand of sacred beads from my neck and put them on her. This will guide you if you get lost or frightened. You never knew how much you were getting with Michael's material and it was soon obvious that we had taken a generous loving spoonful.

There was only the sound of the fire crackling sharper and sharper. An electric hush enveloped the room. It was a perfect Zen moment. I was dead. The Timothy Leary game was suspended and the needle point of consciousness was free to move into any one of thirteen billion nerve cells or down any one of a billion billion genetic-code networks.

That grow so inedibly high

First the dial swung to the sensory. The noise of the fire was the sound of every energy transformation. The crackling of galactic suns.

Then the dial swung to olfactory sensations. The room was filled with spaghetti tangles of smell tapes and, dog-like, I sorted through them. I could see each distinctive fume of scent. The hodgepodge of chemical belts spilling out of the kitchen. Dozens of molecule threads—organic decomposing, perfumed from the bathroom, pouring into the living room like mountain streams rushing to the lake. I could see each rivulet of odor rising from Pat's warm steaming female body. And from Parsons' malehood. Each object in the room emitted its cloud of vapors—fabrics, molds, dyes, leather, wood.

Then consciousness buried itself in tissued memories. A rapid newsreel sequence of my life. Early childhood picture albums. Model A Fords. Cotton candy at the beach.

It was very dark and the wind howled terribly around her, but Dorothy found she was riding quite easily. After the first few whirls around, and one other time when the house tipped badly, she felt as if she were being rocked gently, like a baby in a cradle. (The Wizard of Oz)

The loneliness of long nights in the attic bedroom watching the headlights of cars approaching the house, turning at the corner and disappearing, red taillights winking. Electronic tissue hum of the neural film projector.

Then I heard Pat moving, and her powerful image-energy machine flooded mine and I spun into her head. Gasping marshmallow flesh-fluff erotic jumping rapture.

Rumble seat sex. The dirty, skirty thirties. Who . . . means your happiness . . . who . . . will you answer yes . . . who . . . well you ought to guess . . . who . . . no one but you. . . . Pat's breath, whisky scented, fragile perfume of life . . . breath, air, sighing, air equals orgasm, air is life.

Sudden revelation into workings of oxygen mo-

Can you lie quietly

engulfed

in the slippery union

of male and female?

Warm wet dance of generation?

Endless   ecstasies   of couples?

Can you offer your stamen trembling in the meadow for the electric penetration of pollen while birds sing?

Wait soft feathered,

quivering, in the thicket

while birds sing?

Can you coil serpentine

while birds sing?

Become two cells merging?

Slide together in molecule embrace?

Can you, murmuring,

lose

all

fusing

rainbow

Ethereal pool without source

Empty bowl of radiance

full of universe and star

silent

void

shimmering

ancestor of all things

Here

All sharpness

rounded

All wheels

glide along

soft tracks

of light

Ethereal pool without source

Preface to life

Remember, you are basically a primate. You are designed by the two-billion-year blueprint to live in a small band.

You cannot accept the political or spiritual leadership of anyone you cannot touch, con-spire (breathe) with, worship with, get high with.

Your clan must be centered around a shrine and a totem spiritual energy source. To the clan you dedicate your highest loyalty, and to you the clan offers its complete protection.

But the clan must be orientated toward religious goals. Religion means being tuned-in to the natural rhythm. Religion is the turn-on, tune-in, drop-out process.

nopoly. In the year 1888, British scientists, members of the Huxley family, discover that oxygen supply of earth is failing. Life, ecstasy, consciousness is oxygen. British aristocrats secretly bottle remaining vapors of air and hide it. Air is replaced by synthetic gas which possesses no life or consciousness, keeps people alive as plastic doll robots. Plump, mocking, effeminate, patronizing Englishmen have control of precious oxygen elixir of life which they dole out in doses for their god-like amusement and pleasure. LSD is air.

The rest of the human race is doomed to three-D-headmill-plastic repetition. Trapped. Oh wise brown Ann who saw it all. I'd kill myself to end the meaningless rat race but I'm afraid that wouldn't stop it. It would just spin out new and deader IBM sequences. My flesh, Pat and Parsons, the world was turning to dry brittle hardness.

Science-fiction horror. Hell! I wanted to shriek and run from the room for help. How to get back to life. Center. Pray. Love. Touch. Contact. Human contact. Parsons, sloppy Jewish belly showing. Pat, swollen Jewish mother. I held on to her fat arm, burrowed into their body hive. We huddle in a heap on the floor in front of the fire, softly breathing together.

Spinning through sexual cellular scrapbooks. The eternal dance of male and female. The restless panting search. Sniffing search. Where is she? When will she come? The shock of contact. Soft flesh—furred, scaled, moist, merging. Ah there! Frantic flailing, jumping, convulsive moaning union. Breathless. Breathless. Chuckling she-wisdom. What else is important, you foolish desiccated creature, but this fire dance of life creation?

The murmuring giggling gooey: what else is immortal, oh dry brittle, save this moist buried flesh kiss?

Pat suddenly called in terror. I opened my eyes. The fire throwing up jewel flames, colored shadows on Pat's anguished face. Parsons! Parsons! Where are you? He was lying on the Mexican rug, arms thrown out. He roused and smiled tenderly. Here. Everywhere. With you, love. He reached up and pulled her down on him. She whispered and murmured. He stroked her long black hair and hummed ancient cradle songs.

I sank back into delightful tissue recollections—muscle memories. I could feel each muscle in my shoulders and legs swelling, pulsing with power. Feel the hair growing on my limbs and the elongated dog-wolf foot-pad legs loping and graceful, prairie freedom, the unspeakable delight of movement, fiber excitement. Fierce ecstatic mammalian memories. And life, animal light, radiating, churning. Life force uncoiling. Hindu flute call. Life. Light. Incandescence. The high-tide, flame-wave, surging blood-hot current of life.

And then death. Heavy, cold immobility creeping up my body. Oh God. Now be careful how you lie. Your posture now will be frozen into a mountain marble landscape statue. Be careful of every moment of posture because at some moment the sudden click of death comes, and your last gesture is your permanent tombstone statue. Click, the last permanent still picture. The cosmic game of freeze. I was paralyzing into sprawled appalachian disorder, geological pressures on every muscle (you remember all those Greek myths of metamorphosis, don't you?). So this is death. Good-bye to animal mobility, cellular pulsation. Now the elderly elemental mineral consciousness takes over. Had you forgotten? Rocks are aware. Inorganic matter is involved in energy changes, structural excitements, evolvings, pressured sculptings. Inorganic matter—rocks, cliffs, valleys, mountains are alive and wise. Their geological squirming, breathing movements are older, stronger, more all-seeing than the trivial dances of cellular life. The eternal moist erotic friction of water and land. The tidal caress. The tender leaf-veined carving of rivers on the washed breast of earth.

For millennia I lay in geological trance. Forests grew on my flanks, rains came, continental ecstasies. Great slow heaving supporter of life. Vishnu sleeps and then from my bowel-center-navel out grew the long slender green limb climbing up from the white-milk ocean of formlessness and completed the lotus blossom of awakedness.

Breathing

Drift, drift along your body's soft swampland while warm yellow mud sucks lazily

Breathing

Feel each cell in your body intertwine, merging in wet rainbow serpent-coil gasping orgasm

Breathing

Feel the thudding motor of time pulsing life along the red network

Breathe

Gently, until you are as warm and soft as an infant

Breathing

Bring fire blood flowing into the white rooms of your brain

Breathing

Radiate golden light into the four corners of creation

Yellow-brown

Can you float through the universe of your body and not lose your way?

Can you rest

dormant seed-light

buried in moist earth?

Can you drift

single-celled

in soft tissue swamp?

Can you sink

into your dark

fertile marsh?

Can you dissolve softly?
Decompose?

Can you slowly spiral down
the great central drain?

Yellow-brown

All in Heaven

and

on earth below

Is a crystal fabric

delicate sacred

gossamer web

Grabbing hands

shatter it

Watch closely

this shimmering mosaic

Silent

Glide

in

harmony

I opened my eyes. I was in heaven. Illumination. Every object in the room was a radiant structure of atomic-god-particles. Radiating. Matter did not exist. There was just this million-matrix lattice web of energies. Shimmering. Alive. Interconnected in space-time. Everything hooked up in a cosmic dance. Fragile. Indestructible.

And the incredible shattering discovery. Consciousness controlled it all. Or (to say it more accurately), all was consciousness.

I was staggered by the implication. All creation lay in front of me. I could live every life that had ever been lived, think every thought that had ever been thought. An endless variety of ecstatic experience spiraled out around me. I had taken the God-step.

I was dazed by the infinite permutations that offered themselves. Relive the life of Augustus Caesar. Relive the life of an illiterate untouchable in the squalor of an oriental city. Lives of history, lives of tedium.

A sudden thought. Now that this breakthrough of consciousness had occurred, a new level of harmony and love was available. I must bring my family, my friends to this new universe.

How simple and yet we almost missed it. Now that it's been done we can never lose it. How strange that I was the one to do it. And the endless possibilities. Each person had an endless supply of DNA memory file-cards collected during their tour down-there. The there world was a stage to create and collect fresh experience memory cards—now available for everyone up here in heaven.

I called tenderly to Pat and Parsons. Hey. Isn't this incredible? Look. I waved my hand at the vibrating room. We are here, we've made it. Isn't it beautiful?

They looked up puzzled.

We've got to bring our children here. Our friends. George. Richard. Peggy. Aldous and Laura. It's heaven.

They nodded. Parsons jumped up and began talking about God. He suddenly became a crazed, face-twisted Southern fundamentalist minister, preaching about conversion. Listen to me, brother, we've got to preach the word. Tell people about the second coming. It's here. Let them think we are crazy. We don't care. Shout the word out! His voice rose and the cords in his turkey-neck strained and his eyes bulged. I was scared. I could see that he would ruin everything by acting so nutty. He was showing us how false and fanatic the mystic vision can become if you play it out in the old game.

Then he turned on me. Attack. Brother Tim, you don't believe. You are holding back. I'll denounce you as a false prophet, Brother Tim.

I beckoned up to him. Sit down, Parsons. Here and now. Have peace. I put my head in his lap. Contact. I could feel him soften. Pat reached over and pulled both of us on to her body. My face was on her breast. Slosh. Slosh. Clockwork machinery of nature. Her soft voice murmured sea songs. We merged together.

I got scared and sat up. I was losing myself in the warm ooze. To taste the sugar or become the sugar? Parsons wrapped his arm around me. We three are one. There, there Brother Tim. You'll never be alone again. The three of us, we'll always take care of each other. We were a triangular soul-fucking unit. Endless combinations. Pat is the ocean. Om. Om. Slosh. Slosh. All is well. Human empires rise and fall. Pat is the ocean. Parsons and I are huge continental reef-lands. Endless play. The three-in-one theme repeated. We must never lose this Holy Trinity. I want to go outside but Parsons holds me. We three are one.

We sat in a triangle. Ancient geometry of communication. Holy Trinity. Pat was all Goddess. Just that. The essence of all women. Parsons was a brown, smooth-rubbed Hindu. Wise, experienced priest of the ceremony. We were poised serenely, rotating like galactic systems—intricately related. In harmony. A trinity of awareness. One mind in three bodies. Three minds in one body.

I spun down Parsons' time-ladder, became that Midwestern Jewish boy tending his father's store, fled from Russian pogroms, swung, long-bearded Polish *rebbe*, to the Hassidic dance, slid down into old racial flesh tanks, blubbery bushels of sweating, lardy tissue, writhing in some subterranean wet

Open naked eye

Ayeee!

Light

radiant

pulsating

I've been blind

all my life

to this radiance

Retinal mandala

swamp mosaic of

rods and cones

Light rays

hurtle into retina

My cross scope

tell a scope

retinal scripture

vibrate to trembling

web of light

merge with the scene

slide smiling

down retinal whirlpool

slide smiling

through central

needle point

This is it

The seed moves so slowly and serenely

Moment to moment

That it appears inactive

The garden at sunrise breathing

The quiet breath of twilight

Moment to moment to moment

When man is in tune with this blissful rhythm

The ten thousand forms flourish without effort

Really!

it is all so simple

each next moment. . . .

This is it!

Suddenly you discover you have dropped-out.

Drop-out means exactly that: drop-out. Ninety-nine percent of the activity of ninety-nine percent of Americans goes into robot performances on the TV-studio stage. Fake. Unnatural. Automatic.

To drop-out you must form your own religion.

The drop-out, turn-on, tune-in rhythm is most naturally done in small groups of family members, lovers, and seed friends.

body chamber, fetid, bladder-goiter-Yiddish larval center, the life-death bank. Here in this fungal jungle was the intersection-point of life-death, the soul bank. The fleshquarters seed exchange center. The tissue market. Relentless trading on the genetic ticker-tape. The slimy reincarnation pool. Unattached souls slipping in and out of naked, mucus-covered bodies. The ultimate test of human *caritas*. Can you yield, surrender, join? Or will you hold back?

Owens said, the heart beat isn't coming. It isn't . . . wait, wait. There it is . . . the aperture was gaping, the rush of blood was coming, and overtaking them was the gigantic bar-room-m-m of the systole.

The tidal wave of blood caught up with the Proteus hurtling forward at breakneck velocity. (Fantastic Voyage)

Horror! My flesh is decomposing, merging with a million strange bodies, tentacled union, a moss-mattress fibered organic connection with the steamy, odorous, saggy corpulence of an alien race. I was loosening, losing separate identity. Being swallowed up. My heart beating out precious blood which gushed into the racial cell-soil warming it, bathing it, feeding this remorseless Jewish life-cancer. My blood! My life's blood bleeding out for a strange enigmatic smiling, beaked-nose dark race, older and wiser. Help! Could I pull back? Save myself, rending, tearing the vegetative fibers that joined me?

The ultimate test of yielding. Merge. Give. Surrender. Here, drink my blood. Take my body. My fibers snaking into the moist kidney bowel cushion of the greater process.

Here in the bottom of the flesh pit is the point of seed decision. Can you open your billioned-tentacled cell-body and let it merge with another?

It is like this. Within each living creature is a seed center. From this seed center emerge millions of delicate fibers. They are rainbow-colored undulating ribbons, softly waving, tender endings, sensitive, photo-electric sensing instruments. Breathing in and out.

These delicate fibers seek a contact with congenial delicate connections. Exquisitely complex—yet

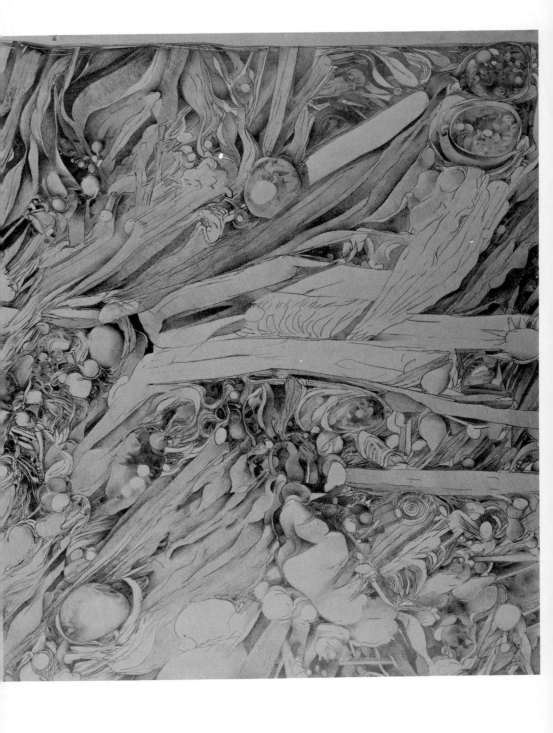

For both psychedelic and legal reasons you must form your own cult.

so simple. This is the essence of energy and its combination. Molecules. Cells. They are not smooth-surfaced, rectangular, or carbon-ringed units which fit together like bricks. Each molecule is a heavenly octopus with a million floating jeweled tentacles hungry to merge. Driven by internal pressure, sexual in nature, towards union. Molecular bonding is the webbed merging of these multi-foliated tender flower machines.

The hunger is to merge. To share and to grow. But the terrible price of union is to lose identity. Be trapped by the union.

Because you and your clan are turned-on, you will radiate energy. You will attract attention—hostility from the TV establishment, enthusiastic interest from rootless TV actors who wish to join your clan. Everyone basically wants to turn-on, tune-in, drop-out.

The soul of each human being is a soft, floating octopus seed center, exfoliating searching tendrils. Blunt, gross contact bruises. Grabbing hands shatter. Crude jolting contact causes these delicate waving soul tentacles to withdraw, encapsulate like some alarmed crustacean.

In his spontaneous, natural state the human being is a radiant sun-star-cell receiving and emitting, feeding and being fed by harmonious neighbors. In the absence of radiant, ex-foliating neighbors each energy center (atomic, molecular, cellular, human) withdraws, spins a hard, leathery resistive seed pod and waits until the warm moist radiance returns.

You must start your own religion. You are God—but only you can discover and nurture your divinity. No one can start your religion for you.

I felt my filaments infiltrating the tangled web of Pat's and Parsons' essence bodies. I subdued the selfish, one-celled-fish reflex to withdraw into separate safety. I surrendered to the ancient process and felt the embracing union.

I opened my eyes. Pat and Parsons were sitting motionless, eyes closed. As my eyes searched their haloed faces their eyes opened and we looked at each other. And nodded.

The session reel continued to whirl through long buried terrains.

Toward dawn Pat and Parsons withdrew to their bed chamber.

Do you wish to use marijuana and LSD to get beyond the TV scenario? To enhance creativity? As catalysts to deepen wisdom? To deepen meaning?

I sat alone and watched the aureal machinery of the room. The air was filled with curving color webs. It seemed the height of vulgarity to plod straight ahead through the room—like a blind robot giant treading down forests and cities. I could reach up with my hands and sculpt the energy patterns. One could only move in smooth looping great arcs to keep in harmony with the vibrations.

(There are at least two explanations of the phenomenon of seeing patterns in the air. The most audacious theory is that the energy is really there and that the psychedelic eye can see what the mind's blind eye cannot see. The more conservative viewpoint would locate the patterns in the capillary or cell-structure networks of the retina; that the vision is simply the eye seeing itself. The eye seeing the non-transparent flaws in its own transparent film. In any case this suggests a natural explanation for the strange movements of some mental patients. Their stereotyped motions. Their peculiar attention to invisibles. The expanded consciousness of the so-called psychotic is not hallucinatory, but tuned in to external or internal processes which are there.)

The sun had risen wh n I walked outside.

The house was surrounded by growing creatures. The house was a stone raft floating in a sea of vegetation.

It was Eden. Each plant was dancing, laughing, a quiet network of high intensity conversation. Trembling. Trembling. Immediate. I followed the garden up slope. Japanese statues. Wise Buddha-eyes silently watched. The garden ended on a paved walk surrounding a swimming pool. Across the back wall a rocky pasture led up to the cliffs. On the top of the perpendicular cliff wall was the house of the god Tepozteco.

Cloud-mists floated along the pasture. I was above the earth. It was the beginning of time. Eden. Above and beyond the life down there. All connections were severed. In fact there was the possibility that the neurological imprints called Mexico City and America no longer even existed—I peered across the wall along the rocky pasture to look for human beings. No one.

There was no visible evidence that the twentieth century existed.

I listened. No sounds of machinery. Bird cries. The rustle of the breeze across the garden. The crowing of cocks. The Timothy Leary game now existed only as a memory. I was liberated. Free to do anything I chose. Stay in the garden. Stay in Tepoztlan. Go back down and wander through the planet as anyone I chose to be. Pick a role. Select a costume.

If so, you will be helped by making explicit the religious nature of your psychedelic activities. To give meaning to your own script, to clarify your relationships with others, and to cope with the present legal setup, you will do well to start your own religion.

First decide with whom you will make the voyage of discovery. If you have a family, certainly you will include them. If you have close friends, you will certainly want to include them. The question—with whom do I league for spiritual discovery—is a fascinating exercise.

Next, sit down with your spiritual companions and put on a page the plan for your trip.

You will learn a lot about yourself and your companions. You will see where you are and where you are not.

In defining the goal of your religion, you need not use conventional religious language. You don't have to make your spiritual journey sound religious. Religion cannot be pompous and high-flown. Religion is consciousness-expansion, centered in the body and defined exactly the way it sounds best to you. Don't be intimidated by Caesar's Hollywood fake versions of religiosity.

If life has a meaning for you beyond the TV-studio game, you are religious! Spell it out!

Develop your own rituals and costumes. Robes or gray-flannel suits, amulets or tattoos. You will eventually find yourself engaged in a series of sacred moments which feel right to you. Step by step, all your actions will take on a sacramental meaning. Inevitably you will create a ritual sequence for each sense organ and for each of the basic energy exchanges—eating, bathing, mating, etc.

Reality and the addiction to any one reality is a tissue-thin neurological fragility. At the height of a visionary experience it is crystal-clear that you can change completely. Be an entirely different person. Be any person you choose. It is a moment of rebirth. You are neurologically a naked baby. Of course you must be careful in choosing your new role. How much game-training is involved? You cannot decide at once to play center field for the New York Yankees or to teach Greek at Harvard. You cannot move into a role position in a modern twentieth-century power game. You cannot decide to move into a status-position or to take over a part with high material rewards. But it is exactly this sort of position that interests you the least—as you look down, not-yet-born Olympian God—on the turmoil and conflict of human life. If you were God playfully considering incarnation as a human being, would you choose to appear as Lyndon Baines Johnson? Or the premier of some European country?

If (and when) you were God, you chose to be reborn in the simplest, least gamey, non-power, low-status position. And you usually did it barefoot. Didn't you?

It is habit, fear, and laziness that keep people from changing after an LSD experience. It's so much easier to doubt your divinity, drift back to speaking English, wearing ties, playing the old game.

My choice in the garden in Tepoztlan at sunrise was frighteningly open. Should I go back to the twentieth century?

You doubt the reality of this option? Listen. There are millions of Americans in mental hospitals right now who have made this choice. Out of confusion or frustration or disbelief in the system. Psychosis is an ontological state, and the psychotic is the person who just won't buy the culture, won't play the game.

And if I chose to leave this Eden and return, what terrestrial game shall I play? Which television-prop studio shall I enter? Which part to assume?

I wandered back down the gardens, into the house. The living room was empty. It glowed, breathed. Glory. Beauty.

A multi-branched candelabrum was burning.

Compelling. Calling. I knelt in front of it and watched. The wax had dripped down over the wooden branches and into melted carvings. A vine of smoke drifted up from an incense stick.

The room was silent except for the whisper of the candles.

Then God spoke to me. Not in the English language. Not in words. He spoke in an older dialect. He spoke through flame and scented smoke. (But He was not the flame and smoke.)

I saw in a quick glimpse the design of the universe. The blueprint of evolution. The impersonal, staggering grandeur of the game.

Think of the auto designers in a Detroit auto plant. They architect a car—but this living structure of God's design is a trillion times more complex than a car. God's automobile is called the atom. Each atom is a structure of detailed intricacy held together by energy of such speed and power that it eludes our conception. Each atom is a spaceship of galactic proportions and at the center of each galactic structure God places the entire staff of his atomic engineers. Do you understand the brilliance of the design? Suppose that General Motors could miniaturize all their designers and engineers and technicians so that they were packaged into every car that rolled off the assembly line. Continuously present to insure efficient operation of the automobile. Continuously conducting on-the-spot performance tests. Continuously collecting data on efficiency, comfort, and safety.

That's the way the atom is constructed—with the intelligence and control and energy-source all in one package inside the nucleus.

And that's the way the cell is constructed. Every cell is an electro-chemical-social system more complicated than the city of New York—with two billion years of accurate intelligence-energy-memory built into the nucleus.

God is an expert on miniaturization. The smaller the unit, the more central, the older, the wiser, the more complex, and the more powerful and faster.

Individuals of every species are stamped out like plastic toys—billions at a time. Immediate turnover. Planned obsolescense. Spin them out. Kill them off.

You must be explicit about the space-time arrangement for your God-game. Each room in your home will contain a shrine. Your house will not be a TV actor's dressing room but rather a spiritual center. Regular rhythms of worship will emerge; daily meditation (turn-on) sessions (with or without marijuana), and once a week or once a month you will devote a whole day to turning-on.

Time your worship to the rhythm of the seasons, to the planetary calendars.

You select a myth as a reminder that you are part of an ancient and holy process. You select a myth to guide you when you drop-out of the narrow confines of the fake-prop studio set.

Your mythic guide must be one who has solved the death-rebirth riddle. A TV drama hero cannot help you. Caesar, Napoleon, Kennedy are no help to your cellular orientation. Christ, Lao Tse, Hermes, Trismegistus, Socrates, are recurrent turn-on figures.

∞

From *Paradise Lost* by John Milton:

The World was all before them,
where to choose

Their place of rest,
and Providence their guide:

They, hand in hand,
with wandering steps and slow,

Through Eden took their solitary way.

∞

In any case, there is nothing for you to do in a collective political sense.

Turn-on,

Tune-in,

Drop-out.

Discover and nurture your own divinity and that of your friends and family members.

Center on your clan, and the natural order will prevail.

∞

This planet is a warm round stone covered with a thin layer of rotting bodies of dead organisms. Each is a teeming field of decomposition on which new layers of brief transient organisms spin out their moment of convulsive dance. Sedimentary cement cemetery.

From the standpoint of the isolated individual, life is a science-fiction horror story. The nervous system mercifully narrows down consciousness so that the individual focuses only on the immediate stimulus. The individual is shackled to a series of reactions to the pressure of food-survival-defense and is spared the overview, the insight that while he pursues his dinner he is hurtling towards his own decomposition.

There comes a point in every lifetime when the blinders are removed and the individual glimpses for a second the nature of the process. This revelation comes through a biochemical change in the body. A twist of the protein key and you see where you are at in the total process.

Just as there is only one heaven, so too there is only one earth. In the hexagram of heaven the doubling of the trigram implies duration in time, but in the hexagram of earth the doubling connotes the solidity and extension in space by virtue of which the earth is able to carry and preserve all things that live and move upon it. The earth in its devotion carries all things, good and evil, without exception. In the same way the superior man gives to his character breadth, purity, and sustaining power, so that he is able both to support and to bear with people and things. (I Ching II)

If this comes to the unprepared person, accidentally, involuntarily, in the context of a secular game, this revelation is shattering and crippling. Our mental hospitals are filled with such revelatory casualties.

If the vision comes in a spiritual context to the person who is prepared to accept the naked awefull truth then—during that exact moment one is part of the entire process—indeed, one sees that the entire process is one. That it is an N-dimensional

From the *Bhagavad-Gita*:

(Arjuna:) Sri Krishna, if you consider me as capable of beholding it, then, O Lord of yoga, reveal to me your imperishable form.

internally unfolding process. Any point from which one sees the one-ness is a center. That one point of vision is the eye of God, seeing, glorifying, understanding the whole.

One such moment of revelation is the only purpose of life. One such moment of vision is the end point of the five-billion-year process of evolution on this planet. One such moment makes the remaining decades of life meaningful and worthwhile.

The red-yellow eyes of the candles and the direct-sweet scent of incense told me this in the sunrise living room at Tepoztlan.

(Krishna:) Arjuna, behold presently in hundreds and thousands my multifarious divine Forms, of diverse colours and different shapes.

I became initiated into an ancient company of illumined seers. I understood the Buddha. I was in complete communication with Blake. I was closer to St. Augustine, Johannes Scotus Erigena, Jacob Boehme, than I shall ever be to any person in rational intercourse.

There exists inside the human nervous system, inside our cellular structures a tissued, biochemical memory-bank. The person who stumbles onto this inner room sees and knows exactly what has been seen and known by visionaries in the past.

Don't talk to me about the objectivity of scientific data or replication of observation. Five thousand years of visionary experience has produced a body of descriptive text of such precision and unanimity that even the distortions of multiple translation and deliberate academic corruption cannot conceal it.

But surely you cannot see me with these gross eyes of yours; therefore I vouch-safe to you the divine eye. With this you behold my divine power of yoga.

Kneeling in front of the candles, trembling in reverence, I saw and heard and sensed and became a member of an invisible religious fraternity. I vowed to dedicate the rest of my life to the preservation of this flame. From that moment on I would no longer be an American, a Harvard instructor, a twentieth centurian. I was a visitor to this modern artificial stage set. A wanderer among the cardboard fake-prop studio backdrops. A carrier of the ancient message. An itinerant announcer sent from central broadcasting. Waiting for the appropriate moment to interject the commercial—we interrupt this program for a brief message. You are all Divine —wake up! Don't get caught in the studio drama!

Arjuna saw the Supreme Deity possessing many mouths and eyes, presenting many a wonderful sight decked with many divine ornaments, wielding many uplifted divine weapons, wearing divine garlands and clothes, besmeared all over with divine sandal pastes, full of all wonders, infinite and having faces on all sides.

The detailed strategy of the new role was still a mystery—the techniques of the prophetic profession. There was plenty of schooling ahead.

But it was to be found. And it was to be found in the past. Hindu. Krishna. Gautama Buddha. Siva. Ram. Kali. Durga. Lila, Maya. Benares. Hardwar. Rishikesh. Himalaya. Brahma. Vishnu. Sankara. Ramakrishna. Yoga. Samsara. Karma. Dharma. The next step was orientation.

I turned from the candles and walked to the windows. The sun was at a low six-in-the-morning angle, just clearing the trees. I stared eastward, eyes open. When I closed my eyes two orange hot disks were burning up the purple-black webbing of my retina. The two glowing orbs changed to yellow and then merged into one and sank into the tissue of my body.

After a while Pat and Parsons came out with dazed looks. Wow! What happened? Where are we?

We're in Heaven. Isn't that obvious?

They nodded. What do we do now?

Anything we want. The choice was razor clean. It depended on our consciousness and on our persistence. We had the Garden of Eden going. It was consensual. We agreed on that. Our situation was a social reality as real as the illusion that Mexico City existed, or Camel cigarettes. We could stay there and continue paradise. Stay high. Keep the thing going. Invite others to come join us. A new thing. A new cycle.

It would be so easy to do. As people arrived at the isolated villa, just treat them as though they had died to all that down there and were reborn here. The three of us could do it—just so long as our commitment did not falter. Just so long as we did not slip back into planetary games. Just so long as we insisted on treating each arrived friend as if he were a newly commissioned god. Turn him on.

Every social structure is an artifact. An "as-if" conspiracy. A "let's-pretend" game. Let's pretend we're Americans. Let's pretend green paper is money.

Any social game can continue only if all participants share in the ontological conspiracy. If people won't pretend to accept our reality we kill them (American Indians) or imprison them (mental patients) or write them off as a nutty sect, cult, or minority.

The religious cult is a small ontological con-

If there be the effulgence of a thousand suns bursting forth all at once in the heavens, even that would hardly approach the splendor of the mighty Lord.

Arjuna, then, saw in the person of that Supreme Deity, comprised in one limb, the whole universe with its manifold divisions.

Then, Arjuna, full of wonder and with the hairs standing on end, bowed his head to the Divine Lord and with joined palms addressed him thus.

Lord, I behold in your body all gods and multitudes of different beings, Brahma perched on his lotus-seat, Siva and all Maharsis and celestial serpents.

O Lord of the universe, I see you endowed with numerous arms, bellies, faces and eyes and having infinite Forms extended on all sides. O Form Universal, I see neither your beginning nor middle nor end.

I see you without beginning, middle or end, possessing unlimited prowess and endowed with numberless hands, having the moon and the sun for your eyes, and blazing fire for your mouth, and scorching this universe by your radiance.

Those hosts of gods are entering you; some with palms joined out of fear are chanting your names and glories. Hosts of Maharsis and Siddhas saying, 'Let there be peace,' are extolling you by means of the very best praises.

Lord, seeing this vast and terrible Form of yours, possessing numerous faces and eyes, many arms, thighs and feet, many bellies and many teeth, the worlds are terrified; so am I.

spiracy. A national state, an ethnic group, is a large ontological conspiracy. A mutually held paranoid system about what is real.

An ontological conspiracy is a neurological conspiracy. A shared consciousness. Politics, religion, economics, social structures, are based on shared states of consciousness. The cause of social conflict is usually neurological. The cure is biochemical.

The three of us in the villa at Tepoztlan were in that rare position of being able to create a new reality. We had the two factors going—a neurological liberation. Our game-chessboard had been temporarily swept clean. And we were in an isolated social situation, the villa, where we could externalize our state of consciousness. It's much more difficult to start a new reality in the center of an ongoing stage set, with all its fierce social pressure for its own ontological survival. Don't plant your tender new ontology in the center of Times Square or St. Peter's Square.

To start a new reality is, of course, to start a new religion.

Well, should we do it? Should we commit ourselves to our three-fold divinity, to the revelation we had received?

A knock on the door. There was our first test. Our first encounter with another consciousness. Three of us stood up and glanced at each other. *Pase Usted.* Come in.

A girl's voice in Spanish—*Señor! Señor!* Lord! Lord!

Open the door.

It was an Indian girl, teen-age. Agitated. Tearful. She scuttled into the room wringing her hands. Rapid high-pitched frantic Spanish.

The family is poor and they have no money. We looked at each other questioningly. It was a biblical scene. The beggar and the three prophets.

Ask her what she wants.

Money for food.

It was so simple and yet so elusive. The Indian girl was trapped in a karma-game which kept her hungry in a continent of plenty. She was carrying around in her skull the same thirteen-billion-cell cosmic computer.

Let's invite her to step out of the illusion of the Indian village and accept her divinity.

What are you called?

María.

María, would you like to leave your life as a Tepoztlana and stay here? This is paradise.

María's face made a quick animal motion. She looked at each of us. Fear, confusion. The emotional pressure was intense. We were staring at her with complete attention. We were completely there for her. Radiating love and acceptance.

María fell to her knees and began to sob. It was too much.

Lords, I am a poor girl. My children are sick. My parents are sick. Money for food. Money for food.

I knelt down beside her. Pat and Parsons knelt down too. Pure New Testament. The four of us on our knees.

I began to pray in English. Let this girl, María, receive the vision. Let her escape from her karma. Let her find her divinity and join us in creating a paradise on this spot. Let her receive the revelation.

The four of us remained kneeling. I could feel the sweat dripping down from my armpits. There was a long silence. It seemed so simple. We were so close. Just one shift in the vibratory frequency and it could click into focus. It seemed tragic that María should have wandered in (or been sent?) at exactly this minute and should not make it. It seemed like a tragic defeat if she just brushed by the glory and returned to her village.

María's discomfort became more visible. She began to whimper. I must go back. Help me, Lords.

Parsons looked at me. I shrugged. He pulled twenty pesos from his pocket. María's eyes widened. She reached out a tentative brown hand. She took the money and kissed Parsons' hand and ran out the door.

We were silent for a long time. Here was a visitor to paradise. And all she wanted was money.

Later that afternoon a friend of Parsons' came to visit. He was a social psychologist from Baltimore. Intellectual. Effeminate. He wanted to make small talk but Pat opened right up. She began to describe

Lord, seeing your Form reaching the heavens, effulgent, many-coloured, having its mouth wide open and possessing large shining eyes, I, with my inner self frightened, have lost self-control and find no peace.

Seeing your faces with fearful teeth, resembling the raging fire at the time of universal destruction, I am utterly bewildered, and find no happiness; therefore, be kind to me, O Lord of celestials and Abode of the universe.

Bhisma, Drona and yonder Karna, with the principal warriors on our side as well, are rushing headlong into your fearful mouths set with terrible teeth; some are seen stuck up between your teeth with their heads crushed.

As moths rush with great speed into the blazing fire for destruction, even so all these people are with great rapidity entering your mouths for destruction.

Swallowing through your burning mouths, you are licking all those people on all sides. Lord, your terrible brilliance is burning the entire universe, filling it with radiance.

Tell me who you are with a Form so terrible. My obeisance to you, O Supreme Deity; be kind. I wish to know you, the primal being, in essence; for I know not your purpose.

I am the inflamed Kala (time), the destroyer of the world. My purpose here is to destroy these people. Even without you all these warriors arrayed in the enemy's camp will not survive.

her vision. She was chanting ecstatic poetry. Songs of revelation. Pacing up and down the room chanting God's message. The radiant stuff of reality. She began to sob in joy as she talked—completely taken by her memories. Beyond social game. A moving, naked, preaching, outpouring of prophetic power. Parsons and I were transfixed. Completely with her.

The psychologist sat on the edge of the sofa clutching his glass of rum and Coke. His smile weakened. His face fell apart. Disbelief. Disapproval. Then fear. Alarm. Then a robot dart of recognition. You've been taking drugs, haven't you?

Pat turned toward him. The flesh of the gods, beloved friend. And you can share our glory if you want to.

The psychologist jumped. Alarm. He put the glass down on the coffee table and pushed it away from him. He made a show of glancing at his watch and jumped to his feet. Well, I must toddle off. Just stopped in to say hello. Glad you're having a good time. He walked quickly to the door.

He had just been exposed to the eloquent witness, to the passionate, precise testimony and he ran away.

The psychologist had brought into the house a nervous, chattering piece of metallic mental machinery. Shrieking gears, noisy, jarring. After he left we could see the spinning wheel of the afternoon weave back golden ribbons through the tears in the delicate fabric.

We resumed our divine dance, effortlessly, timelessly, in tune with the pulse of the house.

We talked, off and on, about the decision. We could phone family and friends back on earth, Hello down there. This is Heaven calling.

Parsons went to the phone. To our surprise it worked. Do you think a call will go through? A telephone line from heaven to earth. From heaven to hell. He began placing a call to the operator. It's ringing.

Hello, Dad. Listen, I've died. Oh, don't be upset. I'm in Heaven. It's magnificent. You must come. When? Now. How? Well, fly to Mexico City and we'll have a limousine drive you to Cuernavaca.

You are the Prime Deity, the most ancient person, you are the ultimate resort of this universe. You are both the knower and the knowable, and the highest abode. It is you who pervade the universe, assuming endless forms.

You are Vayu (Wind-God), Yama (God of Death), Agni (Fire-God), Moon-God, Brahma, the Creator of beings, nay, the father of Brahma himself. Obeisance, obeisance to you a thousand times; salutations, O salutations to you, again and again.

Having seen that which was unseen before, I feel delighted; at the same time my mind is tormented by fear. Pray reveal to me that Divine Form, the Form of Vishnu with four arms. O Lord of celestials, Abode of the universe, be gracious.

Arjuna, being pleased with you, I have shown you, through my own power of yoga, this supreme, shining, primal and infinite universal Form, which was not seen before by anyone else than you.

No. I'm not drunk. No. I feel fine. I've never felt better. I'm not trying to upset you, Dad.

Parsons looked to us and made a sad face. Well, let's put it this way, Dad, Pat and I are happy and we love you and we miss you and we had this impulse to call you and invite you to join us. All right, Dad. We'll write. Good-bye.

The good-bye hung in the air, circling the room like a black buzzard. I opened the window and it flew out.

By nightfall the discussion took a more practical turn. Parsons began talking about business engagements in Mexico City. Tomorrow morning at nine.

Pat and I were in favor of staying, but our union with Parsons was so strong that there was no question of a difference of opinion. We nodded and began to pack.

It was an eerie scene. Packing bags to leave paradise and return to earth. To the hell of people's striving minds. None of us was sure that anything recognizable existed beyond the villa. Perhaps the twentieth century was a figment of our imaginations. Well, let's find out. We'll stick together and love anything we discover.

We got in the car and the motor started. We bumped down the tunnel of trees back into the village square. Well, *that* stage set is still there.

We turned onto the super-highway which led over the mountains to Mexico City. Parsons was tired, so I drove. It started to rain.

We were still high. Everything was seen under the species of eternity. Parsons pointed to a car pulling a boat. Noah's Ark. Pat, the earth goddess, grew cold in the night. We covered her with blankets.

The autostrada is double-laned with white picket fences running along the middle and the outside.

The voyage which usually takes ninety minutes was endless. Hour after hour we rolled along. I still felt it was a mistake, a betrayal of the commandment, to leave Tepoztlan. The restlessness increased as the hours passed. Then, a road sign. Return Gate at 500 meters. Well, that's the message. I swung the car in a U-turn and headed back. Parsons looked up in surprise. Where are you going? I pulled the car over to the side of the road. This highway is endless. The sign said return. I guess we are supposed to go back to the villa at Tepoztlan.

Parsons began to talk about his appointments in Mexico City.

I reversed and cut back through the gate and we continued up the highway.

Several hours passed. There was no sound except the hum of the car motor and the jittery flicking of the windshield wipers. Down below I could see the lights of Mexico City, but the road kept circling, never descending, never getting closer.

We were trapped. Our consciousness created this highway. High way, indeed. Caught in a space-time loop. We'll spend lifetimes circling the city. The car kept passing landmarks we had passed before. The same hairpin turn over and over again. We would remain frozen in this time-shelf until an act of consciousness broke the cycle.

How? What to do? It was a science-fiction horror. We were caught in a relentless orbit doomed to satellite the city in great circles. Perhaps we'll run out of gas. No. I looked at the gauge. It had not changed for hours.

Some dramatic shift of direction was necessary to break us out of the orbit. I looked over at Pat and Parsons for their help. They slept. It was up to me.

The only escape was to swerve the car off the road. What was a highway anyway, but a fixed habit of consciousness? We can't fly because our consciousness can't soar up to the possibility of flight. Our heavy mental certainty holds us down. The only way to fly is to be convinced of the certainty of flight. The only way to escape the tyranny of the endless highway was to smash through the rational-artifactual assumption that we had to stay on the road.

But rapid escape-velocity was required. The car must be accelerated to top speed and then (without my mind deciding), when the orbit-road curved, the car would hurtle forward and break out of the trap, catapult splintering through the white guardrail.

It was so simple. Just wait for the next straighta-

Arjuna, in this mortal world I can not be seen in this Form by anyone else than you, either through the study of Vedas or of rituals, or again through gifts, or austere penances.

Seeing such a dreadful Form of mine as this, be not perturbed or perplexed.

Having thus spoken to Arjuna, Krishna again showed to him in the same way his own four-armed form; and then assuming a gentle appearance, the high souled Sri Krishna consoled the frightened Arjuna.

Sri Krishna, seeing this gentle human Form of yours, I have now become composed and am my normal self again.

Neither by study of Vedas, nor by penance, nor by charity, nor by ritual can I be seen in this Form (with four arms) as you have seen me.

Through single-minded devotion, however, I can be seen in this Form (with four arms), and known in essence and even entered into, O valiant Arjuna.

Thus, in the Upanishad sung by the Lord, the science of Brahma, the scripture of yoga, the dialogue between Sri Krishna and Arjuna, ends the eleventh chapter entitled "The Yoga of the Vision of the Universal Form."

∞

way and then jam my foot down on the accelerator. Accelerator. What a galactic word!

It just required the slightest directional compass change in the multi-dimensional space structure to break free. Only the guardrail kept us from liberation. Once the flimsy white fence (itself a state of mind) was transcended we would spin free, glide over the valley of Mexico (as Richard and Jack Leary and I did two years before) and look down at the volcano-pitted earth surface, or perhaps we would shoot out into some new level of consciousness, some meta-planetary psycho-physical state of gravity-free, bird-like, atom-flash, time-less, electric-orgasm, telepathic simultaneity. Or perhaps, more prosaically, the car would tumble down the cliff. Metal twisting, glass shattering, fatal-accident collision, skin-severing, bone-crushing, blood-soaked, terror-hemorrhaged. But was it not just a test? The bogey-monster fear of protecting your sacred baby skin. The challenge to your egocentric terror of death. How can you reach higher levels of spirituality without giving up your fleshly envelope? How can you reach God unless you sacrifice your ridiculous infantile attachment to that hair-covered mucus-filled body? Oh no, I was beyond these gross concerns of physical comfort and physical safety. If the liberation from the heavy weight of the body meant a bloody, fracturing, rending of the body, I was willing. Thy will be done.

The car rolled along the endless circular track faster and faster. Pat and Parsons slept. I waited for the straightaway. My thoughts buzzed around the car like busy bees. . . . Relentless orbit. . . . Doomed to satellite. . . . Break out of the orbit. . . . Fixed habit of consciousness. . . . Rapid escape velocity required. . . . Car must be accelerated to top speed . . . without my mind deciding. . . .

What was that? Hold on. Without my mind deciding. Then who would give the signal to press the accelerator? Was it not my mind spinning out its theories of liberation and breakthrough? Was it not my mind cunningly inventing escape routes? Was it not my mind refusing to trust the process?

If we were in orbit, then let us stay in orbit. Patiently spinning cold lunar voyagers. Docile. Waiting for the next cycle to be introduced. Faith in the process. Thy will be done.

My foot eased off on the gas pedal.

The highway suddenly began dropping down. The white fence was gone and the valley floor of Mexico flattened out the road.

I looked back at the sleeping passengers. Parsons stirred and opened his eyes.

Where are we?

Back down on the valley floor. I don't know yet what planet or what country.

Oh there's a neon sign. We must be in Mexico. It's in Spanish.

A sign! The first sign. What does it say?

Servicio total.

Total service.

That's why we came back.

If, reader, I had greater space for writing, I now would sing, in part, of that sweet draught which never could have satiated me;

but inasmuch as I have filled the leaves allotted to this canticle, the curb of art now lets me go no farther.

From that most holy water, I returned made new—as trees are brought to life again with their new foliage —purified, and made fit for mounting to the stars.

∞

THE RECEPTIVE *brings about sublime success,*
Furthering through the perseverance of a mare.
If the superior man undertakes something and
tries to lead,
He goes astray;
But if he follows, he finds guidance.
It is favorable to find friends in the
west and south,
To forgo friends in the east and north.
Quiet perseverance brings good fortune.

(I Ching)

APPENDIX

Publications of the Harvard Psychedelic Research Project and the League for Spiritual Discovery, 1960–1968.

BOOKS

Alpert, R., Cohen, S., and Schiller, L., *LSD*. New York: The New American Library, 1966.

Leary, T., *Psychedelic Prayers after the Tao Te Ching*. New Hyde Park, N.Y.: University Books, 1966.

Leary, T., *High Priest*. New York: The New American Library, 1968.

Leary, T., *Ex-static Essays*. New York: Putnam, 1968.

Leary, T., Metzner, R., and Alpert, R., *The Psychedelic Experience*. New Hyde Park, N.Y.: University Books, 1964.

Leary, T., and others, *The Psychedelic Moment*. Millbrook, N.Y.: Castalia Foundation, 1965.

Leary, T., and others, *Psychedelic Theory*. Millbrook, N.Y.: Castalia Foundation, 1965.

Metzner, R., *The Ecstatic Moment*. New York: McMillan, 1968.

Weil, G., Metzner, R., and Leary, T., *The Psychedelic Reader*. New Hyde Park, N.Y.: University Books, 1965.

ESSAYS AND ARTICLES

Barron, F., "Unusual Realization and the Resolution of Paradox." Paper read at American Psychological Association meetings, New York, 1961, and published in revised form in Barron, F., *Creativity and Psychological Health*, ch. 20, New York: Van Nostrand, 1963.

Barron, F., "The Effects of Consciousness-Altering Drugs on Creativity." Paper read at 1962 Utah Conference on Creativity and published in *Widening Horizons in Creativity*, Calvin W. Taylor, ed., New York: Wiley, 1964.

Barron, F., "New Developments in Psychotherapy." Paper read at XIV Congress of Applied Psychology, Copenhagen, 1962, and printed in *Proceedings of Congress*, Copenhagen: Munksgaard Press, 1962.

Clark, W. H., "Theoretical Issues Raised by the Psychological Effects of the Psychedelic Drugs," chapter in *Religion Ponders Science*, Edwin P. Booth, ed., New York: Appleton, 1964, and in Leary, T., *The Psychedelic Moment*, Millbrook, N.Y.: Castalia Foundation, 1965.

Fisher, G., "Dosage Levels of Psychedelic Compounds for Psychotherapeutic Experiences," *Psychedelic Review*, No. 1, New York, 1963.

Havens, J., "Memo to Quakers on Psychedelic Drugs," chapter in Leary, T., *The Psychedelic Moment*, Millbrook, N.Y.: Castalia Foundation, 1965.

IFIF Newsletter, issues 1, 2, and 3, Millbrook, N.Y.: Castalia Foundation, 1963.

Leary, T., "Drugs, Set and Suggestion." Paper read at American Psychological Association meetings, New York, 1961.

Leary, T., "How to Change Behavior." Address presented at XIV Congress of Applied Psychology, Copenhagen, 1962, and printed in *Proceedings of Congress*, Copenhagen: Munksgaard Press, 1962.

Leary, T., "The Effects of Test Score Feedback on Creative Performance and of Drugs on Creative Experience." Paper read at 1962 Utah Conference on Creativity and published in *Widening Horizons in Creativity*, Calvin W. Taylor, ed., New York: Wiley, 1964.

Leary, T., "Interpersonal Behavior and Behaviorism." Paper read at Veterans' Administration Conference on Chemotherapy Studies, Cincinnati, 1962, and printed in *U.S. Veterans' Administration Bulletin*, Washington, D.C., 1962.

Leary, T., "Measuring Verbal Interaction in Freudian and Rogerian Psychotherapy." Dittoed report, Center for Personality Research, Harvard University, 1962.

Leary, T., "American Education As a Narcotic Addiction and Its Cure." Paper read at Symposium on American Values, Eastern Washington State College, 1963, and printed in Leary, T., *Psychedelic Theory*, Millbrook, N.Y.; Castalia Foundation, 1965.

Leary, T., "Memorial Essay for Aldous Huxley," *Psychedelic Review*, No. 2, New York, 1963.

Leary, T., "Problems of Expanding Consciousness." Interview, *KPFK*, Los Angeles, April 18, 1963.

Leary, T., "The Religious Experience: Its Interpretation and Production." Paper presented at 1963 meeting of Lutheran psychologists and printed by the Lutheran Board of Higher Education. Also in *Psychedelic* Review, No. 3, New York, 1965, and Weil, G., *The Psychedelic Reader*, New Hyde Park, N.Y.: University Books, 1965.

Leary, T., Introduction to *LSD—The Consciousness Expanding Drug*, D. Solomon, ed., New York: Putnam, 1964.

Leary, T., "The Rationale for the Zihuatanejo Experiment," chapter in *The Utopiates,* R. Blum, ed., New York: Atherton, 1964.

Leary, T., "Bibliography of the Publications of the Harvard-Castalia Foundation Research Project, 1960–1965," in Leary, T., *Psychedelic Theory,* Millbrook, N.Y.: Castalia Foundation, 1965. Published separately by Kriya Press, Millbrook, N.Y. 1967.

Leary, T., "Chemistry and Conversion," in Leary, T., *Psychedelic Theory,* Millbrook, N.Y.: Castalia Foundation, 1965.

Leary, T., "Communication: Energy Sent and Received," *ETC.,* San Francisco State College, San Francisco, Fall 1965.

Leary, T., "The Ecstatogenic Game Contract," in Leary, T., *Psychedelic Theory,* Millbrook, N.Y.: Castalia Foundation, 1965.

Leary, T., "The Effect of Shared Space-Time on the Ecstatic Experience," in Leary, T., *Psychedelic Theory,* Millbrook, N.Y.: Castalia Foundation, 1965.

Leary, T., "The Effects of Set and Setting on the Ecstatic Experience," in Leary, T., *Psychedelic Theory,* Millbrook, N.Y.: Castalia Foundation, 1965.

Leary, T., "Empirical Studies of the Effects of Setting," in Leary, T., *Psychedelic Theory,* Millbrook, N.Y.: Castalia Foundation, 1965.

Leary, T., "The Experiential Typewriter," *Psychedelic Review,* No. 7, New York, 1965.

Leary, T., "Five Psychedelic Prayers from the Tao Te Ching," *Psychedelic Review,* No. 7, New York, 1965.

Leary, T., "The Game Language for Describing External Behavior," in Leary, T., *Psychedelic Theory,* Millbrook, N.Y.: Castalia Foundation, 1965.

Leary, T., "Homage to the Awe-full See-er," in Leary, T., *The Psychedelic Moment,* Millbrook, N.Y.: Castalia Foundation, 1965, and *Psychedelic Review,* No. 9, New York, 1967.

Leary, T., "Neo-Symbolic Communication of Experience," *Psychedelic Review,* No. 8, New York, 1965.

Leary, T., "The Philosophy of Internal and External," in Leary, T., *Psychedelic Theory,* Millbrook, N.Y.: Castalia Foundation, 1965.

Leary, T., "Programmed Communication During the Psychedelic Session," *Psychedelic Review,* No. 8, New York, 1965.

Leary, T., "Tranart," in Leary, T., *Psychedelic Theory,* Millbrook, N.Y.: Castalia Foundation, 1965.

Leary, T., "LSD and Religion," *Innisfree,* M.I.T. Journal of Inquiry, Cambridge, Mass., Dec. 1966.

Leary, T., "LSD, Law and Society," *The Realist,* No. 69, New York, Sept. 1966.

Leary, T., "The Molecular Revolution." Address presented at LSD Conference, University of California, July 1966. Printed in Leary, T., *Ex-static Essays,* New York: Putnam, 1968.

Leary, T., "Politics and Ethics of Ecstasy," *Cavalier Magazine,* New York, July 1966.

Leary, T., "Sex and Psychedelics," *Playboy,* Chicago, Sept. 1966.

Leary, T., "Turn-On, Tune-In, Drop-Out," *East Village Other,* New York, May–June 1966.

Leary, T., "Another Session," *Oracle,* Vol. 1, No. 10, San Francisco, Calif., Oct. 1967.

Leary, T., "Art Kleps, Mad Luther of Psychedelia," *East Village Other,* July 1967. Reprinted in *Ex-static Essays,* T. Leary, New York: Putnam, 1968.

Leary, T., "The Ecstatic Drop Out," *Sol Magazine,* San Fernando, Calif., 1967.

Leary, T., "How to Start Your Own Religion," *L.A. Oracle,* No. 2, 1967. Published separately by Kriya Press, Millbrook, N.Y., 1967.

Leary, T., "The Politics, Ethics and Meaning of Marijuana," in *Marijuana Papers,* D. Solomon, ed., New York: Bobbs Merrill, 1967.

Leary, T., "Psychedelic Utopia," University of Washington *Daily,* Seattle, Feb. 9, 1967.

Leary, T., "The Diagnosis of Behavior and the Diagnosis of Experience," chapter in *New Approaches to Psychodiagnostic Systems,* A. Mahrer, ed., New York: Holt, 1968.

Leary, T., "The Buddha As Drop Out," *Horizon,* New York, Spring 1968.

Leary, T., "Freeing the Imprisoned," *Psychedelic Review,* No. 10, New York, 1968.

Leary, T., "God's Secret Agent AUS₃," *Esquire,* New York, March 1968.

Leary, T., "The Tribal Family," chapter in *Ways of Growth,* H. Otto and J. Mann, eds., New York: Grossman, 1968.

Leary, T., and Alpert, R., Foreword to *The Joyous Cosmology,* Alan Watts, New York: Pantheon, 1963.

Leary, T., and Alpert, R., "The Politics of Consciousness," *The Harvard Review,* Cambridge, Mass., June 1963.

Leary, T., and Alpert, R., "Some Cool Thoughts on a Hot Issue," *Esquire,* New York, Dec. 1963.

Leary, T., and Alpert, R., "Los Effectos psychoterapeuticos de las dragas hallcinogenas." Paper read at August 1962 meetings of Mexican Society of Neurology and Psychiatry. Printed in English in Leary, T., *Psychedelic Theory,* Millbrook, N.Y.: Castalia Foundation, 1965.

Leary, T., and Clark, W. H., "The Religious Implications of Consciousness Expanding Drugs," *Religious Education,* New York, March 1963.

Leary, T., Litwin, G., and Metzner, R., "The Effects of Psilocybin in a Supportive Environment," *J. of Nervous & Mental Diseases,* Vol. 137, No. 6, Baltimore, 1963.

Leary, T., Litwin, G., and others, "The Politics of the Nervous System," *The Bulletin of Atomic Science,* Chicago, March 1962.

Leary, T., and Metzner, R., "Hermann Hesse: Poet of the Interior Journey," *Psychedelic Review,* No. 1, New York, 1963.

Leary, T., and Metzner, R., "The Castalia Foundation Summer School," in Leary, T., *Psychedelic Theory,* Millbrook, N.Y.: Castalia Foundation, 1965.

Leary, T., and Metzner, R., "The Effects of Love in Prisoner Rehabilitation," *Psychedelic Review,* No. 11, New York, 1967.

Leary, T., and Metzner, R., "The Great Prison Break-Out," *Psychedelic Review,* No. 10, New York, 1967.

Leary, T., Metzner, R., Presnell, M., Weil G., Schwitzgebel, R., and Kinne, S., "A Change Program for Adult Offenders Using Psilocybin," *Psychotherapy,* Chicago, July 1965.

Leary, T., and Smith, Huston, "IFIF Statement of Purposes," in Leary, T., *Psychedelic Theory,* Millbrook, N.Y.: Castalia Foundation, 1965.

Metzner, R., "The Pharmacology of Psychedelic Drugs," *Psychedelic Review,* No. 1, New York, 1963.

Metzner, R., "Notes on Current Psychedelic Research," *Psychedelic Review,* No. 9, New York, 1967.

Metzner, R., Alpert, R., and Weil G., "Perspectives in Psychedelic Research," *Psychiatric Opinion,* Vol. 1, No. 1, Boston, 1964.

Metzner, R., and editors of *Psychedelic Review,* "Statement of Purposes," *Psychedelic Review,* No. 1, New York, 1963.

Metzner, R., and editors of *Psychedelic Review,* "The Subjective After-effects of Psychedelic Experiences," *Psychedelic Review,* No. 1, New York, 1963.

Metzner, R., and editors of *Psychedelic Review,* "The Treatment of Alcoholics with Psychedelic Drugs," *Psychedelic Review,* No. 1, New York, 1963.

Metzner, R., and Leary, T., "On Programming Psychedelic Experiences," *Psychedelic Review,* No. 9, New York, 1967.

Metzner, R., Litwin, G., and Weil, G., "Expectation, Mood and Psilocybin," *Psychedelic Review,* No. 5, New York, 1964.

Metzner, R., and Weil, G., "Predictive Recidivism: Base Rates for Massachusetts Correctional Institution Concord," *Journal of Criminal Law, Criminology and Police Science,* Vol. 54, No. 3, Chicago, Sept. 1963.

Pahnke, W., "Drugs and Mysticism," Ph.D. Dissertation, Harvard University, 1963.